C0-AJZ-084

BEYOND BOUNDARIES:
SEX AND GENDER DIVERSITY IN COMMUNICATION

Edited By

Cynthia M. Lont
George Mason University

Sheryl A. Friedley
George Mason University

George Mason University Press
Fairfax, Virginia

Copyright © 1989 by

George Mason University Press

4400 University Drive
Fairfax, VA 22030

All rights reserved

Printed in the United States of America

British Cataloging in Publication Information Available

Distributed by arrangement with
University Publishing Associates, Inc.

4720 Boston Way
Lanham, MD 20706

3 Henrietta Street
London WC2E 8LU England

Library of Congress Cataloging–in–Publication Data

Beyond boundaries.

Includes bibliographies.
1. Communication– –Sex differences. I. Lont, Cynthia M.
II. Friedley, Sheryl A.
P96.S48B48   1988   305.3   88–24414 CIP
ISBN 0–913969–21–4 (alk. paper)

All George Mason University Press books are produced on acid-free
paper which exceeds the minimum standards set by the National
Historical Publications and Records Commission.

Dedication

To the little things that make life great – Baby and Holli.

Acknowledgements

The authors wish to thank the following individuals for their willingness to review manuscripts for this project: Barbara Bate, Judy C. Pearson, Lea P. Stewart, Paul J. Traudt, Lynn Turner, and Virginia Wheeless. In addition, we would like to thank the Organization for the Study of Communication, Language, and Gender as well as George Mason University's Department of Communication for its assistance with sponsoring and hosting the 9th Annual Conference from which many of these chapters were taken. Finally, we would like to thank the Office Support Services at George Mason University for its assistance with the production of this book as well as Daniel C. Clark for his computer assistance throughout the project.

Table of Contents

Unit III

Sex and Gender Diversity in the Interpersonal Setting

Unit IV

Sex and Gender Diversity in the Organizational Setting

Unit V

Sex and Gender Diversity in Popular Culture 231

Unit VI

New Directions for the Study of Sex and Gender ... 299

Beyond Boundaries: Sex and Gender Diversity in Communication

Cynthia M. Lont and *Sheryl A. Friedley*
George Mason University

Introduction

As infants, we were surrounded by our cribs, our playpens, and our parents' arms. Each boundary encompassed our world, and we developed our identity in relation to the people and places within those boundaries. As children, this space grew. Though we were not able to cross the street alone, our world expanded to include our homes and neighborhoods. We took comfort in the familiarity of this world and felt secure within those boundaries.

As adolescents, our boundaries were not dictated as much by immediate space as they were by time and others' expectations. Though our world expanded as far as we could walk or drive a car, we were usually expected to account for our time and return home by "a reasonable hour." While we felt constrained by others who dictated boundaries, we also felt protected by those boundaries established out of love and concern. We learned to appreciate the necessity for boundaries that provided guidance, direction, and focus.

As adults, boundaries prompt both negative and positive reactions in each of us. We may be grateful for the boundaries that define us as students, spouses, parents, and workers—they reduce the ambiguity of these roles as we enact them in our lives. But how do we feel if those boundaries begin to confine us? For example, boundaries reflect the expectation that middle–age persons *do not* return to school, married couples *do not* work in cities miles apart, men *cannot* stay home to care for children, and women of color *will not* rise to top management. Suddenly, the boundaries no longer represent safety and security; instead, they become limitations and restrictions.

Boundaries—they usually define us, sometimes refine us, and often confine us. Like the lines on a map, boundaries show us where we are, where we've been, and where we are going. Boundaries are necessary—they separate what we are from what we are not. If the distinctions become blurred, then the boundaries must be stretched and re-defined to provide new direction and a clearer focus. It is no coincidence that the authors of this book carefully chose its title—*Beyond Boundaries: Sex and Gender Diversity in Communication*. Some chapters in the book reinforce traditional boundaries while other chapters extend or even eliminate them; as a result, this book challenges and extends our thinking about boundaries.

Beyond Boundaries contains six units of study that include twenty-one individual chapters. The units of study as well as the individual chapters provide a diverse examination of sex and gender issues related to the process of communication. Such unit topics as methodology, language, interpersonal communication, organizational communication, and popular culture are explored within its contents. While some chapters re-establish the more traditional boundaries typically associated with issues related to these areas, other chapters reconceptualize those traditional boundaries to stretch and challenge our thinking. Each unit is introduced with an overview of its central focus and general content, and each chapter is followed by "thought provokers"—questions that are designed to stimulate thinking as well as discussion of the individual chapters. Whether the text is used as the primary source of study or as a supplement to other course materials, *Beyond Boundaries* will serve as a source of both information and stimulation for the reader.

UNIT I

Methodological Approaches to Sex and Gender

Methodology may be defined as the underlying principles, rules, and procedures that organize a philosophical system of inquiry. It is a perspective or frame from which a particular subject is studied. Instruments, on the other hand, are the tools used to draw out information that can then be seen through a methodological frame. Specific methods and instruments are popular within particular areas of study, but this popularity may change over time.

The methodologies discussed in this section, although not new or traditional within the study of communication, language, and gender, stretch boundaries by the innovative ways the authors propose they be used. Therefore, this unit will not parade the wide range of methodologies currently popular in the study of communication, language, and gender. In fact, other units within *Beyond Boundaries: Sex and Gender Diversity in Communication* contain more traditional methodologies: rhetorical analysis, conversation analysis, content analysis (written essays, interviews, questionnaires, advertisements, children's books, and children's cartoons), descriptive historical analysis, statistical analysis (including the use of frequencies, analysis of variance, multiple regression and meta–analysis) and grounded theory. In addition, you will read about the various instruments used to support specific methodologies ranging from semi–structured interviews and open–ended questionnaires to Bem's Sex–Role Inventory. You will read both quantitative and qualitative studies, some focusing on the receiver, others on the sender, and one study that focuses on both. In many ways, the entire book exemplifies the aim and focus of various methodological perspectives currently used in the study of communication, language, and gender.

What we strive for in this methodology section, then, is not a list of the most often used methodologies; instead, we will examine three methods atypical to the study of communication and gender. These methods include a non–traditional form of study (oral history), and an expansion of boundaries within two more traditional methods (content analysis and meta–analysis), thus exploring options for future methodologies used in the study of communication and gender.

In the first chapter, "Weaving the Web: Oral Histories as a Feminine Methodological Stance," Linda Perry discusses the controversy that revolves around qualitative versus quantitative research methods. She details the strengths and weaknesses of one qualitative method, oral history. An important contribution to this section on methodology is Perry's focus on the instruments and procedures used within oral histories, unfolding its practical application.

In Chapter Two, "Content Analysis and Public Policy," David Vest clearly outlines the limitations of content analysis especially confirming "the match between the intention of the sender, the understanding of the receiver, and the beliefs of the researcher." Vest takes the premise underlying content analysis and intertwines it with audience perceptions to form a less restricted perspective on this traditional methodology.

In the final chapter of this unit, "Can We Talk?? A Meta–analytic Review of the Sex Differences in Language Literature," Mary–Jeanette Smythe and David W. Schlueter detail both the background and rationale for the use of meta–analysis in the social sciences and the humanities. This summary is followed by a meta–analysis of the literature on sex differences in communication.

The point on which these chapters pivot rests in the subjectivity and biased nature of all science, qualitative or quantitative in method. Since there are limitations to any single perspective, the chapters within this unit propose an integration of methods in order to more fully uncover the intricacies of communication, language, and gender.

CHAPTER ONE

Weaving the Web:
Oral Histories as a Feminine
Methodological Stance

Linda A. M. Perry
University of San Diego

When I was a child I observed that people, sometimes total strangers, would approach my mother and tell her their deepest secrets, their life stories. To me this was quite a nuisance as it could make any trip to the grocery store or post office drag on for hours. I blamed my mother—she was too friendly, too tolerant. As I became an adult myself, people began to approach me and tell me their life stories. Again, I blamed my mother. After all, whether by nature or nurture, it was from her that I mysteriously learned to give off signals that said, "Tell me your woes, your thrills, your hopes and I will listen." Now, as a researcher who depends on life stories, I thank my mother. We have all heard again and again that females are the nurturers; we may have even noticed differences in the ways in which we view the world versus our male counterparts. However, when it comes to doing research, women have hidden behind quantitative, masculine methods—things my mother never taught me.

Gilligan (1982), in fact, explains that a major flaw in social science research is that the methods used by investigators do not adequately reveal women's lives, attitudes, and/or beliefs. The methods have been predominantly quantitative and the researchers, male. Gilligan argues that "Among the most pressing items on the agenda for research on adult development is the need to delineate *in women's own terms the experiences* of their adult life" (p. 193). She espouses "new modes of analysis and a more ethnographic approach" (p. 169). In other words, the pursuit of knowledge will be broadened by including studies of women, accomplished by women researchers using qualitative methods. Oral histories is one such method with which to capture more closely the essence of the differences between men and women that Gilligan points out. More specifically, oral histories as a method of research will help to describe and understand better the webs in which both women and men weave their lives.

3

Additionally, the use of a qualitative approach such as oral histories is most important for the study of communication, language, and gender because it offers a conceptually different orientation to these phenomena than the traditional quantitative methods. Quantitative research aims to predict and control; qualitative research aims to describe and understand. Although the stances of researchers in these two camps often seem opposed to each others' methods, it will be pointed out later that the two methods combined may make for the most valid and reliable findings.

There are, of course, both advantages and disadvantages to using oral histories as a research method. First, oral histories are gathered through extensive interviews which allow subjects the opportunity to tell their life stories, or portions thereof, in their own words. The clear advantage is that description begins with the object of study. It is the subjects' perceptions, memories, and beliefs that shape the categories *during* analysis. This is very different from quantitative methods whereby the researchers provide categories in which to structure data. Other advantages include the opportunity to gain insights into the subjects' experiences, to expand into areas which did not occur to the researcher prior to the interview, to pry deeply into salient issues, and, in sum, to achieve thicker descriptions.

Disadvantages to oral history gathering, however, are serious considerations. The greatest disadvantage is the insistent argument that plagues all qualitative research: qualitative research is neither reliable nor valid. Kaplan (1964) points out that *all* research is affected by the researchers' attitudes, beliefs, values, past experiences, and future aspirations. From deciding what to observe to drawing final conclusions, researchers bring themselves into their studies. In the end, the best one can do is to make an earnest attempt to use replicable methods and then to challenge oneself constantly every step of the way. One must remain open to, even seek, the opposite of every finding. The other major disadvantage to using oral histories is that it is time–consuming. Data collection takes time, patience, and a flexible schedule. Recording, transcribing, and sorting piles of notes and hours of tape–recordings can be tedious. Finally, analysis is a long struggle to discover themes across many subjects and situations to make some sense of what, on the surface, might appear to be unrelated stories and memories. The purpose of this paper is to offer the reader a replicable method of gathering and analyzing oral histories so that some of these disadvantages will be lessened and more of the benefits reaped.

Gathering the Data

Research is inherently a social and cultural process with deeply rooted moral, political, and personal overtones. By directly confronting such issues, qualitative research is perhaps assuming a kind of legitimacy denied other techniques whose practitioners seem to regard nonscientific matters as things to be swept under the proverbial rug (or, at least, the public rug). (Van Maanen, Dabbs, and Faulkner, 1982, p. 14)

Being scientific entails paying attention to detail; it entails methodically selecting and following clear and logical procedures. The guiding principle, in any case, should be an earnest attempt to remain true to the phenomenon under investigation. An oral history, as defined by Sitton, Mehaffy and Davis (1983), "is the recollections and reminiscences of living people about their past" (p. 5) gathered during interviews. But what does the procedure entail?

Ives (1980) recommends that a minimum of two interviews per subject be conducted. The first interview provides data and the second, clarification and amplification. Sitton, et al. (1983) suggest several additional reasons for conducting the second interview: (1) the interviewees will have had time to recollect new information, (2) the interviewer will have had time to review the notes and the tape recording, (3) the interviewees and interviewer will know each other better and will be more relaxed, and (4) the descriptions will be thicker.

Before the interviews a protocol should be developed. A protocol for an oral history should be specific enough to gather relevant information yet flexible enough to allow the subject freedom of discussion. As Flanagan (1954) explains, the wording should maximize communication and minimize misunderstanding. An orientational statement guides the interviewee toward the kinds of information one is seeking. The total number of questions should be at a minimum, but each will include several implicit questions (Dexter, 1970). For example, "How did that make you feel?" is an implicit question in response to a description of an incident the subject might report. The journalistic probes of "who," "what," "when," "where," "why," and "under what conditions," will be embedded within the questions (Morrissey, 1970). (See Appendix A.)

The possible subjects should be contacted far in advance of the planned interview period. Advance notice will ensure as many opportunities to set dates as possible and allow the interviewee to reflect on his/her experiences (Hoopes, 1979). Each potential subject needs to be informed about who is doing the investigation, why this person was selected to be a subject, and the purpose of the investigation.

The initial phase of the interview is used to orient the subject toward the interview process. Flanagan (1954) and Dexter (1970) stress that the initial moments of the interview set the atmosphere for much of the remainder. In brief:

1. Remind the interviewees of:
    a) your name, and provide them with an identification card,
    b) the sponsoring agent, and
    c) the general purpose for the interview.
2. Request of the interviewees:
    a) permission to take notes,
    b) permission to tape record, and
    c) signature on the Release Form
        (Appendix B).
3. Provide or promise the interviewees:
    a) a copy of the Release Form, and
    b) confidentiality of information.

Interviews are transactional; therefore, the interviewer should secure a professional image as soon as possible. This same stance needs to be maintained throughout all interviews with each subject to prevent unnecessary tangents and irrelevant information from affecting the data. Equally important, according to Hoopes (1979), is that the interviewer attempt to maintain a consistent image across interview subjects to limit the possibility of the data incurring inconsistencies based on personality factors. At the same time, one must make the subjects feel secure and relaxed in order to gain their confidence and trust. Thus, one must be both professional and personable. The context within which the interviewing occurs is also important. Attempt to conduct each interview in a place that is comfortable, and most important, free from interruptions.

The researcher will usually find that the presence of a tape recorder is soon forgotten by the subject so it should be used because it offers several advantages. It is a convenient way to document the interview and it is much less tiring than note–taking. Nonverbal qualifiers such as vocal qualities can be captured and referred to when analyzing the data. Tape recording helps to maintain the interactive aspects of interviewing. Listening to the tapes can help interviewers realize some of the possible ways they affected the process. Above all, tape recordings are accurate.

In addition to tape–recording, notes should be taken. Inferences made by the investigator can be included in notes; the nonverbal, nonvocal cues or perceived messages can be noted, and note–taking implies to the interviewee that she is being listened to and understood. Notes from the initial interview should be expanded as soon as possible to capture description and detail that might be forgotten and lost over time (Dexter, 1970; Hoopes, 1979; and Sigman, 1984). This elaboration includes such additions as inferred messages, observation about nonverbal impressions, an estimate of the subject's reaction to the interview, and an overall evaluation.

Next, the tape recordings should be listened to and the following questions addressed: (1) Was the subject cooperative? (2) Were there trouble spots? Why? (3) How did the interviewer affect the process? the subject? (4) What needs to be clarified, expanded, and/or amplified? And, (5) did the subject seem reliable, consistent, or contradictory? Dexter (1970, pp. 126–127) offers four additional questions investigators can ask during this period to judge whether the information provided by the subjects was distorted. First, is the information plausible? Does it fit common sense? Does it seem logical and believable?

Second, is the subject reliable? Contradictions may show across repeated interviews. Third, what is the subject's mental set? Does what was said by the subject indicate strong biases, ideologies, beliefs, attitudes, and/or feelings that might cause an extreme slanting of the information? And fourth, does what different subjects say seem to complement or contradict in any major ways? Given the answers to these questions, a new list of questions for the second interview protocol can be developed. The same steps—what to do before, during, and after an interview—are then repeated for the second interview. Finally, the data can be analyzed.

Analyzing the Data

Analysis of data is accomplished by qualitative methods. Several principles of qualitative research have been isolated by Van Maanen, et al. (1982), and can serve as a guideline for collecting and analyzing the data. These are: (1) *Analytic Induction:* attempt not to commit oneself to a theoretical model. Categories and generalizations should be generated by the data rather than the data made to fit pre-existing categories. (2) *Proximity:* The collection of data needs to be as close to the phenomena as possible. Dean and Whyte (1970) express this same concern:

> The informant's statement represents merely the perceptions of the informant, filtered and modified by his cognitive and emotional reactions and reported through his personal verbal usages. Thus we acknowledge initially that we are getting merely the informant's picture of the world as he sees it. (p. 12)

Still, the gathering of verbal accounts is closer to the phenomenon than are other forms of data-gathering techniques. Oral histories are closer to the phenomenon than pure observation, but not as close as participant observation. When compared to more quantitative forms, such as questionnaires, however, oral histories provide a more in-depth look at the phenomena. (3) *Ordinary Behavior:* The data should be gathered from the subjects' real-life experiences. (4) *Structure as Ritual:* People act in ways and perceive in ways that make sense to them. Thus, the researchers must rely on the subjects' perceptions more so than their own. And, (5) *Descriptive Focus:* The objective is to discover and describe rather than to predict and control. Address the question, "What's going on here?"

The process of analyzing data is initially inductive; that is, the categories evolve from themes that seem to repeat themselves throughout the data. Miles and Huberman (1984) note that

> When one is working with text, or less well–organized displays, one will often note recurring patterns, themes, or "Gestalts," which pull together a lot of separate pieces of data. Something "jumps out" at you, suddenly makes sense. (p. 216)

To get to the place where these themes will evolve one must be willing to get very close to the data, to listen to the tapes, and read the notes over and over. Researchers must become like children with a new set of building blocks—they must build thematic houses, see if they can be blown over, and be willing to build and rebuild until patterns appear and do "suddenly make sense." To begin this process, the tape recordings must be transcribed. Next, references to communicative acts should be transferred individually onto index cards. Along with the statement, notations should be made concerning the relationship between the sender and receiver of the message, at what stage of the subject's life it occurred, and what effect it had. This is a major break from quantitative orientations. Researchers must bring themselves into the process and offer personal observations about the emotional experiences of the subject along with the actual data. For example, the data on the card might read, "In front of the whole committee he said 'You don't know anything about this so just shut up'." The notation might be that the interaction was between the subject and her boss and that when the subject reported this interaction she lost eye contact, had tears come to her eyes, and spoke with a shaky voice. The researcher might also note a translation: "She appeared to be embarrassed and angry about this incident." This information can then be used to locate associations between variables after the themes evolve.

Themes are isolated by piling similar messages together. That is, once all the transcripts and notes are read many times the researcher will begin to "see" similarities across subjects' experiences. The result is a categorization of messages about communication. However, the process does not end here. Once the categories are established, one should return to the tapes to insure that the intended meaning of the messages remains. Miles and Huberman point out,

> The human mind finds patterns so quickly and easily that it needs no how–to advice. Patterns just "happen," almost too quickly. The important thing, rather, is to be able to (a) see

real added evidence of the same pattern; (b) remain open to disconfirming evidence when it appears. (p. 216)

The major flaw in taking oral histories, however, is that researchers are dependent upon their abilities and predispositions in analyzing the data. Strict attention to consistency throughout this process is important because it increases the objectivity of the procedure (Van Maanen, et al., 1982; Flanagan, 1954).

To enhance reliability and validity, qualitative researchers could use qualitative data linking (Fielding and Fielding, 1986) or triangulation (Webb, Campbell, Schwartz, and Sechrest, 1965). Qualitative linking of data, as suggested by Fielding and Fielding (1986), is the use of ethnographic interviews (such as oral histories) along with participant observation to verify findings. This combination could be very helpful in such settings as organizations. However, if one is investigating such groups as the elderly, participation might be difficult (depending upon the researcher's age). One could work in a home for the elderly, but at best one would simply be an observer.

Triangulation, on the other hand, does offer more opportunities to cross-validate one's findings. Triangulation is the use of independent variables to demonstrate validity. In this case, one has many options. First, one could combine any variety of qualitative methods. Second, one could go to a variety of sources. One might interview others in the same situation or role of the subjects, people closely associated with the subjects, or other researchers of the phenomenon. Finally, researchers from qualitative and quantitative orientations could cross-validate their findings (Jick, 1983). Until recently, most quantitative researchers seemed to be saying, "You qualitative researchers have no methods to your madness," while qualitative researchers were responding, "You quantitative researchers have madness in your methods." Getting beyond these stances means a mutual recognition of the merits to both orientations. Through cooperative efforts, the future of all research will benefit.

Oral histories add both depth and breadth to data collection. How subjects respond sometimes communicates more than the content of the response. The twinkling of an eye, a curling of the lips, or a glance to the ceiling signals an attitude beyond the reply—evidence that cannot be captured with other procedures. We will be better able to describe the female and male experiences in relation and contrast to each other once more qualitatively–based oral histories of communication, language, and gender are provided. The findings can then be grated through the sieves of time, tests, and quantitative measurement. Hopefully, the outcome will be a better understanding of how *both* women and men weave the webs in which they live their lives.

References

Dean, J.P. & Whyte, W.F. (1970) How do you know if the informant is telling the truth? In L.A. Dexter (Ed.), *Elite and Specialized Interviewing*. Evanston, IL: Northwestern University Press, 120–131.

Dexter, L.A. (1970) *Elite and Specialized Interviewing*. Evanston, IL: Northwestern University Press.

Fielding, N.G. & Fielding, J.L. (1986) *Linking Data*. Beverly Hills: Sage Publications.

Flanagan, J.C. (1954) The critical incident technique. *Psychological Bulletin, 51* (4), 327–358.

Gilligan, C. (1982) *In A Different Voice*. Cambridge, MA: Harvard Press.

Hoopes, J. (1979) *Oral History: An Introduction for Students*. Chapel Hill: The University of North Carolina Press.

Ives, D.D. (1980) *The Tape-Recorded Interview*. Knoxville: The University of Tennessee Press.

Jick, T.D. (1983) Mixing qualitative and quantitative methods: Triangulation in action. In J. Van Maanen (Ed.), *Qualitative Methodology*. Beverly Hills: Sage Publications.

Kaplan, A. (1964) *The Conduct of Inquiry*. New York: Harper & Row Publishers.

Miles, M.B. & Huberman, A.M. (1984) *Qualitative Data Analysis*. Beverly Hills: Sage Publications.

Morrissey, C. (1970) On oral history interviewing. In L.A. Dexter (Ed.), *Elite and Specialized Interviewing*. Evanston, IL: Northwestern University Press, 109–118.

Oral History: What? Why? How? (1975) Harrisburg, PA: Division of Arts and Humanities, Bureau of Curriculum Services, Pennsylvania Department of Education.

Sigman, S.J. (1984, March) Some rather mundane items concerning the doing of ethnography. Paper presented at the Eastern Communication Association Annual Meeting, Philadelphia, PA.

Sitton, T., Mehaffy, G.L., & Davis, O.L., Jr. (1983) *Oral History: A Guide for' Teachers (and Others)*. Austin, TX: University of Texas Press.

Stohl, C. (1983, May) "You can't understand us unless you dust our shelves": The role of memorable messages in organization socialization. Paper presented at the Eastern Communication Association Annual Meeting, Ocean City, MD.

Van Maanen, J., Dabbs, J.M. Jr., & Faulkner, R.R. (1982) *Varieties of Qualitative Research*. Beverly Hills: Sage Publications.

Webb, E.J., Campbell, D.T., Schwartz, R.D., & Sechrest, L. (1965) *Unobtrusive Measures*. Chicago: Rand McNally.

APPENDIX A

Interview Protocol[1]

"Think of a time that someone said something to you that indicated to you what you should do in order to succeed at this job or in order for you to fit in around here." (Pause until the subject has an incident in mind.)

"Did this statement cause a significant change in the way you behave on your job or the way you felt about it?"

(If the answer is "NO," say) "I wonder if you could think of the last time that someone did or said something that did affect your behavior or feelings about your job—that is, made you realize what is appropriate or inappropriate behavior for this job?"

(When the subject has such a situation in mind ask the questions below. Allow the subject to carry the conversation unless s/he strays far from the intended purpose of this study.)

1. "What were the general circumstances leading up to this incident?"
2. "Tell me exactly what this person did or said that was so helpful/ harmful at that time."
3. "Why was it so helpful/hurtful in changing your behavior?"
4. "When did this incident happen?"
5. "What was the other person's job?"
6. "How long had the other person been on the job?"
7. "What was your relationship to him/her?"
8. "Why do you suppose this incident had such a strong effect?"
9. "What, if any, effect did this have on your behavior outside of this organization?"
10. "Since that incident, have you told other new employees the same thing? Why or why not?"

---

[1]This protocol was adapted from one suggested by John C. Flanagan in "The Critical Incident Technique," *Psychological Bulletin*, Vol. 51, No. 4, July 1954 with suggestions from Cynthia Stohl in "You Can't Understand Us Unless You Dust Our Shelves: The Role of Memorable Messages in Organizational Socialization," unpublished paper presented at Eastern Communication Association meeting, Ocean City, MD, May 1, 1983.

APPENDIX B

Informed Consent Form[2]

This is to certify that I, _____, hereby agree to participate as a volunteer in a scientific investigation as an authorized part of the education and research program of the _____ University under the supervision of _____.

This investigation and my part in it have been defined and explained to me by _____, and I understand his/her explanation. _____ has informed me that (1) this is an investigation into _____, (2) my participation is voluntary, (3) I will not receive monetary or other compensation, (4) it will take approximately two to three hours of my time, (5) this time will be divided between two separate interviews spaced approximately two weeks apart, and (6) both interviews will be tape recorded.

I have been given the opportunity to ask whatever questions I may have had and all such questions and inquiries have been answered to my satisfaction. I understand that I am free to deny answers to specific items or questions asked during either interview. I understand that any data or answers to the questions will remain confidential with regard to my identity. I further understand that I am free to withdraw my consent and terminate my participation at any time.

I hereby give to _____ for whatever scholarly or educational purposes may be determined, the tape recordings, transcriptions, and contents of these interviews.

_____   _____   _____
Subject's Name   Date   Subject's Signature

I, the undersigned, have defined and fully explained this investigation to the above subject. In addition, I have promised confidentiality in exchange for the information provided.

_____   _____   _____
Investigator's Name   Date   Investigator's Signature

---

[2]Pennsylvania State University approved Informed Consent Form with suggestions made by T. Sitton, G.L. Mehaffy, and O.L. Davis, Jr. in *Oral History: A Guide for Teachers (and Others)*, Austin: The University of Texas Press, 1983, p. 127.

THOUGHT PROVOKER

Although our memories of the past may be less than exact, the interpretation of past actions may communicate more to the researcher than "objective" information such as time, date, and action obtained through quantitative analysis. Discuss the advantages and disadvantages of using qualitative methodology such as oral history.

CHAPTER TWO
Biting the Bullet: A Hybrid Approach to Content Analysis

David Vest

University of Michigan

Content analysis sorts observations according to clearly defined and pre-established categories in order to obtain an objective measure of the frequency with which relevant message units are displayed. Researchers construct their perceptual nets according to their beliefs about the significance of the content for events in the real world, but an inherent problem of content analysis involves the difficulty of conforming the match between the intention of the sender, the understanding of the receiver, and the beliefs of the researcher. This problem is most acute when highly charged issues of public policy are involved. As Sestrup (1981) notes, content analysis results are frequently consistent with the expectations of policy advocates; because of the manner in which the categorization scheme is fashioned, findings become both the proof of the problem and the program for its solution.

When a researcher takes content as the focus for study, there are two general perspectives available. One perspective understands media to reflect the prevalent values and norms; messages are evidence of problems which exist in society, and one does not kill the messenger. From the other perspective, media instruct the audience; the media must exercise social responsibility in this role or be subject to criticism and possible content control. According to the chosen viewpoint, content analysis directs policy implementation for changing society (which will then be reflected in content changes) or for changing the messages in order to improve society.

Although an extensive literature review is beyond the space limitations of this paper, these two themes are evident in the earliest research on portrayals of males/females on television. Head (1954) saw content reflecting (in a distorted manner) actual or idealized understandings of relationships held by a culture, and he made no explicit statement about effects and policy. DeFleur (1964) felt, on the other hand, that the distortions evident in television programming could influence future choices made by viewers, and there was a clear policy implication that television should be more realistic in its presentation. The research of the 70's followed DeFleur's lead with Seegar and Wheeler (1973) suggesting, for instance, that television should reflect representative demographics and demonstrate symbolically what is required in the real world for an individual to be as successful as television models. The authors were advocating a systematic distortion of portrayals toward an ideal based upon quota and realistic presentation of the strategies necessary to attain these goals.

Due in part to its dominance in the violence and television research, social learning theory became the theoretical foundation for much of the content analysis reported in journals (although no mention of theory was common during this period). The other major theoretical perspective involved the linking of cultural indicators and cultivation analysis (Gerbner, Gross, Morgan, and Signorielli, 1980). Since measurable "effects" of viewing were by no means uniform, both theoretical systems sought to identify conditions which attenuated or exaggerated changes in beliefs and behaviors. The controversy over the impact of television centered on category schemes and analysis methodology (see McNeil, 1975 and Seeger, 1975; also Hirsch, 1980). The debate involved how to identify category schemes which could be agreed upon by various research positions and which would be demonstrable as adequate and accurate predictors of effects. This effort was not, by and large, successful; indeed, the history of unsuccessful attempts to link exposure to media content with measures of actual behavior and attitude contributed to the ascendancy of uses and gratifications research as a meaningful alternative to various effects models.

The problem is not, however, that media have no effects; rather, it is the underlying assumption by researchers that they can simultaneously have high inter-rater reliability and high concept validity across the important domains of viewer perception which generates significant difficulty. While it may be the case that observers trained to interpret images identically amongst themselves *may* have perceptions similar to those of viewers using television in their daily lives, it is more likely the case that constraining the variance through rater training uncouples the experience of the coder from the experience of the audience. The resulting analyses can reflect both culturally shared meanings as well as methodologically imposed meanings which produce statistically significant outcomes. These outcomes are then claimed to be socially significant statements and serve as the basis for policy advocacy. The difficulties are further compounded by the public's general belief in the power of media messages; although Bullet theory has long since been discredited, the popular notion of direct and powerful effects has been the underpinning for policy debates from the Payne Fund studies to the 99th Congress' hearings on rock music lyrics.

To this point, the paper has been critical of content analysis as an instrument of policy formation because its methodology tends to obscure important distinctions between domains of perception where there is little ambiguity and domains of perception where there is a great deal of ambiguity. When content is uniform and unambiguous, social learning theory, cultivation analysis, as well as a wide range of cultural approaches suggest that the media provide a pressure toward accepting its representations as normal and natural. When content is more ambiguous and open to interpretation, the ability of individuals to impose their personal understanding of the world becomes important. The central questions are, therefore, under what conditions are content categories likely to reflect the understanding of the audience, and under what conditions are these categories likely to misrepresent these understandings in favor of policy advocacy? The remainder of this paper deals with an effort to identify theoretically and empirically how audience perceptions can be used to inform content analysts of domains where ambiguity exists; using this information, researchers can restructure their categorization schemes to examine the relationship between media, content, and audience.

An Alternative Approach

To establish the sociological framework for an analysis of media content and audience perception of issues revolving around the sex of group members, this paper will draw upon an idea of group conflict which directs attention to the importance of positive affect and symbolic negotiation as primary mechanisms for maintaining structural inequalities. The following statements outline the strategies which are seen as the primary methods for achieving low conflict subordination of one group to another:

a) Given that a power differential exists between two groups, overt displays of power are the last resort of the dominant group;

b) Control of the subordinate group is best maintained by consistent displays of positive affect on the part of the dominant group;

c) Any overt conflict which does surface between the groups will be muted; the dominant group will assert that the alleged inequalities are misconceptions, and the subordinate group will contend that the inequalities are unfavorable to both groups.[1]

The three dimensions which serve to map out the relevant terrain are group affiliation, inter–group closeness, and attitude toward power sharing. Power struggles are played out in the process of the dominant group attempting to persuade the subordinate group that everyone really likes one another and that the division of labor and rewards is equitable and beneficial to all. The smoothness of this operation is largely dependent upon the inter–group closeness perceived by the subordinate group; to the extent that the subordinate group can effectively distance itself from the dominant group, the possibility of significant conflict can arise. This distancing is also identified as gender consciousness (Gurin, 1985), and this term makes clear the connection to concepts of class consciousness; while identity as males or females may describe recognition of group membership, this consciousness identifies a shared fate contingent upon the resolution of inter–group conflict.

Also of interest in this study is the degree to which individual attitudes account for the variance within each group, and whether or not there are differences between groups in the relationship between attitudes and perceptions. This paper draws upon cognitive psychology, particularly the work of Cantor and Kihlstrom (1987) on personality, as the theoretical basis for the hypotheses. These authors describe the pattern of human growth as a repeated movement through the following cycle: self and social concepts lead to perceptions of life tasks and the selection of preferred strategies to deal with them; then, evaluation of outcomes results in changes in self concepts, reframing of tasks, and modification of strategies. The model suggests an elaboration of self concepts through a repeated working through of tasks which are defined by self and social concepts and resolved through preferred strategies. An important implication of this model is that highly elaborated self–concepts permit greater freedom in the framing of tasks as well as in the selection of strategies to deal with them. In this sense, high expertise (a highly developed self–concept domain such as gender identity, for instance) is a double–edged sword; it can be used to filter stimuli in such a manner as to support elaborate, carefully fashioned constructs, or expertise can be used to differentiate accurately complex stimuli to gain additional information about the environment. Clearly, when used to support *status quo* constructs which have become inappropriate, expertise is seen to have a maladaptive side; in its alternative application, expertise allows the individual to recognize the need for change and to mobilize the resources appropriate to adaptation.

Cognitive personality theory intersects with social theories of paternalism, therefore, in the following manner. If an individual is dealing with a central domain in race or sex, members of dominant groups should be more likely to project their own attitudes into portrayals because they do not have to face the constraints experienced by members of the subordinate groups. On the other hand, subordinate group members should be less likely to project their own attitudes into portrayals because they have to cope with the effects of unequal power distribution in a more realistic fashion.

The focus of this study is to assess the position of young adult viewers of prime–time television within the space defined by reported attitudes and to make predictions concerning their understanding of media symbols of inter-group behavior. The following assumptions are in effect:

1) Power differentials exist between groups in both the race and sex contexts;
2) Intergroup behavior can be characterized according to principles of paternalism;
3) The mass media are embedded in this paternalistic social structure;
4) The meanings of media portrayals are negotiated over a wide but finite range of possible interpretations by both the media and the audience.

Based on these assumptions, media production can been seen as process in which images are presented to viewers, and these images have preferred interpretations (Hall, 1979), particularly in terms of inter-group affect; interpretation of power arrangements is likely to be more negotiable. Audience perception is expected to be more uniform for affective components of portrayed relationships and more diverse according to individual and group attitudes for the power component of portrayed relationships. Specifically, the expectation is that under conditions of paternalism (closeness between the groups with a deferential attitude toward power arrangements accepted by the subordinate group) portrayals of dominant group power will be clearly understood by groups; if a paternalistic relationship does not exist between the groups, images of power will be interpretable differentially with each group perceiving its own members as being more powerful in television relationships. Although no inter-group relationships can be described as perfectly paternalistic or purely conflictual, the following hypotheses are based on the notion that sex and race relationships are distinctly different in this domain, with sex being more likely than race to be accepted as the basis for a paternalistic relationship. The hypotheses are:

H1: Regardless of the actual distribution of reported attitudes toward the other group, the distribution of perceived attitudes will be highly skewed toward images of intergroup cooperation and liking; there will be no difference according to sex and race in perceptions of affect.

H2: If dominant and subordinate groups feel close to one another, portrayals of power will be construed by both groups as residing with the dominant group; men and women will tend to see men as dominant.

H3: If dominant and subordinate groups feel distant from one another, portrayals of power will be construed differently by each group, with power being seen as held by one's own group; whites and Blacks will tend to see members of their own group as powerful.

H4: *For members of the dominant groups only,* perceptions of portrayals of shared inter-group power and closeness will be related to their actual attitudes toward the subordinate group.

Results

Using a measuring concept similar to one used by Jackman (see Note 1) in her work on paternalism and deference in issues of race, sex, and class, and adding a similar measure of perceived intergroup behavior on ten popular prime television programs, responses to 393 questionnaires given to college age individuals in a pilot study were analyzed. A comparison between the well constructed survey of Jackman and the biased sample of the pilot study yielded some minor discrepancies, but the following essential relationships between groups were unaffected:

1. Mean values for men (0.05) and women (-0.34) rest about the mid-point on a scale anchored at -4 for "I feel very much closer to (the other group)", 0 for "About equal between the two", and +4 for "I feel very much closer to (my own group)", indicating no strong preference for one's own group;

2. Mean values for whites (2.17) and Blacks (1.52) on the same scale demonstrated marked preference for one's own group;

3. Mean values for women (2.52) and Blacks (2.82) were significantly higher than mean values for men (1.14) and whites (1.58) on a scale anchored at -4 for "I feel the government should do much less than it is doing now to insure equal employment opportunities", 0 for "No more, no less", and +4 for "I feel the government should do much more than it is doing now to insure equal employment opportunities."

Looking more closely at the distribution of closeness and willingness to share power of the dominant and subordinate groups in the pilot study, it is clear that men and women hold similar affective attitudes toward each other (Table 1), but their attitude toward affirmative change is significantly different, with men more resistant to change (Table 2). For race, it is a different story. Both Blacks and whites show a strong preference for their own group, with whites exhibiting an even stronger tendency in this direction (Table 3). It is equally clear that Blacks want more change than whites (Table 4).

Table 1
Distribution of Reported Attitudes
(Male/Female Closeness)

Thinking about members of the opposite sex, do you feel closer to members of your sex or the opposite sex?

Very much closer to other	Men (n=170)	Women (n=222)
-4	X	XX
-3	XX	XXX
-2	XXXX	XXXX
-1	XX	XXX
0	XXXXXXXXXXX	XXXXXXXXXXXX
1	XXXXX	XXXX
2	XXX	XXX
3	XXX	
4	X	XX
Very much closer to own	(mean=0.05)	(mean=-0.34)

Significance tests:
Male mean = 0: n.s.
Female mean =0: p<.01 (toward other)
Male/Female means equal: p<.05

Table 2

Distribution of Reported Attitudes (Male/Female Policy)

Compared to what is being done now, how much do you think should be done in terms of equal employment opportunities for women?

Should do much less	Men (n=168)	Women (n=221)
-4	X	
-3		
-2	X	
-1	XX	
0	XXXXXXXXX	XXX
1	XXXXXX	XXXX
2	XXXXXXX	XXXXXXX
3	XXX	XXXXXXXXXX
4	XXXX	XXXXXXXXX
Should do much more	(mean = 1.14)	(mean = 2.52)

Significance test:
Male/Female means equal: p<.001

Table 3

Distribution of Reported Attitudes
(Race Closeness)

Thinking about (Blacks if R is white, whites if R is Black), do you feel closer to (members of your race) or (the other race)?

Very much closer to other	Whites (n=319)	Blacks (n=65)
-4		X
-3		X
-2		
-1		X
0	XXXXX	XXXXXXXXX
1	XXXXX	XXX
2	XXXXXXX	XXXXXXX
3	XXXXXXX	XX
4	XXXXXXXX	XXXXXXXXX
Very much closer to own	mean=2.17	mean=1.52

Significance test:
Whites/Blacks means equal: p<.02

Table 4

Distribution of Reported Attitudes
(Race Policy)

Compared to what is being done now, how much do you think should be done in terms of equal employment opportunities for Blacks?

Should do much less	Whites (n=320)	Blacks (n=65)
-4	X	
-3	X	
-2	X	
-1	X	X
0	XXXXXXX	XXX
1	XXXXX	XX
2	XXXXXX	XXXXXX
3	XXXXXX	XXXXXXXX
4	XXXXXX	XXXXXXXXXXXXXX
Should do much more	mean= 1.58	mean= 2.82

Significance test:
White/Black means equal: p<.001

Now, how do these groups actually perceive intergroup behavior in terms of cooperation, liking, and sharing of power? The survey respondent identified a favorite character from a favorite show and indicated if this character had interactions with members of the opposite sex and/or race. The respondent was then asked to rate the quality of interaction on both affective (Tables 5 and 6) and balance of power measures (Table 7).

Table 5

Distribution of Perceived Attitudes
and Behaviors of Preferred Characters (Cooperation)

If yes, thinking about the relationship between these two characters, generally speaking, how well or how poorly do they cooperate?

Very poorly	Men(n=151)	Women(n=206)
−4	X	
−3	XX	
−2	X	XX
−1	XX	XX
0	XXX	XXX
1	XX	XX
2	XXXX	XXX
3	XXXXXX	XXXXXX
4	XXXXXXXXXXXXXX	XXXXXXXXXXXXXXXXXX
Very Well	(mean=2.16)	(mean=3.08)
Very Poorly	Whites (n=142)	Blacks (n=30)
−4		
−3		
−2		
−1		
0	XXXX	XXXX
1	X	XXXX
2	XXXXX	XX
3	XXXXXXX	XXXXXXXX
4	XXXXXXXXXXXXXX	XXXXXXXXXXXX
Very Well	(mean=2.69)	(mean=2.67)

Significance tests:
All groups p<.001 for means less than or equal to +1
Male/Female means equal: p<.05
White/Black means equal: n.s.

Table 6

Distribution of Perceived Attitudes and Behaviors of Preferred Characters (Liking)

How well do these characters generally like each other?

Strongly dislike	Men(n=151)	Women(n=206)
-4	X	
-3		
-2	X	
-1		
0	X	XX
1	XX	X
2	XXXX	XXX
3	XXXXXX	XXXXX
4	XXXXXXXXXXXXXXXXXXX	XXXXXXXXXXXXXXXXXXXX

Strongly like	(mean=3.02)	(mean=3.08)

Strongly dislike	Whites(n=143)	Blacks(n=32)
-4		
-3		
-2		
-1		
0	XXX	XXX
1	XXX	XXX
2	XXXXX	XXXXX
3	XXXXXXXXX	XXXXXXXXXXX
4	XXXXXXXXXXXX	XXXXXXXXXXX

Strongly like	(mean=2.66)	(mean=2.69)

Significance tests:
All groups p<.001 for means less than or equal to +1
Male/Female means equal: n.s.
Blacks/Whites means equal: n.s.

Table 7

Distribution of Perceived Attitudes and Behaviors of Preferred Characters (Power-sharing)

When an important decision which affects both characters needs to be made, how often does your favorite character have the final say in what to do?

Woman Decides Almost Always	Men(n=150)	Women(n=203)
−4	XX	X
−3	XX	
−2	X	XX
−1	XX	XX
0	XXXXXXXXXXXX	XXXXXXXXXXXXXX
1	XX	XX
2	XXXXXXX	XX
3	XXXXX	XXXX
4	XXX	XXXX
Man Decides Almost Always	(mean=0.88)	(mean=0.59)

Black Decides Almost Always	Whites(n=203)	Blacks(n=31)
−4	XX	XXX
−3	XX	XXXX
−2	X	XXXXXXX
−1	X	X
0	XXXXXXXXXXXXXXX	XXXXXXXXXXXX
1	X	XX
2	XXX	
3	XXX	
4	XXXX	X
White Decides Almost Always	(mean=0.40)	(mean=−1.16)

Significance tests:
Male and Female means equal: n.s.
Female mean less than or equal to 0: p<.001
White mean less than or equal to 0: p<.05
Black mean greater than or equal to 0: p<.001

Regardless of the reported affective orientation of the group, race and sex being distinctly different along this dimension, perceptions of intergroup positive affect dominate portrayals. Simply put, intergroup liking and cooperation is the message. Hypothesis 1 is supported in this sample. For perceptions of power by sex, these distributions indicate that both men and women see males as the dominant decision maker; hypothesis 2 is supported. For race, white response is significantly different from 0 in the direction of whites perceived as controlling inter-racial decision making, while Blacks clearly see Blacks as controlling decision making in inter-racial situations. While whites and Blacks prefer their own groups and construe inter-racial portrayals as full of positive effect, they are nevertheless able to construe the same relationships as having dramatically different power arrangements. Hypothesis 3 is supported.

Now, what can be said concerning differences in perceptions of members within each of these groups? Taking each subgroup and running a regression analysis, perceptions of cooperation, liking, and power emerge as significantly related to the predictor variables of actual feelings of closeness and willingness to share power in four of six dominant group models (Table 8). None of the relationships was statistically significant in the subordinate group models. Two cautions are in order, however; the sample size for Blacks was very small (30 to 32), and the degree of the significant relationships is, for the most part, modest. Nevertheless, although the variance of perceptions is similar between groups, this variance appears to be related to attitudes only in the case of the dominant groups. Hypothesis 4 receives limited support from the data.

Discussion

Although the above study appears to be a survey of audience perceptions and to have little to do with traditional content analysis, it is important to note that the focus of the study is similar to many content analyses. Within the domain of major prime-time character behavior toward members of other groups, the study examined issues of cooperation, liking, and power sharing which have been operationalized in prior studies as pawn-like/origin-like conception of causation (Hodges, Brandt, and Kline, 1981), socio-emotional/task-oriented behavior (Mackey and Hess, 1982), order taking/giving (Henderson, Greenberg, and Atkin, 1980; and Seegar, 1975), dominance and submissiveness (Reid, 1979; and Lemon, 1977), and so on; but instead of using a group of raters with a theoretical variance approaching 0, the study allows the variance in the audience as measured by their perceptions of relationships which they actually attend to come into play.

Table 8

Regression of Perceived Attitudes on Reported Attitudes

Dependent (Perceptions by Men)	Independent (Attitudes of Men)	Beta	T Value (p>|T|)
Cooperation	Intercept	1.66	
	Closeness to Men	0.03	0.25,(n.s.)
	Desire for Change	0.38	3.60,(.001)
Liking	Intercept	2.80	
	Closeness to Men	0.07	0.93,(n.s.)
	Desire for Change	0.17	2.19,(.05)
Power Sharing	Intercept	0.91	
	Closeness to Men	0.23	2.55,(.02)
	Desire for Change	-0.05	-0.54,(n.s.)

Dependent (Perceptions by Whites)	Independent (Attitudes of Whites)	Beta	T Value (p>|T|)
Cooperation	Intercept	2.68	
	Closeness to Whites	-0.09	-0.98,(n.s.)
	Desire for change	0.13	1.68,(.05,1tail)
Liking	Intercept	2.67	
	Closeness to Whites	-0.08	-0.99,(n.s.)
	Desire for Change	0.11	1.53,(n.s.)
Power Sharing	Intercept	0.24	
	Closeness to Whites	-.20	1.62,(n.s.)
	Desire for Change	-0.14	-1.37,(n.s.)

The study suggests categorization schemes normally employed in content analysis may be more appropriate in some domains than in others. There seems to be, for instance, a more commonly-held understanding of the affective nature of relationships than there is of the power component of relationships. If one is to conduct content analysis with the intent of demonstrating that portrayals teach individuals about the world, it would be helpful to test by experiment or survey whether or not the categorization scheme has meaning to people who are supposedly being affected. If operationalization of power sharing is problematic, the issue is not resolved by causing the coders to conform to group standards; rather, it would be better to allow inter-rater reliability to slip *provided* a strong theoretical basis is established. Although trading off inter-rater reliability and rigid categorization schemes may disqualify this approach as content analysis in the minds of many, researchers who are interested in finding links between content, perception, and behavior need not accept reified notions of content from either the traditional content analysis or the limited effects approach. What is necessary, however, if one abandons the rigid methodology of content analysis, is to find major theoretical constructs which tap into the relationship between media content and variable audience understanding.

Conclusion

This paper has made a plea for caution on the part of policy advocates when interpreting findings from a-theoretical research. Additionally, it is a reminder to researchers that positivistic, empirical work is inherently loaded with value judgments which are neither universally understood nor agreed upon; it is in the best interest of the research community and the users of research findings if all relevant assumptions (particularly in the area of effects) are carefully laid out for inspection.

Beyond the above comments, the paper offers an hybrid research methodology to explore the relationship between images and perceptions of intergroup behavior. Should these findings be verified under better sampling conditions, there are implications for reformulating content analysis categorization on the basis of audience rather than researcher perceptions.

Finally, the paper speculated on the possibility of combining sociological (paternalism) and psychological (cognitive personality) approaches to form a theory centering on an important mass media topic: the relationship between content, perception, and behavior. Underlying the studies presented and proposed is the critical notion that research should proceed from a theoretical rather than a policy driven perspective.

Footnote

[1]This formulation of the dynamics of inter-group conflict presented here was central to the discussion in a seminar taught by Mary Jackman at the University of Michigan, Fall, 1985; her insights were extremely valuable in framing the question of interpreting content from this theoretical perspective. Additional discussion of symbolic negotiation can be found in Jackman and Muha (1984).

References

Cantor, N., & Kihlstrom, J. (1987). *Personality and social intelligence*. Englewood Cliffs: Prentice–Hall.

Curran, J., Gurevitch, M., & Woollacott, J. (Eds.), (1979). *Mass communication and society*. Beverly Hills: Sage Publications.

DeFleur, M. (1964). Occupational roles as portrayed on television. *Public Opinion Quarterly, 28*, 57–74.

Gerbner, G.L., Gross, L., Morgan, M., & Signorielli, N. (1984). The mainstreaming of America: Violence profile no. 11. *Journal of Communication 34*(3), 14–29.

Greenberg, B.S. (1980). *Life on television: Content analysis of U.S. TV drama*. New York: Ablex Publishing.

Gurin, P. (1985). Women's gender consciousness. *Public Opinion Quarterly, 49*, 143–163.

Hall, S. (1979). Culture, the media, and the "ideological effect." In J. Curran, M. Gurevitch, & J. Woollacott (Eds.), *Mass Communication and society*. Beverly Hills: Sage Publications.

Head, S. (1954). Content analysis of television drama programs. *Quarterly of Film, Radio, and Television, 9*(1), 175–194.

Henderson, L., Greenberg, B.S. & Atkin, C.K. (1980). Sex differences in giving orders, making plans, and needing support on television. In B.S. Greenberg, *Life on television: Content analysis of U.S. TV drama*. New York: Ablex Publishing.

Hirsch, P. (1980). The "scary world" of the nonviewer and other anomalies. *Communication Research, 7*(4), 403–456.

Hodges, K.K., Brandt, D.A., & Kline, J. (1981). Competence, guilt, and victimization: Sex differences in attribution of causality in television dramas. *Sex Roles, 7*(5), 537–546.

Jackman, M., & Muha, M. (1984). Education and intergroup attitudes: Moral enlightenment, superficial democratic commitment, or ideological refinement? *American Sociological Review, 49*, 751–769.

Lemon, J. (1977). Women and Blacks on prime–time television. *Journal of Communication, 27*(4), 74–79.

Mackey, W.D. & Hess, D.J. (1982). Attention structure and strategy of gender on television: An empirical analysis. *Genetic Psychology Monograph, 146*(2), 199–215.

McNeil, J.C. (1975). Feminism, femininity, and the television series: A content analysis. *Journal of Broadcasting, 19*(3), 259–272.

Reid, P.M. (1979). Racial stereotyping on television: A comparison of the behavior of both Black and white television characters. *Journal of Applied Psychology, 64*(5), 465–471.

Rosengren, K.E. (Ed.). (1981) *Advances in content analysis*. Beverly Hills: Sage Publications.

Seggar, J.F. (1975). Imagery of women in television drama: 1974. *Journal of Broadcasting, 19*(3), 273–282.

Seegar, J.F., & Wheeler, P. (1973). World of work on TV: Ethnic and sex representations in television drama. *Journal of Broadcasting, 17*(2), 201–214.

Sepstrup, P. (1981). Methodological developments in content analysis? In K.E. Rosengren (Ed.), *Advances in content analysis.* Beverly Hills: Sage Publications.

THOUGHT PROVOKER

Direct effects of content on audience members has always been a theoretical leap researchers have been unable to make. A researcher may study the content of a communication message and assume it emits a certain message but how can that assumption be demonstrated? In what way does Vest attempt to make this theoretical leap?

CHAPTER THREE
Can We Talk??
A Meta–analytic Review of the Sex
Differences in Language Literature

Mary–Jeanette Smythe
University of Missouri

David W. Schlueter
Baylor University

Introduction and Rationale

Traditionally, literature reviews in the social science and humanities have been cast in a literary mode, wherein research results are analyzed and summarized in a descriptive or critical narrative. Emphases may be theoretical, as the reviewer attempts to assess the merits of competing explanations for a critical phenomenon based on available data, or may be methodological, as the reviewer explores the research strategies and operational definitions that have been applied to a particular research problem. It is less common to see single reviews that address both issues simultaneously, although such integrative reviews are fairly common in the physical sciences. Regardless of type, however, all reviews share the same basic functions. As Cooper (1984) has noted, the cumulative nature of science, burgeoning numbers of outlets for research reports, and simple time constraints on the individual consumer of research literatures have increased reliance on research reviews. In short, if knowledge building is to be an orderly process, then trustworthy accounts of past research are imperative. Nowhere is this more essential than in an area characterized by inconsistencies in research findings, such as the language and gender–related literature.

Studies of the relationship between gender and language behaviors have proliferated briskly in the past two decades. Early reviews by Thorne and Henley (1975) or Eakins and Eakins (1978) are clearly dated and even the most recent summaries (Pearson, 1985; Stewart and Ting–Toomey, 1987; Smythe, *in press*) are cast in a traditional textbook or literary format. It is to this swiftly accumulating body of work that the current analysis is directed. Two characteristics

31

of the gender and language research literature make a fresh review particularly appropriate and potentially revealing. The most distinctive of these is the high level of contradictions and inconsistencies among findings in the area. The field is peppered with studies that appear to indicate opposite effects. A typical illustration involves the question of which sex talks most. Evidence may be cited that supports both of the popular stereotypes about sex effects in conversation. On the one hand, some studies reflect a pattern associated with the allegedly chattering female, while others sustain the image of males exerting dominance through longer speaking turns. Equally diverse findings are common in the area of linguistic forms (tentativeness, politeness, questions) and also in studies of differential perceptions of male/female language (Smythe, *in press*; Pearson, 1985).

Meta-analysis

Traditional, so-called literary reviews have been the dominant mode of analysis for literatures in linguistics (Philips, 1980) and communication (Pearson, 1985; Smythe, *in press*; Thorne, Kramerae, and Henley, 1983). The essence of this approach is consensual validation. Studies supporting various positions on a hypothesis are enumerated. The position which can claim the largest number of valid and statistically significant effects or synthetic papers in support is presumed to be the most accurate reflection of the phenomenon in question. While eminently familiar and acceptable, this technique has several shortcomings which invite unwarranted inferences. First, the literary method is biased in favor of large-sample studies (Glass, *et al* 1981), an inevitable problem because the probability of finding a significant effect increases as the sample size of the study increases. Two or three large sample studies with anomalous findings may therefore skew a pattern of results because significant findings are, after all, far more likely to be published. Second, the traditional technique is subject to the idiosyncrasies of the individual reviewer. As Glass (1976) has indicated:

> A common method for integrating several studies with inconsistent findings is to carp on the design or analysis deficiencies of all but a few studies—those remaining frequently being one's students or friends—and then advance the one or two "acceptable" studies as the truth of the matter (p. 4).

Though broadly drawn, Glass's description is not without foundation. All reviewers bring to their task a set of prejudices concerning methodologies, constructs, and explanatory paradigms. Standards for determining what constitutes "acceptable" evidence vary dramatically; a linguist is far less concerned with empirical issues of sample size or randomization than a social psychologist or communication researcher.

An alternative method of reviewing research findings that is especially appropriate to a variety of research areas in communication is meta–analysis. Generally, this technique includes all of the attributes of the more familiar forms described above with a significant addition: a statistical procedure for evaluating patterns in research findings. In this respect the meta–analytic review provides several distinct advantages. First, the somewhat common procedure of decrying the design or analysis flaws of several studies with inconsistent findings is replaced by a straightforward assessment of the extent to which specific characteristics of studies are related to patterns of results. For instance, Cooper (1984) reported a series of studies which explored the relationships among social class, ethnic group differences and achievement motivation, sex differences in conformity, and locus of control and academic achievement by combining studies instead of merely reporting the numbers of studies that obtained influences on any of these topics.

Similarly, meta–analysis enables estimates of the strength of association among gender–linked variables across studies, as well as indicating the direction of any differences. This asset is especially useful because it reveals how much confidence may be placed in an overall pattern of results. Since most scholars acknowledge that published studies represent a biased sample (toward publication of statistically significant findings) of all studies completed on a topic, the robustness of any gender–linked effect may be questioned. Rosenthal (1978), however, has developed a technique for identifying the number of non–significant findings that would have to be buried in scholars' files to refute an effect located by the meta–analysis. In this way, the predictive power of a relationship between gender and some specific communication behavior may be indexed.

As a procedure for reviewing literatures, meta–analysis is not without its own set of problems and highly vocal critics. Of the various objections, two seem especially relevant to this project. One frequently cited disadvantage of meta–analytic techniques is that the procedures ignore the quality of studies by integrating results of poorly done studies with those from well–executed investigations, thereby threatening the integrity of any overall hypothesis tests. This reasoning is intuitively appealing but basically spurious. Glass *et al* (1981), Rosenthal, (1984), and Cooper (1984) concur that the relationship between the quality of single studies and the results of a meta–analysis is quite minimal. Moreover, the preoccupation with research "quality" smacks of reviewer bias. It is perfectly reasonable to argue that flawed studies may point toward an overall pattern of effects. As Glass *et al.* (1981) have noted, "Respect for parsimony and good sense demands the acceptance of the notion that imperfect studies can converge on a true conclusion" (p. 221–222).

Another objection to statistical summaries of literature addresses clear biases associated with published research results. Statistically significant findings, particularly those supporting current trends or beliefs, predominate. If a review is dominated by these published findings, it is argued, then the likelihood of an erroneous or distorted account of the phenomenon may result. Some authors (Hall, 1984; Rosenthal, 1978) have suggested that the remedy to this dilemma is to include as many unpublished studies as possible, reasoning that null and/or unpredicted results may be more adequately represented in this way. In this instance, the strategy has not been employed, primarily because the effort to obtain unpublished materials such as doctoral dissertations or convention papers not locally available arguably offsets any probable gains in precision. Moreover, inclusion of materials not readily available for general scrutiny seems counterproductive, at least from the consumers' (of a review) perspective. It is also important to note that the published literature on sex differences may not be so biased as in the case with other phenomena (Hall, 1984). Many studies reporting sex differences were less studies of this phenomenon than of persuasion, attraction, or some other substantive construct. Quite often researchers include the sex variable in statistical analyses merely to increase precision, or to achieve methodological completeness rather than because of an intrinsic interest. Thus the magnitude and direction of sex differences would have been only marginally related to whether or not a given study was published. At least to some extent, this may offset the representativeness problem.

Finally, it is appropriate to note the simplifying nature of the type of analysis reported in this paper. Consumers unfamiliar with meta-analytic reviews may be troubled by the absence of in-depth presentations of specific studies either in the text of an article or its tables. For a corpus of studies as large as the gender and language literature, it is not feasible to discuss studies individually. Additionally, the focus here is exclusively on those overall tests of the sex differences hypotheses, resulting in the omission of studies in which, for instance, sex interacted with other factors in a research design. Too few studies are sufficiently similar to enable meaningful comparisons of such interaction effects, so that domain of data remains lost to this analysis.

Language Differences Literature

As noted earlier there exists a robust and flourishing literature documenting sex–associated differences in communication behaviors. Much of that research has focused on language. Integrating a literature that evolves from so many disciplinary perspectives and whose abundance is rivaled only by its diversity is a formidable undertaking. Given the limitations of this method, the review is necessarily selective. Further, several factors inherent in the sex differences in communication literature make synthesis difficult. First, distinctions among data drawn from actual behaviors, self-reported behaviors, and other-perceived behaviors are not always clearly drawn. The vast majority of studies are populated by white, upper-middle-class university students, interacting in public, mixed-sex situations. Obviously this forced homogenization of data has effects, some of which may obscure relationships among variables of interest, and none of which are easily assessed.

Additional problems derive from the fragmentary character of this literature. Many studies report differences in language, but these are frequently buried in studies of some other phenomenon such as self-disclosure. Because the findings are often tied to the goals of specific studies, there is little continuity in the selection and measurement of variables, or the reporting and discussion of results. As Philips (1980) noted, comparability across disciplinary perspectives is especially problematic. The absence of agreement concerning definitions of key concepts, constructs, and operationalizations creates an incongrous array of variables and associated findings rather than a set of basic, well-researched linguistic categories.

Problems notwithstanding, the accumulation of findings and the apparent discrepancies within the literature warrant exploration. For this preliminary analysis, the two most dominant tributaries of research on sex-associated differences in language, male/female differences in language production and differences in perceptions elicited by male/female language were selected. Regarding language production, early studies of language and gender were focused on conversations. They revealed differences between men and women, which generally reinforced stereotypic conceptions of masculine and feminine speech. Careful scrutiny, however, suggested that no language cues appeared to be solely characteristic of either sex. Rather, any sex differences reflected in these studies were sex-preferential rather than sex-exclusive. Previous reviews (Kramer, Thorne and Henley, 1978; Haas, 1979) have suggested that the literature is organized around research related to form, topic, content, and use of spoken language. The form and use variables which have appeared to discriminate male and female language include talkativeness, tentativeness, correctness, questions, and interruptions.

While men and women exhibit patterns of discourse that may vary in consistent ways, the social consequences of these cues appear considerably *less* variable. What is most striking about initial studies in this area is the strength and enduring character of sex-based linguistic stereotypes. Jespersen's (1922) allegations that women's discourse was more hyperbolic, euphemistic, and refined while men's' talk was more vivid, innovative and slang-ridden were corroborated more than fifty years later in Kramer's (1977) study of the perceptions of male/female speech among college students. Therefore, it is hardly surprising that authors repeatedly describe perception of women's speech as weaker and less forceful than men's speech.

Research on language judgments has focused on the attributions listeners make about speakers on the basis of linguistic cues, the evaluations associated with certain configurations of language cues (powerful/powerless speech) and the specification of linguistic markers of sex (gender–linked–language effect) (Mulac and Lundell, 1980). As was the case with language production studies, the findings associated with the perceptions of language typically reveal differential sex–associated effects. While the two literatures are related, investigations of evaluations elicited by men's and women's language appear considerably more imbued with sex stereotypic judgments. Edelsky (1979) describes the enigma, noting that while language production clearly is not a reliable reflection of social fact, language attitudes persist as if it were. The results of the meta–analysis should yield a far clearer picture of the relationship between sex and language than has been available to date.

Based on the foregoing rationale, the following research questions were posed.

RQ 1. Do male and female speakers use different specific language forms?

RQ 2. Are male and female speakers evaluated differently?

Another impetus for the meta–analysis derives from Eagly's (1983) assertion that the sex of the researcher may be associated with the magnitude and direction of differences in behaviors of men and women uncovered. Specifically, Eagly and Carli (1981) have determined that female investigators have been more likely to discover a sex effect that favors women (i.e., decoding nonverbal cues accurately), while male investigators have displayed a corresponding tendency to uncover differences that favor men (i.e., more resistant to persuasion). In the often politicized domain of language differences research, the implications of this assessment warrant serious consideration.

RQ 3. Does the sex of the researcher relate to the results of a study?

Procedures

Literatures as Documentary Evidence

No restrictions were used in terms of sample populations, methodologies, or constructs. Thus subjects of all ages, assuming mental and physical normality, were included. Research methods of the studies incorporated in the review were principally systematic observations and objective testing. Finally, no disciplinary boundaries were imposed on this synthesis; the only requirement was that the study had to report empirical findings (e.g., significance tests). Regrettably, a number of intriguing and widely cited studies such as the Zimmerman and West (1975) account of interruptions were excluded on these grounds, as were a number of linguistic studies. An initial pool of more than one hundred investigations was thus reduced to approximately seventy–one studies.

In the process of identifying studies for this meta–analysis, two problems with important methodological implications became apparent. Each arose because it was sometimes necessary to make judgments about how to group the data. If a researcher reported more than a single study within an article, the independent samples were treated as two separate studies. The trickier decision entailed those studies in which multiple behaviors were measured within a single study. On the one hand, it is generally desirable to keep observations independent by assuring that each result is drawn from a separate sample of subjects. In some instances, however, this practice becomes unrealistic, in that researchers measured several different types of language cues in a given sample. Though these observations were not independent, it seemed too profligate to disregard all measures save one, and too arbitrary to devise some scheme to average across diverse measures to obtain a single result per sample (Hall, 1984; Rosenthal, 1984).

Quantitative Analysis

Three outcome measures are frequently used in meta–analytic studies. Each is generally recognized as an effective means of summarizing literature and each has found application in a number of research reviews. Direction is a straightforward tally of which way a result turned out, regardless of statistical significance, effect size, or other mathematical considerations. Thus, the three possible outcome indices for direction are those indicating higher levels of an attribute for females (F+), males (M+), or no differences between males and females (NSD). Data summarized in Tables 1 and 2 exemplify directional information.

A second measure is effect size, an index of the magnitude of an effect or a relationship. In most instances, effect size estimates enable the researcher to assess how robust or powerful a pattern of findings may be by comparing standardized effect size estimates such as d, a statistic that standardizes mean differences between groups based on the amount of variance in the sample (Cohen, 1969). Computation of effect sizes frequently permits comparisons among studies on other attributes including sample characteristics, methods, and the like.

A third index, statistical significance, is recommended as the initial level of analysis and is reported in this paper. This most familiar of a reviewer's inferential tools reveals how much confidence may be placed in the accuracy of a sample difference. When a group of p values is obtained, these may be analyzed in various ways as summarized by Rosenthal (1984). The techniques deemed most relevant for

these data set entailed a comparison of significance tests through con-
version of p values to Z–scores. Following Rosenthal's (1984) conservative recommendation, all nonsignificant findings for which no p
values were reported were assigned a Z–score of 0 and probability
level was presumed to be .05.

Results

The initial phase of meta–analysis focused on comparisons across
studies to determine the presence and degree of a sex difference effect in terms of language production and the perceptions occasioned
by those differences. In essence this procedure is what Rosenthal
(1984) calls a "diffuse test," in that it reveals at the broadest level
whether a group of studies differ among themselves with regard to
some quantitative outcome measure (e.g., statistical significance). In
a literature like the one summarized here, the diffuse test is arguably
the appropriate beginning point and may indicate whether focused
tests or contrasts exploring specific hypotheses within a set of studies
are warranted. In the present instance, studies were compared across
significance levels using the formula, $(Zj - \bar{Z})^2$, with K–1 df.

RQ 1. Regarding the performance or production studies, a total
of 65 hypothesis tests were identified and Z–scores computed. The
average Z–score was 1.609. A value of 225.69, 64 df p > .0001 was
obtained, indicating that the significance levels were heterogeneous.
That is, no consistent sex–associated effect emerged in this group of
studies.

RQ 2. In assessing the strength of association among the studies
of perceptions elicited by men's and women's speech, identical procedures were followed. A total of 68 hypothesis tests were computed
and the Z–scores compared to an average Z–score of 2.188. A significant value of 381.96, 67 df p > .0001 was obtained. As before the
question of whether male and female speech elicits differential patterns of evaluations is answered negatively.

RQ 3. Research question 3 had to be abandoned due to the
ludicrously small number of studies conducted solely by male investigators. In addition to providing the authors with a ready object lesson
in humility, this miscalculation attests to the efficacy of limiting biblio-
graphic entries to surnames and initials only. It was only following a
tally of the studies conducted by male investigators had been completed that the discrepancy became apparent. Regrettably this state of
affairs does little to assuage the doubts aroused by Eagly and Carli's
(1981) findings. The threat of researcher bias in the language literature has not been removed, merely obscured.

Some cautionary comments about the meta–analytic work completed thus far seem warranted here. The effect size analyses have
not yet been completed, and while inspection of the F and t values
reported in Tables 1 and 2 suggests that effect sizes would be modest,

they would nonetheless reveal important patterns related to specific behaviors. Displayed in Table 2, for instance, are data that might be used in a focused analysis on interruptions. Similarly, alternative strategies for combining the studies are being explored. Since variance across dependent variables might obscure some patterns of effects favoring one sex or another, it is possible that a more sensitive test might be better suited to this set of studies.

Discussion and Implications

Depending upon one's general orientation toward language differences research, the findings of this initial meta–analysis indicate several alternative interpretations. The meta–analysis could be rejected out–of–hand as spurious, or its results might be construed as an accurate depiction of social reality. Between these two positions lies one which would suggest that the meta–analysis is a strong commentary on the quantity, and indirectly, the quality of evidence available to support knowledge claims regarding the relationship between gender and language. It is our contention that these findings expose more about the questions that cannot be answered from available empiricism than anything else. In this sense, the current analysis echoes the observation of earlier literary reviews by Kramer, Thorne, and Henley (1978), Haas (1979), and Philips (1980) to the effect that strikingly few actual differences have been reliably and validly documented. While the need for more research is clear, the observation that no more of the same sort of research reviewed here is needed appears clearer still. Therefore, it seems appropriate to comment briefly on some conceptual and empirical characteristics of the literature summarized here that support this contention.

It is impossible to perform a quantitative review of this literature without becoming acutely sensitive to several recurrent empirical flaws. First, there is a troublesome lack of consistency across studies in terms of operational definitions. The measures of talkativeness summarized in Table 1 illustrate this problem well. It is far from certain that word production per unit of time and total talk time are precisely comparable. While few contemporary researchers employ quixotic or idiosyncratic measures of language variables the discrepancies associated with disciplinary differences are substantive. A linguist's approach to the notion of a "speaking turn" is quite different than that of a communication researcher. Greater attention to definitional and measurement matters of this sort would facilitate synthesis of findings vastly. Moreover, use of a common set of operational definitions would enable researchers to explore the effects of other process variables more precisely. At present, process variables are often confounded with or obscured by the differences across definitions and studies.

Table 1
Language Production
Talkativeness

Study	DV	N	NSD	F+	M+	**F	df	p
Kimble, et al 1981	word rate	144	X					
Ruben & Nelson (1983	total talk	40	X					
Wood (1966)	utterance length	36			X	6.43	22	.01
Gleser, et al (1959)	word rate	90	X					
Brouwer, et al (1977)	word rate	587	X					
Graves & Price (1980)	word rate	80			X	5.31	1,78	.05
Dabbs & Ruback (1984)	total talk	100		X		2.58	18	.05
Gall, et al (1969)	word count	39		X		2.40	1,36	.05
	word variability					2.90	1,36	.05
Ickes, et al (1979)	verbalizations	120		X		3.60	2,54	.05
Haas (1981)	total talk	24	X					
Smythe, et al (1983)	total talk	160	X					
Markel, et al (1976)	total talk	60			X	7.15	1,32	.05
Martin & Craig (1982)	word count	40	X					
Ickes & Barnes (1977)	verbalizations	124		X		10.75	1,48	.005
Ickes & Barnes (1978)	verbalizations			X				
Schultz, et al (1984)	total talk	90		X		4.81	1,84	.03
Crosby, et al (1981)	number of words			X				
Argyle, et al (1968)*	total talk	48						
Brownell & Smith (1973)	total talk	56		X		4.75	1,54	.05
Cherulnik (1979)	duration	36	X					
Chaiken (1979)	word rate	68			X	9.52		.001
Frances (1979)	speaking turns	88			X	6.49	1,86	.01
Nemeth, et al (1963)	Bales categories	168			X	3.02	1,144	.10
Feldstein, et al (1963)	word rate	96	X					
Cherulnik, et al (1978)	duration	134	X					
Levin & Silverman (1965)	word rate	48			X	3.57	1,46	.05
Shaw & Sadler (1965	talk time	36	X					

*No statistical data reported. Included for direction of effects.
**Values may also indicate t.

A related empirical matter concerns the impact of experimental conditions (e.g., tasks, etc.) upon language behaviors. Describing a stimulus picture in a room with a tape recorder can hardly be considered comparable to an initial interaction with a stranger of the opposite sex. Neither is particularly comparable to those situations in which a superordinate goal such as problem–solving, allocating rewards, or persuading another is imposed on participants. Indeed, the ecological validity of the laboratory setting for studies of language might be questioned, for while this domain has proven a fertile ground for investigating sex differences in other social behaviors, language may be an exceptional instance. Specifically troublesome is the fact that the equivalence of males' and females' roles as experimental subjects does not comport with the realities of social life. The idea that observed sex differences in language might accrue from the particular roles occupied by men and women is not new. What is surprising is that so little attention has been directed toward clarifying this potential confound. In many respects, this potential limitation on the generality of language performance findings corresponds to the language–as–fixed effect fallacy that is frequently attributed to the perceptions of language differences studies. These and other methodological errors produce endless qualifications to any generalizations about the discourse of men and women, which in turn erode the descriptive and predictive power of the literature.

The pattern of differences presented in Tables 1 and 2 might suggest that the variance within sex groups is substantially greater than that between the sexes. To the extent that this observation may not be dismissed as the cumulative effect of artifacts throughout the studies, it would indicate that our interest in sex as a causal factor is misleading. The comparative absence of simple linear relationships

Table 2
Language Production: Interruptions

Study	N	NSD	F+	M+	F	df	p
Lawrence & Carmen (1980)	72		X		4.24	1,72	.05
Shaw & Sadler (1965)	36		X		4.8	1,33	.01
Smythe, et al (1983)	160	X					
Rogers & Jones (1975)	36	X					
Roger & Schumacher (1983)	72	X					
Martin & Craig (1982)	40	X					
Dabbs & Ruback (1984)	100	X					
Eakins & Eakins* (1976)				X			
Zimmerman & West* (1975)				X			
West* (1979)				X			

*Studies did not provide statistical data; included here for information on direction of differences

between sex and discrete language variables suggests that sex might be more usefully examined as a moderating variable, affecting the patterning and organization of language cues at the macroscopic level rather than the microscopic level. Investigating the gender variable in this way implies an entirely different empirical approach, but one which could materialize the differences that seem to elude efforts to date.

One solution to the dilemmas described here is to shift toward methodologies which enable researchers to study language in natural contexts, through ethnographies, oral histories, or participant observation. Studies of speech as it occurs in natural settings offer powerful descriptions which frequently capture subtle shadings and nuances of conversational style that rarely emerge from more structured laboratory studies. Returning language to its social context is by now a familiar theme in the gender and communication literature, and one whose promise is being realized gradually, as more qualitative works are published. While some advocates renounce quantitative methods altogether, the contributions of both methodologies are critical to the development of theory in this area. At this phase, questions of incidence are no less important than questions of meaning and application. Quantitative methods are particularly well-suited to the former pursuit, while qualitative methods afford a richer analysis of how individuals organize their communication behaviors in response to situational demand, to coordinate their interactions, and/or to achieve specific goals.

On a more conceptual level, there are two noteworthy matters. In considering the various main effects for sex sprinkled throughout the literature, Ickes, Schermer, and Steeno (1979) would recommend the following caveat, "...virtually all of the previous studies in this area...represent comparisons in which biological sex is confounded with the subjects' sex role identifications" (p.378). This so-called natural confounding of effects represents a problem of undetermined magnitude. Some strong evidence suggests that androgyny, while far from the panacea originally promised in terms of explaining differences in social behaviors (Deaux, 1984), may be of singular importance in conversational analyses. LaFrance (1981) has suggested that rather than predicting the range of lifestyle and dispositional variables originally thought, androgyny's value may lie in the specification of very concrete and local behaviors. Her own work as well as that reported by Cook (1985), Smythe *et al* (1983) and Crosby *et al* (1981) would suggest that language may be among those behaviors affected to a significant degree. Too little is known to afford generalizations, but the likelihood that the androgyny construct might account for some of the within-sex variation in language behaviors should not be taken lightly. The relevance of gender schema theory (Bem, 1981) for the perceptions of language literature is less well explored. Although some theoretical linkage might exist (e.g., androgynes presumed flexibility might make them more tolerant of others' styles), Warfel's (1984) test of this relationship provided little clarification.

A final issue concerns the problem that Block (1976) labeled slippage in the evaluational sequence. In part, this problem is inherent in the way the gender and language literature has developed. The sequence is set in motion when a study documents a sex difference. The researcher then proceeds to speculate on the causes for that difference. Other researchers adopt that explanation to account for differences obtained in their studies and in time an entire explanatory framework has evolved without ever being tested directly.

An obvious quarrel with this tradition involves the number and types of inferences drawn in the latter half of the process. Very often the causal factors identified are those which are either popular in contemporary literature or which reflect a researcher's political or paradigmatic predilection among explanations. Quite often the causal force so identified is linked to the hypotheses or measurements taken in the study by nothing more than the author's personal opinion. Sex differences, however, are often very difficult to explain; the compelling and essentially unknowable combinations of biological, social, personal and behavioral factors that constitute femaleness and maleness defy easy or universal explanations. Unfortunately, researchers' and reviewers' own values on occasion appear to disrupt the orderly and logical interpretation of the extant data. Block drew from the classic Maccoby and Jacklin (1974) *Psychology of Sex Differences* to illustrate the problem. In summarizing sex differences on a continuum ranging from "well established" to "open questions" to "unfounded," the authors placed the dominance effect associated with male behavior in the "open question" category. Their earlier discussion of the effect, however, had concluded:

> We have seen that males tend to be the more dominant sex in the sense of directing more dominance attempts toward one another, toward authority figures, and perhaps toward females as well; it does not follow that females are submissive. It is possible, in fact, that dominance–submission is not a single continuum (p. 265).

In the context of a review of dominance studies, the relevance of another variable (submissiveness) left unmeasured in many of the studies is questionable, and in no way affects the balance of findings on male dominance. In an apparent effort to refute the stereotypic conception of women as "submissive" interactants the authors came precipitously close to misrepresenting the sum of their findings. Such slippage in the evaluative sequence, whether at the level of a single study or in summarizing dozens of investigations is unquestionably avoidable. The implication is actually quite simple; the documentation of a sex difference and the determination of its likely causal antecedents represent two, not *one*, empirical questions.

Taken together, the forgoing analyses recommend a two–pronged research attack. The primary goal of building an adequate data base for theory construction remains critical. Popular treatments of sex differences research notwithstanding, the number of language behaviors about which virtually no data are available is disquieting. Too many questions await answers. Thus, further studies, preferably of a programmatic nature, are needed to distinguish among those differences observed in the discourse of the sexes and document those which reliably discriminate. The same recommendation applies to the perceptions of language literature. In the strictest sense, the current practice of defining key concepts (e.g., powerful speech) as the absence of certain cues is conceptually indefensible. Without a substantial data base, our knowledge claims are at best no better than naive observations. At worst, they become dogma.

The second line of research should focus on developing and comparing explanatory paradigms for language behaviors. There is a deplorable lack of work in this critical aspect of theory development. Efforts like those of Schultz *et al* (1984) in the study of genderlect acquisition are excellent exemplars of this sort of research. For the perceptions of language literature, the gender–linked–language effect construct represents an instance of research in desperate need of an explanatory framework. If, as those studies seem to suggest, the speech of women is perceived as superior in socio–intellectual status and aesthetic quality, why are there no correspondingly high attributions of competence, attractiveness, or power made to women's speech? Finally, the call by Thorne, Kramerae, and Henley (1983), Smythe (*in press*) and others to develop models that incorporate both differences and similarities in male and female language identifies another important conceptual focus for research.

Should such a research scheme develop, it seems reasonable to infer that as each tributary evolves, the synergism between them would go far toward unraveling the complexities of the language and gender relationship. For the time being, however, global statements about the nature of this relationship should be held in abeyance.

References

Argyle, M., Lalljee, M., & Cook, M.(1968). The effects of visibility on interaction in a dyad. *Human Relations, 21*, 31–36.

Bem, S.L. (1981) Gender schema theory: A cognitive account of sex–typing. *Psychological review, 88*, 354–364.

Block, J.H. (1976) Issues, problems and pitfalls in assessing sex differences: A critical review of the psychology of sex differences. *Merrill–Palmer Quarterly, 22*, 283–308.

Brouwer, D., Gerritsen, M. & DeHaan, D. (1979). Speech differences between women and men: On the wrong track? *Language in Society, 8*, 33–49.

Brownell, W., & Smith, D. R. (1973). Communication patterns, sex, and length of verbalization in speech of four–year–old children. *Speech Monographs 4*, 310–16.

Chaiken, S. (1979). Communicator physical attractiveness and persuasion. *Journal of Personality and Social Psychology, 37*, 1387–97.

Cherulnik, P.D. (1979). Sex differences in the expression of emotion in a structured social encounter. *Sex Roles, 5*, 413–24.

Cherulnik, P.D., Neely, W.T., Flanagan, M., & Sachau, M. (1978). Social skill and visual interaction. *Journal of Social Psychology, 104*, 263–70.

Cohen, J. (1969). *Statistical power analysis for the behavioral sciences.* New York: Academic Press.

Cook, E.P. (1985) Psychological androgyny. New York: Pergamon Press.

Cooper, H.M. (1984) *The integrative research review: A systematic approach.* Beverly Hills: Sage Publications

Crosby, F., Jose, P., & Wong–McCarthy, W. (1981). Gender, androgyny and conversational assertiveness. In *Gender and nonverbal behavior.* C. Mayo & N.M. Henley (Eds.). New York: Springer–Verlag.

Dabbs, J., & Ruback, B. (1984). Vocal Patterns in Male and Female Groups. *Personality and Social Psychology Bulletin, 10*, 518–525.

Deaux, K. (1984). From individual differences to social categories: Analysis of a decade's research on gender. *American Psychologist, 39*, 105–116.

Eagly, A.H. (1983) Gender and social influence: A social psychological analysis. *American Psychologist, 38*, 971–981.

Eagly, A.H., & Carli, L.L. (1981). Sex of researchers and sex–typed communications as determinants of sex differences in influenceability. *Psychological Bulletin, 90*, 1–20.

Eakins, B. & Eakins, G. (1976). Verbal turn–taking and exchanges in faculty dialogue. In *The Sociology of the languages of Ameri-*

can women. B.L. DuBois & I. Crouch (Eds.). San Antonio, Texas: Trinity University Press.

Eakins, B.W., & Eakins, R.G. (1978). *Sex differences in human communication*. Boston: Houghton Mifflin.

Edelsky, C. (1979). Question intonation and sex roles. *Language in Society, 8*, 15–32.

Feldstein, S., Brenner, M.S., & Jaffe, J. (1963). The effect of subject sex, verbal interaction and topical focus on speech disruption. *Language and Speech, 6*, 229–39.

Frances, S.J. (1979). Sex differences in nonverbal behavior. *Sex Roles, 5*, 519–35.

Gall, M.D., Hobby, A.K., & Craik, K.H. (1969). Non–linguistic factors in oral language productivity. *Perceptual and Motor Skills, 29*, 871–74.

Glass, G. (1976) Primary, secondary, and meta–analysis research. *Educational Researcher, 5*, 3–8.

Glass, G. V., McGaw, B., & Smith, M.L. (1981). *Meta–analysis in social research*. Beverly Hills: Sage Publications.

Gleser, G. C., Gottschalk, L.A., & Watkins, J. (1959). The relationship of sex and intelligence to choice of words: A normative study of verbal behavior. *Journal of Clinical Psychology, 15*, 182–191.

Graves, R.L. & Price, G.B. (1980). Sex differences in syntax and usage in oral and written language. *Research in the Teaching of English, 145*, 147–53.

Haas, A. (1979) Male and female spoken language differences: Stereotypes and evidence. *Psychological Bulletin, 86*, 616–626.

Haas, A. (1981). Partner influences on sex–associated spoken language of children. *Sex Roles, 7*, 925–35.

Hall, J.R.(1984). *Nonverbal sex differences*. Baltimore: The Johns Hopkins Press.

Ickes, W., & Barnes, R.D. (1977). The role of sex and self–monitoring in unstructured dyadic interactions. *Journal of Personality and Social Psychology, 35*, 315–30.

Ickes, W., & Barnes, R.D. (1978). Boys and Girls together—and alienated: On enacting stereotyped sex roles in mixed–sex dyads. *Journal of Personality and Social Psychology, 36*, 669–83.

Ickes, W., Schermer, B., & Steeno, J. (1979). Sex and sex–role influences in same–sex dyads. *Social Psychology Quarterly, 42*, 373–85.

Jespersen, O. (1922) *Language: Its nature, development and origin*. London: Allen and Unwin.

Kimble, C., Yoshihawa, J., & Zehr, D. (1981). Vocal and verbal assertiveness in same sex and mixed–sex groups. *Journal of Personality and Social Psychology, 40*, 1047–54.

Kramer, C. (1977). Perceptions of female and male speech. *Language and Speech, 20,* 151-61.

Kramer, C., Thorne, B., & Henley, N. (1978). Perspectives on language and communication. *Signs, 3,* 638-51.

LaFrance, M. (1981). Gender gestures: Sex, sex-role, and nonverbal communication. In *Gender and nonverbal behavior,* Mayo, C. & Henley, N. (Eds.), New York: Springer-Verlag. 129-150.

Levin, H., & Silverman, I. (1965). Hesitation phenomena in children's speech. *Language and Speech, 8,* 67-85.

Maccoby, E.E., & Jacklin, C.N. (1974). *The psychology of sex differences.* Stanford: Stanford University Press.

Markel, N.N., Long, J.F., & Saine, T.J. (1976). Sex effects in conversational interaction: Another look at male dominance. *Human Communication Research, 2,* 356-364.

Martin, J.N. & Craig, R.T. (1983). Selected linguistic sex differences during initial social interactions of same-sex and mixed-sex student dyads. *Western Journal of Speech Communication, 47,* 16-28.

Mulac, A. & Lundell, T. (1980). Differences in perceptions created by syntactic-semantic productions of male and female speakers. *Communication Monographs, 47,* 111-118.

Pearson, J. (1985). *Gender and communication.* Dubuque, Iowa: Wm. C. Brown Publishers.

Philips, S.U. (1980). Sex differences and language. *Annual Review of Anthropology, 9,* 523-544.

Piliavin, J.A., & Martin, R.R. (1978) The effects of the sex composition of groups on style of social interaction. *Sex Roles, 4,* 281-296.

Rogers, D.B. & Schumacher, A. (1983). Effects of individual differences on dyadic conversational strategies. *Journal of Personality and Social Psychology, 45,* 700-705.

Rogers, W.T. & Jones, S.E. (1975). Effects of dominance tendencies on floor holding and interruption behavior in dyadic interaction. *Human Communication Research, 1,* 113-122.

Rosenthal, R. (1984). *Meta-analytic procedures for social research.* Beverly Hills: Sage Publications.

Rosenthal, R. (1978). Combining results of independent studies. *Psychological Bulletin, 85,* 185-93.

Rubin, D., & Nelson, M. (1983). "Multiple Determinants of a Stigmatized Speech Style: Women's Language, Powerless Language, or Everyone's Language?" *Language and Speech, 26,* 273-288.

Schultz, K., Briere, J. & Sandler, L. (1984). The use and development of sex-typed language. *Psychology of Women Quarterly, 8,* 327-336.

Shaw, M.E., & Sadler, O.W. (1965). Interaction patterns in hetero-sexual dyads varying in degree of intimacy. *Journal of Social Psychology, 66,* 345–51.

Smythe, M.J., Arkin, R.M., Nickel, S. & Huddleston, B. (1983). Sex differences in conversation: The stereotype revisited and revised. Paper presented at the International Communication Association, Dallas, Texas.

Smythe, M.J. (*in press*) Gender and communication behavior: A review of research. In *Progress in Communication Sciences Vol 10* B. Dervin (Ed.). Norwood, N.J.: Ablex.

Stewart. L., and Ting–Toomey, S. (1987) Communication, gender, and sex role in diverse interaction contexts. Norwood, N.J.: Ablex.

Swacker, M. (1975). The sex of the speaker as a sociolinguistic variable. In *Language and Sex: Difference and dominance.* B. Thorne & N. Henley (Eds). Rowley, MA.: Newbury House.

Warfel, K.A. (1984). Gender schemas and perceptions of speech style. *Communication Monographs, 51,* 253–267.

West, C. (1979). Against our will: Male interruptions of females in cross–sex conversation. In *Language, sex and gender: Annual New York Academy of Science.* Orsanu, J., Slater, M.K., & Adler, L.L. (Eds.) 81–100.

Wood, M.M. (1966). The influence of sex and knowledge of communication effectiveness on spontaneous speech. *Word, 22,* 112–37.

Zimmerman, D.H., & West, C. (1975). Sex roles, interruptions and silences in conversation. In *Language and sex: Differences and dominance.* (Ed.) B. Thorne & N. Henley. Rowley, MA.: Newbury House.

THOUGHT PROVOKER

What are the limitations of using meta–analysis as a research method? What information does meta–analysis provide for researchers that individual studies, when viewed alone, might not provide?

UNIT II
LINGUISTIC ISSUES RELATED TO SEX AND GENDER

One of the first areas of study researchers explored to distinguish differences in male/female communication was "how men and women speak differently." As a result, women's language was often labeled "deferential language" that carried relatively little power; common language choices included women's excessive use of qualifiers, empty adjectives, tag questions, and hedges. From this initial base of study, researchers have continued to explore such areas as male/female language choices, the impact of these choices on masculine and feminine images, and conversational control.

The four chapters included in this unit all focus on the use of language. The first two chapters are quantitative studies that measure male/female differences in usage and interpretation of pronoun choices. The third chapter is a quantitative study that focuses on the control of both social and task–oriented conversations. The final chapter is a qualitative study that examines specific language choice as it relates to persuasive messages that are feminist and anti–feminist in nature.

In Chapter Four, "Generic 'Man': Distribution, Acquisition, and Perception," Susan J. Wolfe, Cindy Struckman–Johnson, and Judy Flanagin examine sixth–graders' masculine/feminine associations with the generic pronoun "man." Since the authors posit that the generic value of all forms of the pronoun "man" is significantly reduced at age eleven, they encourage researchers to pursue exploring at what age these associations are acquired. In addition, the authors challenge educators to play a vital role in altering these associations since this language association appears to be acquired at a relatively young age in language development.

Miriam Watkins Meyers' chapter, entitled "Adult Writers' Generic Pronoun Choices," documents the fact that the use of the singular *they* is becoming well–established in the public writing of adult Americans. This study also suggests that the pronoun form *he or she* provides a viable alternative to the singular *they* or the generic masculine pronoun. Meyers' study clearly establishes the fact that traditional, grammatical boundaries are being altered to adapt to a nonsexist, inclusive use of pronouns.

From these initial studies concerning the impact of generic pronoun usage, Sally K. Murphy's research in Chapter Six entitled
"Gender Influences and Topic Management in Initial Interactions"
focused on the broader context of conversation. Murphy's study specifically examines the verbal strategies males and females use to introduce, maintain, decline, and terminate the topics of both
task–oriented and social conversations. While previous research
clearly suggests that males control conversations through control of
these specific strategies, Murphy's research concludes that the purpose of the conversation may be a stronger indicator of control than
the sex of the conversants. If we accept Murphy's findings as
generalizable, the power of conversational control may no longer be
almost exclusively associated with males.

Finally, in Chapter Seven, entitled "The Language of Opiniona-
tion and Controversy: Sexism," Virginia L. Chapman provides the
only qualitative examination of language choice in this unit. Chapman's research examines feminist/anti–feminist literature to discern
differences in language style and choices as well as their impact on
persuasibility. Chapman concludes that the intensity of language, the
sex of the author/speaker, and the sex of the audience act inter-
dependently to create a persuasive message. If the blend of these
variables is not appropriate, persuasion may not occur.

From the impact of generic pronoun usage to the impact of conversational control and linguistic choices in persuasion, these four
chapters focus on the use of language related to sex and gender issues. While some of the chapters reinforce the traditional findings of
previous research, other chapters suggest that traditional boundaries
are being redefined. These authors challenge future researchers to
break new ground in exploring these issues in greater depth.

CHAPTER FOUR

Generic "Man": Distribution, Acquisition and Perception

Susan J. Wolfe,
Cindy Struckman–Johnson and Judy Flanagin
University of South Dakota

Since 1970, a body of literature has emerged linking the use of masculine generics in English with sexism in American society. Bos-majian (1972), for example, labels "man" and its variants examples of "masculine supremacist language," while Bate (1975) attributes the existence of "invisible woman" to the use of "generic man." In a review of the literature on masculine generics, Todd–Mancillas (1981, p. 108) cites a number of representative articles providing "philosophical and humanistic arguments vying against usage of 'man'–linked words and masculine pronouns." Thorne, Kramarae and Henley (1983) list 44 books and articles which have focused on generics, in addition to a number of other sources which advocate changes in use, discuss changes which have occurred, or analyze reasons for opposition to change.

Murray (1973) claims that the supposedly generic (sex–neutral) meaning of the term is often confused with the male meaning, resulting in referential shifts from the generic to the male–specific within a single discourse, or even within a single paragraph. In related research on the history of the feminine pronoun, Stanley and Robbins (1978) show that authors occasionally manipulate the ambiguity of the masculine generic pronoun, quoting from Taylor (1973, p. 12), whose shift from generic to masculine reference in the following passage is obviously intended as humorous:

> When he has grown safely to adulthood he can wake up in the morning in his heated or air–conditioned house, use the latest techniques to prepare food for himself, drive off in his heated or air–conditioned car, and spend the day in a glass and plastic office...or even be one of the select few who have voyaged to the moon. And to cap it all he may, if he really so desires, stay at home and change into a she!

Empirical research demonstrates that generic "man" has strong male associations which affect the perceptions of language users.

Schneider and Hacker (1973) describe a study in which 603 students in their sociology class were asked to submit photographs illustrating sections of an introductory text. Half of the subjects were given such titles as "Social Man" and "Urban Man," while the others were asked to submit photographs representing, for instance, "Culture" and "Family." When generic "man" was included in the titles, 64% of the subjects submitted photographs depicting only males, often in stereotypically male occupations. "Urban man," for example, would elicit photographs of male police officers and construction workers. Only about 50% of the subjects receiving non-"man" titles submitted male-only photographs.

Kidd (1971) provided 68 subjects with declarative sentences containing forms of "man." After nine of 18 sentences, open-ended questions asked subjects to describe the sex of the individuals mentioned in the declarative sentences; 66% of the subjects identified the referents as male, whereas only 29% assigned generic reference to "man"– words. In the remaining half of the sentences which were followed by forced-choice alternatives, male associations were even more marked, with 86% of all subjects identifying referents as male.

Martyna (1980) claims that her studies of pronoun usage demonstrate the sex-exclusiveness of masculine generics. Investigating primarily generic "he," she (1978a; 1978b) found that males use the pronoun more frequently than females, who more often resort to "they" or "he or she." Males also more readily imagine themselves as included within a category referenced by generic "he"; in fact, males in her study saw themselves as included in generic "he" with seven times the frequency of females. Martyna (1980) further contends that the ambiguity of "he" (as either specific or generic in reference) allows it to be read as male-specific even in contexts which should force a generic reading (as, for instance, in sentences with indefinite antecedents like "someone" and with no sex-specific imagery; e.g., "When someone goes for a walk, he should wear comfortable footwear.")

Martyna (1983, p.31) also cites as evidence that "man" is normally read as male the fact that "startled laughter often greets such sentences as ...Man, being a mammal, breastfeeds his young." The data which she compiled on sex-specific versus sex-generic reference of "he" in educational materials indicate that the pronoun is twice as likely to be sex-specific; hence, speakers tend to avoid the use of generic "he" with female-dominant meanings, instead using "she" to refer to hypothetical nurses and librarians (a finding reported in a 1975 study conducted by the American Psychological Association). Martyna questions why a truly generic pronoun would ever necessitate a shift to a female pronoun.

Wolfe and Struckman-Johnson (1987) observe that "man," in addition to its strong male associations and potential ambiguity, has grammatical patterns unique among English generic nouns. Most English generics are count nouns; they co-occur with the articles "a" and "the," and take plural forms:

1. The student must spend two hours preparing for each hour of class.
2. A student must spend two hours preparing for each hour of class.
3. Students must spend two hours preparing for each hour of class.

Sentences 1 and 2 have one reading which is generic; sentence 3 is generic only. Generic "man," however, does not pattern in this way; sentence 4 is ungrammatical if intended as a generic reference (the asterisk denotes ungrammaticality):

4. *The man must work to earn a living.
5. A man must work to earn a living.
6. Men must work to earn a living.

Even sentence 6 is likely to be read as a plural referring only to males.

They remark that "man" seems to have its most strongly generic reading in the singular without "a," a construction which is ungrammatical for other human nouns:

7. Man must work to earn a living.
8. *Student must spend two hours preparing for each hour of class.

In a survey of 124 college students, Wolfe and Struckman-Johnson (1987) found that the singular form of "man" without an article had greater generic reference value than other forms of "man," while "the man," "a man," and "men" were more likely than other potentially generic nouns to be perceived as male-specific. In their study subjects read 56 declarative sentences followed by forced-choice alternatives requiring that they identify references as specific or generic. Singular non-"man" nouns were interpreted as generics 56% of the time with "the," 48% of the time with "a." While results for "a man" sentences did not differ appreciably, 88% interpreted "the man" as sex-specific. "Man" without an article was seen as generic by 91% of the subjects.

In the second part of the study, subjects were asked to identify the sex of the image categories suggested by human sentence-subjects as those of a single male, a single female, all males, all females, or all males/females of the species. When forced to discriminate between a reference as a male-only generic and true generic, 28% read "man" as referring to all males, while only 68% read it as referring to all human beings. "Men" was read as a male plural over 88% of the time, whereas other plural nouns were read as species-generic nearly 98% of the time (i.e., "workers" was read as "all workers," male or female.) "The man" was interpreted as a single male by 75% of the

subjects, and all males by nearly another 19%; non–"man" words with the article "the" were read as generics by nearly 88%.

As the studies summarized above indicate, forms of "man" are so strongly associated with male imagery that adult subjects interpret them as male–specific, perhaps even when generic reference is intended. It was hypothesized that the ambiguity inherent in generic uses would make generic "man" difficult to learn, and that the irregularity of its grammatical distribution might pose additional difficulties.

Studies of the acquisition of syntactic and morphological structures have demonstrated that complexity of a grammatical element determines its order of acquisition: the most complex structures are learned last. Chomsky (1969), studying the acquisition of syntax in children ages five to ten, has determined that several factors contribute to the relative complexity of sentences and decrease the ease with which they are learned. Two might have a bearing on the ability of learners to interpret generic "man" correctly: (1) A syntactic structure associated with a particular word is at variance with a general pattern in the language; (2) A conflict exists between two of the potential syntactic structures associated with a particular verb. These factors correspond roughly to the specificity of reference of "the man" in contrast to generic uses of e.g. "the tiger," and the ambiguity inherent in all instances of "a man," "the man," and "men."

Chomsky discovered that children first acquire (learn to interpret) a general pattern (for instance, sentence 9 below) in which the object of the main (first) verb is construed to be the subject of the second:

9. Mickey told Donald to turn a somersault.

A correct interpretation of sentence 9 determines Donald, not Mickey, to be the subject of "turn a somersault." Sentences containing the verb "promise," however, are at variance with the general rule.

10. Mickey promised Donald to turn a somersault.

In such sentences, the subject of the main verb is also understood to be the subject of the infinitive "to turn a somersault." Children learn to interpret such sentences later; still later, they learn to interpret sentences containing "ask" and infinitive constructions, for such sentences have two possible interpretations.

11. Mickey asked Donald to turn a somersault.

In sentence 11, the subject may be requesting permission to perform an action himself, or be requesting that the addressee perform the same action.

The present study was undertaken to investigate whether Chomsky's notions of grammatical complexity might also apply to semantic content and its interpretation. Generic uses of "man" should be more difficult for children to interpret correctly, allowing us to infer that they have not been learned, because of the unique grammatical patterns of the generic noun. ("Man" alone is the only form with a generic–only interpretation; in contrast to the other generic nouns, "the man" is specific–only in simple sentences. Moreover, the ambiguity of the forms "a man" and "men" should cause them to be interpreted as specifics by more than 50% of sixth–grade subjects because sex–specific references occur more frequently in speech and in educational materials, and because, as for adult speakers, forms of "man" have strong male associations.

It was thus hypothesized that eleven–year–old children would not only interpret all forms of "man" as specific more frequently than they would non–"man" nouns, as did college students in the Wolfe and Struckman–Johnson study (1987), but that they would also assign inappropriate sex–specific interpretations to "man" (interpreting singular "man" without an article as sex–specific.) In other words, not only would forms of "man," taken as a whole, have less generic reference value than non–"man" counterparts, but the generic–only singular "man" would, perhaps, not be acquired by eleven–year–old subjects.

For this study, "humanity" and "mankind" were included as sentence subjects; since they are consistently singular in form and generic in reference, it was hypothesized that eleven–year–old subjects would interpret them correctly more frequently than they did "man."

Method

Subjects

Subjects were 35 female and 23 male children in two sixth–grade classes in Vermillion, South Dakota. The average age of the children was 11.3 years. All subjects had received parental permission to be in the study and understood that participation was voluntary and anonymous.

Instrument

The questionnaire used by Wolfe and Struckman–Johnson (1987) in their study of college students was modified for the sixth–grade subjects. The number of items was reduced from 56 to 21 and the language of the instructions and of some predicates was simplified. As in the earlier study, sentences with "man" and non–"man" subjects were presented randomly so that neither context nor item similarity would affect their interpretation; singular forms of "man" and non–"man" nouns with the articles "a" and "the" and plural forms were included, as well as the unmodified singular "man."

Part I of the questionnaire contained the following sentence sets:

Man versus *Employee* must be cheerful and cooperative.

Man versus *Worker* must work hard to get ahead.

Man versus *Citizen* must pay taxes to the government.

One *Mankind* and one *Humanity* sentence were added at the end of the 21 sentences of the three Man/Non-Man sets. Instructions read as follows:

This survey is about how students understand sentences which start with different nouns. It is NOT A TEST. There are no right or wrong answers, only your opinions.

Please read the following sentences and answer whether you feel a sentence is about ONE SINGLE PERSON or whether it is about ALL PEOPLE.

For example, in the sentence "Man must work to live," if you think the sentence if about one particular man who must work to live, you would circle the answer "SINGLE PERSON." If you feel the sentence means that all people must work to live, then you would circle the answer "ALL PEOPLE." Please work quickly.

Part II of the questionnaire contained the same 24 sentences found in Part I. The instructions read as follows:

Please read the following sentences and answer whether a sentence makes you picture or think of:

A SINGLE MAN

A SINGLE WOMAN

ALL MEN OR A GROUP OF MEN

ALL WOMEN OR A GROUP OF WOMEN

ALL MEN AND WOMEN TOGETHER

For example, if you read the sentence "Man is a hunter" and picture a single man as being a hunter, then circle the answer, "A SINGLE MAN." If you picture men as being hunters, then circle the answer "ALL MEN OR A GROUP OF MEN." If you picture all people as being hunters, then circle the answer "ALL MEN AND WOMEN TOGETHER."

Procedures

A researcher and the sixth-grade teachers distributed the survey to the children in a classroom setting. Students without parental permission or interest in the study were given alternative activities. Subjects completed the questionnaire within 30 minutes.

Results

Responses of sixth-grade subjects differed from those of the college-age subjects studied by Wolfe and Struckman-Johnson (1987).

"The man" was seen equally often as sex–specific (88.1%); however, non–"man" with "the" was interpreted as referring to a single person or animal 63% of the time. Moreover, "a man" was interpreted as specific 79.4% of the time, versus 72.3% for non–"man" sentences with "a"; such sentences included, for example, "a worker must work hard to get ahead," which adults were unlikely to interpret as singular and specific in reference.

"Man," assigned a generic reading by the majority of college–age subjects, was incorrectly interpreted as specific by 54% of the sixth–grade subjects in sentences like "Man must work hard to get ahead." The plural form "men," on the other hand, was interpreted as referring to an entire class by 95.4%; plurals of non–"man" nouns were said to refer to an entire class by 96.6%.

Finally, sentences containing "humanity" and "mankind," inserted as a control, were interpreted as specific 20.3% and 11.9% of the time respectively. These nouns are abstract and therefore unambiguously generic; though singular, they refer to all humans collectively. Nonetheless, approximately one–fifth of the subjects incorrectly assigned a specific reading to "humanity."

Table 1

Distribution of responses of Eleven–Year–Old Children for Specific Versus Generic Categories for sentences with Man, Non–Man, and Generic Subjects

	Specific Readings Subject Refers To One, Single Person Animal	Generic Reading Subject Refers To An Entire Species Or Class of People-Animal
Man	54.0%*	46.0%
The Man	88.1%	11.9%
The Non–Man	63.0%	37.0%
A Man	79.4%	20.6%
A Non–Man	72.3%	27.7%
Men	4.6%	95.4%
Non–Men	3.4%	96.6%
Mankind	11.9%	88.1%
Humanity	20.3%	79.7%

Refers to the percentage of students who assigned the sentence to the "single person" category for three example sentences combined.

The second part of the questionnaire asked subjects to envision the referents of nouns as either a single male, a single female, all males, all females, or all people. Thus, subjects were forced to select for sex as well as number, unlike the choices they made in Part I of the survey. Here, the identification of "man" with maleness was even more marked: 47.2% of the subjects perceived "man" as referring to a single male and another 12.5% as referring to all males, only 39.8% as referring to all people. "The man" was seen as referring to one male in 84% of the responses, as all males in 4%, whereas non–"man" nouns introduced by "the" were read as generics 63.9% of the time and as sex–specific only 27.2% of the time. "A man" was perceived as sex–specific by 84.6% of the subjects; non–"man" nouns with "a" by 29.5% of the time. Even the plural form "men" was associated with all humans only 17.7% of the time, versus plurals of non–"man" nouns, perceived as generic 83.5% of the time. Finally, "mankind" and "humanity," termed generic in 88.1% and 79.7% of all responses to Part I of the questionnaire, were said to be perceived as generic by only 72.9% and 81% of the subjects.

Table 2

Distribution of Responses of Eleven–Year–Old Children from Sex–Identified Image Categories for Sentences with Man, Non–Man, and Generic Subjects

	A Single Male of the Species	A Single Female of the Species	All Males of the Species	All Females of the Species	All Males/ Females of the Species
Man	47.2%*	0.0%	12.5%	0.5%	39.8%
The Man	84.0%	0.5%	4.0%	0.0%	11.5%
The Non–Man	23.1%	7.1%	4.1%	1.8%	63.9%
A Man	76.6%	0.5%	8.0%	0.0%	14.9%
A Non–Man	25.4%	10.1%	4.1%	1.2%	59.2%
Men	4.0%	1.1%	77.2%	0.0%	17.7%
Non–Men	7.1%	1.2%	5.9%	2.3%	83.5%
Mankind	10.2%	1.7%	14.4%	0.8%	72.9%
Humanity	9.5%	0.9%	5.2%	3.4%	81.0%

Refers to the percentage of students who assigned the sentence to the "Single Male" sex–identified image category for the three example sentences combined.

Conclusions

As was hypothesized, eleven–year–old children assigned specific interpretations more frequently to forms of "man" than to other nouns with possible generic interpretations. When asked to picture forms of "man" as including either males or females or both, the percentage of responses designating forms of "man" as generic tended to decrease, possibly because Part II of the questionnaire clearly isolated sex and number as factors by allowing subjects to select from among "all males," "all females," and "all males/ females." The data thus suggest that forms of "man" are strongly associated with the male sex for sixth–grade subjects, as they are for adults, reducing the generic reference value of all forms.

It should be noted that the use of the terms "male" and "female" may have skewed the responses to Part II of the questionnaire, but it is difficult to envision a forced-choice experiment—whether one requiring selection of pictures or words—which would not have this defect. Indeed, Schneider and Hacker (1973) have speculated that their subjects' free choice of photographs may have tended to produce more pictures of males because the material printed at the time may have contained more photographs of males than females.

Results also substantiated the hypothesis that eleven-year-old children would be more likely than college students to misinterpret "man," a form which is collective and hence conceptually plural though grammatically singular. The subjects in Wolfe and Struckman–Johnson (1987) read "man" (in the singular without an article) as plural in over 90% of all responses, although associating it with "all males" 27.6% of the time in response to Part II of the questionnaire. Sixth-grade students, however, said that "man" referred to a single individual in 54% of the responses to Part I of the questionnaire and in 47.2% of the responses to Part II. Such subjects may be confusing the singular form of the word with its reference, since "the man" was perceived as singular and sex-specific in most of the responses to both parts of the questionnaire.

One unanticipated result was the apparent confusion of the part of some subjects over the interpretation of "mankind" and "humanity," perceived as singular by more than one-tenth of the sixth-graders. Additional research should be conducted to determine the percentage of eleven-year-old subjects who understand these terms and the nature of their comprehension (e.g., to determine whether the nouns are understood to refer to humans rather than animals or inanimate objects).

The results obtained do suggest that some of the subjects did not comprehend the notion of generic reference or, at least, had not mastered the grammatical constructions normally used to indicate it. A plural noun without the article "the" (or quantifiers such as "some," or other modifiers) as in "Workers must work hard to get ahead," is generally construed as referring to all members of the class or species. In this study, however, 8.3% of the subjects' responses to plural non-"man" nouns like "citizens" in Part II of the questionnaire designated them as singular, despite their plural forms. Subjects who have not mastered generic reference for nouns other than "man" cannot be expected to interpret correctly sentences containing "man," given its grammatical irregularity and sex-associated imagery.

Future research is needed to correlate the acquisition of generics in general and masculine generics in particular with the acquisition of other lexical items and grammatical forms. Additional research should be conducted with younger and older subjects to determine the age at which generics are acquired. Furthermore, while this study is suggestive, it does have some methodological flaws. First, as has been mentioned, the use of sex–specific terms in Part II of the questionnaire may have contributed to the tendency for subjects to associate "man" with maleness. Second, it is not clear that all sixth–grade subjects, perhaps with no prior experience using such instruments, were capable of following the directions; or, that having been informed that each questionnaire was "not a test," they completed their responses to the best of their ability. Third, it cannot be determined from the data whether subjects understood any portion of the terms' definitions used (e.g., "male," "female," "humanity," "mankind"), since no other interpretations were elicited. Open–ended questions about words might ascertain whether, for example, "male" was understood as denoting a sex and "mankind" as denoting human individuals. Finally, the results do not isolate the extent to which responses may be attributed to male–associated imagery and ambiguity, or to possible confusion caused by complexity due to grammatical irregularity.

If it can be demonstrated that generics are not acquired by age eleven, they are a comparatively late acquisition. Moreover, the failure of a majority of children in a specific age group to understand generic nouns, particularly masculine generics, would provide some direction for educators and publishers of textbooks and other written materials. Illustrations or specific, unambiguous contexts might be used to render generics comprehensible and to help language learners assimilate their use. In any case, the use of generic nouns should probably be monitored; the linguistic complexity they introduce into a text or discourse may create difficulties in comprehension beyond the ambiguities perceived by an adult speaker.

References

Bate, B. (1975). Generic man, invisible woman: Language, thought, and social change. *University of Michigan Papers in Women's Studies*, 2, 83–95.

Bosmajian, H. (1972). The language of sexism. *Etc.*, 29, 305–313.

Chomsky, C. (1969). *The acquisition of syntax in children from 5 to 10.* Cambridge, MA: M.I.T. Press.

Kidd, V. (1971). A study of the images produced through the use of the male pronoun as the generic. *Moments in Contemporary Rhetoric and Communication*, 1, 25–30.

Lewis, C.S. (1960). *Studies in words.* London: Cambridge University Press.

Martyna, W. (1978b). *Using and understanding the generic masculine: A social psychological approach to language and the sexes.* Unpublished Ph.D. dissertation, Stanford University.

Martyna, W. (1978a). What does "he" mean? Use of generic masculine. *Journal of Communication*, 28, 131–138.

Martyna, W. (1980). Beyond the he/man approach: The case for nonsexist language. *Signs: Journal of Women in Culture and Society*, 5, 482–493.

Martyna, W. (1983). Beyond the he/man approach: The case for nonsexist language. In B. Thorne, C. Kramarae, & N. Henley, (Eds.) *Language, gender and society* (pp. 25–37). Rowley, MA: Newbury House.

Murray, J. (1973). Male perspective in language. *Women: A Journal of Liberation*, 3, 46–50.

Schneider, J. & Hacker, S. (1973). Sex role imagery and the use of the generic "man" in introductory texts. *American Sociologist*, 8, 12–18.

Stanley, J.P. & Robbins, S.W. (1978). Going through the changes: The pronoun *she* in Middle English. *Papers in Linguistics*, 11, 71–88.

Taylor, J.G. (1973). *Black holes.* New York: Random House.

Thorne, B., Kramarae, C. & Henley, N. (1983). *Language, gender and society.* Rowley, MA: Newbury House.

Todd–Mancillas, W.R. (1981 Spring). Masculine generics = sexist language: A review of literature and implications for speech communication professionals. *Communication Quarterly*, 107–115.

Wolfe, S. & Struckman–Johnson, C. (1987). Generic man: grammatical distribution and perception. In M.A. Garnett & M. Hadley (Eds.) *Women in the World: Selected Proceedings* (pp. 109–121). University of South Dakota, Vermillion, SD: Pine Hill Press.

THOUGHT PROVOKER

How do the masculine images and attributes often associated with generic pronouns affect our perceptions of the persons, places, or things they represent? What factors in our everyday lives help us to acquire such perceptions at an early age?

CHAPTER FIVE
Adult Writers' Generic Pronoun Choices

Miriam Watkins Meyers
Metropolitan State University
St. Paul/Minneapolis, Minnesota

That singular generic *they* is firmly established in cultured English speech has long been known by language scholars. Indeed, singular *they* has been in use even in *written* English for centuries, and, as Randall (1985, p. 130) has pointed out, has been attested in the prose of such masters of the language as Austen, Thackeray, Mill, Scott, Dickens, and Trollope. Singular *they* is not an "ignominious legacy of the feminist movement," as one vehement guardian of the language put it in a recent letter to the editor of *The Chronicle of Higher Education* (Ecker, 1986), but a firmly entrenched usage that will not go away, attempts of eighteenth century prescriptive grammarians—and some contemporary English teachers—notwithstanding. Recent citations collected by the researcher include numerous instances of singular *they* in the public writing and speeches of doctors, lawyers, scientists, university officials, U.S. senators, language scholars, and other highly educated users of English—this in spite of the overwhelmingly negative attitude toward this usage on the part of the nation's editors (Kingsolver and Cordry, 1985, p. 4).

For several hundred years (Joesting, 1983, p. 30; Jochnowitz, 1982, p. 199), speakers and writers of English have apparently needed singular *they* to fill a grammatical slot for a pronoun to refer to singular persons of unspecified sex. This need may have become more urgent recently, as concern about inclusive language has grown. Thus, some writers have self-consciously adopted in their published work proscribed singular *they*, rather than the traditionally prescribed masculine generic pronoun, or have used other options, such as *he or she* (also proscribed traditionally), *he* and *she* used alternately within a text, *s/he*, or even created forms such as *hesh* and *hir* (see Baron, 1981, for an extensive listing of created forms), often with some acknowledgment in their preface or in other notes of this departure from standard edited English.

63

A variety of publishers and professional organizations, e.g., McGraw Hill and the American Psychological Association, have published guidelines for inclusive language, often urging writers to avoid the issue by pluralizing singular pronoun referents. In her instructions to 1984 convention program participants, the Chair of the Program Committee for the Conference of College Composition and Communication, a division of the National Council of Teachers of English, took the position that "in all but strictly formal usage, plural pronouns have been acceptable substitutes for the masculine singular" (Hairston, 1983, p. 3).

The literature on generic pronouns is considerable, and other researchers have reported choices made by speakers and writers. Richmond, Gorham and Dyba (1985), for example, have reported research indicating that public school children are more likely to use masculine referents when describing a gender–neutral person, with an increase in neutral treatments as they get older. Green (1977, p. 152) has noted that singular *they* is considered "normal" among junior college students. Martyna (1980, p. 75) found that college women used generic masculine pronouns less than college men.

The purpose of this paper is to report research into approaches taken to the generic pronoun by adult, upper–division college writers of both sexes. In particular, the research attempts to answer these questions:

- To what extent are traditionally prescribed masculine generic pronouns, singular generic *they*, and forms such as *he or she* in use in the writing of working adults who have had at least two years of college?
- What other approaches do these writers take to describe a person of unspecified sex?
- Are these writers in apparent control (i.e., are they conscious) of their pronoun choices, as manifested by consistency of approach?
- What is the relationship between sex of writer or of audience and generic pronoun choices?

These questions came to the attention of the researcher several years ago in studying essays prepared by the population in question for a writing diagnostic exercise. The topic for those essays was "What Makes a Good Class?" and, as one might predict, many writers discussed the hypothetical instructor of such a class. This instructor turned out as often to be a *they* as a *he* or a *he or she*, and often, it appeared, the generic pronoun treatment tended to confusion, with a variety of approaches used within the same passage. Readily accessible, and more recent, essays from other students from the same population, this time focused directly on a topic concerning a hypothetical person, provided the researcher an opportunity to investigate further first impressions about this group of writers' generic pronoun usage.

A preliminary analysis of almost half the samples, reported elsewhere (Meyers, 1986), indicated that more writers chose singular generic *they* than the prescribed masculine generic pronoun and that females were more likely to choose masculine generics and males to choose singular *they*. While these findings contrasted with those of researchers such as Martyna (1978) and Nilsen (1973), the researcher did not find them surprising, given the established tendency of females more closely to approximate prescribed usage. Females in the preliminary sample were also more consistent than males in their pronoun use, but whether this was a real or merely a random difference was not clear. No tests of statistical significance were applied in the preliminary study, nor did the sample size at that time (N=186) appear to be adequate, given the number of different approaches taken by the population. Such concerns prompted the present, extended study.

Method

Subjects. Metropolitan State University of the Twin Cities of Minneapolis/St. Paul, Minnesota is an upper- and graduate- level institution designed specifically for adults returning to college. Students must be certified as juniors to gain admission to a bachelor's degree program. The group of 392 students sampled here had accumulated an average of 111 quarter hours of college credit with at least a "C" average, with a range of from 80 to 242 quarter credit hours. The average age of the group was 34 at the time of sampling, ranging from 22 to 64 years of age. Fifty-five percent of the students were female.

Materials and Procedures. Near the beginning of their tenure at Metro State, all students seeking admission to a bachelor's degree program take a required course in which they plan their upper-division degree programs. One product of this effort is an individual degree plan, which begins with an educational goals statement. In their goals statements, students are asked to address the question "What is an Educated Person?" Faculty and staff within the university, as well as community professionals, review and evaluate each degree plan. Degree candidacy rests on acceptability of the degree plan, and the plan stands as part of the public record. Since the goals statement assignment carries a great deal of weight and involves several drafts and revisions, one could assume the writing represents a student's more careful work. It is this resource that has been used to obtain a corpus of writing to analyze.

Goals statements from all students completing the required class during the Winter and Spring Quarters of 1985 were obtained from official student files, copied, and scanned to locate the passages addressing the educated person topic. Each such passage was then marked, a word count was made, and all pronouns referring to the educated person were circled. Goals statements that did not contain a treatment of the educated person were excluded, leaving 392 student writing samples. These 392 samples were then reread and coded for overall approach and, when a third person singular approach was taken, they were read and coded for consistency, in accordance with generally–accepted principles of standard edited English. All instances of singular *they* and any use of feminine pronouns, whether free–standing or in combination, as in *he or she*, were coded as well.

The preliminary study yielded the following categories for coding consistent approaches to the third–person singular generic pronoun: the "masculine generic"; singular *they*; *he or she*–type treatments, including *she or he* and *s/he*; the "feminine generic" (*she* standing alone); and *one*. (For ease of reading, the nominative form has been used throughout this chapter to represent all forms of a given pronoun.) These categories obtained in the extended study as well.

The two major categories for coding approaches other than a consistent third person singular approach were the inconsistent mix and a catchall "other approaches" category for such treatments as those employing no pronouns, pluralization of the subject, and one–time–only use of a singular pronoun, which renders a judgment on consistency impossible.

The question of consistency bears discussion, since it occupies a prominent place in the study described. As stated above, treatments were judged consistent or inconsistent in accordance with generally accepted standards of edited English, in the sense that choices were sustained throughout the passages. In addition, controlled use of singular *they* and of *he–* or *she*–type choices were judged consistent in spite of much inveighing against these usages by parties who do not accept the proposition that choices of educated users of a language determine what is and is not standard. The usages in question are well established options in English speech and writing.

Excerpts from passages using the most common third person singular treatments will illustrate what consistency might mean within these categories:

Masculine generic: My idea of *an educated person* contains these elements: 1.) *a self–initiating lifelong learner*. This is *a person* who has learned the skills to educate *himself* in unknown areas. *He* has gone through the learning process many times.... *This educated person* is prepared to face any challenge that *he* encounters.

Singular they: I see *an educated person as: a well rounded person* who thinks clearly, has morals and ethics, uses *their* knowledge to the betterment of *themselves* and mankind. *A person* who has taken responsibility for *their* own life.

He– or she–type choices: In my opinion, *an educated person* is *one* who is well–rounded.... *The educated person* does not overlook *his/her* chosen profession.... *An educated person* must consider not only formal education but also the concepts of permanent learning throughout *his/her* lifetime.

One: To me *an educated person* has the willingness to learn new and innovative things while also learning about things of the past. *One* who has a curiosity and open mind...has the skills needed to further and develop *one's* individual potential to the utmost.

Feminine generic: *An educated person* is a *person* who is aware of who *she* is and what *her* place in the world is. *She* is comfortable with *herself*, and unafraid to present that self to others around *her*. *She* feels that *she* has a purpose in *her* life, and *she* understands the environment in which *she* is living.

By contrast, treatments judged inconsistent include the following:

- *An educated person* is one who takes responsibility for *his/her* own learning .... Knowing *one's* own strengths and weaknesses is a great benefit. For, *he/she* will be thinking for *themselves*, and never letting *their* limits be limiting to *them*. *They* will always be trying to achieve beyond the acceptable limits of *their* capacity.

- *A well–educated person* should have a high degree of competence in *their* vocation.... *An educated mind*...has committed values and bases *his* actions on them (,) forms *its* own judgments about works of art, makes *its* own political opinions.

- I agree that a degree doesn't guarantee that *one* is educated..... I have met *many people* that haven't a degree and are still quite educated. *This person* has been educated through life experiences. I feel life experiences provide *one* with a majority of *their* education. If *one* were to have a degree, but block out what is happening around *him*, *he* would be depriving *himself* of a total education.

- In my opinion *an educated person* is *someone* who is aware enough to know what makes *him or her* happy and productive. Just a piece of paper does not make *you* any more educated than *the person* who hasn't obtained *their* high school diploma. To be educated *you* must know what *you* want for *your* self, and once this established, if *you're* smart, *your* goal is....

Judgments on consistency are just that—judgments. Reader/coder judgments of consistency in passages such as the ones in question here are confounded by the complexity and variety of English pronoun treatments, including, for example, perfectly standard use of alternating *one* with other third person singular pronouns to avoid repetition and, sometimes, to mark more formal discourse. But it was important that such judgments be made in this study because consistency suggests control, which in turn suggests conscious editorial choices. Ambiguity about writer purpose is always possible, as in the last inconsistent example, where the writer uses "familiar *you*" as well as a third singular approach. This writer's approach was judged inconsistent not just for his use of familiar *you*, but for other reasons as well; control over approach was simple not apparent in a reading of the passage.

To return to the overall methodology of the study, and to summarize, the following questions were asked of the writing samples:

> What approach was taken to the person of unspecified sex (the educated person)? Did the writer use a third person singular approach (including singular *they*)? If so, was pronoun use consistent or inconsistent, i.e., was the pronoun of choice sustained throughout the passage?
>
> Did the writer use singular *they* at least once in the passage?
>
> Did the writer use any feminine pronoun at least once in the passage?

These data, as well as length of passage and sex of both writer and instructor, were coded in preparation for computer entry, then analyzed to obtain frequencies, cross tabulations, and comparisons of means.[1]

Results and Discussion

Findings with regard to broad approaches are contained in Table 1.

TABLE 1. Adult College Students' Approaches to Generic Pronouns in Writing about "The Educated Person"

N=392 (216 females, 174 males*)

Third Person Singular Approaches
Consistent/controlled	138 (35%)
Inconsistent/variable	65 (17%)
Other Approaches*	189 (48%)

*Sex of two writers proved unavailable; hence the two missing cases in all tests and descriptions of writers by sex. **Examples include pluralizing antecedent nouns, using first or second person pronouns, avoiding pronouns altogether, and using one generic pronoun only.*

Contrary to the researcher's expectations, inconsistency in pronoun use was not as epidemic as an impressionistic reading of the preliminary corpus suggested. On the contrary, over twice the number of writers using more than one third person singular generic pronoun demonstrated control over their chosen approach as did not. Furthermore, if alternating singular *they* with other third person pronouns, especially *he–* or *she*–type choices, had been judged consistent, the record on consistency would have been even higher. Alternating *they* with another consistently chosen third singular approach may be an alternative to alternating *one*, which is accepted in edited American English but sounds formal to many an American ear. Alternating *they* is widespread in the speech and writing of educated speakers of English. Such citations from spoken English as the following are easily collected from the media:

If I had *a secretary, he or she* would just be sitting around waiting for me to tell *them* to do something, and I wouldn't know what to tell *them*. (Walter Matthau, actor, quoted in the newspaper)

If *a person* on welfare loses *his or her* benefits, *their* (Neal Kinnock, head of the British Labor Party, in a radio broadcast)

If *he or she* finishes the program, *they* will automatically be admitted.... (Gerald Christensen, Chancellor of the Minnesota State University System, in a radio broadcast)

While usage conventions for spoken English differ from those of written English, examples of the usage in question are available in writing as well:

The manager needs to be "in control" at all times. *He/she* acts as if *they* are always right and everyone else is wrong.

If *somebody* is really stuck and *he or she* is arguing with you, ...by making *the person* laugh, you've broken the pattern of argument and forced *him or her* to make changes in what *they* say and how *they* say it. (Excerpts from two columns of Kenneth Blanchard, author of *The One–minute Manager*)

We cannot assume that because we have offered a message to *another person they* have received it. *The other person* may not have been able to "catch" our message, may have been preoccupied with "throwing" one of *his or her* own, or may have been distracted by other bombarding stimuli. (Judy Pearson, in *Gender and Communication, 1985*)

It is worth noting that a large number (48%) of the writers in the sample took other approaches than ones requiring decisions on generic pronoun use, perhaps to avoid the issue of consistency, where a commitment to inclusivity compounds the writing task, especially with regard to style. Choices of these writers will not be examined in detail in this paper, which takes as its focus third person singular generic pronoun choices. Generic pronoun choices of those demonstrating consistency in a third person singular approach are summarized in Table 2.

TABLE 2. Choices of Writers Using a Consistent Singular
Approach to the Generic Pronoun
$N=138$

Approach	n	%
Generic he	47	34
Singular they	44	32
He/she-type	30	22
One	11	8
She	6	4

It appears from these results, and from the preliminary study where singular *they* overtook generic *he*, that these two approaches are about equally chosen by this population of writers as the most popular. *He/she* is a strong contender, however.

Table 3 shows all approaches to discussing the hypothetical educated person, by sex of writer.

TABLE 3. Approaches by Sex to Sex–Neutral Person
$N=390$

*Approach	Female		Male		Combined	
	n	%	n	%	n	%
Other than singular	75	34.7	48	27.6	123	31.5
Mix (inconsistent)	37	17.1	30	17.2	67	17.2
Generic He	20	9.3	27	15.5	47	12.1
Singular they	22	10.2	22	12.6	44	11.3
He/she-type	17	7.9	11	6.3	28	7.2
He once	6	2.8	17	9.8	23	5.9
He/she once	10	4.6	7	4.0	17	4.4
They once	10	4.6	6	3.4	16	4.1
One	5	2.3	6	3.4	11	2.8
She	6	2.8	0		6	1.5
One once	4	1.9	0		4	1.0
She once	3	1.4	0		3	.8
It once	1	.5	0		1	.3

*Approaches are in descending order of their selection by writers of both sexes, as indicated in the column headed "Combined."

Sex of writer was found to be a factor in choice of approach to the treatment of person of unspecified sex ($X^2[12,n=390]=25.64$, p <.01). Females were more likely than males (34.7% and 27.6%, respectively) to choose other than third–person singular approaches to the writing task. Furthermore, in contrast to the preliminary study, females in the extended study chose generic *he* less than males (9.3%

and 15.5%, respectively). Only females used *she* as either a consistent or a one-time-only approach. In fact, females used more different approaches than did males. Consistency of approach, however, was not found to be related to sex in tests of statistical significance ($X^2[1,n=201]=.17850$, p $<.6727$).

Given traditional sanctions against the use of both singular *they* and *he or she*—and the radical departure from prescribed generic *he* signaled by generic *she*—the extent of these approaches total use in the corpus seemed worthy of investigation. To what extent, that is, did these adult writers use some traditionally proscribed singular generic pronoun, whether consistently or inconsistently, at least once in their writing? Choices of writers who used a mix of approaches, those who used consistent singular approaches, and those who used one-time-only singular approaches were analyzed to study this question. Of these writers using any third person singular generic pronoun in their essays, 105, or 39%, were found to have used singular *they* at least once. Ninety-two writers, or 34%, used a feminine generic pronoun (either alone or in *he or she*-type combinations) at least once. Chi square tests performed on all writers in the sample showed no significant interaction between sex and use of singular *they* or feminine generic pronouns ($X^2[1,n=390]=.07022$, p<.7910 and 2.10448, p<.1469, respectively).

Sex of instructor was investigated as a possible influence on pronoun approaches, following the suggestion of some researchers (Bate, 1978; Richmond and Dyba, 1982; Todd–Mancillas, 1981) that the teacher may have an effect on student generic pronoun usage. This seemed particularly appropriate in the present study, since student subjects depend on their instructors for support and even advocacy in achieving degree candidacy and need instructor "approval" of their goals statements. Furthermore, a preponderance (over two–thirds) of the goals statements were prepared in classes with female instructors. No effect was indicated, however, on a chi square test ($X^2[24,N=392]=15.41828$, p<.9079).

These results may provide interesting comparisons with those from other, more traditional, college student populations. The Metro State University student is older than most students. As working people in their mid–thirties, typically well on their way to finishing a college degree, Metro State students might be thought to fall somewhere between informants designated Type II (middle–aged, high school educated) and Type III (young, college educated) in dialect studies (Allen, 1964).

Regional comparisons may prove interesting as well. It is worth noting that the social climate in which the writers in this study move is particularly conducive to sensitivity in generic pronoun use. The Minnesota legislature passed a law in 1986, for example, requiring that all masculine generic language in state statutes be revised for inclusivity

(Pinney, 1986, p. 1B). Public speakers who do not use inclusive language are something of a scandal in the Twin Cities metropolitan area. A prominent New York newscaster elicited a loud, in-unison gasp at the annual meeting of the Greater Minneapolis Chamber of Commerce in 1985 when she referred to the many women in the audience as "wives and girlfriends" of the "businessmen" present; this *faux pas* made the front page of the morning newspaper the next day.

Comparisons with young writers may also be instructive to determine trends across generations. The writers whose pronoun use is examined here are typically parents of Minnesota school children. Essays submitted by such children for publication in the "Journal Juniors" feature of the *Minneapolis Star and Tribune* provide a means of studying the status of singular *they* and *he or she*–type approaches in the writing of youngsters and of making comparisons with the adult sample. Preliminary analysis of papers submitted by children on two topics, "The Ideal Teacher" and "The Ideal Adult," indicates that singular *they* is much more prevalent in the writing of Minnesota children than in that of their parents' generation. For reasons which are not yet clear, these children's ideal adult is more likely to be a *they* than is their ideal teacher. It appears as well that the children use masculine pronouns when they have a male model in mind, feminine pronouns when they have a female in mind, and singular *they* when they have no model in mind.

Conclusion

This study documents what many observers of current English usage have suspected to be true: the singular *they* is well–established in the public writing of adult Americans. The study suggests also that generic pronoun constructions of the *he or she* type provide an alternative to singular *they* or the masculine generic pronoun. While writers were twice as likely to maintain consistency in their pronoun choices, more work is necessary to determine what motivates generic pronoun choices and what role inclusive language concerns play in the inconsistency one finds in generic pronoun choices. How is singular *they* analogous to more formal *one*? What regional, social, age and other differences obtain in generic pronoun approaches? What effect does schooling have on willingness to use singular *they* in public writing?

Whatever the results of research into these and related questions, given the current emphasis on inclusivity, the increasing body of scholarship documenting the historic status of singular *they*, and the apparent willingness of a large proportion of writers to use both this form and those of the *he or she* type, it will be interesting to see if these solutions to the generic pronoun problem become more widely adopted and more generally acceptable in edited writing.

Reference List

Allen, H.B. (1964). The primary dialect areas of the Upper Midwest. In A. Marckwardt (Ed.), *Studies in Language and Linguistics in Honor of Charles C. Fries* (pp. 303-314). Ann Arbor: English Language Institute, University of Michigan.

Baron, D.E. (1981). The epicene pronoun: the word that failed. *American Speech. 56* (2), 83-97.

Bate, B. (1978). Nonsexist language use in transition. *Journal of Communication, 28,* 139-149.

Ecker, M.W. (1986, June 19). 'They' is no substitute for the right pronoun (Letter to the editor). *The Chronicle of Higher Education, 30,* 33.

Green, W.H. (1977). Singular pronouns and sexual politics. *College Composition and Communication. 28,* 150-153.

Hairston, M. (December, 1983). Memorandum to participants of 1984 CCCC convention program. National Council of Teachers of English, Urbana, IL.

Jochnowitz, G. Everybody likes pizza, doesn't he or she? *American Speech, 57*(3), 198-203.

Joesting, J. (1983). The psychology of sex differences in the use of masculine and feminine pronouns in written English. *The USF Language Quarterly, 22* (1-2), 30, 38, 43, 46.

Kingsolver, P., & Cordry, H.V. (October, 1985). Gender and the press: an update. Paper presented at the Eighth Annual Communication, Language, and Gender Conference, Lincoln, NE.

Martyna, W. (1978). What does "he" mean? *Journal of Communication, 28,* 131-138.

Martyna, W. (1980). The psychology of the generic masculine. In S. McC. Ginet, R. Borker, and N. Furman (Eds.), *Women and Language in Literature and Society* (pp. 69-78). New York: Praeger.

Meyers, M. (April, 1986). Generic pronoun strategies in adults' writing. Paper presented at the annual meeting of the Minnesota Council of Teachers of English, Minneapolis, MN.

Nilsen, A.P. (1973). Grammatical gender and its relationship to the equal treatment of males and females in children's books. Doctoral dissertation, University of Iowa.

Pinney, G. (July 31, 1986). State laws, revisions take effect today. *The Minneapolis Star and Tribune,* pp. 1B, 4B.

Randall, P. (1985). Sexist language and speech communication texts: another case of benign neglect. *Communication Education, 34,* 128-134.

Richmond, V.P., & Dyba, P. (1982). The roots of sexual stereotyping: the teacher as model. *Communication Education, 31,* 265-273.

Richmond, V.P., Gorham, J. & Dyba, P. (October, 1985). Generic and non–generic gender referent usage among student in grades 3–12. Paper presented at the Eighth Annual Communication, Language, and Gender Conference, Lincoln, NE.

Todd–Mancillas, W.R. (1981). Masculine generics=sexist language: a review of literature and implications for speech communication professionals. *Communication Quarterly, 29,* 107– 115.

Footnotes

[1]Grateful acknowledgment is made of the invaluable help of Vee Verdick, Joanne Brisse, Donna Blacker, Vera Goldberg, Sue Nelson, Paige Reyes, Heather Johnson, Wendy Johnson, and Lin Schroeder for their help in obtaining, copying, and entering the data for this study; to Steve Plummer for providing a data base search; and to Leah Harvey for consultation on statistical analysis.

THOUGHT PROVOKER

What effect does schooling have on our willingness to use the singular "they" or other grammatical adaptations in public writing? How do regional, social, age, or other differences impact on generic pronoun interpretations?

CHAPTER SIX
Influences of
Sex Composition and Topic
Management in Initial Interactions

Sally K. Murphy

University of Pittsburgh

In 1973, Robin Lakoff focused both popular and academic interest on the subject of "female" language. After an introspective examination of her own communication style and consideration of chance conversations, Lakoff identified a number of behaviors which she classified as "typically female": content choices (topics that focused on people or feelings), vocal features (hesitations, declaratives with rising intonation), lexical choices (adjectives, adverbs, mitigators), and grammatical forms (tag questions, modal constructions). Lakoff's suggestions struck a responsive chord for many readers and stimulated investigation of speech patterns of women and men. Had Lakoff identified real or stereotypic language behaviors? The subsequent research has produced contradictory and inconclusive results.

Female–male communication patterns have been studied from two perspectives. One program seeks to answer the questions: Do native speakers of American English identify particular communication styles as female and male? If so, are there varying evaluations of those sex–typical speech styles? Results indicate that there are strongly held stereotypes of and about male and female speech (see, for example, Siegler and Siegler, 1976; Edelsky, 1976; Berryman and Wilcox, 1980; Liska, Mechling, and Stathas, 1980).

While these studies found widespread recognition of sex–specific language, significant questions remain. The research used constructed messages as stimulus for rater evaluation. While constructed messages have the advantage of giving the researcher control of the variables of interest, they also have significant limitations: Do the specific constructed messages used in the research reflect the communication patterns of normal conversation, or do the messages simply reflect the stereotypic expectations of the researchers? Because the sentences/messages were not taken from actual conversation, and because the rate of use of sex–specific markers in the constructed messages was not matched with patterns of natural conversation, the results may only be taken to support the existence of stereotypic assumptions about and evaluations of sex–specific communication patterns.

The second approach to the study of female–male communication asks the question: Do women really use a communication style that is distinct from that used by men? The studies which investigate this question examine interaction data but the results provide little conclusive data for proof or disproof of Lakoff's thesis. While some studies found women and men using different patterns of talk (for example, DuBois and Crouch, 1975; Zimmerman and West, 1975; Crosby and Nyquist, 1977; McMillan, Clifton, McGrath, and Gale, 1977; Fishman, 1977, 1978), not all of the differences were in the direction expected (DuBois and Crouch, 1975), and numerous studies found no sex–specific behavior (Tyler, 1976; Shaw, 1979; Martin and Craig, 1983, among others).

Studies which have identified strongly held stereotypes about female and male speech suffer from the limitations of using constructed messages. Studies which have examined actual interaction data have been inconsistent in which sex–related indicators have been coded, what topics of conversation were assigned, how the experimental groups were constructed, and in what setting the conversations were collected; as a result, making comparisons is difficult.

The effect of conversational context may be particularly critical in explaining inconsistent findings. It may be argued that while speaker sex is (almost) always noticeable in face–to–face interaction, in certain contexts display of sex–typical behavior may be more appropriate than in other contexts. For example, in an initial mixed–sex social interaction, one might expect sex of speakers to be an important aspect of speaker choices. But in conversations where both speakers must accomplish an imposed task, or where both speakers are of the same sex, the sex of the speaker may be less relevant to the strategies speakers choose to construct their conversation.

Additionally, sex difference research has frequently failed to consider the impact of speaker choices when analyzing conversational data. Specific grammatical forms, lexical choices, vocal features, and content choices have been identified and counted so that male-female differences could be described. What has not been investigated is the impact of any particular communication strategy on the structure of the conversation itself. One way to ascertain the importance of speaker choices, and hence the importance of any observed sex difference, is to examine whether different conversational strategies lead to different conversational outcomes. For the purposes of this study, the outcome considered is topic management.

To determine the impact of conversational strategies on the structure of conversation, this study examined the verbal strategies female and male conversants use to introduce, maintain, decline, and terminate the topics of conversation. The following question was asked:

1. Do women and men differ in the ways they offer, pick, maintain, decline, and terminate topics of conversation?

Because conversational context may account for the failure to find sex-linked communication differences in prior research, data was collected in two contexts and a second question was asked:

2. Do women and men in task and social conversations differ in the ways in which topics are picked, maintained, declined, or terminated?

Methods

Data

Six two-person conversations were collected for this study. Three of the conversations were task conversations collected from students who were attempting to decide upon a topic to debate as their final project in argumentation classes. The other conversations were social: volunteer undergraduate students from an introductory communication course were paired, given a tape recorder and tape, and asked to talk until the tape was complete or they had finished their conversation. A total of six females and six males participated. Two female-female, two male-male, and two female-male conversations were analyzed. Participants were asked how long they had known their conversational partner in order to determine if prior acquaintance would figure in the analysis (Sykes, 1984). None of the students in the social condition knew their partner prior to the conversation. The students in the task condition recognized their partners from in-class interactions during the one to five weeks of class prior to data collection. None reported any conversation with their partners outside the classroom.

Data Analysis. Each of the conversations were transcribed and topic sequences were identified. A detailed approach to topic identification was used. Each utterance was coded for potential topics. Any part of an utterance which could reasonably be considered something about which speakers could talk was marked as a potential topic. Each subsequent reference to the potential topic was also coded (1). For the purposes of this study, a topic is one in which partner collaborates and which occupies at least three utterances of conversational space. Based on this analysis, four categories of topics were identified: potential topics, major topics, subtopics, and single-speaker topics.

Potential topics are those issues offered for talk by one of the speakers but which were not developed by either speaker. *Major Topics* are those issues which elicited at least one contribution by each speaker and which were discussed for a minimum of five utterances. *Subtopics* are those issues which were discussed by both speakers, but which occupied only three or four utterances of conversational space. *Single-speaker topics* are those topics which were developed by only one speaker and were at least three utterances long.

The number of potential topics, single-speaker topics, sub-topics, and major topics each speaker contributed to the conversation was counted. This allowed a comparison of both the work done by individual speakers in the conversations and their success rate for various topic types.

After topics had been identified, each utterance was coded for its conversational function using a scheme developed by Burton (1981). This allowed identification of the moves speakers made to offer and take-up topics of talk. Comparisons were made between speakers and conversation types in order to determine whether topic management strategies differed due to speaker sex or conversational context. The same procedures were followed to uncover the strategies of topic maintenance and topic termination. A final step included examination of those potential topics which were not chosen by speakers as topics of talk. In this manner, each topic sequence in the six conversations was fully described in terms of the offer, take-up, maintenance, and termination of topic sequences.

Results

The initial and continuing need to discover topics which are shared between the speakers is at the heart of making conversation. When Schenkein notes that "conversation proceeds as speakers arrange their participation through delicately orchestrated sequences of utterances, ...organized through abstract resources and constraints" (1978, p. 3), he is describing conversation as a joint enterprise between the speakers which requires careful use of the resources available to each. One of the resources which speakers bring to conversation is a cache of potential topics.

Potential Topics

Table 1 summarizes the number of potential topics each speaker offered and the successful topics contributed by each speaker. The richness of speakers' conversational resources is illustrated by the average number of potential topics offered in the conversations: 167.

Table 1

Summary of Conversational Topics

Data	Speaker	Potential Topics	Sub–Topics	Major Topics
10S [a]	Female	131	10	14
	Male	154	14	19
7S	Male	89	18	18
	Male	86	16	14
4S	Female	69	18	15
	Female	64	16	17
9T	Male	60	13	13
	Female	54	12	8
2T	Female	68	11	3
	Female	98	9	19
11T	Male	61	10	10
	Male	79	8	6
Female [b]				
Average success		80.67	25.33	12.67
			31.41%	15.07%
Male		88.17	26.5	13.33
Average success			30.06%	15.12%

[a] S denotes social conversations, *T* denotes task conversations
[b] Success was determined by taking the number of topics as a percentage of the speaker's potential topics

Women in these conversations offered, on average, fewer potential topics than did the men. While women offered fewer topics than men in these data, the difference between women and men is a small one. (2)

Topics

A topic remains a potential topic until it is developed in the conversation. Developed topics of two distinct kinds were found in these conversations: those topics to which both conversational partners contributed and those developed by only one speaker (Single–speaker topics). Both are described below.

Joint Topics. Two different categories of jointly–produced topics were coded for these data: subtopics, those topics which were mentioned for 3 or 4 utterances, and major topics, those which were mentioned for 5 or more utterances.

As is clear from the data summary in Table 1, women in these conversations offered slightly fewer topics for conversation than men and they had a slightly higher success rate than men. The amount of conversational work done by women and men was, in the initial interactions studied, roughly equal.

In these conversations, the differences between speakers are related to the context of the conversation rather than the sex of the speaker. Table 2 describes topic success rates of speakers by conversational context.

Table 2
Comparison of Speaker Success by Conversational Context

Data	Speaker	Successful Topics[a]	Difference Between Speakers
10S	Female	8.42	3.16
	Male	11.58	
7S	Male	20.57	3.43
	Male	17.14	
4S	Female	24.81	0.0
	Female	24.81	
Average difference between social speakers		2.20	
9T	Male	22.81	5.27
	Female	17.54	
2T	Female	8.43	8.44
	Female	16.87	
11T	Male	14.29	4.29
	Male	10.00	
Average difference between task speakers		6.00	

[a] Success was determined by taking the speaker's topics as a percentage of total topics offered.

The difference in success of topics offered and taken up by speakers in social conversations is relatively small. No one speaker seems to be considerably more successful than her partner. In the task conversations, the situation is different. In each task conversation, there is similarity in the total number of topics taken up, while the success rate of individual speakers, measured as a percentage of total topics offered for talk, is markedly different.

Single-speaker topics. Single–speaker topics are problematic: If conversation is a jointly created act, topics which are monologic challenge the notion of topic as co–created. Yet for a speaker to be able to create an embedded monologue, partner must permit, by suspending her claim to a turn, the development of a single–speaker topic.

Table 3
Single–Speaker–Only Topics
by Sex of Speaker
and
Conversational Context

	Female Speakers	Male Speakers
	15	11
	8	4
	10	7
	4	7
	5	5
	12	8
	54	42
Avg.	9.0	Avg. 7.0
	Social Conversations	Task Conversations
	26	11
	11	17
	18	13
	55	41
Avg. 8.33		Avg. 13.63

Table 3 summarizes the incidence of single–speaker topics by the sex of the speaker. Women and men in these conversations differed in their development of single–speaker topics; women developed an average of nine single–speaker topics per conversation while men developed an average of seven.

Again, conversational context provides additional information about single–speaker topics. As Table 3 indicates, single–speaker topics occur most frequently in social conversation and occur less frequently in task conversations.

Topic take–up strategies

Potential topics become topics of conversation when they are taken up by one's partner and developed in the conversation. Regardless of the specific number of contributions made by either speaker, for a potential topic to qualify as a conversational topic, both speakers must be oriented to the topic. Describing how this co-orientation is signaled is the purpose of this section.

By examining the utterance in which a topic was first offered and the partner's first utterance which continued the topic, four patterns of topic take-up were identified: 1) informative-comment; 2) informative-elicit; 3) elicit-reply; and 4) informative/elicit-challenge. Table 4 summarizes the frequency with which each of the patterns were found in the conversations.

Table 4
Patterns of Topic Offer and Take Up
By Conversation

Data	Inform/ Comment	Inform/ Elicit	Elicit/ Reply	Inform/ Challenge
10S				
# of moves	23	23	11	0
% of moves	40.35	40.35	19.30	0.00
7S				
# of moves	25	24	17	0
% of moves	37.88	36.36	25.76	0.00
4S				
# of moves	27	20	19	0
% of moves	40.91	30.30	28.79	0.00
11T				
# of moves	25	2	6	1
% of moves	73.53	5.88	17.65	2.94
2T				
# of moves	17	13	6	6
% of moves	40.48	30.95	14.29	14.29
9T				
# of moves	19	6	10	11
% of moves	41.30	13.04	21.74	23.91
Total	136	88	69	18
Percentage	43.73	28.30	22.19	5.79

Each conversational pair demonstrated a preference for offering topics in informative utterances and taking them up with comments on the informative. Indeed, the relative frequency of use of the four patterns of offer and take–up is the same in all but one of the conversations. While overall patterns are similar; there are differences among the conversations. Does the sex of the speakers account for them?

Table 5 organizes the data by sex composition of the dyad and by sex of the speaker. Again, the data suggest a general similarity of the strategies used by these speakers. The relative frequency of particular pairings is the same whatever the combination: female/female, male/male, and female/male pairs all used the informative/comment pattern most often, the inform/elicit pair with the next highest frequency, the elicit/reply sequence less frequently, and the informative/challenge pairing least of all. While the male/male pairs demonstrated a stronger preference for the informative/comment sequence, the difference is minor. In general, the data support the view that male and female speakers' strategies are more similar than different.

Table 5

Topic Offer/Take Up Strategies
By Sex Composition of Dyads
and
By Sex of Speaker

	Inform/ Comment	Inform/ Elicit	Elicit/ Reply	Inform/ Challenge
Female/ Female				
#	46	33	25	6
%	41.82	30.00	22.73	5.45
Male/ Male				
#	49	25	23	1
%	50.00	25.51	23.47	1.02
Female/ Male				
#	40	27	20	11
%	40.82	27.55	20.41	11.22
Females				
#	61	46	37	11
%	39.36	29.68	23.87	7.1
Males				
#	76	39	30	7
%	50.0	25.66	19.74	4.61

There are few notable differences between males and females in these data. While the men in these conversations seem to show some preference for comments, and while the women preferred to take up a topic with an elicit or a reply, the differences are not striking. The one obvious difference among the conversations is the more frequent use of the informative/challenge pattern (3) in dyads with female speakers. Table 5 also indicates that the use of challenges is not a sex-specific behavior. Of the eleven challenges found in the female/male conversation, five were used by the female and, six were used by the male. Sex differences were not found to influence the process of topic offer and take-up in these conversations.

What accounts for the differences in topic offer and take-up found? The differences in topic offer/take-up strategies are associated with the nature of the conversation rather than the sex of the speakers (Table 6). Even here, the pattern of topic offer/take-up is similar. Speakers demonstrated a strong preference for taking up a partner's topics with comments. While that preference appears to be stronger in task than in social conversations, and while social speakers used the inform/elicit pattern with a greater frequency than did task speakers, the rank order of the topic take-up patterns was more similar than different.

Table 6
Topic Offer/Take-Up Strategies
By Conversational Context

	Inform/ Comment	Inform/ Elicit	Elicit/ Reply	Inform/ Challenge
Social				
#	75	67	57	0
%	37.7	33.7	28.6	0
Task				
#	61	21	22	18
%	50.0	17.2	18.0	14.8

Topic Termination: Each topic sequence in each conversation was examined to identify the terminating utterance(s). Five topic termination strategies were used by the speakers in these conversations: topics were ended with informatives or comments, with a summary or restatement, with acceptance or acknowledgment, with passing moves, or with elicitations. Table 7 summarizes the frequency with which each of the topic terminating moves were used.

Table 7
Frequency of Topic Termination Moves by Conversation

	Inform/ Comment	Summary/ Restatement	Accept/ Acknowledge	Passing	Elicit
4S					
#	30	19	11	5	1
%	45.45	28.79	16.67	7.58	1.52
10S					
#	42	11	3	0	1
%	73.68	19.30	5.26	0.00	1.75
7S					
#	33	21	9	2	1
%	50.00	31.82	13.64	3.03	1.52
Social Totals #	105	51	23	7	3
%	55.56	26.98	12.17	3.7	1.59
#	23	5	12	0	2
%	54.76	11.91	28.57	0.00	4.76
11					
#	20	9	3	2	0
%	58.82	26.47	8.82	5.88	0.00
9T					
#	21	18	5	2	0
%	45.65	39.13	10.87	4.35	0.00
Task Totals #	64	32	20	4	2
%	52.46	26.23	16.39	3.28	1.64

There are few consistencies in the use of these strategies. The different preferences individuals displayed should not hide the fact that in both task and social conversations, the rank order of topic termination moves was the same: comments or informatives were the most frequently used, summaries or restatements second, acceptances or acknowledgments third, passing moves fourth, and elicitations the least frequently used strategy for topic termination.

In order to determine whether topic termination preferences were influenced by sex pairing, female/female, male/male, and female/male conversations were compared. Table 8 includes these data. No clear pattern is displayed.

Table 8 also displays the strategies used by males and females in all six conversations. Similarity between women and men rather than difference is apparent in the choices for terminating topics. Women used utterances which accept or acknowledge their partner's earlier utterance more frequently, but the rank order of the move is the same as for men. More interesting than this difference in frequency is the overall similarity. Men and women made comparable choices of topic termination strategies.

Table 8
Topic Termination Moves
By Sex Composition of Dyads
and
By Sex of Speakers

	Inform/ Comment	Summary/ Restate	Accept/ Acknowledge	Passing Moves	Elicit
Female/Female					
#	53	24	23	5	3
%	49.07	22.22	21.3	4.63	2.78
Male/Male					
#	53	30	12	4	1
%	53.0	30.0	12.0	4.0	1.0
Female/Male					
#	63	29	8	2	1
%	61.17	28.16	7.77	1.94	.97
Females					
#	86	39	28	7	4
%	52.44	23.93	17.18	4.29	2.45
Males					
#	83	44	14	4	2
%	56.46	29.93	9.52	2.72	1.36

Topic termination strategies discriminate the least between conversation type of any of the conversational moves examined so far. The strategies discriminate neither speaker sex nor conversation context.

Maintaining Topics

Topic offer, take-up, and termination moves have been examined. But once the topic is established, how do speakers keep the talk on topic? Although there may be many strategies available, one was the focus of this study: storytelling. Storytelling is the one topic management strategy which distinguished these conversationalists by sex; in these data, women told six times as many stories as men. Conversational context also influenced whether speakers told stories. Over 70% of the stories were told in social conversations.

Whether the data is examined from the perspective of the gender pairing of the conversation, the sex of the speaker, or the conversational context, storytelling is a discriminator. Table 9 summarizes the data on stories in these conversations.

Table 9
Storytelling

	Sex composition of conversations		
	Female/Female	Male/Male	Female/Male
#	14	2	6
%	63.6	9.1	27.3
	Sex of speaker		
	Female	Male	
#	19	3	
%	86.4	13.6	
	Conversational Context		
	Social	Task	
#	16	6	
%	72.7	27.3	

Stories are one of the strategies speakers have at their disposal for establishing, maintaining, and shifting topic talk. They are the one strategy for managing topics of conversation which differentiated women and men.

Discussion
1 – "What do you want to talk about?"
2 – "Ah, I don't know."

Conversation is jointly created, a product of the collaborative efforts of the speakers. The conversational snippet above makes explicit the problem of finding mutually-acceptable topics of conversation. This study examined speakers' strategies for managing conversational topics and found that women and men use similar strategies to offer, take-up, and terminate conversational topics. Only one aspect of topic management, maintaining topics by telling stories, differentiated women and men in these data.

Rather than finding sex–related differences in topic management strategies, this study found differences associated with the conversational context. That is, speakers in task conversations, regardless of sex, displayed inequality in the numbers of topics offered for talk and inequality in the success rate of topics taken up for talk. Additionally, speakers in task conversations differed in the frequency with which they used particular strategies to initiate, take–up, maintain, and terminate conversational topics.

Sex Differences. Earlier research suggests that women offer more topics for conversation than do men, but that they are less likely to be successful in having their topics discussed than men (Zimmerman and West, 1975; Fishman, 1977, 1978). Fishman's study of married couples' conversations found that the women offered 62% of the conversational topics while the men offered only 38% of the conversational topics. An even more dramatic difference was found when the success of topics was examined. Fishman found that the topics offered by men succeeded 96% of the time while women's topics succeeded 36% of the time. (Unfortunately, Fishman does not explain her criteria for identifying a successful topic. The comparison, hence, must be taken as tentative.) This study found that women and men worked equally hard to establish conversational topics and their work was equally successful; women and men offered essentially equal numbers of potential topics and had equal success in having their topics developed in the conversations. In the conversations examined for this study, the conclusion that women work harder for fewer returns was not supported.

A possible explanation for the difference in these results and Fishman's conclusions may be the difference in the relationship between the speakers in the two studies. Fishman's conclusions were based on conversations of married couples. It seems reasonable to assume that the patterns of interaction found in the conversations of couples with a relatively long history would differ from the patterns found in initial interactions. Additionally, the conversationalists who constituted these data are younger than those studied by Fishman. The three couples who comprised Fishman's data set ranged in age from 25 to 35, while the speakers in the current investigation ranged in age from 18 to 26 with the average age about 21 years. The differences found between the data sets may reflect differences in the behaviors of younger, unmarried men and women and older, married ones.

One difference in topic sequences found in these data was the more frequent incidence of single–speaker topics in women's contributions to the conversation than in the men's. While the difference between women and men was not large (women averaged nine single–speaker topics per conversation, men averaged seven), one possible explanation can be offered. The greater frequency of single-speaker topics may be due to the larger number of stories told by women in the conversations. Of the 29 single-speaker topics which were a part of a storytelling sequence, 26 were from female speakers while only 3 were from males.

Having found general equality in topic offer and success rates for speakers, the strategies speakers used to offer and take-up topics were examined to determine whether women and men used different means for getting their topics "on the floor." Again, similarity rather than difference was found. Women and men used the same set of conversational strategies with the same frequencies to offer and take-up conversational topics. The consistent pattern in selection of offer/take-up strategies suggests that the strategies available to speakers for managing topics of conversation, perhaps grounded in norms for initial interactions, are more influential than the sex of the speakers.

The failure to find differences in the strategies women and men use to offer and take-up topics suggests that there may be a repertoire of strategies available to speakers regardless of sex. It suggests that, at least in initial interactions between college students, the repertoire is equally available and similarly used by both female and male speakers.

One strategy for maintaining topics was identified in these data—storytelling. Females in these data told 70% of the stories identified. This was the only topic-relevant strategy which distinguished women and men. These results are inconsistent with those found by McLaughlin, et al. (1984). In their study of sex differences and stories, they found no difference in the frequency of storytelling by women and men.

Obviously, with such limited data, and conflicting results found by McLaughlin, explanations can be only tentative. Some of the functions stories perform in maintaining topics are politeness or coorientation tasks. Perhaps women in these data were displaying conversational caretaking by telling stories in order to maintain coordination and a polite atmosphere. Yet another explanation is possible; women may tell stories to secure the floor and avoid interruptions. Research suggests that women take shorter turns at talk then men, and that women are interrupted more frequently (see Eakins and Eakins, 1978; Pearson, 1985). The dynamics of storytelling counteract these patterns. A story demands that normal turn-taking procedures be suspended to allow for the telling (Jefferson, 1978). Additionally, stories have a compelling nature—they resist interruptions from partner. Additional research on stories as strategy for maintaining topic talk would help clarify the ways in which stories can function as a topic management strategy.

Topic termination strategies were the final topic management behavior examined in this study. Again, no differences in the choices made by women and men were found. Women and men chose from among the same set of utterance types to end topic sequences.

Conversational Context. For each of the topic management moves examined in this study, with the exception of topic termination strategies which did not display any pattern, context of the conversation accounted for the variation in speaker choices. In social conversations each conversational partner offered and had taken up equal numbers of topics, regardless of speaker sex or sex composition of the dyad. The same was not true for task conversations. In task conversations, inequality rather than equality described the amount of work individual speakers did and the success rate of speakers' topics.

There are at least two reasons for the differences found between speakers in the task and social conversations. One reason for the difference may be the difference in topic expertise exhibited by speakers in the task conversations. Since the task required finding a topic to present in debate, the speaker who had the greater interest in or knowledge of the potential debate topic would be the one more likely to initiate the topics which were taken up. In the social interactions, the speakers did not have to discover anything more than topics about which they both could converse.

A second explanation for the difference between the speakers in the two conversation types may be a politeness rule that requires that speakers should share talk time and by implication, share topic work, in initial interactions. The rule may be stated in the following way: if engaged in an initial interaction, each speaker should have a roughly equal opportunity to set the conversational topic. Speakers who have an interest or goal that overrides the normal rules of initial interaction, (e.g. accomplishing the task) may feel free to violate the rule.

The differences between speakers in task conversations is of considerable interest. However, it should not overshadow the remarkable equality of topic success displayed by the female and male speakers overall, and by speakers in the social conversations. How this equality comes about remains an unanswered question. Surely no individual keeps count of the topics she offered which were taken up by her partner. Yet, without consciously keeping track of the success of one's own and one's partner's topics, the conversationalists seem to manage their interaction in such a way that both speakers should feel they shared equitably in the management of topics of conversation.

Single–speaker topics were also found more frequently in social conversations. Again, politeness rules of initial interaction may explain why partner allowed the embedded monologue in initial interactions. In the task conversations, a topic which did not involve both speakers would not be a likely choice for a debate topic and so may be abandoned as soon as partner fails to take up the potential topic.

Speakers in task and social conversations used topic take–up strategies with different frequency. These differences may be explained by the differences in speaker goals in the two types of conversation. Social speakers, who were simply getting to know their partner, were more likely to use strategies which sought information about partner or encouraged continuation of partner's topics. Speakers in task conversations, more interested in the goal of finding a mutually–acceptable debate topic, were more likely to use strategies which allowed them to discover, efficiently, potential debate topics.

Storytelling also distinguished task and social speakers. Stories were more frequently told in social rather than task conversations. Again, the demands of the context can explain this difference; stories may take up a considerable amount of conversational space. They are not an efficient way to determine shared topics which would make good debate topics.

Conversational context, then, exerts an influence on speakers' choices that was not found when sex of speakers was examined.

Conclusions

Do women and men use different strategies to manage conversational topics? Not noticeably, at least in these conversations. This study began with the argument that before evaluating (what may be) sex–typical behavior, the impact or function of behaviors ought to be understood. The women and men who spoke these conversations used the same strategies to offer, take–up, and terminate topics. In these conversations, women and men worked equally to discover topics and were roughly equal in the success they had with their topics. Only storytelling differentiated the speakers by sex. Women told stories as a part of their "on topic" talk.

These results should not be taken to dismiss sex differences in speaker style. The women and men chose different strategies when in task or social conversations. The context of the conversation made more difference than speaker sex in topic management. The role that context played in this study may also explain why sex differences are inconsistently found; sometimes speakers may choose to display sex–typical behavior, sometimes not.

Obviously there is a need for continuing research to investigate these issues. The results of this study may be due to the use of initial interaction data. Perhaps the results may reflect peculiar patterns of speech displayed by students in the upper Midwest; however, the results are encouraging. They suggest that when sex is not a critical variable in an interaction, women and men have equal access to conversational strategies and relatively equal success in managing topics of conversation.

Notes

1   Only the verbal components of topic sequences were coded. Previous research suggests that topic identification is not affected by excluding nonverbal components of messages. Planalp and Tracy

(1980) found no differences in subjects' ability to identify topic segments whether coding from videotapes or transcripts. Their results suggest that judgments about topic changes are made on the basis of textual material not nonverbal cues.

2   Statistical analysis of differences was not computed for these data. The sample size, six conversations, is too small to allow for statistical comparison. Although the number of moves contributed by each speaker seems large, the moves are not independent and cannot be treated as such.

3   In Burton's coding scheme, challenges are those utterances which distract from or sidetrack the topic. They may be friendly and supportive of the partner and they do not necessarily indicate disagreement with the topic.

References

Aries, E. Interaction patterns and themes of male, female, and mixed groups. *Small Group Behavior*, 1976, *7*, 7-18.

Berryman, C.L. & Wilcox, J.R. Attitudes towards male and female speech: experiments on the effects of sex-typical language. *Western Journal of Speech Communication*. 1981, *44*: 50-59.

Burton, D. Analyzing spoken discourse. In R.M. Coulthard and M.M. Montgomery (Eds.), *Studies in discourse analysis*. 1981: 61-81.

Crosby, F. & Nyquist, L. The female register: An empirical study of Lakoff's hypothesis. *Language and Society*. 1977, *6*: 313-322.

Dethman, L.F. & Hoffman, S.F. Controlling in conversations: Tactics and situations. Paper presented to the Western States Communication Association convention, Portland, OR: 1980.

DuBois, B.L. & Crouch, I. The question of tag questions in women's speech: They don't really use more of them, do they? *Language and Society*. 1975, *4*: 289-294.

Eakins, B. & Eakins, G. *Sex Differences in Human Communication*. Boston: Houghton Mifflin Co., 1978.

Edelsky, C. Recognizing sex linked language. *Language Arts*. 1976, *53*: 746-752.

Ellis, D. & McCallister, L. Relational control sequences in sex-typed and androgynous groups. *Western Journal of Speech Communication*. 1980, *44*: 35-49.

Jefferson, G. Sequential aspects of storytelling in conversation. In J. Schenkein (Ed.), *Studies in the organization of conversational interaction*. 1978: 219-248.

Key, M.R. *Male/female language*. Metuchen, N.J.: Scarecrow Press, 1975.

Lakoff, R. Language and women's place. *Language and Society*. 1973, *2*: 45-79.

Liska, J., Mechling, E., & Stathas, S. Differences in subjects' perceptions of gender and believability between users of deferential and non-deferential language. Paper presented at the Western Speech Communication Association convention, Portland, 1980.

Martin, J. & Craig, R.T. Selected linguistic sex differences during initial interactions of same-sex and mixed-sex dyads. *Western Journal of Speech Communication*. 1983, *47*: 16-28.

Murphy, S. Measuring conversational control. Unpublished manuscript. 1982.

Murphy, S. & Martin, J. Measuring conversational control in dyadic interaction. Paper present at the Speech Communication Association, Louisville, 1982.

Parlee, M.B. Conversational politics. *Psychology Today*. May 1979: 48-56.

Planalp, S. & Tracy, K. Not to change the topic but...: A cognitive approach to the management of conversation. In D. Nimmo (Ed.), *Communication Yearbook IV*. New Brunswick: Transaction Books, 1980: 237–258.

Schenkein, J. *Studies in the organization of conversational interaction*. New York: Academic Press, 1978.

Shaw, M. Observed variations in language behavior in female and male interviewers and applicants. Paper presented at the Western Speech Communication Association convention, Los Angeles, 1979.

Siegler, D.M. & Siegler, R.S. Stereotypes of males' and females' speech. *Psychological Reports*. 1976, *39*: 167–170.

Sykes, R.E. Initial interaction between strangers and acquaintances: A multivariate analysis of factors affecting choice of communication partners. *Human Communication Research*. 1983, *10*: 27–54.

Tyler, M. Why sex based language differences are elusive. ERIC, E.D. 142–092, November 4, 1976, 18.

THOUGHT PROVOKER

Recall conversations with the opposite sex. Who more often controls the topics discussed in these conversations? What *verbal* and *nonverbal* strategies are used to control these conversations? Other than sex of conversants, what variables might account for conversational control?

CHAPTER SEVEN
The Language of Opinionation and Controversy: Sexism

Virginia L. Chapman
Anderson University
Anderson, Indiana

The effect that the sex of a speaker has on communication has been an ongoing area of concern. The majority of studies has been concerned with the difference of how men and women use language and the effect of how sex identifying terms such as he/she, lady/man, chairman/chairperson affect perception. Many of these studies conclude that language has a measureable effect on perception and that there are differences in how men and women communicate. The purpose of this paper is to examine feminist and antifeminist literature to discover if the specialized language of feminists and the sex of the speakers interact affecting the persuasive ability of the literature.

Feminists, representing the frontier of change, often use newly–created words or specialized meanings of words. These new words and specialized meanings of words may create reactions in the audience which prevent or hinder the audience's consideration of the real issue. The words, in themselves, may become the source of contention or basis from which the retort or argument is launched rather than the original issue set forth by the language. Adding to this effect may be the audience's reaction to the combination of the sex of the communicator and the language choices.

Realization of this block to genuine communication could be instrumental in the persuasive approach taken by feminist and antifeminist rhetoricians. Campbell (1973) speculates that the rhetoric of feminism "unearths tensions woven deep into the fabric of our society and provokes an unusually intense and profound 'rhetoric of moral conflict'" (p. 75). Campbell concludes that women's liberation rhetoric is of a separate genre with its own distinct features that requires attention apart from other principles of persuasion and rhetoric. Kramer (1974) concludes that women's rhetoric has been largely ignored except for information that she terms the "folk view: how people think women speak or how people think women should speak" (p. 24).

Although there are no studies which have specifically dealt with this area of feminist/antifeminist language, there are other studies which seem to apply to this area of research. Rich (1971) conducted a case study of interracial communication identifying and cataloguing statements which seem to contribute to racial tension. Rich speculated that some terminology may cause an "allergic reaction" psychologically and "words which we once accepted in conversation with little or no emotional reaction we now find intolerable and offensive" (p. 229). As a result, Rich speculated that the perceiver may have an extremely negative reaction or perceive the source of the communication as insincere. Extrapolating this principle of "allergic reaction" in racially–associated terms to feminist and antifeminist terminology seems a reasonable perspective. The issue itself may not be carefully considered if the receiver of the communication cannot overcome the "allergic reaction" to the language contained in the communication itself.

Other related studies discuss the effects of language used by males and females. Jones, Burgoon and Stewart (1975) conducted a study to determine interactions between sex of the source, situational anxiety, source credibility and language intensity. They determined that there is an interaction between language intensity and sex of the source. A female source was most effective with low–intense language while a male was least effective with low–intense language.

Firestone, as cited in Kramer (1974), supports the concept that women use language differently than men: "A man is allowed to blaspheme the world because it belongs to him to damn—but the same curse out of the mouth of a woman or a minor, i.e., an incomplete 'man' to whom the world does not yet belong, is considered presumptuous, and thus an impropriety or worse" (p. 22). Wiley and Eskilson (1985) compared the use of powerful versus powerless speech on perceptions of male and female managerial job applicants. They found that women are more sensitive to perceiving the differences in powerful versus powerless speech, and applicants using powerful speech were related more positively regardless of sex. However, they conclude that "discouragingly for supporters of equal rights, the expectation held by female respondents that women using powerful speech styles will be socially accepted is not mirrored in the responses of males" (p. 1004). They further remarked that males did not expect females using powerful speech to be well–liked and noted that these language standards may create a conflict for females between success and positive personal relationships.

A study by Liska, Mechling and Stathas (1981) concluded that deferential language is perceived as less powerful by males as well as females, choice of language does significantly affect believability, and deferential language is associated with femininity. Prior studies (Bostrom and Kemp, 1969; Berryman and Wilcox, 1980) dealt with language differences between males and females and persuasibility. Bostrom and Kemp concluded women were more persuasive when they advocated non–institutional norms while the reverse was true for men. Berryman and Wilcox found that raters could identify the correct sex of a message source and distinguished the female message as less commanding.

The literature revolving around sex and language seems to indicate that men and women do use language differently, the perception of this difference is obvious, and the effect of this perception of sex and language usage differences affects persuasibility.

The awareness that perception of meaning may be contained in the receiver as well as the sender, and the interesting data collected about women's language usage and male/female differences in communication style and believability, lead to questions about the rhetoric surrounding a specifically female–related issue. If, as Campbell believes, feminist rhetoric is an oxymoron and if the other studies about the interaction of powerful/powerless speech and sex are reliable, one could speculate that the language choices which create speech style and enhance perception may be the major issues in themselves regarding feminist rhetoric. If these words are a pivotal issue in feminist/antifeminist rhetoric, what explanations, if any, can be found in the scholarly literature regarding perception and persuasibility? It seems only natural that an answer to this question can be found through examination of feminist and antifeminist literature.

Bowers (1964) refers to terms that convey the attitudinal state of the communicator as perceived by the receiver as intensity or "the quality of language which indicates the degree to which the speaker's attitude toward a concept deviates from neutrality" (p. 416). The Bowers study pre–tests for intensity of words and then compares the intensity and metaphorical quality of the words to conclude that there were "perfect correlations between intensity and the two types of metaphor—those conventionally associated with sex and those conventionally associated with death" (p. 420). Bowers defined a term as metaphorical when its denotation could not be directly transferred from conventional association to its association in the context of the communication. For this study, Bowers' definition of intensity and metaphor will be used to identify intense terms in the literature of feminists and antifeminists.

Representative samples of feminist and antifeminist rhetoric that have generated response and action by its advocates should contain intense language as described by Bowers and may be assumed to have language that produces an allergic reaction as noted by Rich. The major works *Outrageous Acts and Everyday Rebellions* by Gloria Steinem, a well–known feminist advocate, and *The Power of the*

Positive Woman by Phyllis Schlafly, a noted antifeminist, were selected for review in this study. Steinem and Schlafly were chosen because both are publicly well-known in their advocacy regarding feminist and antifeminist issues respectively. In addition, review of speeches and activities of Schlafly by *Ms. Magazine* (edited by Steinem) were reviewed to determine feminist attitudes toward Schlafly's language choices. All of the literature revolves around the Equal Rights Amendment issue, thus providing a common focus around which a variety of language could be examined. These works were reviewed to identify a list of terms and phrases that seem to be "intense" and that may cause an "allergic reaction" in the audience.

As the literature was reviewed, a list of intense words and phrases was generated (See Appendix). In some instances the juxtaposed literature produced categories of contrasting language; however, an interesting phenomenon seemed to develop that not only words and phrases but concepts needed to be compared in the literature. The natural implications of categories of terms and ideas seemed to develop from this list similarly to the development of Bowers' categories of sex and death metaphors of intense language. The literature of the theory of persuasion was then examined relative to these categories to provide a basis for analysis and explanation of possible allergic reactions to feminist and antifeminist literature.

The list of words generated from the literature of feminists and antifeminists seems to assemble naturally into categories referring to people, the E.R.A. issue, and concepts held about the people and the issue. Steinem and Schlafly compare to one another in their approach to the issue in that each has made a career-like commitment to the E.R.A. issue, but from opposite opinion bases.

As in any debate, the affirmative advocates a change in the status quo; thus, the affirmative advances a definition of terms. Since the E.R.A. proponents advocate change, i.e. E.R.A., the discussion of the list of terms shall proceed from the affirmative perspective to the opponents' terminology that seems equivalent.

References to people surprisingly include overlap in usage from Steinem and Schlafly. Steinem refers to E.R.A. proponents as liberationists while Schlafly may also on occasion. However, Steinem discusses feminists, sisters, liberals, radical feminists, and activists, while Schlafly refers to macho–feminists, militants, bitter women's libbers, libbers and lesbians.

Words referring to the E.R.A. issue forwarded by Steinem are the following: equality, E.R.A., a wave, a revolution, a movement, activism, empowerment and liberation. Schlafly refers to the E.R.A. issue as an assault on the family, marriage and children; she equates it to abortion; and, she calls it a "Jewish scheme" to destroy marriage, the family, home and motherhood.

Concepts that are expressed by Steinem include the generic title of address, Ms. for a female, equal pay, sexual harassment and equality. Schlafly is more colorful and approaches the concepts from a reversed point of view. Schlafly refers to her opposition to E.R.A. as "putting America back on track"; she identifies it as the existent "special privilege" women enjoy and the protection of womankind.

The lists of parallel but seemingly unequal terms generated from these works lead to the questions: Are words and their manipulation the actual battleground, and how do we account for this? As Weaver explained in *Ethics of Rhetoric*, there may be "God" and "Devil" terms. A God term embraces a universal value generally regarded as good or desirable and a Devil term embraces an unfavorably viewed word (Golden, Berquist and Coleman, 1978, p. 274). Schlafly's list of concepts and reference to the E.R.A. as well as people certainly refer to accepted principles in the lifestyle such as family and marriage while reminding the audience of abhored concepts such as lesbianism, abortion, and macho–feminists. The identification of the E.R.A. issue with such negative concepts while it negates such positive ones can be categorized as use of God and Devil terms. Steinem is espousing terms that are relatively new in concept to the listener such as sisterhood, empowerment, and sexual harassment. Simply because of their unfamiliar usage, these terms may be suspect to the listener or create an allergic reaction. For example, many traditional females may experience a sense of uneasiness or uncertainty about the connotations of words like sisterhood used to describe a political or ideological organization. It may be even more of a concern for males in the audience. The term brotherhood, however, has long been used to describe established, credible organizations without concern for sexual connotations. The term sisterhood, associated with the feminist movement and the description of feminists as lesbians, may interact to create an allergic reaction in the audience.

Another interesting difference between proponents and opponents is the style of language use. Steinem tends to use powerful speech. As Kramer (1974) points out, that includes fewer tag questions, more discussion or talk, and hyperbole. Steinem uses her speeches, books, and articles to present issues heretofore kept out of general public discussion. For instance, she discusses the attitudes of men toward working wives and proclaims that many men expect their wives to have a "jobette" rather than a job because a job interferes with the whims of the males' world, while a less important job—or "jobette"—can be ignored and devalued when the man prefers. The creation of the word "jobette" and the open discussion of such an issue elevating it to a degree of importance and contention for purposes of attracting proponents and elevating male and female consciousness is daring, contentious, and powerful. This language style may be perceived very negatively when used by a female.

Elshtain (1982) believes that the feminist who wants power must consider questions of meaning and the nature of language. Her discussion of the philosophy behind various categories of feminist language concludes that feminists should recognize that individuals who are put on the defensive with language will respond defensively. It is ironic that language, the very means used to persuade, and the heart of much controversy regarding the E.R.A., may be the very means of dissuasion and cause of controversy.

Schlafly's choice of reference to the people, the issue, and the concept seem to allude to common metaphors that deal with sex and family. She attempts to equate abortion, lesbianism, unisex, female underwear and motherhood with the proponents of E.R.A.—an obvious reference to sex and family status. Steinem, however, uses terms that are not directly equated in this manner. Her terms, such as sisterhood, liberal, militant and activist, equal pay, and Ms. are relatively neutral and new to the vocabulary. They seem to be specialized uses of the language. A study by Franzwa (1969) concerning the use of negatively and positively evaluated language and dynamic and non-dynamic language usage concluded that there is a tendency to use dynamic language when speaking to partisans and non-dynamic language when speaking to hostile audiences. Language selected for an opposing speech uses non-dynamic language more frequently than that selected for a proposing speech. Thus, Schlafly may target more dynamic, pro-feminist literature to use as the basis for her counterattack and addresses her audience of proponents in even more dynamic language which is positively perceived by her audience and negatively perceived by her opponents. If this is true in the reverse regarding Steinem, the escalation of the language war is like the moot point of nuclear overkill—ultimately, no one wins.

Burgoon and Miller (1971) concluded in their study of message style and attitude change that attitude change is directly related to the intensity of the counterattitudinal message. For instance, a low intensity, belief discrepant message is encoded more positively than one of high intensity. A prior study by Bowers (1963) denies that intensity alone is the issue; rather, it suggests that the ethos of the speaker may be operating in an indirect manner through language intensity to influence the listener as in a boomerang effect. Additionally, Bradac, Bowers and Courtright (1979) generalized that language intensity and maleness interact regarding attitude change in such a way that intensity enhances the effect of males but inhibits the effect of females. Thus, proponents and opponents of the E.R.A. may be unintentionally persuading only their prior advocates with the use of intense language. Especially of concern is the sex of the audience addressed. Since males do not positively evaluate intense, powerful female language, the rhetoric of Steinem may fall on deaf ears. Schlafly, using God terms and positive values, may be communicating to a larger audience. Although the language of Steinem may seem to be less intense, it may be perceived as very powerful for a female, thus reducing its acceptance among both males and females.

Ultimately, feminist/antifeminist language may be repelling the very sectors of society it purports to attract. Feminists' powerful language and female speakers may cause an allergic reaction to males and females alike. The specialized use and style of language by feminists may be an accepted style only within the ranks of the believers, but serve to attract few, if any, converts while the intense, dynamic language of antifeminists may be more positively perceived because it falls within the range of "acceptable" language style.

Further observation of the language effects of feminist/antifeminist literature may lead to implications about persuasibility and language style within the E.R.A. issue. Additional research may specifically identify such terminology, its frequency of use, and its persuasive effects. The results of such studies may also be useful in studying the effect of perception of female language in the work environment.

The research surrounding feminist/antifeminist rhetoric, in conjunction with the body of research on language in general, join to set forth an important lesson: The intensity of the language, the sex of the author/speaker and the sex of the audience act not independently but with great interdependence. The interdependence of the factors is such that an incorrect mix may cause an allergic reaction among opponents that has been camouflaged by positive feedback from proponents; as a result, persuasion will not occur. Was Mother wrong when she said, "Sticks and stones may break your bones, but words will never hurt you..."?

References

Berryman, C.L., & Wilcox, J.R. (1980). Attitudes toward male and female speech: Experiments on the effects of sex–typical language. *The Western Journal of Speech Communication, 44,* 50–59.

Berryman–Fink, C.L., & Wilcox, J.R. (1983). A multivariate investigation of perceptual attributions concerning gender appropriateness in language. *Sex Roles, 9,* 663–681.

Bostrom, R.N., & Kemp, A.P. (1969). Type of speech, sex of speaker, and sex of subject as factors influencing persuasion. *Central States Speech Journal, 20,* 245–251.

Bowers, J.W. (1963). Language intensity, social introversion, and attitude change. *Speech Monographs, 30,* 345–352.

Bowers, J.W. (1964). Some correlates of language intensity. *The Quarterly Journal of Speech, 50,* 415–420.

Bradac, J.J., Bowers, J.W., & Courtright, J.A. (1979). Three language variables of communication research: Intensity, immediacy and diversity. *Human Communication Research, 5,* 257–269.

Burgoon, M., & Miller, G.R. (1971). Prior attitude and language intensity as predictors of message style and attitude change following counterattitudinal advocacy. *Journal of Personality and Social Psychology, 20,* 246–253.

Burgoon, M., Jones, S.B., & Steward, D. (1975). Toward a message–centered theory of persuasion: Three empirical investigations of language intensity. *Human Commmunication Research, 1,* 240–256.

Campbell, K.K. (1973). The rhetoric of women's liberation: An oxymoron. *The Quarterly Journal of Speech, 59,* 74–86.

Chase, L.J., & Kelly, C.W. (1976). Language intensity and resistance to persuasion: A research note. *Human Communication Research, 3,* 82–85.

Elshtain, J.B. (1982). Feminist discourse and its discontents: Language, power and meaning. *Signs, 7,* 603–621.

Franzwa, H.H. (1969). Psychological factors influencing use of "evaluative–dynamic" language. *Speech Monographs, 36,* 103–109.

Golden, J.L., Berquist, G.F., & Coleman, W.E. (Eds.). (1978). *The rhetoric of western thought.* Dubuque, Iowa: Kendall/Hunt.

Jaggar, A.M., & Struhl, P.R. (1978). *Feminist frameworks.* New York: McGraw–Hill Company.

Jarrard, M.E.W. & Randall, P.R. (1982). *Women speaking: An annotated bibliography of verbal and nonverbal communication 1970-1980.* New York: Garland.

Kramer, C. (1974). Women's speech: Separate but unequal? *The Quarterly Journal of Speech, 60,* 14–24.

Liska, J., Mechling, E.W.. & Stathas S. (1981). Differences in subjects' perceptions of gender and believability between users of deferential and nondeferential language. *Communication Quarterly*, *29*, 40–48.

O'Reilly, J. (1982). Schlafly's last fling. *Ms. 11*, 41–45.

Rich, A. (1971). Some problems in interracial communication: An interracial group case study. *Central States Speech Journal, 22*, 228–235.

Rowland, R. (Ed.). (1984). *Women who do and women who don't join the women's movement*. Boston: Routledge & Kegan Paul.

Schlafly, P. (1977). *The power of the positive woman*. New York: Arlington House.

Steinem, G. (1986). *Outrageous acts and everyday rebellions*. New York: Signet.

Vetterling–Braggin, M., Elliston, F.A. & English, J. (Eds.). (1977). *Feminism and philosophy*. New Jersey: Rowman and Littlefield.

Wiley. M.G., & Eskilson,. A. (1985). Speech style, gender stereotypes, and corporate success: What if women talked more like men? *Sex Roles, 12*, 993–1007.

Wohl, L.C. (1974). Phyllis Schlafly: The sweetheart of the silent majority. *Ms., 2*, 54–57+.

Appendix

	Steinem	*Schlafly*
People	Liberationists Feminists Sisters Liberals Radical feminists Activists	Macho feminists Militants Bitter women's libbers Lesbians Libbers
Issues	Equality E.R.A. A wave A revolution A movement Activism Empowerment Liberation	Assault on the family, marriage and children Abortion Jewish scheme to destroy marriage, family, home and motherhood
Concepts	Ms. Equal Pay Sexual harassment Equality	Putting America back on track Special privilege of womenkind

---

THOUGHT PROVOKER

Since female language has traditionally been labeled as "deferential," how does language used by the feminist movement violate traditional sex–role expectations? Why might such language choice create an "allergic reaction" with some audiences?

UNIT III
Sex and Gender Diversity
in the Interpersonal Setting

'erpersonal communication focuses on the study of immediate, ᵗ̣ -face communication behaviors between and among persons. Typically, same-sex and mixed-sex interactions in friendships, romantic relationships, marriage, and families are explored within the interpersonal communication setting. As a result, this setting encompasses a variety of communication topics that typically includes the following: self-disclosure, communication style, trust, power and influence, conflict, and the developmental stages of relationships.

Since researchers often find it difficult to observe actual relationships in progress, much of the data for research in the interpersonal setting is based on individual perceptions and recollections of specific or generalized interpersonal behaviors. All four chapters in this unit examine interpersonal communication in this manner. Through perceptual data, examined both qualitatively and quantitatively, these researchers explore the male and female descriptions of communicator style (the way one communicates), communicator style as it relates to perceived competence, locus of control during conflict, and the component processes of romantic jealously. While some of the research reinforces the traditional male and female norms, some studies or portions of the studies provide new and provocative insight into these perspectives on interpersonal communication.

In Chapter Eight, entitled "Male and Female Communicator Style Differences: A Meta-analysis," Brenda Faye McDonald examines eight separate studies that focus on perceived communicator style including both "self" and "other." Using the quantitative method of meta-analysis, findings indicate that males and females differ on all dimensions except impression leaving. For example, men are perceived as more dominant, dramatic, and contentious; women are perceived as more animated, attentive, open, and friendly. In general, the researcher notes that these findings are consistent with traditional social expectations and norms that link males to instrumental (task-oriented) behaviors and females to expressive (affiliative) behaviors.

Brian H. Spitzberg and Claire C. Brunner explore the instrumental/expressive behaviors related to communication competence in Chapter Nine, entitled "Sex, Instrumentality, Expressiveness and Interpersonal Communication Competence." Specifically, 496 college students were asked to recall "the most satisfying, and the most dissatisfying, face–to–face dyadic conversation you have experienced over the last two weeks." While the authors discovered that males and females differ in their use and evaluation of behaviors, they also suggest that the differences are far more complex than the instrumental–expressive dichotomy allows. These findings extend our knowledge concerning male and female perceptions of the specific cues associated with communication competence.

In the third chapter of this unit, entitled "Attitudes and Control Behaviors Associated with Gender–Based Meanings of Personal Control," Judi Beinstein Miller uses the qualitative method of content analysis to explore responses from semi–structured interviews combined with several quantitative methods to compare internal and external men's and women's recall of social experience and estimates of response in interpersonal conflict. Specifically, the researcher explores the similarities and differences between male and female internals (persons who believe they are responsible for outcomes) as well as male and female externals (persons who believe chance, fate, or powerful others are responsible for outcomes). The findings suggest that *both* sex and locus of control account for differences in the recollection of social experience, including interpersonal conflict.

Finally, in Chapter Eleven, entitled "Gender Differences in the Social Construction of Romantic Jealousy: An Exploratory Study," Susan Parrish Sprowl and Cindy L. White explore male and female perceptions of romantic jealously based on their own relationships as well as their observations of others' relationships. By analyzing the responses to a set of questions, the researchers compared male and female responses centered around nine component processes that emerge from the data: envy, violation of relational boundaries, direct prompts for behaviors, indirect prompts for behaviors, competition, physical release, seeking support, cognitive reframing, and withdrawal. The findings on each of the component processes suggest some provocative differences in the male and female conceptualization of romantic jealousy. The authors caution that this study represents exploratory research, but encourage further in–depth exploration of how individuals and couples construct and enact the jealously syndrome.

While these chapters represent only a small portion of the topics that could be examined in the interpersonal setting, they extend our knowledge on such topics as communication style, communication competence, control within conflict, and romantic jealousy. Some of the chapters validate our knowledge by reinforcing socially–accepted expectations and norms while other chapters extend our knowledge by presenting new and provocative views of male and female perceptions. Throughout this unit, the authors challenge the reader to place these findings in the context of previous research and to continue study of these topics in greater depth.

CHAPTER EIGHT
Male and Female Communicator Style Differences: A Meta Analysis

Brenda McDonald Pruett

West Virginia University

Few studies consider differences in communicator style usage and biological sex (Norton, 1983; Porter, 1982; Jablin, 1985; Nussbaum, Robinson & Grew, 1985; Duran & Zakahi, 1984; Bednar, 1982; Stohl, 1981). In addition, none consider style differences due to biological or psychological sexual orientations. Studies that have specifically examined at the style variables and biological sex have found few sex differences (Norton & Montgomery, 1981; Gudykunst & Lim, 1985). These articles conclude that males and females have more similarities in style than differences. However, style dimensions found to differ significantly in one study may not be the same across studies (Montgomery & Norton, 1981; Gudykunst & Lim, 1985; Stohl, 1981; Baird & Bradley, 1979; Honeycutt, Wilson, & Parker, 1982).

Style refers to the way one communicates. Watzlawick, Beavin, and Jackson's content and relational communication model (1967) defines the study of style. This model focuses on the message's interpretation by the receiver and its impact on what is being said and how it is being said. Until recently, style had been studied more extensively by scholars outside the communication field than those within it. For example, Blake and Mouton (1977) examined managerial style in the business field while Jurma (1979), a psychologist, studied leadership styles usage in small groups.

Communicator style is "the way one verbally, nonverbally, and paraverbally interacts to signal how literal meaning should be taken, interpreted, filtered, or understood" (Norton, p. 11, 1983). Norton's Communicator Style Scale (1983) examines nine variables. A person's style is a mixture of some or all of these variables: dominant, dramatic, contentious, animated, impression leaving, relaxed, attentive, open, and friendly variables. A dominant communicator takes charge of the conversation, while a contentious style is more argumentative. A dramatic communicator uses stories, metaphors, exaggerated movements, etc., while an animated style refers to the use of subtle nonverbal cues. Relaxed communicators show low tension levels, while an attentive communicator lets others know that he or she is listening. A person who readily reveals information about him or herself is described as open, and a person that leaves an impact on the receiver's memory has used an impression leaving style. The friendly style positively recognizes others (Norton, 1983). The appropriate mixture for the situation leads to a good communicator image (Norton, 1983).[1]

Literature reviews on sex differences in male/female communication show mixed conclusions on what differences exist between the sexes (Fairhurst, 1986; Hall, 1984; Pearson, 1985). However, one difference is consistent: women are perceived to be and report being expressive communicators while men are more often perceived as and report being instrumental communicators (Pearson, 1985; Wood, Polek, & Aiken, 1983). The studies which specifically address communicator style and biological sex (Gudykunst & Lim, 1985; Lamaude & Daniels, 1984; Montgomery & Norton, 1981; Seiffert & McDonald, 1986) find some style dimensions to be significantly different for men and women. Those studies which have used biological sex as a variable, relating sex and styles to other factors (i.e., attraction, job satisfaction, marital happiness) have found noticeable style differences between males and females (Baird & Bradley, 1979; Honeycutt et al., 1982; Stohl, 1981). Due to the inconsistencies across studies, the argument for a re-analysis of the findings on communicator style (Norton, 1983) and biological sex may be made.

Another argument which points toward a re-analysis is the problem of "power" within many of the studies. The communicator style construct has nine variables; thus, in order to test adequately for an effect, a larger than normal sample is required. Failing to find significant difference in small samples might, therefore, be more a result of the sample size than the fact that differences do not exist.

In addition, the style variables are correlated with each other. Thus, when using multivariate statistics, one variable may emerge as the significant predictor and in another study another variable may emerge as a more significant predictor of differences. This phenomenon is a function of the correlation among variables and how and when the variables entered the statistical model. Meta-analysis allows researchers to re-evaluate these two problems by looking at differences that were not found significant in one study but may be consistent across studies.

Since men and women may perform the same behavior and these behaviors may be perceived differently (Pearson, 1985), the self-report methods used in many of the studies looking specifically at sex and style, may be inadequate. Analysis should consider the impact of others' perceptions on these behaviors, especially when examining outcomes from style use. A style which is effective for men may not be effective for women. Therefore, this chapter will analyze studies using self and other reports separately, but due to the small number of studies concerned with style, a third analysis examining all studies will be completed, presenting a transactional result.

The main research questions to be addressed by the meta-analysis are: 1) On what dimension(s) of the communicator style construct (Norton, 1983) do males and females significantly and consistently differ? 2) If differences are found, are the differences meaningful at the $p < .05$ criterion? 3) Does the method used to collect data (i.e., self or other reports) impact the style dimensions found to be significantly different for men and women?

Literature Review

Norton and Montgomery (1981) report two studies that address the issue of biological sex and communicator style. Both studies use self reports data by students in interpersonal communication classes at Purdue University. In the first study, males and females differed significantly on the precise, friendly, and animated dimensions. In the second study, contentious, precise, and animated dimensions were significantly different. Females reported higher scores on the friendly and animated dimensions; males reported higher means on the contentious and precise dimensions. Differences, although not all significant, were reported on all dimensions. Dominant, precise, relaxed, attentive and animated had mean differences in the same direction for both studies.

In a follow-up study, Gudykunst and Lim (1985) again used self report data from college students in communication classes. All dimensions were administered, but four of the dimensions were eliminated due to low reliabilities. The remaining dimensions, with the exception of communicator image, were found to differ significantly. Men reported higher scores on all dimensions studied: dominant, contentious, impression leaving, relaxed, dramatic, and communicator image.

A study which examined style differences between male and female managers concluded that men's and women's styles were expected to differ. In addition, expectations for women managers were higher than for men managers (Baird & Bradley, 1979). In this study, women were perceived to be more attentive and show more concern than men. Men were perceived as more dominant, contentious, and more likely to direct the conversation (Baird & Bradley, 1979). A follow-up study (Lamude & Daniels, 1985), using both self and other reports of managers, discovered that "other" reports perceived females as more dramatic and open. Male managers self-reports were more animated than female managers self-reports.

An unpublished study (Seiffert & McDonald) examined other reports. Two friends and two acquaintances of each subject were used to rate each subject. Using 145 male and 132 female college students, males were found to be more contentious and have a better communicator image. Females were found to be more friendly, open, and animated.

A study, which examines self reported style differences between happily married couples, demonstrates that men and women report differences in style usage both inside and outside the marital context (Honeycutt et al., 1982). Stephen and Harrison (1985), using items from Norton's Communicator Style measure as well as other style measures, found differences by both biological sex and psychological sex (gender). Numerous other studies use different operationalizations of style or concepts related to style report sex differences (Fairhurst, 1986; Hall, 1984; Pearson, 1985).

With such a small number of studies examining communicator style and sex, conclusions are difficult to draw. A meta–analysis of these studies, therefore, which quantitatively compares results of each style dimension across studies, may provide a more thorough understanding.

Method

A meta–analysis is the study of quantitative values generated in each study and, using a simple statistical procedure, adds these values to calculate one overall value for all studies. The results are summarized numerically. Instead of dealing with eight different studies with eight varying conclusions, one deals with one value generated from the eight studies.

This analysis examines eight available studies which report communicator style and biological sex. For the purpose of the analysis, sex is one's sexual identity: what he or she would respond when asked if male (man) or female (woman) (Hall, 1984).

This analysis employed the Stouffer method, reviewed by Rosenthal (1978) and employed by Hall throughout her 1984 text. This method uses unweighted Z scores, and Z scores were calculated from p values. The formula is EZ/vN where EZ is the sum of the unweighted Z for the variable and vN is the square root of the total number of studies being used. P was set at the .05 criterion and all tests were assumed to be two–tailed (Hall, 1984). The mean direction and sample size are given as reported in the study.

Actual p values were used for each study, whether or not the results were significant. Studies which did not give p values were treated as follows: Stephen and Harrison (1985) study used a Q–sort by item; Baird and Bradley (1979) study did not give statistical results for all dimensions of communicator style. If the variable was not known to be included in the study reviewed, the study results for the variable could not be included in the meta–analysis.

The Stohl (1981) study gave the direction of the means. This finding was noted, but since non–significant p's were not included in the Stohl results, they were not included in this analysis when the mean direction was consistent with other studies or if no consistency were shown across the studies reviewed. If the mean direction were not consistent with other studies reviewed (i.e., favored females when others favored males), a significant Z value (p = .05) was set for this opposite result. This value was actually higher than what was found, thus allowing for more conservative results (Hall, 1984).

The Lamude & Daniels (1984) study conducted statistical analysis on both self and other reports. The largest N was 11 with the average N being 7.7. As discussed earlier, with the lack of power, few significant differences were found. Because power was stronger for the other reports and more p's were reported for these reports, the Lamude & Daniels study was used in the other analysis. Nonsignificant, nondirectonal results were included by giving them a p of .50 and a Z of 0. This again allowed for conservative results (Hall, 1984). However, the nonsignificant self reports (Lamude & Daniels, 1984) were dropped from this analysis for two reasons: 1) only one variable's means direction and p were given in the results; 2) the population was small and was already being used in the other analysis for the overall meta–analysis. However, one exception was made on the animated variable where the other report was not reported and the self report was in the opposite direction of all other studies used in the analysis, thus allowing for conservative results.

The Honeycutt et al. study (1982) was not included in the analysis because statistics for male–female differences were not consistently reported. In addition, dimensions that were reported were not clearly specified and were not consistent with Norton's dimensions.

Meta–analysis offers a much more objective look at study results than does a literature review (Glass, McGaw, & Smith, 1981; Rosenthal, 1978). This study examined the complex research results on communicator style and biological sex to discern on which style dimensions (if any) males and females differed by averaging the probability of the studies reported. Variables on which males means were higher were given negative probabilities (p's and Z's); females were given positive probabilities.

Because of differences between perceptions of male and female behaviors as well as self and other reports, three separate analyses were conducted. Studies using other reports were analyzed and an overall p was reported for how others perceive males and females. Studies using male and female self reports were combined to arrive at an overall p to see if differences exist between male and female self–perceptions. Finally, all studies examining communicator style and biological sex were combined to produce an overview of differences and/or similarities between males and females.

Reported reliabilities for the communicator style measure ranged as follows: dominant (.70 to .86), dramatic (.64 to .76), contentious (.60 to .81), animated (.56 to .69), impression leaving (.69 to .81), relaxed (.66 to .71), attentive (.57 to .73), open (.67 to .69), and friendly (.37 to .63) (Gudykuntz & Lim, 1985; Norton, 1977; Seiffert & McDonald, 1986).

Results

A total of four studies used other reports of males and females. The overall p's were found to be significant on the following dimensions of communicator style: dominant ($p<-.005$); contentious ($p<-.0001$); attentive ($p<+.005$); open ($p<.012$). Females were perceived to be more open and attentive than males. Males were higher on all other dimensions where p's were significant.

Table 1.   **Studies Using Other Reports[2]**

Study	1	2	3	4	Overall P
N	277	m=69 f=81	m=11 f=11	m=26 f=26	
Dominant	p<+.4398	p<-.0034	NS	p<-.005	P<-.005
Dramatic	p<+.7890	p<-.2533	p<+.04	p<-.005	P<-.3669
Contentious	p<-.0090	p<-.0029	NS	p<-.005	P<-.0001
Animated	p<+.0001	*	NR	p<-.005	P<+.2981
Impression leaving	p<+.3046	*	NS	p<-.005	P<-.114
Relaxed	p<-.6436	p<+.9227	NS	* NR	P<+.27
Attentive	p<+.0466	p<-.0033	NS	* NR+NS	P<+.005
Open	p<+.0011	p<+.8727	p<=+.025	NS	P<+.012
Friendly	p<+.0004	p<-.2186	NS	* NS	P<+.072

- indicates means were higher for males
* indicates not included in this analysis (see
Method for justification)
NR = Not Reported
NS = Not Significant

A total of five studies used self reports of males and females with an average of three studies used in each analysis. The overall p's on studies using self reports were found to be significant on the dominant ($p<-.0062$), dramatic ($p<-.02$), contentious ($p<-.000$), animated ($p<+.00003$), relaxed ($p<-.005$), and attentive ($p<-.0008$) dimensions. Females reported being more animated and attentive than men. Men reported higher means on the dominant, dramatic, contentious, and relaxed style variables.

Variables found to be significant across all studies were dominant ($p<-.001$), dramatic ($p<-.0495$), contentious ($p<-.0000$), animated ($p<.0004$), attentive ($p<+.0000$), open ($p<+.0068$), and friendly ($p<+.04$) (See Table 3). Women's mean scores were higher on the attentive, animated, open and friendly dimensions while males' scores were higher on the dramatic, contentious and dominant dimensions.

Table 2.   Studies Using Self Reports

Study	3	5	6	7	8	Overall P
N	m=11	m=44	m=253	m=473	m=238	
	f=11	f=181	f=232	f=263	f=144	
Dominant	*	*	p<-.01	p<-.159	p<-.154	P<-.0062
Dramatic	*	p<.01	p<-.01	p<+204	p<-.436	P<-.02
Contentious	*	* NR	p<-.001	p<-.019	p<-.0001	P<-.0000001
Animated	p<-.018	p<+.001	* NR	p<+.0001	p<-.0001	P<+.00003
Impression leaving	*	p<+.001	p<-.01	p<-.419	p<+.792	P<+.2451
Relaxed	*	* NR	p<-.01	p<-.072	p<-.270	P<-.005
Attentive	*	p<+.01	* NR	p<+.010	p<+.209	P<.0008
Open	*	* NR	* NR	p<+.050	p<-.462	P<+.1587
Friendly	*	* NR	* NR	p<+.001	p<-.945	P<+.1446

− indicates means were higher for males
* indicates not included in this analysis (see
Method for justification)
NR = Not Reported
NS = Not Significant

Table 3.   Summary

Variable	Other	Self	Overall
Dominant	Men higher p<+.005	Men higher p<-.0062	Men higher p<-.0001
Dramatic	Men higher p = NS	Men higher p<-.02	Men higher p<-.0495
Contentious	Men higher p<-.0001	Men higher p<-.000	Men higher p<-.000
Animated	Women higher p = NS	Women higher p<.0003	Women higher p<.0004
Impression leaving	Men higher p = NS	Women higher p = NS	Men higher p = NS
Relaxed	Women higher p = NS	Men higher -.005	Men higher p = NS
Attentive	Women higher p<+.005	Women higher p<.0008	Women higher p<.000
Open	Women higher p<.012	Women higher p = NS	Women higher p<.0068
Friendly	Women higher p = NS	Women higher p = NS	Women higher p<.04

Discussion

Research question 1 asks on what communicator style dimensions males and females significantly and consistently differ. Results clearly show that men are more dominant and contentious than women, and women are more attentive than men. These results are consistent with the expressive/instrumental difference found in other studies (Hall, 1984).

This study also clearly illustrates that neither males nor females are more likely to leave an impression. This finding suggests that simply whether one is male or female is not important as to whether another remembers the person; other factors seem considerably more important.

Men definitely perceive themselves as more dramatic than do females. Overall, males are perceived as more dramatic. Women are perceived as more open and, overall, are significantly more open than men. These slightly mixed results are consistent with stereotypical, conflicting, traditional male and female norms. Traditional males strive to be respected and admired, in control of the situation yet should be emotionally demonstrative (Thompson, Grisanti, & Pleck, 1985). Traditional females should be entertaining and responsive, yet proper (Hall, 1984; Pearson, 1985) These results may suggest that women may be perceived as more open than men; however, men may *feel* that they are more open than others perceive them to be. Women may be perceived by others as more open than what they perceive themselves to be. This is consistent with Pearson's (1985) findings on perceived sexual differences between males and females.

The relaxed dimension was found to have very mixed results. Men report being more relaxed; however, others do not necessarily see them as more relaxed. This may be due to the fact males are expected to be in control of the situation (Thompson et al., 1985). They are more dominant and less expressive (Hall, 1984; Pearson, 1985). Thus, others see these characteristics and do not perceive men as relaxed. Possibly, males feel social pressure to report being relaxed because they do not want to be perceived as emotionally uptight or too expressive (Thompson et al., 1985). More studies need to be conducted before any conclusion can be reached on this dimension.

Overall, women seem to be more animated and friendly than men; however, these conclusions are drawn tentatively because of the mixed results across studies and methods. These mixed results may be due in part to the low reliabilities on these dimensions, especially on the friendly dimension (Alpha reliability = .37) (Norton, 1977). Women report being more animated; however, others do not consistently perceive them to be more animated. Again, this may be due to social pressures to be the bubbly, vivacious conversationalist; as a result, women perceive themselves as more animated because they feel this behavior is expected of them.

Research question 2 examines whether these differences are meaningful at the $p<.05$ criterion. Overall differences which are meaningful include the following: men are more dominant, dramatic, and contentious while women are more animated, attentive, open, and friendly. These differences were consistent across self and other reports. However, studies using other reports on the dramatic dimension had a probability which was not significant, but in the same direction as self and overall reporting methods. Self-report studies did not show significant differences on the open variable.

Relaxed and impression leaving dimensions did not give meaningful results except on self-report studies; in these studies men reported being more relaxed. In this meta-analysis, most results were meaningful, thus suggesting that males' communicator style and women's communicator style do differ.

These results lead us to question 3: Does the method used to collect data (i.e., self or other reports) impact the style dimensions found to be significantly different for men and women? The only two dimensions where mixed results were found across methods were impression leaving and relaxed. Impression leaving provided no significant results no matter how studied. Relaxed provided significant results only on studies using self reports. Whether this was due to actual differences in self and other report methods, due to the number of studies involved, or due to actual differences in those reporting cannot be concluded at this time. However, little difference in results were found in self, other, and combined methods. This finding may be a result of the nature of the concept studied rather than true for all types of studies.

Most of the results, especially those significant to or in the same direction across methodologies, may be explained by social expectations and norms. Masculine (traditional) men have been seen as the dominant, more powerful, more contentious sex. Traditionally, men tell stories (dramatic) while women listen (attentive). Women have been and still are expected to be responsive (animated), open and friendly. They are touched and touch more than men; they allow their personal space to be invaded more often than do men (Hall, 1984). Therefore, these results are not surprising.

Although changes may be seen in the roles and expectations of the sexes, this analysis shows that differences between the sexes still exist. The way males and females report communicating and the way males and females are perceived by others to communicate is also different.

To communicate better, one must recognize the similarities and differences in the person with which he or she wishes to communicate. Thus, realizing that subtle differences exist in male and female communication styles allows one to adapt better to that individual and allows for less chance of misunderstanding and disagreement. This study shows that traditional male and female roles still impact upon our communication style. The results also suggest that male–female communication style differences should not be excluded from future analysis, especially when examining variables such as attraction and effectiveness.

The meta–analysis allows for stronger, more objective conclusions to be drawn because conclusions from numerous studies were analyzed statistically. Several suggestions and problems still exist. Only a small number of studies were analyzed because only a small number were reported using biological sex and communication style. Not all results in the original studies were reported: therefore, the analysis was more difficult as decisions had to be made about nonsignificant or unreported variables. If this type of objective analysis is to be conducted, more nonsignificant results need to be reported in journals. Further, the communication style dimensions are not all reliable (Gudykunst & Lim, 1984); therefore, there is a greater chance of error and mixed results.

Meta–analyzing studies using psychological sex (gender orientation) and communication style such as Talley and Richmond (1980) would be an interesting comparison to biological sex and style results. More studies need to be conducted in this area before such analysis is possible. Also, examining who is completing other reports (i.e. males or females) might lead to some interesting insight into male and female perception of each other.

The results of this analysis clearly indicate that communicator style variables differ consistently between the sexes. Men are more dominant, dramatic, and contentious. Women are more animated, attentive, open, and friendly. Analyses such as the one conducted in this study allow for stronger conclusions to be made because a larger, more varied population is studied. The meta–analysis quantifies results and allows for more objective results. Since this method is fairly simple and results in a wealth of information, more review of this nature should be attempted.

References

Baird, J.E. & Bradley, P.H. (1979). Styles of management and communication: A comparative study of men and women. *Communication Monographs, 46,* 101–111.

Blake, R.R., & Mouton, J.S. (1977). *The new managerial grid.* Houston: Gulf Publishing Company.

Bednar, D.A. (1982). Relationships between communicator style and managerial performance in complex organizations: A field study. *Journal of Business Communication, 19,* 51–76.

Duran, R.L. & Zakahi, W.R. (1984). Competence or style: What's in a name? *Communication Research Reports, 1,* 42–47.

Fairhurst, G.L. (1986). Male–Female communication on the job: Literature review and commentary. In M.L. McLaughlin (Ed.) *Communication Yearbook, 9,* (Beverly Hills: Sage Publications).

Glass, G. McGaw, B., & Smith, M.L. (1981). The problems of research review and integration. (Ch. 1.) in *Meta–analysis in social research.*

Gudykunst, W.B. & Lim, T. (1985). Ethnicity, sex, and self perceptions of communicator style. *Communication Research Reports, 2,* 68–75.

Hall, J.A. (1984). *Nonverbal sex differences:* Communication accuracy and expressive style. Baltimore: Johns Hopkins University.

Jurma, W.E. (1979). Effects of leader structuring style and task–orientation characteristics of group members. *Communication Monograph, 46,* 282–295.

Lamude, K.C., & Daniels, T.D. (1984). Perceived managerial communication style as a function of subordinate and manager gender. *Communication Research Reports, 1,* 91–96.

Honeycutt, J.M., Wilson, C., & Parker, C. (1982). Effects of sex and degrees of happiness on perceived styles of communication in and out of the marital relationship. *Journal of Marriage and the Family, 44,* 395–406.

Jablin, F.M. (1985). An exploratory study of vocational organizational communication socialization. *The Southern Speech Communication Journal, 50,* 261–282.

Montgomery, B.M. & Norton, R.W. (1981). Sex differences and similarities in communicator style. *Communication Monographs, 48,* 121–132.

Norton, R.W. (1978). Foundation of a communicator style construct. *Human Communication Research, 4,* 99–112.

Norton, R.W. (1983). *Communicator style: Theory,* applications, and measures (Beverly Hills: Sage Publications).

Nussbaum, J.F., Robinson, J.D., & Grew, D.J. (1985). Communicative behavior of the long–term health care employee: Implications for the elderly resident. *Communication Research Reports*, 2, 16–21.

Pearson, J. (1985). *Gender and Communication*. Dubuque, IA: Wm. C. Brown.

Porter, D.T. (1982). Communicator style perceptions as a function of communication apprehension. *Communication Quarterly, 30*, 237–244.

Rosenthal, R. (1978). Combining results of independent studies. *Psychological Bulletin, 85*, 185–193.

Seiffert, M.A., & McDonald, B.F. (1986). The effects of gender on perception of communicator style. (Unpublished manuscript, WVU).

Stephen, T.D. & Harrison, T.M. (1985). Gender, sex–role identity, and communication style: a q–sort analysis of behavioral differences. *Communication Research Reports, 1*, 53–67.

Stohl, C. (1981). Perceptions of social attractiveness and communicator style: A developmental study of pre–school children. *Communication Education, 30*, 367–476.

Stohl, C. (1982). Sugar or spice: Teachers' perceptions of sex differences in communicative correlates of attraction. In Burgoon, M. (Ed.), *Communication Yearbook, 6*, 811–830 (Beverly Hills: Sage Publications).

Talley, M.A., & Richmond, V.P. (1980). The relationship between psychological gender orientation and communicator style. *Human Communication Research, 6*, 326–339.

Thompson, E.H., Grisanti, C., Pleck, J.H. (1985). Attitudes toward the male role and their correlation. *Sex Roles, 13*, 413–427.

Watzlawick, P. Beavin, J., & Jackson, D. (1967). *Pragmatics of human communication: A study of interpersonal patterns, pathologies and paradoxes*. New York: Norton Company.

Wood, W., Polek, D., & Aiken, C. (1985). Sex differences in group task performance. *Journal of Personality and Social Psychology, 48*, 63–71.

Endnote

1. Communicator image was not used in this analysis because Norton intended it to be an anchor variable around which the others work. In addition, only three of the eight studies reported this variable.

Information for Tables

2. Code for Studies
   1. Seiffert & McDonald (1986)
   2. Baird & Bradley (1979)
   3. Lamude & Daniels (1984)
   4. Stohl (1981)
   5. Stephen & Harris (1985)
   6. Gudykunst & Lim (1985)
   7. Montgomery & Norton (Study I) (1981)
   8. Montgomery & Norton (Study II) (1981)

The author would like to thank Drs. Melanie Booth–Butterfield and Virginia Eman Wheeless for their input into this paper.

THOUGHT PROVOKER

What variables, other than biological sex, may account for communicator style differences? In what ways do you think the findings from a meta–analysis of communicator style based on psychological sex (gender orientation) would differ from those reported in this study?

CHAPTER NINE
Sex, Instrumentality, Expressiveness and Interpersonal Communication Competence

Brian H. Spitzberg
North Texas State University

Claire C. Brunner
University of Cincinnati

Social scientists have long speculated that males and females vary both quantitatively and qualitatively in their interaction behavior. These speculations appear to be borne out in empirical research. Men and women differ in their language usage (Smyth, Arkin, Huddleston & Nickel, 1983), conversational cues (Hall & Braunwald, 1981), nonverbal communication skills (Hall, 1980), disclosure preferences (Dosser, Balswick & Halverson, 1986), power strategies (Offermann & Schrier, 1985), leadership tendencies (Fairhurst, 1985), superior–subordinate communication (Steckler & Rosenthal, 1985), conflict management tendencies (Fitzpatrick & Winke, 1979; Kelley, Cunningham, Grisham, Lefebvre, Sink & Yablon, 1978; Roloff & Greenberg, 1979; Shockley–Zabalak & Morley, 1984), control symmetry and complementarity (Heatherington & Allen, 1984), and a variety of objective, interpersonal behaviors (e.g., Ickes & Barnes, 1977). One of the most parsimonious frameworks for encompassing these interaction differences is the proposition that females tend to behave expressively whereas males tend to behave instrumentally (Parsons, 1955). The instrumental versus expressive distinction has been used to define relationship types (Fitzpatrick, 1984; Fitzpatrick & Indvik, 1982), explain sex–role incompatibility (Ickes, 1985), and to predict differences in behavioral tendencies and psychological outcomes in interpersonal interactions (Ickes, 1981). The distinction appears to be so resilient that it often shows up in studies not designed to find such differences. For example, Barnes and Buss (1985) identified four factors of inferentially grounded and objectively coded behavior in married couples (i.e., coercive–manipulative, initiative, communal, and flashy attire), which clearly correspond to the instrumental–expressive dimensions.

Clearly the instrumental–expressive distinction seems pervasive. However, while males clearly seem to *behave* more instrumentally, and females clearly seem to *behave* more expressively, the extent to which these behavioral manifestations are reflected in the cognitive structures of interactants is not clear. In other words, do interactants vary in their *evaluation* of males and females on the basis of instrumental–expressive judgments? Furthermore, do males and females differ in their cognitive processing of behavioral evaluations on the basis of instrumental–expressive distinctions? This study seeks to address these issues.

One of the most important types of social evaluation is the inference of communicative competence. Competence in communicating, in one form or another, has been implicated in the etiology and maintenance of a host of undesirable social phenomena, including: depression, loneliness, low self–esteem, stress, anxiety, hypertension, academic failure, occupational failure, and heterosocial inadequacy (see Spitzberg, 1986a). Basically, competence in communicating involves appropriate and effective interaction. Obviously, people who consistently are more competent in interaction stand to receive greater social rewards from their interaction experiences than those who are inappropriate and ineffective. A question arises as to whether or not American socialization practices result in differences in competence and competence judgments between males and females. Assuming that males behave more instrumentally and females behave more expressively, a reasonable conjecture is that such behavioral orientations could produce differences in competence and competence inferences.

While the communicative competence research has hardly been idle on the subject of sex, existing studies provide surprisingly sparse information directly relevant to the links between instrumentality, expressiveness, and competence inferences. To date, competence research indicates that females report themselves (and are reported by others) to be more interpersonally competent than males (Brunner, 1984; Reiser & Troost, 1986; Spitzberg, 1986b; Spitzberg & Hurt, 1987). Such studies point to a consistent pattern, but the effect sizes of the sex differences are generally very small, and measures used typically have combined molar items (i.e., general, subjective) and molecular items (specific, objective) (Bellack, 1983; Spitzberg, 1987), making conclusions regarding behavioral judgments problematic. Finally, such measures may be culturally biased in favor of expressive dimensions. For example, current measures tend to include factors such as empathy, anxiety, listening, and self–disclosure (see Phelps & Snavely, 1980). Other conceptual frameworks might generate more instrumental dimensions, such as Parks' (1985) decision-making effectiveness model or Stricker's (1982) organizational/interview measure.

Some isolated findings suggest that males and females base their inferences of competence along instrumental–expressive lines. When asked to describe behaviors representative of communicative competence, females are more likely to mention characteristics such as "eye contact," "listening," and "attentiveness." Males, on the other hand, appear to be primarily aware of whether or not a person appears "knowledgeable" (Brunner & Pearson, 1984). This finding supports the prediction that differences in competence inferences may be affected both by sex and by the implicit instrumental–expressive schemata used by males and females. By itself, however, the Brunner and Pearson study provides an incomplete picture. First, the competent communicator was a hypothetical target. Some subjects may have conjured up a particular person, and others may have used some cognitive competence prototype (Pavitt & Haight, 1985). Second, and closely related, there was no conversational context or conversational "data" referenced by the subjects. It is one thing to imagine what behaviors are generally competent. It is quite another to consider which behaviors were competent in a particular conversation. Third, considerable evidence now suggests that lay interactants are not very cognizant of which behaviors they pay attention to in interaction (Conger, Wallander, Mariotto, & Ward, 1980; Conger, Wallander, Ward, & Farrell, 1980). Therefore, a preferable strategy would be to supply interactants with a fairly comprehensive and relevant sample of behaviors and allow the interactants to then judge those behaviors. In doing so, the way in which interactants "perceptually organize" sets of behaviors can be studied more comprehensively.

Based on the literature, therefore, we expect that males and females can be differentiated according to their evaluations of interpersonal skills, both in terms of their self perceptions and in terms of their evaluations of conversational coactors. The exact nature of these perceptions is difficult to predict. The research by Brunner and Pearson (1984) suggests that males and females will use different behaviors (i.e., instrumental vs. expressive). Research by Conger et al. (1980) also suggests that females use a broader and richer set of behavioral cues in judging interpersonal skills. Thus, in this study we anticipate that females and males will differ both in the number and nature of their cue utilization in deriving competence inferences.

Method

Subjects

Subjects were 496 students enrolled in communication courses at a medium–sized public university in the southern midwest (n–287) and a large public urban university in the central midwest (n=209). These two groups were sampled in order to increase the generalizability of the results of this study. Demographic analysis revealed nearly identical profiles for the two groups. The total sample contained 49% males and 51% females; 0.8% Asians, 10.5% blacks, 1.4% hispanics, 0.2% middle easterners, 85.4% whites, and 1.4% "others." Age ranged from 17 to 49 with a mean age of 20.5. Reported demographics for the recalled conversational partners were virtually identical.

Instrumentation

The Conversational Skills Rating Scale (CSRS) consists of 25 molecular–level skill items (e.g., "use of eye contact," "speaking rate—neither too slow nor too fast," "expression of personal opinions—neither too passive nor too aggressive" and five molar–level items (e.g., appropriate & effective–inappropriate & ineffective, skillful conversationalist–unskillful conversationalist, expressive–inexpressive, etc.). The 25 skill items are rated on a five–point scale, anchored by "1=INADEQUATE (i.e., use was disruptive, awkward, or resulted in negative impression of his or her/your communicative skill), 3=ADEQUATE (i.e., use was sufficient but not exceptional, had no particular impact in impressions of his or her/your communicative skill), and 5=EXCELLENT (i.e., use was controlled, smooth, or resulted in positive impression of his or her/your communicative skill)." Alternate pronouns were used in self– or actor–reference (i.e., "your") and coactor–reference (i.e., "his or her") forms of the CSRS.

Previous studies (Spitzberg, 1985, 1986c, Spitzberg & Hurt 1987) have shown that the CSRS is related significantly and positively to motivation, knowledge, overall competence, communication apprehension, and contextual typicality. The molecular and molar subscales have been shown to be very reliable. In this study, the five molar items attained a coefficient alpha estimate of reliability of .78, and the 25 molecular items revealed a coefficient alpha reliability of .91. The coefficients for the coactor form of the CSRS were .86 for the molar items and .93 for the molecular items.

For purposes of this study the authors independently coded each item of the CSRS as being more expressive ("E") or instrumental ("I"). After initial comparison of codings, the two items upon which there was disagreement were resolved through discussion. The coding decisions are represented in the tables.

Procedure

Subjects were given questionnaire packets, and were told that they would receive some form of extra credit for their participation. There were two types of induction instructions on the questionnaires: either "recall the most satisfying," or "recall the most dissatisfying," face–to face dyadic conversation you have experienced over the last two weeks. Thus, subjects either received a SATISFYING or a DISSATISFYING induction. Recalled conversation procedures have been shown to be efficient methods for obtaining information on interpersonal communication, especially for exploratory purposes, and generally have produced construct interrelationships similar to actual conversation episode studies (see Cupach & Spitzberg, 1981; Spitzberg & Cupach, 1983; Spitzberg & Hurt, 1987; Spitzberg & Phelps, 1982). In addition to being consistent with many more naturalistic approaches, the recalled conversation approach taps into peoples' "recalled reality." In other words, whether or not the conversation is recalled accurately is a separate empirical question. It is equally important how the "perceived reality" of the conversation is retained over time. Recall procedures capture this perceived reality, which can be considered as important in many ways as the "actual" reality, since it is the recalled images of conversations that form the comparison base from which future decisions regarding the relationship are likely to be made.

Results

The first step was to assess the existence of general level differences in the summed CSRS ratings according to sex. Four analyses of variance were examined. For each condition (i.e., satisfying vs. dissatisfying), the actor self–reference CSRS form and the actor reference of coactor CSRS form served as dependent variables in two–by–two models with sex of actor and sex of coactor as classification factors. In the satisfying condition, female actors rated themselves more competently when they had male coactors ($\overline{X}$ = 123.20) than when they had female coactors ($\overline{X}$ = 119.16), although the difference was not substantial (F = 4.25, p <.05, eta–squared = .02). Male actors did not appear to consider themselves more competent with male coactors ($\overline{X}$ = 118.17) than with female coactors ($\overline{X}$ = 117.72). Furthermore, in the satisfying condition, ratings of coactor competence did not differ by sex of actor or coactor.

An interesting reversal occurs when examining the dissatisfying condition. No significant differences were observed on actor ratings of self according to sex of actor or coactor. In contrast to the satisfying condition, in the dissatisfying condition actor ratings of coactor did differ by sex of self and coactor. Specifically, females viewed male coactors ($\overline{X}$ = 97.47) more competently than female coactors ($\overline{X}$ = 93.63). However, males again did not appear to view male coactors ($\overline{X}$ = 95.04) any differently than female coactors ($\overline{X}$ = 95.50). The overall model was highly significant (F = 12.17, p<.001, eta squared = .10).

Initially, for each discriminant analysis two methods of variable entry were compared. Direct entry resulted in all CSRS items being entered to examine their relative contributions. Stepwise entry was used to examine which particular items were the most statistically important behaviors. The stepwise models were generally more parsimonious and powerful because statistical error and additional degrees of freedom were not forced into the equation. Consequently, only the stepwise results are reported.

Table 1 reports the results of the discriminant analysis of actor sex based on actor self-ratings of interpersonal skills. For the total

Table 1. Stepwise Discriminant Analyses of Actor Sex by Actor Ratings of Actor's Skills.

Item Abstract	Total Sample	Dissatisfied Condition	Satisfied Condition
1. Eye contact(E)	.02		.21
2. Topic initiation(I)	.41	.65	
3. Topic maintenance(I)	−.22		−.35
4. Speaking time(I)			
5. Interruptions(I)			
6. Speaking rate(I)		.40	
7. Speaking fluency(I)		−.31	
8. Vocal confidence(I)	−.26		−.48
9. Articulation(E)			
10. Nervous twitches(E)			
11. Posture(E)	.46		.51
12. Fidgeting(E)	−.22		−.33
13. Questions(E)			.22
14. Head nods(E)	−.22	−.34	
15. Body lean(I)	.33	.30	.25
16. Altercentric speech(E)			
17. Egocentric speech(I)			
18. Encouragements(E		−.53	.30
19. Humor/stories(E)	−.67	−.42	−.50
20. Vocal variety(E)			
21. Volume(E)		−.37	
22. Opinion expression(I)	−.23		
23. Facial expression(E)	.55	.70	.25
24. Gestures(E)	.27		.31
25. Smiling/laughing(E)			
Group Centroids:			
Females:	.29	.31	.42
Males:	−.31	−.33	−.46
Chi−Square	40.18	21.58	42.42
Canonical Corr.	.29	.31	.41
Significance	.01	.01	.01
% Classified	61.12	62.03	68.55

sample, the use of humor and/or stories and facial expression were the most influential behaviors. This would suggest a positive affect function. Posture, topic initiation, and body lean were also important discriminators. It appears that males are discriminated by their signs of positive affect, but that females are judged according to a broader range of nonverbal behavior (e.g., facial expression, posture, etc.). In dissatisfying conversations, facial expression and topic initiation are the most powerful discriminators, associated more with the evaluation of females than with males. Males tended to be discriminated according to their use of encouragements, humor and stories, volume, head nods, and fluency as behavioral referents. In satisfying conversations, males were differentiated more in terms their use of humor and stories and vocal confidence, in contrast to females, who were judged more in terms of their posture. Females may be evaluated more in terms of their ability to establish a "comfortable" or "casual" conversational climate, while males may be judged more in terms of their ability to establish a satisfying climate through confident use of humor and stories. Given that the canonical correlation reduces to a simple Pearson product–moment correlation in the two-group case, the relationship between sex and competence attribution shares between 9 and 16 percent of the variance.

Table 2 reports the discriminant analyses differentiating coactor sex based upon male actor ratings of coactor skills. All stepwise functions were statistically significant, explaining between 21 and 35 percent of the variance. In general, males rely heavily on the cues of humor and/or stories and vocal confidence in evaluating male coactors, and eye contact, egocentric speech, facial expressiveness and vocal variety in evaluating female coactors. In dissatisfying conversations, males refer to smiling and/or laughing in judging male coactors, and attend to eye contact, facial expressiveness, and egocentric speech in judging female coactors. This would appear to represent a positive affect function, and would imply that dissatisfying conversations for males are characterized by males who may seem overly serious, and females who are inattentive. In satisfying conversations males relied heavily on vocal confidence when evaluating male coactors, and facial expressiveness and smiling/laughing when evaluating female coactors. This seems to parallel the prototypical satisfying conversation, in which males can be evaluated in terms of their appearance of power and females in terms of their socioemotional skills.

Table 2. Stepwise Discriminant, Analyses of Coactor Sex by Male Actor Ratings of Coactor's Skills.

Item Abstract	Total Sample	Dissatisfied Condition	Satisfied Condition
1. Eye contact(E)	.49	-.52	
2. Topic initiation(I)			
3. Topic maintenance(I)	-.24		
4. Speaking time(I)			
5. Interruptions(I)			
6. Speaking rate(I)	-.26	.48	
7. Speaking fluency(I)			
8. Vocal confidence(I)	-.52		-.76
9. Articulation(E)		.32	
10. Nervous twitches(E)		-.30	
11. Posture(E)		.43	
12. Fidgeting(E)		.43	
13. Questions(E)	.35		.35
14. Head nods(E)		-.37	
15. Body lean(I)	.24	-.33	.32
16. Altercentric speech(E)		-.27	
17. Egocentric speech(I)	.52	-.45	.31
18. Encouragements(E)			-.35
19. Humor/stories(E)	-.55		-.55
20. Vocal variety(E)	.43	-.41	
21. Volume(E)			
22. Opinion expression(I)	-.27	.44	
23. Facial expression(E)	.54	-.49	.51
24. Gestures(E)	-.39	.40	.39
25. Smiling/laughing(E)		.68	.52
Group Centroids:			
Females:	.40	-.56	.46
Males:	-.65	.84	-.81
Chi-Square	47.19	35.53	33.50
Canonical Corr.	.46	.57	.53
Significance	.01	.01	.01
% Classified	70.72	74.26	71.19

Table 3 shows the results of the discriminant analyses differentiating coactor sex based upon female actor ratings of coactor skills. All stepwise functions are statistically significant, indicating that sex and inferred skills share between 9 and almost 36 percent of the variance. In general, females rely on humor and/or stories, and to a lesser extent, on speaking rate and facial expressiveness, when evaluating male coactors. Females rely on head nods, speaking fluency, and smiling/laughing when judging female coactors. This is not a very interpretable finding, but is clarified by the episode type breakdown. In dissatisfying conversations, females depend heavily on head nods in evaluating female coactors, and mainly refer to speaking time

Table 3. Stepwise Discriminant Analyses of Coactor Sex by Female Actor Ratings of Coactor's skills.

Item Abstract	Total Sample	Dissatisfied Condition	Satisfied Condition
1. Eye contact(E)			.53
2. Topic initiation(I)			
3. Topic maintenance(I)			
4. Speaking time(I)		.62	.94
5. Interruptions(I)			
6. Speaking rate(I)	.50		-.64
7. Speaking fluency(I)	-.66	-.24	.61
8. Vocal confidence(I)			
9. Articulation(E)			
10. Nervous twitches(E)			
11. Posture(E)	.46	.47	-.36
12. Fidgeting(E)			.40
13. Questions(E)			
14. Head nods(E)	-.69	-.96	
15. Body lean(I)	-.34	-.42	
16. Altercentric speech(E)			-.43
17. Egocentric speech(I)	.34		.41
18. Encouragements(E)			
19. Humor/stories(E)	.76	.43	
20. Vocal variety(E)			
21. Volume(E)			
22. Opinion expression(I)		.29	
23. Facial expression(E)	.50	.34	-.25
24. Gestures(E)			.50
25. Smiling/laughing(E)	-.55		
Group Centroids:			
Females:	-.43	-.76	.88
Males:	.25	.46	-.50
Chi-Square	23.07	32.03	42.15
Canonical Corr.	.31	.51	.56
Significance	.01	.01	.01
% Classified	62.35	75.21	75.40

when evaluating male coactors. This suggests that in dissatisfying conversations female attentiveness and male dominance are preeminent concerns in drawing competence inferences. In contrast, in satisfying conversations females rely primarily on speaking time, and to a lesser extent on fluency and gestures in evaluating female coactors, and speaking rate and eye contact in evaluating male coactors. Satisfying conversations may be marked by relative equality of speaking time for females interacting with females, and conversational involvement on the part of male coactors.

Discussion

The question motivating this study concerned the nature of differences between males and females in the way they judge self and coactor competence. A reasonable expectation was put forward that any differences uncovered would reflect instrumental versus expressive interpersonal dimensions, and that males and females would use these cues differentially, both qualitatively and quantitatively.

The first intriguing finding was that the conversational condition made an important difference in how females inferred competence. In satisfying conversations, females considered *themselves* more competent with male coactors than with female coactors. However, in dissatisfying conversations, females viewed their male *coactors* as more competent than female coactors. Attribution theory suggests that, generally speaking, positive outcomes lead individuals to focus on self as a perceptual object, while negative outcomes lead people to focus on the environment or others as the perceptual object (Seibold & Spitzberg, 1982). Females apparently responded to positive conversational outcomes by focusing their attention on self as a locus of causality in the presence of males, and focused on their coactor as a locus of causality in dissatisfying conversations when their partner was male. In both instances, it seems that male coactors served as a catalyst of sorts. It could be that females are generally more capable of attending to or being sensitive to interpersonal behavior, but that this sensitivity is generally only "activated" or "aroused" in heterosexual encounters. Such encounters may be viewed as having a different set of reward contingencies or activity types than those with females, thus stimulating an increased vigilence regarding interpersonal behavior. The affective valence of the conversation (i.e., satisfying or dissatisfying) then determines whether attention is "switched" primarily to self or other. Males, in contrast, do not appear to be sensitive to such nuances.

The general picture that evolves from the discriminant analyses is difficult to characterize in any summary form. Close scrutiny of the functions reveals relatively little similarity across conditions and sexes. Despite this, several qualified conclusions can be conjectured. First, when judging self, males tend to be discriminated according to their ability to use humor and/or stories, whereas females tend to be differentiated according to their facial expressiveness, posture, and topic initiation. Although humor and storytelling are expressive activities, they also are a form of gaining attention, and can even be viewed as a way of achieving control (Derber, 1981). In dissatisfying conversations subjects seem acutely aware of facial expressiveness, suggesting a prevalence of facial expressions of negative affect or perhaps simply a lack of expression for males. In satisfying conversations, posture, humor/stories, and vocal confidence seem more important. This implies that male composure and confidence, combined with their humor and storytelling, are bases for differentiating sex. Posture is used to discriminate females in satisfying conversations. While humor and storytelling may not be the behaviors most typically associated with male social skills, they clearly function to gain attention, and can in this sense be viewed as instrumental. Research needs to examine the control function of humor as it applies to sex differences.

Second, when judging the competence of coactor behavior, sex clearly makes a difference. Between 9 and 36 percent of the variance was shared between sex classification and competence ratings. However, males and females appeared to reveal little commonality in their reliance on various interpersonal cues in deriving these competence judgments. Males tend to rely primarily on smiling and laughing in dissatisfying conversations, and vocal confidence in satisfying conversations. While it is difficult to ascertain from the data, it could be speculated that for males the dissatisfying conversations recalled were negative because female coactors were affectively negative, this affect being primarily displayed through facial affect. In contrast, what is key to males in satisfying episodes seems to be their feeling of confidence or composure. This latter finding seems largely an instrumental basis for differentiation.

Third, somewhat surprisingly, for females the dissatisfying conversations called forth attention to the behavior of head nods. Apparently, females find a lack of this attention behavior (males are viewed as less competent in providing this behavior) particularly indicative of negative conversational episodes. Satisfying conversations, in contrast, clearly revolve around the relative speaking time of the interactants. In this instance the group centroid for males indicates that they are perceived lower on this dimension, suggesting that females view females as more competent at distributing speaking time in satisfying conversations, which itself could contribute to the feeling of satisfaction. For dissatisfying conversations, then, an expressiveness behavior is central, in which females tend to be viewed as more competent. For satisfying conversations, the instrumental behavior of speaking time is emphasized, for which males are considered less competent.

Fourth, it is important and interesting to note just how different the discriminant solutions are between the satisfying and dissatisfying conditions. Very few behaviors are consistently used across conditions to discriminate sex of coactor. What is unclear, and cannot be addressed by this data, is the causal order of information processing. In other words, do negative affective outcomes or reactions cue an actor to attend differentially to behavior in inferring competence, or are competently, or incompetently, used conversational behaviors perceived to accumulate to produce affective reactions? Actors may "overlay" schematic sex expectations upon conversations, at which point deviation from these expectations cue a cognitive focus upon certain conversational behaviors. The degree to which these behaviors either competently negotiate acceptable identities for the interactants, or achieve desired outcomes, in turn influences the affective tone of the episode.

Regarding the number of cues used by males and females, the expectation that females would utilize a richer and broader base of interpersonal behaviors was not supported by the data. From this data set at least, it appears that males are just as differentiated in their cue usage as females when considering competence inferences. This contrasts with the research by Brunner and Pearson (1984) and Conger et al. (1980) in which females generated more cues, and generally more molecular cues, than did males. An important difference between these studies and the study reported here is that in the former subjects generated their own cues in an open-ended format. In this study, the cues were provided for the subjects. When the cues are provided, males seem just as capable of using the entire range of cues as females.

Finally, this study points to some cautions regarding future sex-based research. First, it seems clear that as intuitive and parsimonious as the instrumental–expressive distinction is, it may be far too simplistic to encompass adequately the minutiae of interpersonal behavior and its attendant inference processes. Verbal and nonverbal behavior are multifunctional (Capella & Street, 1985), and are not always appropriately force-fit into an instrumental or expressive category. In this study, males and females showed a remarkable variety in their reliance on specific interpersonal behaviors in deriving competence impressions. Second, and related, research that uses unidimensional rating scales (e.g, attractiveness, power, etc) is likely to miss the complexity of actor behavior. In other words, if provided a wide diversity of behavioral rating dimensions, interactants seem perfectly capable of using them. Studies that attempt to reduce interpersonal behavior to a few particular features (e.g., self–disclosure, structuring behavior, eye contact, etc.), are probably doing violence to the richness of the interpersonal process. Third, and very importantly, the degree to which sex is a relevant perceptual variable depends in part upon the affective valence of the episode being considered and the dyadic sex composition of the stimulus event, as well as the sex of the rater. In this study, females rated themselves differently than males did when they had male coactors in satisfying encounters, and rated their male coactors as more competent than female coactors when involved in dissatisfying conversations. This issue of affective valence appears to have been overlooked in many studies of sex evaluations, or at least simply presumed. The nature of episodic affective valence and its mediating role in defining the relevance and importance of sex seems an important avenue for future research.

References

Barnes, M.L. & Buss, D.M. (1985). Sex differences in the interpersonal behavior of married couples. *Journal of Personality and Social Psychology, 48,* 654–661.

Bellack, A.S. (1983). Recurrent problems in the behavioral assessment of social skill. *Behavior Research and Therapy, 21,* 29–41.

Brunner, C.C. (1984, October). *Gender differences in interaction involvement and interpersonal communication competence.* Paper presented at the Language and Gender Conference, Oxford, OH.

Brunner, C.C. & Pearson, J.C. (1984, November). *Sex differences in perceptions of interpersonal communication competence.* Paper presented at the Speech Communication Association Conference, Chicago, IL.

Capella, J.N. & Street, R.L. (1985). Introduction: A functional approach to the structure of communicative behaviour. In R.L. Street & J.N. Capella (Eds.), *Sequence and pattern in communicative behaviour* (pp. 1–29). London: Edward Arnold.

Conger, A.J., Wallander, J.L., Mariotto, M.J. & Ward, D. (1980). Peer judgments of heterosexual–social anxiety and skills: What do they pay attention to anyhow? *Behavioral Assessment, 2,* 243–295.

Conger, A.J., Wallander, J.L., Ward, D.G., & Farrell, A.D. (1980). *Ratings of heterosocial anxiety and skill: 1+1=1.* Unpublished manuscript, Purdue University, West Lafayette, IN.

Cupach, W.R. & Spitzberg, B.H. (1981, February). *Relational competence: Measurement and validation.* Paper presented at the Western Speech Communication Association Conference, San Jose, CA.

Derber, C. (1981). *In pursuit of attention.* Boston: Schenkman.

Dosser, D.A., Jr., Balswik, J.O. & Halverson, C.F., Jr. (1986). Male inexpressiveness and relationships. *Journal of Social and Personal Relationships, 3,* 241–258.

Fairhurst, G.T. (1985, May). *Male–female communication on the job: Literature review and commentary.* Paper presented at the International Communication Association Conference, Honolulu, HI.

Fitzpatrick, M.A. (1984). A typological approach to marital interaction: Recent theory and research. *Advances in Experimental Social Psychology, 18,* 1–47.

Fitzpatrick, M.A. & Indvik, J. (1982). The instrumental and expressive domains of marital communication. *Human Communication Research, 8,* 195–213.

Fitzpatrick, M.A. & Winke, J. (1979). You always hurt the one you love: Strategies and tactics in interpersonal conflict. *Communication Quarterly, 27,* 3–10.

Hall, J.A. (1980). Gender differences in nonverbal communication skills. In R. Rosenthal (Ed.), *New directions for methodology of social and behavioral science: Quantitative assessment of research domains* (pp. 63–77). San Francisco: Jossey–Bass.

Hall, J.A. & Braunwald, K.G. (1981). Gender cues in conversations. *Journal of Personality and Social Psychology, 40*, 99–110.

Heatherington, L. & Allen, G. J. (1984). Sex and relational communication patterns in counseling. *Journal of Counseling Psychology, 31*, 287–294.

Hinde, R.A. (1984). Why do the sexes behave differently in close relationships? *Journal of Social and Personal Relationships, 1*, 471–501.

Ickes, W. (1981). Sex–role influences in dyadic interaction: A theoretical model. In C. Mayo & N. M. Henley (Eds.), *Gender and nonverbal behavior* (pp. 95–128). New York: Springer–Verlag.

Ickes, W. (1985). Sex–role influences on compatibility in relationships. In W. Ickes (Ed.), *Compatible and incompatible relationships* (pp. 187–208). New York: Springer–Verlag.

Ickes, W. & Barnes, R. D. (1977). The role of sex and self–monitoring in unstructured dyadic interactions. *Journal of Personality and Social Psychology, 35*, 315–330.

Kelley, H.H., Cunningham, J.D., Grisham, J.A., Lefebvre, L.M., Sink, C.R. & Yablon, G. (1978). Sex differences in comments made during conflict within close heterosexual pairs. *Sex Roles, 4*, 473–492.

Offermann, L.R. & Schrier, P.E. (1985). Social influence strategies: The impact of sex, role, and attitudes toward power. *Personality and Social Psychology Bulletin, 11*, 286–300.

Parks, M.R. (1985). Interpersonal communication and the quest for personal competence. In M.L. Knapp & G.R. Miller (Eds.), *Handbook of interpersonal communication* (pp. 171–201). Beverly Hills, CA: Sage.

Parsons, T. (1955). Family structure and socialization of the child. In T. Parsons & R.F. Bales (Eds.), *Family, socialization, and interaction process*. Glencoe, IL: Free Press.

Pavitt, C. & Haight, L. (1985). The "competent communicator" as a cognitive prototype. *Human Communication Research, 12*, 225–242.

Phelps, L.A. & Snavely, W.B. (1980, February). *Toward the measurement of interpersonal communication competence*. Paper presented at the Western Speech Communication Association Conference, Portland, OR.

Reiser, C. & Troost, K.M. (1986). Gender and gender–role identity influences upon self– and other–reports of communicate competence. *Sex Roles, 14*, 431–443.

Roloff, M.E. & Greenberg, B.S. (1979). Sex differences in choice of modes of conflict resolution in real–life and television. *Communication Quarterly*, *27*, 3–12.

Seibold, D.R. & Spitzberg, B.H. (1982). Attribution theory and research: Formalization, critique, and implications for communication. *Progress in Communication Sciences*, *3*, 85–125.

Shockley–Zabalak, P.S. & Morley, D.D. (1984). Sex differences in conflict style preferences. *Communication Research Reports*, *1*, 28–32.

Smythe, M.J., Arkin, R.M., Huddleston, B.M. & Nickel, S. (1983, May) *Sex differences in conversation: The stereotype revisited and revised*. Paper presented at the International Communication Association Conference, Dallas, TX.

Spitzberg, B.H. (1985, May) *Loci of perception in the domain of interpersonal skills*. Paper presented at the International Communication Association Conference, Dallas, TX.

Spitzberg, B.H. (1986a, November). *A critical review of communicative competence measures I: Self–Reference instruments*. Paper presented at the Speech Communication Association Conference, Chicago, IL.

Spitzberg, B.H. (1986b, November). *A critical review of communicative competence measures II: Other–reference instruments*. Paper presented at the Speech Communication Association Conference, Chicago, IL.

Spitzberg, B.H. (1986c, November). *Validating a measure of interpersonal skills*. Paper presented at the Speech Communication Association Conference, Chicago, IL.

Spitzberg, B.H. (1987). Issues in the study of communicative competence. *Progress in Communication Sciences*, *8*, 1–46.

Spitzberg, B.H. & Cupach, W.R. (1983, November). *The relational competence construct: Development and research*. Paper presented at the Speech Communication Association Conference, Washington, D.C.

Spitzberg, B.H. & Hurt, H.T. (1987). The measurement of interpersonal skills in instructional contexts. *Communication Education*, *36*, 28–45.

Spitzberg, B.H. & Phelps, L.A. (1982, February). *Conversational appropriateness and effectiveness: Validation of a criterion measure of relational competence*. Paper presented at the Western Speech Communication Association Conference, Denver, CO.

Steckler, N.A. & Rosenthal, R. (1985). Sex differences in nonverbal and verbal communication with bosses, peers, and subordinates. *Journal of Applied Psychology*, *70*, 157–163.

Stricker, L.J. (1982). Interpersonal competence instrument: Development and preliminary findings. *Applied Psychological Measurement*, *6*, 69–81.

THOUGHT PROVOKER

The authors discovered that in satisfying conversations, females considered *themselves* more competent with male coactors than with female coactors; however, in dissatisfying conversations, females viewed their *male* coactors as more competent than *female* coactors. To explain this difference, the authors suggest that females may be more interpersonally sensitive in heterosexual encounters because they may perceive a different set of rewards or purposes than those encounter with females. Discuss some of the possible perceived rewards or purposes that may activate such sensitivity. How do you account for this phenomenon occurring in females and not in males?

## CHAPTER TEN

Attitudes and Control Behaviors Associated with Sex–Based Meanings of Personal Control

Judi Beinstein Miller
Oberlin College

And why do you think you have a strong sense of personal control?

> I know I can make a difference in my life and that it is a matter of my choice. If I choose to study tonight instead of going out, which is actually what I'm going to do, this will make a difference in what I can do in the future. (Sara)

> I believe that nine times out of ten if what you're doing isn't working, all you have to do is try harder or try a new approach. I think the quality of my life, the quality of my friendships, the quality of my work have all gone up, and I've seen that related to trying harder. (Dan)

And why do you think you do not feel more in control of what happens to you?

> The way I look at it is that everybody else is going on and everybody's doing whatever they're going to do. And so obviously to that extent we don't have control. But I do think you have control over how much you're going to accept it and how much you're going to bring it on you. (Julia)

> I think a lot of misfortunes do happen outside your own control. I mean there are a lot of different people out there that I don't think you can really control, as I've learned, one example is my girlfriend. I really don't think you can control how other people behave. (Mike)

A sense of personal control means different things to different people. As illustrated by the remarks above, it may mean beliefs in contingencies between choices and future outcomes, between trying hard and success, and/or beliefs in the influenceability of other people. Despite such variations in meaning there is general agreement among psychologists that persons who believe their outcomes are contingent upon their own behavior (i.e. internals) do better at adjusting to their physical and social environments than do persons who believe their outcomes depend on chance, fate, or powerful others (i.e. externals). Correlates of internal expectancies for control include, for example, superior assimilation and use of information that is relevant to salient goals, greater persistence at achievement activities, more effective styles of coping with stress, less psychopathology, and a generally better emotional adjustment to life (Lefcourt, 1982). In the social arena internals may fare better than externals, since there is some evidence that they are more popular, more involved in leadership roles, and more assertive than are externals (Nowicki and Duke, 1983; Doherty, 1983). Consequently, all things good are linked to an internal locus of control and all things bad to an external one.

The tendency to view an external locus of control as undesirable is unfortunate for at least three reasons. First, correlations between expectancies for control and behavior are often not very large and concern task–behavior more often than social behavior. Second, external expectancies appear to be associated stereotypically with femininity and internal expectancies with masculinity, even though women and men do not differ much in their locus of control scores (Hall, 1984). Only when they are asked to respond to the scales as though they were super males or super females are differences in their scores very pronounced (Strickland and Haley, 1980). Third, such value judgments overlook differences in beliefs, such as those illustrated initially that might result in the same scale scores. If, for example, persons score as "external" because they do not believe their task outcomes are contingent upon their behavior, they may well be at a disadvantage. If, in contrast, they score as "external" in awareness of constraints that are associated with social interdependence, then this may reflect another kind of adaptation—one that could be associated with positive attitudes and behavior towards other people. The purpose of this study was to discover whether internal and external men and women hold characteristically different cognitions of life experience and whether such differences are associated with characteristic attitudes towards self versus others and characteristic ways of coping with socially problematic situations.

Two lines of evidence indicated that expectancies for control might be associated with different meanings of control among men and women. The first was provided by responses to individual items on Rotter's Locus of Control Scale (1966) by women and men who had been matched for their total scale scores (Strickland and Haley, 1980). Even though there were no significant differences in their summed responses to personal control items, women and men tended to express personal control on different items in different ways. Women tended to check a cluster of items that concerned planning ahead and personal destiny, whereas men tended to check items that were related to leadership and influencing others. These results suggested that personal influence may play a larger part in a man's expectancies for control; in contrast self–direction may play a larger part in a woman's expectancies for control.

The second line of evidence was provided by studies of social antecedents to expectancies for control, particularly of recalled parental behavior. Although results from these studies are not completely consistent, they do indicate that memories of parental warmth, supportiveness, consistent discipline, and early independence training may facilitate development of an internal locus of control (Lefcourt, 1982). In contrast, memories of parental overprotectiveness, restrictiveness, rejection, and hostile control and the experience of parental divorce may facilitate development of an external locus of control. More importantly, studies of social antecedents often uncover different correlates of internality and externality among men and women. In fact in one study, perceptions of internal control were not associated significantly with any parental behaviors unless the sex of the subject was taken into consideration (Levenson, 1973). Internality was associated with memories of maternal instrumental companionship among men but with memories of less maternal protectiveness among women. These results were interpreted as an indication that women may require experiences of rejection to become independent and internal. Longitudinal evidence supports this interpretation, since indicators of maternal coolness and criticality in childhood are correlated positively with an internal locus of control in adulthood more often among women than among men (Crandall and Crandall, 1983). Moreover, external men tend to rate their fathers as more rejecting than do internal men, but external women tend to rate their fathers as less rejecting than do internal women (Johnson and Kilman, 1975).

Two other differences are also worth noting. Internal men tend to recall less maternal affective punishment, but recall more contingent physical punishment and predictable maternal standards than do external men; whereas, internal women recall more maternal achievement pressure than do external women (MacDonald, 1971 and Yates, Kennelly, and Cox, 1975). Thus the self–direction that may impart a sense of personal control to women may be related to memories of maternal achievement pressure and underprotectiveness, whereas beliefs in personal influence that may impart a sense of personal control to men may be related to memories of maternal predictability, companionship, and discipline.

If women's expectancies for control focus more on self–direction and men's focus more on personal influence, then their attitudinal schemata should reflect this difference. When talking about their lives, for example, internal women who recall a larger number of "internal experiences" (e.g. perceptions of maternal rejection) might make more negative statements about other people and relationships with them, but more positive statements about themselves, than do internal women who recall fewer such experiences. External women who recall a larger number of "external experiences" (e.g. greater maternal protectiveness and less rejecting fathers) might, in general, express more feelings about other people, particularly positive ones, and fewer about themselves than do external women who recall fewer such experiences. In contrast, internal experience among men (e.g. certainty regarding family standards and punishment) might be correlated with positive expressions of attitude toward other people and relationships with them, whereas external experience (e.g. uncertainty about family standards and inconsistent discipline) might be correlated with negative attitudes toward other people and relationships with them.

If personal influence is a more important component of men's than women's sense of control, then this should also be reflected in the ways that they cope with interpersonal conflict. Internal and external experience might constrain the conflict responses of men more than those of women, since the former are presumably more concerned with issues of relational control than are the latter. Specifically among men, internal experience might be related to greater self–assertion, whereas external experience might be related to greater aggression if the matter is important, and passivity if the matter is unimportant (Doherty, 1983). Among women, no such relationship may obtain. Indeed, the few studies reported in this domain demonstrate a positive relationship between assertiveness, rather than aggression and passivity, and internality among men but not among women.

Therefore the following three research questions were posed for this study.

1. Would memories that characterize a broad range of social experience differ among internal and external men and women?

2. Would the memories of each subgroup be associated with characteristically different attitudes toward self versus others?

3. Would the memories of each subgroup be associated with characteristically different responses to interpersonal conflict?

Method

To answer these questions, semi–structured, in–depth interviews were conducted with internal and external men and women about their memories of relationships with parents and peers while growing up and about their general activities. Semi–structured interviews were employed rather than a battery of pre–coded questions in order to elicit as wide a variety of salient social experiences as possible and probe responses to general questions. The memories of each subgroup were ascertained through qualitative analysis of the transcribed interviews. Each interview was also coded for expressions of attitude toward self versus others. Memories that were characteristic of each subgroup were used to scale the internal and external experience of men and women. Scale scores were correlated with measures of attitude and with responses to a series of interpersonal conflict situations that had been elicited three months prior to the interview.

Subjects

Interviewees were selected from a pool of 133 undergraduate men and women who had, three months previously, responded to a battery of questionnaires. Included in the battery was Rotter's Locus of Control Scale. Included also was a series of nine hypothetical conflict situations that posed mild threats to friendship relations. Respondents had been asked to write down precisely what they thought they would say in each situation. Their responses had then been coded as aggressive, assertive, neutral, conditionally acquiescent, or acquiescent.[1]

Women and men who scored as "internals" (scale scores of 4 to 9) and women and men who scored as "externals" (scale scores of 13 to 20) each formed a pool of potential interviewees. Each pool was further restricted by the requirement of having scored either relatively high in aggressive and assertive responses or relatively high in conditionally acquiescent and acquiescent responses. Ten interviewees were then randomly selected from each of the internal and external male and female subgroups so that half of each group would be relatively assertive and half relatively acquiescent. These 40 students were contacted by letter and asked to participate in a follow–up study of the initial survey. All agreed but two students, who indicated that they had pressing school work. These two were replaced by comparable students on the list.

The Interview

Interviews lasted from one to one and a half hours. Following a discussion of their earlier responses to the interpersonal conflict situations, and examples of their behavior in recent conflict situations, the interview turned to recollections of their relationships with parents, including their parents' compliance–seeking behavior and flexibility regarding rules and regulations. The presence of siblings in the household was also ascertained, but additional information about sibling relationships was not systematically sought unless the interviewee initiated such discussion.

Interviewees were then asked if they could remember their lives as far back as grade school. They were asked to imagine a continuum with a "social star" at one end and a "loner" at the other and indi-

cate where they would have fallen on that continuum in grade school.
Their response was followed by questions concerning their neighbor-
hood and school friends in grade school as well as the major ways
they spent their leisure time. The same questions were asked about
their lives during junior high and high school. At the conclusion of
these questions, they were asked (if they had not already indicated)
whether there was ever a time that they felt outside of, or rejected by,
a group that they wanted to join. They were asked if they had ever
been shy, if they had ever been teased or picked on, and whether a
significant person in their lives had ever broken off a relationship with
them.

Two final questions were asked. The first required them to describe one of the most important events in their lives. The second
required them to speculate on reasons for their locus of control
scores. All interviews were taped and transcribed verbatim.

Analytic Procedures

Each transcription was summarized by diagramming information
supplied about family, peers, and activities. Additionally, all statements expressing positive or negative evaluation of self and activities
(e.g. "I don't like it when I get angry" or "I really enjoy sports"),
other people (e.g. "I didn't like the girls in that group" or "my
mother was wonderful"), and relationships with other people (e.g. "I
don't like my boyfriend always agreeing with me" or "I like friends
who share my interests") were written down, as were all references to
personal abilities (e.g. "I was never very good at sports" or "I won
many debates").

Coding

Comparison of the diagrammed summaries and information
about moves the families had made produced a list of 24 characteristics for which information was uniformly, or nearly uniformly, available. To this list was added three other characteristics. The first was
the most important event in their lives, which was coded as either a
personal accomplishment (e.g. winning an award or having freedom
and responsibility in college) or a relational experience (e.g. an intimate relationship or loss of a significant other).[2] The second concerned the way they talked about friendships. Every interviewee but
one referred to personal abilities, traits, or interests that bring friends
or make friendship formation difficult, but a substantial number also
referred to their sense of self–esteem or feelings being influenced
(either positively or negatively) by friends. Thus, beliefs about friendship could be coded as basically exchange–oriented (i.e. one gets a
friend in exchange for something) or as additionally self–actualizing.[3]
The final characteristic was extracted from initial discussions concerning responses in conflict situations. If an interviewee indicated
that he/she avoided conflict or didn't have conflicts with others, and

could think of no recent examples of conflicts, his/her conflict style was coded as avoidant or nonconfrontational. If he/she readily produced examples and indicated no hesitation in such exchanges, his/her style was coded as one of engagement. If he/she readily produced examples but also indicated a certain biting of the tongue or holding back so as not to become too angry, his/her style was coded as restrained engagement.

Indices of internal and external experience

Distributions of these 27 characteristics were then compared among internals and externals, using chi square as a criterion for modal differences. All comparisons that produced chi squares with probabilities of .10 or less and that also produced a distinct modal response in a sex subgroup (i.e. a category of a characteristic had to contain at least 7 members) were retained for subsequent analysis. With these criteria, comparisons yielded 11 characteristics on which internals and externals differed and/or sex subgroups appeared to differ (See Figure 1).

A score of internal experience was assigned to each internal male and female by summing the number of indicative categories that he/she shared with members of his/her subgroup. Similarly, a scale score of external experience was assigned to each external male and female by summing the number of indicative categories that he/she shared with members of his/her subgroup. The indicative category for a subgroup was the one into which at least 7 subgroup members fell. If no category of a characteristic contained at least 7 subgroup members, then the characteristic was not considered to be indicative of the subgroup's typical experience. A female internal who recalled such indicative experiences as being threatened and ordered by parents, having only a small group of friends in high school, taking music lessons, and feeling rejected by social groups, but who recalled no other experiences that were indicative of internal experience among women, would have received a scale score of 4. Interviewees thus received one point for each experience that was indicative of their subgroup's typical experience.

Two adjustments were then made to these scale scores. Since research findings had suggested a relationship between broken relationships and externality, and since this association was suggested also by the current data, one point was added to the score of every external whose parents had been divorced or separated and one point was added to the score of every external who had suffered a broken relationship. One point was subtracted from the score of every internal whose parents had been divorced or separated and one point was subtracted from the score of every internal who had suffered a broken relationship (i.e. thereby making his/her experience less internal). For example, if the internal woman who received a scale score of 4 had experienced the divorce of her parents but had not suffered a broken relationship, then her final score would have been a 3.

Measures of attitudes

The total number of positive and negative statements that each interviewee had made in the interview were counted, as were the number that each had made about him/herself and his/her activities, other people and relationships with other people, and his/her abilities.4 The frequencies of these statements, and the degree to which positive ones outweighed negative ones (and vice versa) were then correlated with scale scores of internal and external experience among male and female subgroups.

Measures of behavior in interpersonal conflict

Since nearly all interviewees indicated that their responses to the hypothetical conflict situations were at least pretty much what they would do in real life, these responses were used to measure their probable behavior in interpersonal conflict. The number of aggressive, assertive, neutral, conditionally acquiescent, and acquiescent responses that they had written on the earlier questionnaire were each correlated with their scores of internal or external experience. Separate correlations were run among the 4 subgroups.

Results

Characteristic Memories of Internals and Externals
General differences in social experience

Chi square analyses indicated that internals recalled their parents being stricter but also more inclined to use reasoning when seeking compliance (as opposed to orders and/or threats of punishment alone) than did externals ($X^2 = 6.20$, df = 2, p<.05 and $X^2 = 5.58$, df = 1, p<.05 respectively). More often than externals, they spontaneously recalled playing with siblings ($X^2 = 10.42$, df = 1, p<.01) and participating in music lessons, practice, and performances with orchestras or bands ($X^2 = 4.76$, df = 2, p<.10).

Externals recalled being more popular in high school than did internals ($X^2 = 12.94$, df = 2, p<.01) and feeling outside of, or rejected by, social groups less often ($X^2 = 11.92$, df = 2, p<.01). Internals were not loners in high school, but they also did not consider themselves to be extremely sociable or outgoing. The majority simply had a good set of friends.

The relational histories of internals tended to be more stable than those of externals. Fewer of their parents were divorced, separated, or widowed ($X^2 = 3.13$, df = 1, p<.10) and fewer recalled suffering a broken relationship with a significant other while growing up ($X^2 = 2.85$, df = 1, p<.10). Relational instability may have increased the salience of intimate relationships for externals since the most important events in their lives tended to be relational experiences whereas the most important in the lives of internals tended to be personal accomplishments (X^2 = 6.67, df = 1, p<.05). Moreover, externals more often described friendships in self-actualizing as well as exchange terms alone (X^2 = 8.29, df = 1, p<.01). This difference in perspective may have been influenced also by interpersonal sensitivities that developed through cross-cultural contact, since a significantly larger number of externals than internals had lived in another country during some period when they were younger (X^2 = 4.33, df = 1, p<.05).

Finally, a large majority of internals indicated having conflict styles of engagement whereas half the externals said either that they were not confrontational or avoided conflict (X^2 = 9.86, df = 3, p<.05).

Differences in social experience among women and men

As can been seen in Figure 1, internal women and men shared six indicative characteristics and had different modal responses on two. Another five characteristics were indicative for one group but not the other.

Internal women tended to describe their parents as lenient rather than strict, but also as having sought compliance by means of orders and/or threats of punishment. They did not talk spontaneously about playing with siblings, but they often mentioned being involved with music lessons, practice, and performances with orchestras or bands. For some, this was an important source of social life. Nearly all remembered having a good group of friends in high school, but only one described herself as a "social star." All recalled feeling outside or rejected by a peer group for at least one period of time, but only two recalled feeling that way throughout grade school, junior high, and high school. Their relational environments had been stable. Only two came from broken homes and most had not moved to another town while growing up; none had ever lived in another country. These women were as likely to discuss a personal accomplishment as to discuss a relational experience when asked to describe the most important event in their lives. They talked about friendships in exchange terms. They dealt with conflict through engagement.

Internal men, like internal women, came from stable households; not one came from a broken home and most had neither moved to another town nor lived in another country while growing up. Few recalled a significant other terminating a relationship with them. Unlike internal women, internal men remembered their parents as strict, but also as having sought compliance by reasoning with them, in addition to giving them orders or threatening with them. Most made spontaneous mention of playing with siblings while growing up, but there were as many who didn't mention involvement in music as mentioned it. Their recollections of relationships in high school were fairly

Figure 1. Modal Characteristics of Internal and External Women and Men

Characteristic	Internal women	Internal men	External women	External men
Compliance-seeking by parents	Orders, threats	Also reasons	Orders, threats	Orders, threats
Strictness of parents	Not strict	Strict	-----	Not strict
Play with sibblings	-----	Played	Didn't mention	Didn't mention
High school relationships	Friends, no star	-----	Social star	-----
Feelings of being outside	At least one period	At least one period	-----	-----
Music lessons, practice	Yes	-----	-----	Didn't mention
Important event	-----	Personal achievement	Relational experience	Relational experience
Beliefs about friendship	Personal qualities bring/lose friends	-----	Friendship brings good/bad feelings also	-----
Cross-culture contact	Did not live in a different country	Did not live in a different country	-----	Did not live in a different country
Moved to a different town	Didn't move	Didn't move	-----	Didn't move
Conflict style	Engagement	Engagement	-----	Avoids, doesn't have, or holds back

Note. *Dotted lines occur where responses were fairly evenly spread across categories; all other entries represent the responses of at least 7 interviewees.*

evenly divided between having a good group of friends and being a "social star". The social stars were most often those who were and continue to be involved in team sports. Like their female counterparts, most had felt apart from or rejected by a peer group for at least one period in their lives. Unlike their female counterparts, their descriptions of friendship were fairly evenly divided between perspectives of exchange and perspectives of self-actualization in addition to exchange. Most discussed a personal accomplishment when asked to describe the most important event in their lives. Most also dealt with conflict by engaging in it.

External men and women shared only three indicative characteristics and had the same modal responses on all three. Another seven characteristics were indicative for one group, but not for the other.

External women came from the least stable households. Their parents were almost as likely to be divorced or separated as to be married and living together. Most had moved to another town while growing up. There were nearly as many who had lived in another country as who had not. These women were fairly evenly divided in their recollections of parental strictness. As many recalled their parents being lenient as being strict. Recollections of parental compliance–seeking behavior, however, were more uniform. Most recalled their parents using orders or threats of punishment. Most did not spontaneously mention playing with siblings. These women were nearly evenly divided with regard to mentioning and not mentioning involvement in music. Most remembered themselves as "social stars" in high school. Half had never felt apart from or rejected by a peer group, but half had experienced such feelings during at least one period of their lives. Nearly as many had suffered a broken relationship as had not. All but one discussed a relational experience when asked to describe the most important event in their lives. All talked about friendship in self–actualizing as well as exchange terms. They indicated avoiding conflict or being nonconfrontational as often as engaging in conflict.

Like external women, most external men did not come from intact homes, but unlike external women, most had not moved to another town while growing up or lived in another country. Most recalled their parents as not being strict. All remembered their parents seeking compliance through orders and threats of punishment alone. Most did not spontaneously mention playing with siblings or involvement in music. Their recollections of popularity in high school were fairly equally spread among being a loner, having friends, and being a social star. Recollections of feeling outside of, or rejected by, a peer group were similarly distributed. Half did not recall such feelings and half had felt this way during at least one period of their lives. As many had suffered broken relationships with significant others as had not. Like their female counterparts, most discussed a relational experience when asked to describe the most important event in their lives. Unlike their female counterparts, they were fairly evenly divided in ways they described friendship. Nearly as many described it without as with self–actualizing terms. These men also tended not to engage in conflict. A majority indicated avoiding conflict, being non-confrontational, or consciously holding back in conflict situations.

Attitudes and Conflict Responses Associated with Internal and External Experience

Internal women

Correlations (r) between the internal experience and attitudes of internal women partially confirmed expectations regarding the foci of their attitudes. The more internal were the experiences of these women, the more attitudes they expressed about other people and relationships with other people (r = .69, p<.01) and the more negatively balanced were these attitudes (r = −.66, p<.05). The more internal were their experiences, the more they tended to say about their abilities and the less they tended to say about their activities (r = .47, p<.10 and r = −.47, p<.10 respectively). There was also a tendency for women who scored high in internal experience to express more negatively balanced attitudes in general than did women who scored low (r = −.46, p<.10).

Correlations between the internal experience and interpersonal conflict responses of these women indicated two trends. Women who recalled more internal experiences tended to be more assertive (r = .51, p<.10) and less neutral (r = −.47, p<.10) than those who recalled fewer such experiences.

Internal men

Correlations between the internal experience and sentiments of internal men yielded no particularly characteristic focus of their attitudes. The more internal were the experiences of these men, the fewer attitudes they expressed about other people and relationships with other people (r = −.68, p<.05) and the more positively balanced were their attitudes in general (r = .48, p<.10). There was also a tendency for men who scored high in internal experience to say less about their personal abilities than those who scored low (r = −.46, p<.10).

Correlations between the internal experience and interpersonal conflict responses of these men confirmed predictions from the research literature. The more internal were their experiences, the less aggressive (r = −.74, p<.01) but the more assertive (r = .54, p<.05) and neutral (r = .55, p<.05) were their responses.

External women

As anticipated, recall of external experiences was clearly related to a focus on other people and relationships with other people among external women (r =.80, p<.01). Women who scored high in external experience did not express more positively balanced attitudes about other people and relationships with other people than those who scored low, but neither were their attitudes more negatively balanced. Women who scored high in external experience, like their internal counterparts, expressed fewer attitudes about their activities than did those who scored low (r = −.56, p<.05). Unlike their internal counterparts, they did not focus their remarks on their personal abilities.

Correlations between recall of external experience and interpersonal conflict responses among these women indicated only one trend. The more external their experiences, the more assertive were their responses (r = .50, p<.10).

External men

As anticipated, the more external the experiences of external men, the more attitudes they tended to express about other people and relationships with other people (r =.53, p<.10) and the more negatively balanced were these attitudes (r = −.62, p<.05). Men who scored high in external experience also tended to express more negatively balanced attitudes about themselves and their activities than men who scored low (r = −.51, p<.10).

Correlations between recall of external experience and interpersonal conflict responses confirmed predictions from the research literature. The more external the experiences of these men, the more aggressive (r = .44, p<.10) and less assertive (r = −.62, p<.05) their responses tended to be.

Discussion

The results from this study provide tentative answers to the three research questions that were posed early on and suggest directions for future sex research. The first question concerned memories that characterize the social experience of internals and externals and the extent to which these might differ among men and women. Although the typical social experiences that were reported by internal men and women in this study were similar in some respects, there were more differences than similarities between them. Internal men and women both came from stable home environments, but internal men recalled a strict home environment in which reasons often accompanied parental requests for compliance; in contrast, internal women recalled a flexible or lenient home environment in which orders and threats accompanied parental requests for compliance. To the extent that strict rules and reasoning reinforce and clarify parental standards, the internal men in this study would have been particularly cognizant of their parents' expectations and of contingencies between their own behavior and their parents' treatment of them. To the extent that threats and orders may appear unreasonable when delivered in the context of flexible rules, the internal women in this study would have been particularly cognizant of unreasonable parental demands.

Internal men and women both felt outside of, or rejected by, social groups during at least one period of their lives, but only the women typically recalled having a small group of friends in high school. The men were as likely to recall being "social stars" as having only one small group of friends. The women also may have spent more time in solo activities than did the men. Part of their leisure time was typically devoted to practicing music, whereas the men more often participated in team sports. These differences in memories of parents and peers may be symptomatic of greater expectations for autonomy and interpersonal difficulty among the women than the men, especially since the women were the only ones who typically described friendship in exchange terms alone.

The experiences that were recalled by external men and women in this study were also similar in some respects, but there were more differences than similarities between them as well. Although neither recalled their parents reasoning with them to seek compliance and although a significant number from each subgroup had experienced the divorce of their parents and/or termination of an important peer relationship, residential stability was a typical experience of the men but not of the women. To the extent that stability of the home environment provides a sense of predictability, these women would have experienced greater uncertainty, and perhaps therefore greater dependence on other people, than would have the men. External men and women both tended to describe a relational experience as one of the most important events in their lives, but the women were the only ones who typically described friendship in self-actualizing terms. They were also the only ones who typically recalled being a social star in high school. These differences in memories suggest a greater capacity on the part of the women than the men to cope with the uncertainties of life by utilizing relational resources constructively.

The second research question concerned the extent to which characteristically different attitudes would be associated with the memories of internal and external men and women. As anticipated, negatively balanced sentiments about other people and relationships with other people tended to characterize internal women who exemplified the memories of their subgroup. These women did not express more positive sentiments about themselves than did other internal women, but they did say more than the others did about their personal abilities. Internal men who exemplified the memories of their subgroup did not express more positively balanced sentiments about other people and relationships with other people than did other internal men. They also tended to say less about their personal abilities than did the others; however, their expressions of attitude, in general, were more positive than negative. These differences in focus of attitude support earlier speculations that internal women may expect greater difficulty in relationships with other people than do internal men and may be more concerned with their personal autonomy.

As anticipated, external women who exemplified the memories of their subgroup did express fewer sentiments about themselves and more sentiments about other people and relationships with other people than did other external women. Their sentiments about other people and relationships with other people, however, were neither more positively nor negatively balanced than were those of other external women. External men who exemplified the memories of their subgroup tended also to express more sentiments about other people and relationships with other people than did other external men, but their sentiments were significantly more negatively balanced than were those of other subgroup members. Moreover, their sentiments about themselves and their activities also tended to be more negatively balanced than were those of other external men. These differences in focus of attitude support earlier speculation that external women may be more capable than external men of adapting to the uncertainties of their environment by utilizing relational resources.

The third research question concerned the extent to which characteristically different interpersonal conflict responses would be associated with the memories of internal and external men and women. As anticipated, these memories proved to be somewhat more constraining for the men than the women. Internal men who exemplified the memories of their subgroup were significantly more assertive and less aggressive than were other internal men. External men who exemplified the memories of their subgroup were significantly less assertive and somewhat more aggressive than other external men. Similar differences were not apparent in the responses of internal and external women. Exemplars of both groups tended to be somewhat more assertive than other members of their subgroups. Assuming that assertive responses represent constructive ways of coping with conflict and that aggressive responses represent relationally destructive ones, it was external experience among men primarily that was characterized by destructive responses to conflict.

In general, the results from this study suggest that the experience of externals does not necessarily place them at risk, at least not in the social arena. Only among men, who may be less well–equipped than women to utilize relational resources, may this experience have a negative impact. Indeed, internal rather than external experience may place women at somewhat of a social risk.

The results from this study suggest also that future research on sex differences stress the reasons why men and women score similarly as well as differently on various psychometric and other tests. As the current study has demonstrated, men and women may acquire similar beliefs about the world and their relation to it but may come to these conclusions for very different reasons.

References

Crandall, V.C. & Crandall, B.W. (1983). Maternal and childhood behaviors as antecedents of internal–external control perceptions in young adulthood. In H.M. Lefcourt (Ed.), *Research with the locus of control construct*, (Vol. 2). New York: Academic Press.

Doherty, W.J. (1983). Locus of control and marital interaction. In H.M. Lefcourt (Ed.), *Research with the locus of control construct* (Vol. 2) New York: Academic Press.

Hall, J.A. (1984). *Nonverbal sex differences: Communication accuracy and expressive style.* Baltimore, Maryland: Johns Hopkins University Press.

Johnson, B.L. & Killmann, P.R. (1975). The relationship between recalled parental attitudes and internal–external control. *Journal of Clinical Psychology, 31,* 40–42.

Lefcourt, H.M. (1982). Locus of control: Current trends in theory and research. Hillsdale, New Jersey: Lawrence Erlbaum Associates.

Levenson, H. (1973). Perceived parental antecedents of internal, powerful others, and chance locus of control orientations. *Developmental Psychology, 9,* 260–265.

MacDonald, A.P., Jr. (1971). Internal–external locus of control: Parental antecedents. *Journal of Consulting and Clinical Psychology, 37,* 141–147.

Nowicki, S., Jr. & Duke, M.P. (1983). The Nowicki–Strickland lifespan locus of control scales: Construct validation. In H.M. Lefcourt (Ed.), *Research with the locus of control construct* (Vol. 2) New York: Academic Press.

Rotter, J.B. (1966). Generalized expectancies for internal versus external control of reinforcement. *Psychological Monographs, 80.*

Strickland, B.R. & Haley, W.E. (1980). Sex differences on the Rotter I–E scale. *Journal of Personality and Social Psychology, 39,* 930–939.

Yates, R., Kennelly, K., & Cox, S.H. (1975). Perceived contingency of parental reinforcements, parent–child relations, and locus of control. *Psychological Reports, 36,* 139–146.

Footnotes

[1]In 3 of the situations a friend expressed disagreement with an opinion of the respondent; in 3 he/she was critical of something the respondent had said or done; and in 3 his/her plans conflicted with those of the respondent. Aggressive responses were defined as attempts to control interaction by severely restricting the other's options. These included challenges, accusations, sarcasm, abusive or derogatory statements, and orders. Assertive responses were defined as attempts to control interaction without severely restricting the other's options. These included simple disagreements, justified disagreements, disagreements that recognize the other point of view, and instructions. Neutral responses were defined as noncommittal. These responses were most often extensions of what had been said in the situation and minimized the rights of both to control it. Conditional acquiescence was defined as acceptance of the other's point of view or wishes with reservations or qualifications. It included qualified statements of favor–doing, agreement, giving in, and admission of fault. Acquiescence was defined as acceptance of the other's point of view or wishes without reservations or qualifications. It included simple statements of favor–doing, agreement, giving in, and admission of fault. Coding agreement was estimated at .95, pi (Scott) at .91.

[2]Coding agreement was estimated at .95, pi (Scott) at .91.

[3]Coding agreement was estimated at .90, pi (Scott) at .79.

[4]Coding agreement was estimated at .95, pi (Scott) at .91.

THOUGHT PROVOKERS

Discuss the similarities and differences experienced by *internal* males and females in their recall of social experience, including conflict. What factors may account for the similarities as well as the differences? What factors may account for similarities and differences in *external* males and females? How might the age group of the sample studied affect the findings?

## CHAPTER 11

Gender Differences in the Social Construction of Romantic Jealousy: An Exploratory Study

Susan Parrish Sprowl
University of Massachusetts

Cindy L. White
San Francisco State University

In a recent paper on emotion and interpersonal communication, Bowers, Metts, and Duncanson (1985) suggest "the fact that emotions are an important aspect of interpersonal relationships is self-evident to anyone who has ever been closely involved with another person" (p. 500). While acknowledging the obvious relationship between communication and emotion, they also point out that this area of research has been neglected for the most part by communication scholars. One emotion that should be of special significance to those researchers interested in intimate communication is romantic jealousy.

While jealousy is experienced by an individual, that experience is a function of his/her communication transactions. When an individual experiences jealousy, it is because s/he has attached a particular meaning to some external event. Indeed, the meaning that is attached to the event is what distinguishes one emotion from another. If a woman observes her husband in the company of another woman, any number of emotions may result depending on the wife's interpretation of the situation. Males and females learn the rules for attaching meaning to an event such as this through their ongoing interactions with others. Therefore, an individual's experience of jealousy at any given moment is a function of his/her past experiences with the emotion (i.e. past relationships), the dynamics of the current relationship, as well as broader cultural rules and expectations relating to the emotion. These factors help to create a cognitive schemata through which stimuli are filtered and thus given meaning. It is in this sense that an individual constructs his/her emotional reality. Understanding how individuals construct particular emotions can give us insight into the meaning and function these emotions serve in the broader sociocultural system. In the case of heterosexual romantic jealousy, we have the additional concern of accounting for the differences in male and female constructions of relational reality. Scholars (see, for example, Gilligan, 1981) have repeatedly demonstrated these differences —particularly with regard to emotional experience. Therefore, any systematic effort to understand the construction of romantic jealousy must acknowledge gender (i.e. the social/cultural construction of female and male roles) as a central concern. This study begins to explore the nature and function of romantic jealousy by examining how males and females socially construct jealous episodes in heterosexual romantic relationships.

Romantic Jealousy

Despite the pervasive nature of romantic jealousy in the general population, our knowledge of its function and scope is limited for several reasons. First, empirical research on the normative, as opposed to the pathological, operation of the emotion did not begin until the mid 1970's. Researchers have not yet had an adequate opportunity to fully explore the function and scope of jealousy as a non-idiosyncratic emotion operative in normative interpersonal relationships. A second reason our knowledge of jealousy is limited is that most of the research has been singular in its methodological approach. The vast majority of the research is quantitative and utilizes some self-report measure of romantic jealousy. That, in and of itself, is not problematic. However, because there is minimally acceptable evidence of the psychometric quality of these scales (Bringle & Buunk, 1985), the validity of findings generated from their use is questionable.

An individual confronting the jealousy literature for the first time would be bombarded with a series of articles relating jealousy to a variety of variables, often in inconsistent ways, with little notion of how these variables are related in terms of the indivdual's construction of the jealous episode. This is particularly true of studies examining jealousy as it relates to the characteristics of the individual experiencing the emotion. For example, theoretical conceptualizations suggest a strong relationship between jealousy and self-esteem. However, the research has produced mixed results, with some studies supporting this hypothesized relationship (Bringle, 1981; Jaremko & Lindsey, 1979; Manges & Evenbeck, 1980), while other studies fail to support the relationship or actually report a *positive* correlation between jealousy and self-esteem (Buunk, 1980, 1982; Mathes & Severa, 1981; White, 1981(a), 1981(b)). With regard to the research on the cognitive, affective, and behavioral responses associated with jealousy, Bringle and Buunk (1985) conclude that some very basic questions have been left unanswered.

For example, it has yet to be determined which affective, cognitive, and behavioral responses are characteristic of jealousy. A related question concerns whether there is only one typical response that can manifest itself in several ways or several clearly distinctive types of jealousy. Furthermore, we wonder whether the nature of the threat, affective response, and coping strategies are not more closely interrelated...Possibly, specific types of threats go together with specific affective responses and coping strategies (p. 251).

The research examining the relationship between jealousy and gender differences is fraught with problems as well.[1] This research is characterized by small effect sizes, inconsistent findings (Bringle & Buunk, 1985), and a failure to understand how the parts relate to the whole. After reviewing the available literature in this area, Bringle & Buunk (1985) conclude that "there has been no systematic, integrated attempt at understanding gender differences in jealousy; typically, these differences assume an ancillary status while other issues receive the primary attention" (p. 261). Unfortunately, after more than a decade of research, we still have very limited knowledge about male and female constructions of jealous episodes, how they behave in light of these constructions, and what purpose(s) the constructions serve. These questions can be most appropriately answered if one conceptualizes jealousy within a social constructivist view of emotion.

A Constructivist View of Emotion

James Averill provides the most extensive conceptualization and analysis of emotion from the constructivist perspective. Averill (1980) defines emotion as "a transitory social role (a socially constituted syndrome) that includes an individual's appraisal of the situation and that is interpreted as a passion rather than as an action" (p.312). He suggests that the three most important aspects of this definition are syndrome, appraisal, and passion (Averill, 1985). He argues that a syndrome is "an organized set of responses (behavioral, physiological, and/or cognitive)" (p. 98). All elementary responses to stimuli are based on the same physiological and psychological processes. It is the systematic organization and interpretation of these responses within a social context that gives them meaning. The elementary responses can be grouped together to form component processes. These component processes are not necessarily mutually exclusive, either within or across different emotions. The manner in which these elementary responses group and the complex relationships between the component processes, both of which are socially determined, reveals the nature of the emotional syndromes, thereby differentiating it from other emotional syndromes.

According to Averill (1977), the experience of an emotional syndrome "represents the enactment of a transitory social role" (p. 8).

In other words, the syndrome represents a socially constructed phenomenon that involves the processes of role-making (responding from your own role) and role-taking (placing yourself in the other's role). Symbolic interaction theory specifies that role-taking can occur on two levels, taking the role of the specific other and taking the role of the generalized other (the expectations of the cultural group to which one belongs). By doing this, we, as actors, learn the socially derived rules for playing out our own roles.

The second aspect of Averill's definition of emotion that deserves attention is "appraisal." Experiencing an emotional syndrome requires that an individual appraise some situation (object) in such a way as to trigger the enactment of the appropriate syndrome. Averill (1985) suggests that "the appraised object is usually the most distinctive or distinguishing feature of any emotion... [and may] consist of any or all of three aspects: the instigation, the target, and/or the aim (objective) of the [emotional] response" (Averill, 1985, p. 99). The target is the person(s) (or objects) at whom the emotional response is directed; the instigation is what provokes the response; and the aim is what function or purpose the response serves. The important point to note here is that the appraisal process is bound by social rules that give the event meaning within a broader social context.

The final aspect of Averill's definition that we wish to discuss is that of emotion as passion. Several authors have discussed the notion of emotions as passions (something beyond our control) rather than actions (something within our control) (Averill, 1977, 1980; Peters, 1962, 1969; Solomon, 1976). The argument most frequently made with regard to this distinction is that emotions are "remnants of our biological heritage" (Averill, 1977, p. 11) and are mediated by physiological factors. Emotions are passions because they are a result of involuntary physiological responses rather than cognitive processing. Averill (1977) rejects this notion by suggesting that social, rather than biological, factors explain why emotions are interpreted as passions. Although he acknowledges that involuntary physiological responses to a situation play a part in the individual's labeling of the emotional response as "passive," he argues that this explanation is incomplete. In order to explain how a response may be socially constructed to be "beyond self-control," Averill (1977, 1980) defines three kinds or paradigms of emotion: impulsive, transcendental, and conflictive.

The impulsive paradigm "represents straightforward desires and aversions that have become so 'second nature' that they are not regarded as self-initiated. Examples are grief, joy, hope, sexual desire..." (Averill, 1980, p. 331). Conflictive emotions refer to emotions that result from two (or more) conflicting sets of social norms. The emotion is a "passionate" response to that conflict. Averill (1985) has analyzed romantic love as a conflictive emotion. He argues that:

...the conflict is between norms that encourage independence, self-reliance, and economic self-interest, on the one hand, and unselfish commitment to a spouse and children, on the other. The conflict is resolved by falling in love which – if the script follows its traditional course – typically results in marriage and family. (Averill, 1980, p. 333).

The final type of emotional paradigm is known as transcendental. This paradigm describes emotional responses that result from the breakdown of normative cognitive structures. This can happen for a variety of reasons, including meditation, brain damage, drugs, etc. (Averill, 1980). These states are transcendental because they "involve a transcendence of the self, and because they tend to be diffuse, ineffable, and difficult to describe in ordinary language" (Averill, 1980, p. 333). It is important to note that the paradigms are not mutually exclusive and any particular emotion may contain aspects of all three paradigms. Viewing emotion from this paradigmatic perspective allows one to conceptualize emotions as socially constructed rather than biologically based passions.

Rationale

Viewing jealousy from a constructivist perspective means conceptualizing it as a syndrome (transitory social role) which involves the appraisal of some person or object and is interpreted as a passion rather than action. However, we know very little about the syndromic, appraising, and passionate nature of romantic jealousy, and thus, how the emotion represents the enactment of a social role. Conceptualizing jealousy within this perspective poses a great many questions. If jealousy is a syndrome, it should be characterized by an organized set of responses that can be interpreted by examining the social context within which they occur. In other words, we should be able to identify how responses are related to one another to determine the component processes that distinguish jealousy from any other emotional syndrome. If jealousy is a syndrome, and therefore a transitory social role, then we must begin to explore how that role is played out in different cultural contexts. Since the syndrome involves appraisal, we must identify the object (aim, instigation, and/or target) of the jealousy. This will give us insight into the meaning and function of this particular emotion within a given sociocultural system. In addition, we need to understand which paradigm(s) of emotion best explains the operation of jealousy as a socially constructed passion. Finally, since we know that gender largely determines role enactment in romantic relationships in general (Gilligan, 1982; Schaef, 1981), researchers must examine the role of gender when attempting to discover how the jealous role is constructed. In an effort to increase our understanding of romantic jealousy as a socially constructed role, this exploratory study posed the following research question: What are the component processes of heterosexual romantic jealousy and how do males and females conceptualize these processes?

Method

Questionnaire Construction

Several factors influenced the design of the questionnaire. First, our desire to understand how individuals construct episodes required the use of open–ended questions that allowed respondents to describe their constructions. Secondly, we had to develop a series of questions that would give us insight into the component processes of the syndrome. Because of the importance of the appraised object in distinguishing one emotion from another, we asked questions designed to ascertain the aim, the instigation, and the target of the emotional response. A third factor which influenced our questionnaire construction was the concept of role–taking and role–making. On the one hand, we were interested in how individuals enact or make their own roles. On the other hand, we were concerned with the individual's perception of how others take this role. Therefore, we constructed two questionnaires (given to two different samples), one which assessed individual experiences and one which assessed normative expectations of the role. These will be referred to hereafter as the individual data set and the normative data set, respectively. For the individual data set, respondents were asked to think of a specific situation during which they experienced feelings of jealousy in a romantic relationship and to provide the following information with respect to that situation. (1) Explain the situation by identifying the participants, their sex, their relationship to you and to one another, and what *specifically* made you jealous. (2) Describe how you communicated your feelings of jealousy about this situation to your partner, both verbally and nonverbally. (3) What behaviors did you engage in to help you cope with your jealous feelings? (4) If you discussed this situation with anyone other than your partner, identify who you talked to (specify sex), their relationship to you, and why you chose to discuss the situation with them.

Individuals in the normative data set were told to answer the following questions based on their own relationships as well as their observations of the relationships of others. (1) What provokes romantic jealousy in males? (2) What provokes romantic jealousy in females? (3) How do males communicate their feelings of romantic jealousy to their partner, both verbally and nonverbally? (4) How do females communicate their feelings of romantic jealousy to their partner, both verbally and nonverbally? (5) What do males do to help them cope with their feelings of romantic jealousy? (6) What do females do to help them cope with their feelings of romantic jealousy? In addition to the above questions, subjects in both samples responded to a variety of demographic items.

Sample

Respondents were individuals enrolled in a basic communication course at a medium–size Eastern university. The sample consisted of 73 males (28 in the individual data set and 45 in the normative data set) and 71 females (33 in the individual data set and 38 in the normative data set) for a total N of 144.

Data Analysis

The data were analyzed by listing all of the elementary responses and inductively deriving component processes from the clustering of these responses. The clusters were based on the notions of aim (what purpose does the jealousy serve as revealed by individual's responses to the situation), instigation (what prompts the enactment of the role) and the target (at whom or what is the jealousy directed). We examined the individual experiences data from the males first and then repeated the process with the individual experiences data from females. The above procedures were then repeated with the normative data set. We first examined how males perceive male jealousy and how they perceive female jealousy and then looked at how females perceive male jealousy and how they perceive female jealousy.

Findings & Discussion

Two observations must be made before a discussion of the component processes is offered. First, the data suggest that romantic jealousy can best be conceptualized as an emotional syndrome enacted for the purpose of protecting self and relationship (aim) and prompted by an uncertainty over relational role position (the instigation) because of the partner's (target) actual or potential relationship with a rival, resulting in a fear of loss of a perceived/desired primary relationship. It should be noted that the above definition suggests that the enactment of the jealous role does not necessarily depend on the jealous individual being the partner's *primary* romantic interest. Many traditional definitions of jealousy suggest that jealousy occurs when an individual fears losing something s/he already possesses while "envy stems from the desire to acquire something possessed by another" (Foster, 1972, p.168). Within that definition, jealousy could only occur when an individual is actually in a primary relationship. However, the data in the current study indicate that a person may experience what s/he considers jealousy even if s/he is not the "partner's" primary romantic interest. That is, when asked to describe an experience of jealousy, many individuals chose to describe situations in which they were not necessarily the primary partner. Their descriptions of their experiences, however, reflect the same underlying processes. Since we are concerned with understanding how individuals construct the romantic jealousy experience, our definitions must reflect the meaning imposed by those experiencing the emotion rather than the arbitrary distinctions imposed by researchers.

It could be that this finding is idiosyncratic to the current sample, to college students, or to *dating* relationships. Systematic research designed to clarify this issue is clearly needed.

A second observation that should be made before proceeding to a discussion of the component processes is that the categories which emerge from the data are consistent across males and females and across individual and normative data sets. However, the conceptualizations and enactment of the component processes often differ and that difference seems to be gender–based.

Component Processes

Instigations

The first two component processes can be considered instigations (processes that prompt the enactment of the role) and are qualitatively different aspects of the overarching instigation of romantic jealousy, which is uncertainty over relational role position. Uncertainty over relational role position occurs when an individual perceives s/he is or wants to be the partner's primary romantic interest and either the partner or a third party does something that causes the individual to question his/her role position. The two component processes which reflect this overarching instigation are envy and violation of relational boundary expectations.

Envy. This provocation involves social comparison processes between the jealous individual and the third party. For females, this process can best be described as "attribute envy." Females tend to focus on the physical, and to a lesser extent, the psychological attributes of themselves and "the other woman." This process can prompt the fear that the partner will prefer the attributes of the rival. The following two examples capture the essence of this attribute envy.

> I now think that my jealousy towards her was due to her character. She's a nice girl, very intelligent, beautiful, nice figure, etc. She is no one that an 'ordinary' person like me could ever hope to compete with if Scott ever decided that he would rather be with her. (FEMALE)

> She had a perfect figure, she was wearing a bathing suit and jeans and she had straight blond hair which ran from her shoulder to her behind. She was pretty. The way she dressed and her impeccable figure made me feel jealous. (FEMALE)

The male conceptualization of this process can best be described as "status envy." A male is more likely to be concerned with other males "winning his role" or taking away "his property."

> A female, Erin, who was my girlfriend for about a month, went on a date with someone else. We were fairly close and I became extremely jealous. The fact that someone else would try to get what I had made me jealous. (MALE)

Another guy in the dorm, Tom, also liked this girl very much and at dorm parties we found ourselves competing for her attention, often until late in the evening. One night, Tom made his move on her, before I did, and she ended up with him for a brief period. I was jealous of Tom because he had taken the initiative and it had paid off. I, at that time, did not have the courage to take initiative and I paid for it. (MALE)

Violation of relational boundary expectations. A person develops a relational reality that includes expectations of how participants in a romantic dyad should behave both within and outside of the relationship. These expectations serve as boundaries for the perceived/desired primary relationship. Violation of these boundaries may take on several forms. An individual may fear that the partner *will* violate the boundaries, s/he may *suspect* that the partner has violated the boundaries, or s/he may actually *know* that the partner has violated the boundaries. The gender differences in this category seem to revolve around broader societal expectations of the male role.

The traditional male role places a great deal of pressure on a man to display his sexual prowess. This is reflective of the centrality of sex in defining his universe (Schaef, 1981). The pressure to prove sexual prowess in adolescence is a well-known characteristic of the transition from boyhood to manhood. In the current analysis, males reflect this attitude by stressing the lack of trust they have in other males when it comes to their partners. Many of the males do not want their partners in the company of any other male when they cannot be present.

Males a lot of the time don't relax. They are not willing to and don't feel at ease letting their girl out in the streets. (MALE)

Females easily provoke jealousy in males through other males. They can mention other guys' names in certain ways that make you jealous. They can spend a lot of time with other guys which may be just friends, but it makes you jealous. Sometimes they just talk to other guys and you get jealous. (MALE)

Jealousy is provoked by romantic advances by other males toward my girlfriend. This really pisses me off. Overhearing guys talk about her might be considered flattering, but to me, it seems threatening. (MALE)

The emphasis on sexuality in the male role forms the basis for the female's conceptualization of this component process as well. However, female enactment of this process involves not trusting the male around another woman because he might evaluate her as a more worthy partner based on her attributes. In addition, many females do not feel comfortable when their boyfriends go out with their male friends. One respondent discussed what provokes jealousy in females this way:

> When the male partner is with his male friends and they talk about all the good–looking girls they have known (romantically) and know (nonromantically). (FEMALE)

The fear seems to be that the peer pressure males feel around other males, particularly in this age group, makes a male think about, and possibly do, things that he "should not." Perhaps there is some basis for this fear. A male thought of the provocation of female jealousy in this way:

> A misunderstanding of wants and needs within a relationship does not help. Females need to let loose a little when males want to go their way. Females don't realize a male's drives and needs. (MALE)

Interestingly, the normative data set suggests that both males and females have a fairly low threshold for jealousy. Depending on the nature of the relationship, a conversation with a third person or even a simple look can provoke jealousy. This could be characteristic of the uncertainty and instability of dating relationships in college which results in a greater fear that relational boundaries will be violated.

Aim

The aim of the jealous response is protection of self and relationship. This is consistent with past research on jealousy which indicates these two factors are an integral part of the emotional experience (White, 1981a). When a person enacts the jealous role, s/he does so with the intent of eliminating the rival relationship and eliciting confirmation of his/her primary status, thus protecting his/her relationship. However, because of the influence others have on self–image, particularly in love relationships, a threat to the relationship is a threat to self as well. Ellis and Weinstein (1986) suggest "the jealous person must now be on guard against threats to the boundaries of and meanings for self as well as against loss of partner. Intrusion by the third party brings about a sense of 'what about me?'" (p.346). The component processes that can be considered methods of protecting self and relationship are direct prompts for behavior, indirect prompts for behavior, competition, physical release, seeking support, cognitive reframing, and withdrawal.

Direct prompts for behavior. This category consists of behaviors enacted by the jealous individual which directly prompt behavior or interaction on the part of the partner. This includes talk, arguments, and seeking information about the specific jealousy–evoking situation. Many females in the normative data set seem to think that males seldom engage in this behavior. However, the report of individual experiences, as well as the normative male data, suggests that males often engage in direct interaction about the event. A potential explanation for this discrepancy will be offered in the discussion of the next component process.

Indirect prompts for behavior. This category consists of behaviors enacted by the jealous individual which indirectly prompt behavior or interaction on the part of the partner. Males seem to enact this component process by engaging in affect withdrawal.

Males communicate their feelings of jealousy be being uncommunicative, unemotional, and temperamental. They get an "I don't care" attitude but in reality their feelings are hurt. (FEMALE)

Females engage in affect withdrawal also, but they report using a wider variety of indirect prompts for behavior, including nonverbal expressions of hurt and anger, sarcasm, and humor. The normative male data confirm this finding.

Females become agitated, emotional and betrayed and visually communicate much more fully about this. Nonverbally, they become sullen, pouty, and sorry for themselves. (MALE)

[If I were jealous] I would speak nastily (in anger) to the person, not want him to touch me, sulk, avoid eye contact. (FEMALE)

[I communicated my jealousy] by getting angry about it and making snide comments about it. (FEMALE)

Many respondents specify that they use indirect prompts first and then use more direct prompts for behavior. However, it is unclear as to whether or not the direct prompt is used after an indirect prompt because the indirect prompt does not work or because it does work and that prompts direct communication on both parts. Indeed, it is possible that the two are "unrelated" and that, in certain situations, individuals feel compelled to act out both protective mechanisms. There are three pieces of evidence to support the notion that males use direct communication only after their indirect communication "works." First, females in the normative data set seem to feel that males do not directly communicate their jealousy. If a male only communicates his jealousy *after* his partner responds to his indirect prompt (usually affect withdrawal), it is not surprising that females do not feel males *directly* confront the issue. Secondly, some males actually report that they directly communicate about their jealousy only after their girlfriends "drag it out" of them. Finally, both males and females in the normative data set indicate that males do not like to admit they are jealous because it is inconsistent with their male role.

Competition. The gender differences in the conceptualization of this component process parallel the forms of envy that can instigate the jealousy syndrome. Females tend to compete on an "attribute" dimension.

[Females] tend to try harder or look better for their man next time so he won't go to someone else. (FEMALE)

[Females] do anything so the male finds them more attractive. (MALE)

If a girl has jealousy, she tends to be sweeter and nicer to the guy in hopes that he will realize that she is the right girl for him and not the other girl. (MALE)

Males demonstrate their status envy by confronting the other person, denigrating and disconfirming the third person, and directly expressing territoriality.

[Males] tend to become much more protective and overbearing which only turns the female away. (FEMALE)

[Males communicate their jealousy] by telling the guy to take a hike.... (MALE)

Verbally, [males] ask who is the male in question who evoked the jealousy. Usually it's very careful questions such as how do you know that jerk? (FEMALE)

Physical release. This component process describes the physical expression of the jealousy syndrome. Males displace their anger by engaging in athletic activities, e.g., running and basketball. They also drink excessively and yell.

Sometimes I drank, other times I did something athletic like run or play sports. Sometimes just a good all out fight did the trick. (MALE)

The normative data set strongly suggests that male responses are often violent (hitting walls or another person). The individual data set does not support this. However, it is possible that a strong social desirability factor is operating. Females also engage in physical release, but usually it consists of screaming, yelling, crying, and/or eating.

Seeking support. This component process involves elementary responses which express need for emotional support from others. This can manifest itself in two ways: seeking support from partner and seeking support from others. Both males and females seek support from their partners. The normative data set indicates that females are more likely to go to their friends for support than males. However, in the individual data set, virtually every male respondent indicates talking with friends for emotional support.

I talked to my other close male friends. They reinforce my feelings. I chose them because I knew they would be honest with me. (MALE)

Both males and females in the normative data set think females go to their friends for support and the individual data set supports this.

> [I talked to] my best friend because I felt foolish having acted like a child, and needed to release the tension of my embarrassment. (FEMALE)

Cognitive reframing. This process involves attempts to "intellectualize" the emotion by talking with friends to "sort things out," as well as rationalizing the situation. Both males and females report engaging in this process. They tend to minimize the relationship between the partner and the third party, or themselves and their partner.

> I tell myself that anyone who tries to get me jealous is not worth my time and I also tell my partner that in various ways. (MALE)

> I just kept saying to myself that they were only friends and that there was nothing to worry about. (FEMALE)

Interestingly, unlike the males in this sample, females expressed a need to have others evaluate their situations to determine the "appropriateness" of their feelings.

> I discussed the situation with his sister. I talked to her about it because I wanted to know if I had the right to be jealous or if I was just acting immature and insecure. (FEMALE)

Withdrawal. A final set of elementary responses can be classified as relationship withdrawal or leaving the relationship. In the individual data set, very few respondents indicate they leave a relationship because of jealousy. Those that did, however, were males. Both males and females in the normative data set think that males are more likely to leave a relationship when jealous.

Target

If jealousy is the enactment of a social role designed to protect a relationship, and in turn the self, then the target of the emotional syndrome must be the partner. Ultimately, it is the partner who determines the "outcome" of the syndrome. That is, it is the partner who must provide the confirmation of the relationship. While a particular response may be directed at self or rival, the syndrome as a whole is aimed at somehow controlling the partner's behavior.

Role Enactment

Several patterns relating to the enactment of the jealous role emerge from the data. It appears that romantic jealousy operates under a conflictive paradigm. An emotional syndrome is conflictive when it is a response to two competing sets of social norms. As discussed earlier, Averill (1985) sees romantic love as an emotional response to the conflict between social norms which call for unselfish commitment to partner and family and norms stressing independence and self–reliance. Falling in love (the romantic ideal) is the emotional syndrome that resolves the conflict and holds the family unit together for the good of society. The conflicting sets of social norms that seem to create the jealousy syndrome are similar to those that create love: social norms stressing commitment and the social norms that comprise the male sex role. Males experience jealousy as a result of conflict between norms stressing they stay in a relationship and norms saying they should protect their ego and maintain their independence. For a male, jealousy is a passionate response, beyond his control, that allows him to engage in interaction that will resolve the conflict.

Females also experience jealousy as a result of conflict between norms stressing commitment and independence. Females understand the nature of the male role's demand for independence and must engage in behavior that will encourage the partner to remain in the relationship. As with males, enactment of the jealousy syndrome allows the female to prompt interaction which will, if the script is carried out, remove the conflict. If falling in love is the syndrome that brings the couple together, it is possible that jealousy is a socially developed role to protect the romantic dyad and thus the family unit. When an individual's commitment to his/her partner is threatened, the partner has a socially sanctioned, yet passionate (beyond his/her control), syndrome that initiates action/interaction to thwart that threat. The notion that both males and females experience jealousy as a response to conflict surrounding the male role supports Schaef's (1981) notion of a primary male system (the White Male System) and a Reactive Female System, a system which develops its characteristics in response to those of the White Male System. This would suggest that the roles enacted in the jealousy syndrome might be gender–based and, more specifically, a function of the interaction between the White Male System and The Reactive Female system. Indeed, the construction of the jealousy syndrome that emerges from the data in the current study suggest an interaction pattern that is very characteristic of the interaction between the two systems: ownership/commodity.

The roles the males and females in this sample seem to be acting out can best be explained metaphorically. The operative metaphor is ownership/commodity. The emphasis on status envy for males and attribute envy for females suggests that males are concerned with the status of "owning" a prized commodity, i.e., an attractive female. Several males report that they get jealous of another male simply because he has a good–looking girlfriend. Females participate in this marketplace mentality by attending to that which makes them desirable to males, namely physical attributes. A female's physical attributes seem to determine her market value which is why she engages in social comparison processes evaluating that dimension of herself. Thus the data in the current study suggest role enactment in the jealousy syndrome is a function of traditional male/female interaction patterns.

Conclusion

This paper attempts to provide an initial conceptualization of romantic jealousy as a transitory social role. The results indicate that romantic jealousy can best be conceptualized as an emotional syndrome enacted for the purpose of protecting self and relationship (aim) and prompted by an uncertainty over relational role position (the instigation) because of the partner's (target) actual or potential relationship with a rival, resulting in a fear of loss of a perceived/desired primary relationship. The component processes which emerged from the data are envy, violation of relational boundaries, direct prompts for behavior, indirect prompts for behavior, competition, physical release, seeking support, cognitive reframing, and withdrawal. The first two component processes can be considered aspects of the instigation, while the last seven reflect the aim of the syndrome. We posit an argument that the conceptualizations of these dimensions are gender-based and reflect traditional male/female interaction patterns. We further suggest that jealousy may serve a functional role in our society by providing a means through which individuals can resolve a conflict between a (male) norm of independence on the one hand, and a norm of unselfish commitment to partner and family on the other. While the findings discussed above are enlightening as well as provocative, it is important to note that this study represents only a first, very exploratory step in the process of conceptualizing romantic jealousy as a social role and therefore the interpretations of the current data are tentative. Future research should address these issues with larger and more varied samples. In addition, we could benefit from in-depth interviews with individuals and couples designed to discover how they construct and enact the jealousy syndrome in their ongoing communication transactions.

Notes

1. For a review of the literature on gender differences and jealousy, see Bringle and Buunk (1985) and Sprowl (1987).

References

Averill, J.R. (1977, November). *Anger*. Paper presented at the Nebraska Symposium on Motivation.

Averill, J.R. (1980). A constructivist view of emotion. In R. Plutchik & H. Kellerman (Eds.), *Emotion: Theories, research and experience. Volume 1: Theories of emotion* (pp. 305–339). Orlando, Florida: Academic Press, Inc.

Averill, J.R. (1985). The social construction of emotion: With special reference to love. In K.J. Gergen & K.E. Davis (Eds.), *The social construction of the person* (pp. 89–109). New York: Springer–Verlag.

Bowers, J.W., Metts, S.M., & Duncason, W.T. (1985). Emotion and interpersonal communication. In M.L. Knapp & G.R. Miller (Eds.), *Handbook of interpersonal communication* (pp. 500–550). Beverly Hills: Sage Publications.

Bringle, R.G. (1981). Conceptualizing jealously as a disposition. *Alternative Lifestyles, 4*, 274–290.

Bringle, R.G. & Buunk, B. (1985). Jealousy and social behavior: A review of person, relationship, and situational determinants. In P. Shaver (Ed.), *Self, situations, and social behavior: Review of personality and social Psychology*, Vol. 6 (pp. 241–264). Beverly Hills: Sage Publications.

Buunk, B. (1980). *Intieme relaties met derden. Een sociaalpsychologische studie*. Alphen a/d Rijn: Samsom.

Buunk, B. (1982). Strategies of jealousy: Styles of coping with extramarital involvement of the spouse. *Family Relations, 31*, 13–18.

Ellis, C., & Weinstein, E. (1986). Jealousy and the social psychology of emotional experience. *Journal of Social and Personal Relationships, 3*, 337–357.

Foster, G.M. (1972). The anatmoy of envy: A study in symbolic behavior. *Current Anthropology, 13*, 165–202.

Gilligan, C. (1982). *In a different voice*. Cambridge, Massachusetts: Harvard University Press.

Jaremko, M. E., & Lindsey, R. (1979). Stress coping abilities of individuals high and low in jealousy. *Psychological Reports, 44*, 547–553.

Manges, K., & Evenbeck, S. (1980). *Social power, jealousy, and dependency in the intimate dyad*. Paper presented at the meeting of the Midwestern Psychological Association, St. Louis.

Mathes, E., & Severa, N. (1981). Jealousy, romantic love, and liking: Theoretical considerations and preliminary scale development. *Psychological Reports, 49*, 23–31.

Peters, R.S. (1962). Emotions and the category of passivity. *Aristotelean Society Proceedings, 62*, 117–134.

Peters, R.S. (1969). Motivation, emotion, and the conceptual scheme of common sense. In T. Mischel (Ed.), *Human Action,. conceptual and empirical issues.* New York: Academic Press.

Schaef, A.W. (1981). *Women's reality.* Minneapolis: Winston.

Solomon, R.C. (1976). *The passions.* Garden City, New York: Anchor Press/Doubleday.

Sprowl, S. Parrish (1987). Cognitive, affective, and behavioral correlates of romantic jealousy: An analysis of gender differences. In L.B. Nadler, M.K. Nadler, & W. Todd–Mancillas (Eds.), *Advances in gender and communication research.* Lanham, Maryland: University Press of America.

White, G. (1981a). A model of romantic jealousy. *Motivation and emotion, 5,* 295–310.

White, G. (1981b). Some correlates of romantic jealousy. *Journal of Personality, 49,* 129–142.

THOUGHT PROVOKERS

The authors suggest that jealousy may serve a "functional role" in our society by providing a mechanism for resolving the conflict between a norm of independence and a norm of unselfish commitment to partner and family. Since jealousy is often perceived as a negative emotion, how might you justify it as functional and necessary in light of this interpersonal conflict?

SEX AND GENDER DIVERSITY IN THE ORGANIZATIONAL SETTING

As women have increasingly entered the paying workforce since World War II, researchers have focused more attention on male and female job performance. Traditionally, researchers have examined such concerns by developing demographic descriptions of males and females on the job, exploring the impact of sex–role stereotypes in the workplace, and identifying differences in male and female management styles. Today, we continue to address these issues and many others to determine both similarities and differences of men and women on the job. In reviewing this research, it is not uncommon to discover inconsistent findings among studies exploring the same issues.

The three chapters in this unit represent quantitative research using questionnaires and surveys. From the data collected, some of the findings support the traditional male management model as preferred in the workplace while other findings suggest a shift to perceived male and female equality as managers. Whether examining specific issues such as conflict resolution and sexual harassment or examining general views toward the job, exploring perceptions and attitudes in the workplace is the common thread that runs throughout these chapters.

In Chapter Twelve, "Sex–Role Stereotypes in Organizational Conflict," Lawrence B. Nadler and Marjorie Keeshan Nadler examine the impact of sex–role stereotypes in the perception of conflict-resolving behaviors. While previous research generally concludes that females approach conflict cooperatively while males approach conflict competitively, these research findings suggest that both males and females perceive a cooperative approach as more effective in resolving conflict. The authors do note that some methodological limitations may account for this discrepancy from previous findings; however, the authors also suggest that the traditional sex–role stereotype may simply be incorrect.

In Chapter Thirteen, "An Investigation of Sexual Harassment, Gender Orientation, and Job Satisfaction," Marcia A. Brusberg studied the effects of sex and gender orientation on the tendency to label communication behaviors as sexually harassing. Through analysis of perceptual data gathered from subjects, Brusberg concludes that females are more likely to perceive sexual harassment on the job than males. With this finding, the author then challenges the reader to consider how knowledge of this perceptual difference may be valuable to managers in the workplace.

Finally, Linda McCallister and Donald Gaymon collected survey data to measure male and female attitudes toward the workplace. Specifically, Chapter Fourteen, entitled "Male and Female Managers in the 21st Century: Will There Be A Difference?" identifies several attitudinal differences and similarities concerning the workplace that males and females hold. Such specific work–related issues as attitudes toward human relations, job scope, and a contract model for evaluating job performance are explored. Perhaps one of the most interesting findings is that *both* males and females are increasingly rated as equal in their competency as managers—a definite shift from the traditional male model in management.

Using quantitative research methods, the authors of all three chapters gather perceptual and attitudinal data concerning males and females in the workplace. While some traditional boundaries differentiating male and female perceptions and attitudes toward the organizational setting are reinforced, many of those boundaries are either redefined or completely eliminated by the findings of the authors. As you conclude this unit, consider the impact of such changes in both males and females in the workplace as we prepare to enter the next decade.

CHAPTER TWELVE
Sex-Role Stereotypes in Organizational Conflict

Lawrence B. Nadler and *Marjorie Keeshan Nadler*

Miami University

Introduction

Reported inequities in sex-related success patterns in American corporations highlight the need to explore women's ability to negotiate successfully within their work organizations. Estimates of the sex salary gap range from women earning 31% to 38% less than men (*Changing Times*, 1984). In addition to wage inequities, women have been limited in gaining entry to managerial or executive positions. Harris (1978) indicates that in 1940, only 4% of company executives were women; by 1978, this figure had not topped 6%. Clearly, women have not been as successfully integrated into positions of power and authority in business (Terborg, Peters, Ilgen, Smith, 1977). Women experience considerable difficulty in earning promotions to management level positions, receiving equal pay for performing the same work as men, and possibly even selling their ideas and gaining recognition for their work. While various reasons (e.g. lower need for income, interruptions for child-rearing, and the nature of their occupations) have been advanced to account for these disparities, it appears that a gap still exists. As *Changing Times* (1984) reports, "most researchers agree that anywhere from 1/3 to 1/2 of the earnings gap can be explained by male-female differences in work experience, job tenure and advanced training...but that still leaves a so-called residual gap (p. 10)."

We believe that obtaining raises, promotions and other forms of organizational support are at least partially related to the individual's negotiation ability and that women are at a negotiation disadvantage relative to men. This paper will briefly examine the research on the role of sex-role stereotypes' influence in the negotiation area and present the results of an experimental study examining and comparing perceptions of cooperative and assertive/competitive behaviors for and by males and females in an organizational negotiation situation.

Sex–Role Stereotypes

A primary aspect of negotiation outcomes involves sex–role stereotypes and related role prescriptions which influence behavioral choices. An interesting illustration of the connection between expectations and behavior involves self–fulfilling prophecies. Here, an individual's expectations of the other person's behavior, based upon stereotypical judgments, produce actions which are likely to reinforce those role–based predictions. If managers expect less of female subordinates, they are likely to receive less. Some studies have demonstrated this relationship with regard to on–the–job training. According to Zellman (1976), employers are often reluctant to offer on–the–job training to female employees.

Fink (1982) notes that studies depict the perception that males are better suited to and more capable of assuming management positions. In fact, Bowman, Worthy, and Grayser (1965) report that managers do not perceive women as having the decision–making skills or competitive aggressiveness needed for these positions. Instead, women are viewed as too emotional for managerial positions (Orth and Jacobs, 1971; Schein, 1973). This lack of training and exposure to critical experiences reinforces the prophecies by ensuring that females will be unprepared to assume managerial roles.

In a negotiation setting, sex–role stereotyping can increase the likelihood of women obtaining negative outcomes relative to men. This assertion is supported by the literature on sex–related norm violations. As Grotjahn (1957) states, "the women of our contemporary scene have to be careful, because any show of aggression, open or disguised, is taken by every man in our competitive culture as a challenge...to which he has to rise (p.37)." This point, though somewhat overstated, still possesses relevance. As Sereno and Weathers (1981) maintain, women are caught in conflict between traditional female roles and new emerging behavioral alternatives. They frequently encounter the following double bind: if they conform to norms of passivity and dependence, they might fail to attain desired outcomes; on the other hand, if they act assertively, they risk the consequences associated with any norm deviation. While cultural conditions are changing, Sereno and Weathers accurately observe that "in the midst of this social change, women often find themselves in anxiety–provoking situations for which they do not have effective responses (p. 2)."

Certainly, the existence of sex–role stereotypes exerts strong influence on how women view themselves in communication situations, especially intraorganizational negotiation settings. These perceptions, in turn, affect the manner in which women present themselves and the outcomes they obtain. According to Horner (1968), females are often motivated to avoid success, believing that femininity and intellectual achievement are desirable, but mutually exclusive goals. In other words, women often modify their behavior to be more socially acceptable, even if certain goals must be sacrificed in the process. Bentley (1982) identifies the lack of risk–taking and assertive behaviors as limiting factors in women's entry into high–level management positions. According to Lange and Jakubowski (1976), women are often non–assertive because they believe the stereotypical notion that assertive behavior will be construed as aggressive and masculine.

Nadler and Nadler (1984) studied male and female orientations to negotiation in an organizational setting. Subjects were presented with a hypothetical job performance evaluation and were asked what percentage pay raise they ideally wanted, thought was realistic, and would minimally settle for given that the company's average pay raise would be 6% and the subject received a very good evaluation. On all three items, males had significantly higher expectations. Subjects were also asked to predict their supervisor's view concerning the employee's ideal pay increase, realistic raise level, and minimum acceptable salary gain. Again, males had significantly higher expectations concerning their supervisor's bargaining stance for all three items. Thus, the results of this study would suggest that males approach organizational negotiation settings in a more personally advantageous manner than females.

Nadler and Nadler (1987) followed this study with an experimental analysis of the outcomes of subjects placed in the organizational setting identified above. Subjects were randomly placed in pairs so that the sex of the supervisor and subordinates were varied. All possible combinations (i.e., male supervisor–male subordinate, male supervisor–female subordinate, female supervisor–male subordinate, female supervisor–female subordinate) were employed. The findings of this study supported the results predicted by the prior experiment which focused upon expectations entering the situation. Specifically, male supervisors produced lower pay raises for their subordinates than female supervisors, and female subordinates received lower pay increases than male subordinates. The lowest final outcomes were accrued in the male supervisor–female subordinate condition.

The results of this prior research strongly suggest that sex plays a role in the outcomes of negotiation and conflict situations. It also suggests that the differences in results may be a combination of sex–role stereotypes brought to the situation and differences in behavior between the sexes in conflict and negotiation situations. It is also quite likely that sex–role stereotypes may contribute to the differences in behaviors exhibited in these areas.

The following study is designed to examine the role of sex–role stereotypes in perceptions of conflict resolving behaviors. Specifically, it has been suggested that women avoid more assertive and confrontive behavior due to fears of being perceived negatively, while men do not hesitate to engage in such behaviors due to lack of fear of negative expectations associated with them. Thus, it has been suggested that females are more cooperative in conflict situations due to social rewards for conforming to societal stereotypes and are discouraged from displaying aggressive or competitive behaviors for fear of punishment for violating norms. Conversely, the same literature implies that males lack these concerns and thus feel free to adopt the behavior most likely to yield successful outcomes in the same conflict situations. By examining reactions of male and female subjects to males and females engaging in either cooperative or assertive/competitive approaches to the same organizational conflict situation, we hope to identify the role that sex-role stereotypes play in influencing outcomes in negotiation settings. While prior research has focused upon expectations brought to conflict situations and outcomes generated by different sex-related behaviors, this study will focus on subject's perceptions about the appropriateness and effectiveness of the two approaches for males versus females in an organizational conflict setting.

Methodology

Independent Variables

This study explored the effects of four independent variables on perceptions of negotiation behavior. Biological sex was examined, as was psychological gender. In the latter regard, a revised version of the Bem Sex-Role Inventory (BSRI) was administered to subjects (Wheeless and Dierks-Stewart, 1981). Using a median-split procedure advocated by Rancer and Dierks-Stewart (1983), subjects were classified as masculine if they scored above the median for masculinity but below the median for femininity; feminine if they scored above the median for femininity but below the median for masculinity; androgynous if they scored above both medians; and undifferentiated if they scored below both medians. Further, sex of actor was explored, as was form of negotiation behavior. In the latter regard, approximately half of the subjects read protocols depicting competitive behavior in an organizational environment, while the remaining subjects read protocols describing cooperative behavior in the same situation. In dealing with an undesirable job assignment, competitive behavior was operationalized as being prepared to quit and go to work for a competitor, whereas cooperative behavior involved being prepared to accept the situation.

Sample

Our sample consisted of 277 undergraduate students at Miami University. The 126 male subjects and 151 female subjects were enrolled in introductory communication courses and were fulfilling a class requirement via their experimental participation. While these students were drawn from introductory level courses, most participants were juniors and seniors.

Procedures

Upon entering the experimental situation, subjects were told that we were performing research concerning perceptions of communication behavior and that they would be asked to read about how an individual dealt with a particular situation and to assess the person's behavior afterward. Thus, subjects were asked to read the following situation description (Note: this description is one of four that were employed in crossing sex of actor with form of negotiation behavior):

> John is an account executive with MNA Corporation. Recently, his boss assigned him the account with PDL, Inc. Through the grapevine, John found out that working with PDL was a difficult, unpleasant task. In fact, several associates had indicated that the PDL account was available only because PDL's prior account representative had resigned the account. Given this information, John, who had been with MNA for five years, badly desired not to be assigned this account with PDL. As a result, John scheduled a meeting with his boss. At the meeting, John planned to tell the boss that he preferred that the account be assigned to another executive. If this were not possible, though, John was prepared to accept the situation and handle the account to maintain his position in the company.

After reading the description, subjects were asked to assess the stimulus person's behavior. Specifically, they rated the account executive's conflict resolution behavior along the following dimensions: appropriateness, assertiveness, effectiveness, productiveness, professionalism, realism, selfishness, and successfulness. In all cases, seven-point scales ranging from "very" to "not at all" were employed for these dependent measures. Additionally, subjects were asked their sex, age, and class standing. On the next page, subjects completed the revised 20 item BSRI. Afterward, they were told that the experimenters were studying sex and gender differences in evaluations of conflict-related behaviors and they were thanked for their participation.

Hypotheses

Based upon prior research concerning the appropriateness of male and female sex roles, the following hypotheses were advanced and subjected to experimental examination:

H1. Males will view competitive behavior more favorably than will females.

H2. Male actors will be viewed more favorably than female actors for competitive behavior, while female actors will be viewed more favorably than male actors for cooperative behaviors.

H3. Masculine subjects will view competitive behavior more favorably than will feminine subjects.

In all cases, Analysis of Variance tests were performed with a probability level of .05.

Results

The eight dependent measures yielded few statistically significant results. No main effects were predicted or found for sex of subject, while only one main effect was obtained for sex of actor (Table 1).

Table 1
Realistic

	Sum of Squares	DF	Mean Square	F	Sig. of F
Sex of Actor	19.493	1	19.493	8.931	.003

	Cell Means	
	Male	Female
	F4.08	3.57

Specifically, the female account executive was seen as more realistic than her male counterpart across both conflict–related behavior conditions. Also, no main effects occurred for gender, as measured by the revised BSRI. The conflict–related behavior variable produced significant differences for all eight dependent measures. Cooperative behavior was perceived as more appropriate, more effective, more productive, more professional, more realistic, and more successful than competitive behavior. Similarly, competitive behavior was viewed as more assertive and more selfish than cooperative behavior. Clearly, the conflict behavior manipulation was successfully implemented.

The number of significant interaction effects was also quite limited. There were four such effects for sex of actor with conflict–related behavior. Surprisingly, males were perceived as more appropriate (Table 2), productive (Table 3), and realistic (Table 4) when they displayed cooperative behavior, whereas females were

Table 2
Appropriate

	Sum of Squares	DF	Mean Square	F	Sig. of F
Sex of Actor X Conflict – Related Behavior	15.361	1	15.361	5.835	.016

Cell Means
Conflict–Related Behavior

		Competition	Cooperation
Sex of Actor	Male	5.21	3.05
	Female	4.60	3.41

Table 3
Productive

	Sum of Squares	DF	Mean Square	F	Sig. of F
Sex of Actor X Conflict – Related Behavior	14.949	1	14.949	6.468	.012

Cell Means
Conflict–Related Behavior

		Competition	Cooperation
Sex of Actor	Male	5.22	3.74
	Female	4.93	4.36

Table 4
Realistic

	Sum of Squares	DF	Mean Square	F	Sig. of F
Sex of Actor X Conflict – Related Behavior	27.422	1	27.422	12.563	.000

Cell Means
Conflict–Related Behavior

		Competition	Cooperation
Sex of Actor	Male	5.06	3.12
	Female	3.91	3.23

seen more favorably along these three dimensions when they exhibited competitive behavior. Further, females who behaved competitively were viewed as more assertive than their competitive male counterparts, who were perceived as more assertive than females when they acted in a cooperative manner (Table 5). One significant result was obtained for the sex of subject–BSRI interaction (Table 6).

Table 5
Assertive

	Sum of Squares	DF	Mean Square	F	Sig. of F
Sex of Actor X Conflict – Related Behavior	14.516	1	14.516	6.965	.009

		Cell Means Conflict–Related Behavior	
		Competition	Cooperation
Sex of Actor	Male	2.82	3.05
	Female	2.20	3.22

Table 6
Assertive

	Sum of Squares	DF	Mean Square	F	Sig. of F
Sex of Subject X BSRI	30.776	3	10.259	4.922	.002

		Cell Means BSRI			
		Feminine	Masculine	Andro-gynous	Undif-ferentiated
Sex of Subject	Male	3.71	3.11	2.07	2.83
	Female	2.98	2.56	2.92	2.26

Table 7
Selfish

	Sum of Squares	DF	Mean Square	F	Sig. of F
Sex of Subject X BSRI	28.661	3	9.554	2,750	.043

		Cell Means BSRI			
		Feminine	Masculine	Andro-gynous	Undif-ferentiated
Sex of Subject	Male	3.71	2.88	3.05	4.00
	Female	3.68	3.59	3.08	3.00

Specifically, androgynous males saw the account executive's behavior (across both conflict–related behavior conditions) as more assertive than did androgynous females; in all other cells, regardless of sex–typing, female subjects viewed the account executive's behavior as more assertive than did male subjects. Further, the sex of actor–BSRI interaction for selfishness was statistically significant (Table 7). Here, masculine and feminine subjects viewed males as more selfish than females, whereas undifferentiated subjects saw females as more self–ish than males. Finally, one significant result was garnered for the three–way interaction of sex of subject, sex of actor, and BSRI. This result was obtained for the measure of realisticness, but it permitted no intelligible interpretation and was thus dropped from the analysis.

Discussion

In linking the experimental results to the research hypotheses, it is clear that virtually no support has been garnered for the theoretical predictions. In fact, the few significant results are in the opposite direction of the hypotheses. The first hypothesis, that males would view competitive behavior more favorably than would females, was not supported, as the sex of subject–conflict behavior interaction yielded non–significant results for all eight dependent measures. The second hypothesis, that male actors would be viewed more favorably than female actors when behaving competitively, and that the reverse pattern would be exhibited for cooperative behavior, also lacked ex–perimental support. While the sex of actor–conflict behavior interac–tion was statistically significant for four of eight measures, all four results were counter to theoretical expectations. Specifically, females were viewed more favorably (i.e., assertive, appropriate, productive, and realistic) than males when acting in a competitive fashion. Fi–nally, the prediction that masculine subjects would view competitive behavior more favorably than would female subjects was not sup–ported. In this case, the BSRI–conflict behavior interaction was not significant for any of the eight dependent measures. It should be noted that while three other interaction effects were obtained, these results lend no support to the experimental predictions. On the whole, then, the research hypotheses were in no way buttressed by the experimental results.

Given this pattern of results, it is necessary to consider why they occurred, as well as their practical importance. In the former regard, a few methodological aspects can be cited as possible contributors to the non–significant pattern of results. First, the situation description was perhaps too brief to permit reasonable judgments by subjects. While time constraints and the fear of introducing other variables mediated against a more detailed description of the negotiation situ–ation, an assessment of another person's behavior in actual interac–tion would often be based upon more information than was provided. Second, the wording of the situation, based upon subjects' feedback, may have been somewhat ambiguous. While we intended for students

to evaluate the stimulus person based on his/her conflict–related behavior, some subjects indicated after the experimental sessions that
they were assessing the actor in terms of his/her utilization of rumor-
based information regarding the history of the PDL account. Finally,
it should be realized that subjects were evaluating planned versus actual behavior.

It is difficult to determine whether these factors influenced the
experimental results. In either event, two interesting potential implications of this research warrant attention. First, the conflict–related
behavior main effect for all eight dependent measures indicates a
strong preference for cooperative versus competitive behavior. Here,
cooperation was viewed as more appropriate, more assertive, more
effective, more productive, more realistic, more successful, and less
selfish. This overwhelming preference, by male and female respondents, merits additional research. Second, and perhaps even more
provocative, is the relationship of this study's results with prior research in this area. Specifically, our prior research has suggested that
males and females behave differently in negotiation situations. This
study, though, indicates that males and females are not, on the
whole, evaluated differently when engaging in competitive or cooperative negotiation behavior. In fact, some support exists that women
are even viewed more favorably than men when performing the same
conflict–related behavior. One reason for this discrepancy could be
based on this study's focus on attitudes about behavior versus the
prior research's focus on behaviors. Part of the reason males and
females behave differently in conflict situations may involve expectations about how those behaviors will be evaluated by others. Indeed,
the classic double bind suggests that women may fear loss of social
approval if they behave too aggressively. This research suggests that
the double bind affecting women in organizations may be more apparent than real. In other words, women may conform to sex–role
prescriptions because they falsely fear the sanctions which would accompany non–normative behavior. As women were not evaluated
more negatively than men when behaving competitively, perhaps the
double bind they perceive in such situations would not be substantiated by other people's reactions, especially when they choose to devi-
ate from perceived social norms in acting assertively. Certainly, this
issue is thought–provoking and worthy of future research.

References

Bentley, N.W. (October 1982). An historical perspective: Where did the mentor system come from and how has it affected women to date? Fifth Annual Communication, Language, and Gender Conference, Ohio University.

Bowman, G.W., Worthy, N.B. & Grayser, S.A. (1965). Problems in review: Are women executives people? *Harvard Business Review*, *43* (4), 14–28, 164–178.

_____. (1984). Why do women earn less than men? *Changing Times*, April, 10.

Fink, C. (October 1982). Perceptions of women's communication skills related to managerial effectiveness. Fifth Annual Communication, Language, and Gender Conference, Athens, Ohio.

Grotjahn, M. (1957). *Beyond Laughter*. New York: McGraw–Hill.

Harris, M. (1978). One–upwomanship: Six books on women executives. *Money*, *7*, 118, 120.

Horner, M.S. (1968). Sex differences in achievement motivation and performance in competitive and non–competitive situations. Unpublished doctoral dissertation, University of Michigan.

Lange, A.J. & Jakubowski, P. (1976). *Responsible Assertive Behavior: Cognitive Behavioral Procedures for Trainers*. Champaign, Illinois: Research Press.

Nadler, L.B. & Nadler, M.K. (March 1984). Communication, gender and negotiation: Theory and findings. Eastern Communication Association Conference, Philadelphia, Pennsylvania.

Nadler, M.K. & Nadler, L.B. (1987). The influence of gender on negotiation success in asymmetric power situations. In L. B. Nadler, M.K. Nadler, & W.R. Todd–Mancillas (eds.) *Advances in Gender and Communication Research*. Lanham, Maryland: University Press of America.

Orth, C.P. & Jacobs, F. (1971). Women in management: Pattern for change. *Harvard Business Review*, *49* (4), 139.

Rancer, A.S. & Dierks–Stewart, K.J. (October 1983). An examination of biological and psychological gender differences in trait argumentativeness. Sixth Annual Communication, Language, and Gender Conference, New Brunswick, New Jersey.

Schein, V.E. (1973). The relationship between sex role stereotypes and requisite management characteristics. *Journal of Applied Psychology*, *57*, 95–100.

Sereno, K.K. & Weathers, J. (1981). Impact of communicator sex on receiver reactions to assertive, nonassertive, and aggressive communication. *Women's Studies in Communication*, *4*, 1–17.

Terborg, J., Peters, L., Ilgen, D., & Smith, F. (1977). Organizational and personal correlates of attitudes toward women as managers. *Academy of Management Journal, 20,* 89–100.

Wheeless, V.E. & Dierks–Stewart, K.J. (1981). The psychometric properties of the Bem sex–role inventory: Questions concerning reliability and validity. *Communication Quarterly, 29,* 173–186.

Zellman, G.L. (1976). The role of structural factors in limiting women's institutional participation. *Journal of Social Issues, 32* (3), 33–46.

THOUGHT PROVOKERS

How might the nature of the conflict influence men's and women's approaches to conflict resolution? What are some typical "on–the–job" conflicts that may carry impact for men and women depending upon how they resolve these conflicts?

CHAPTER THIRTEEN

An Investigation of Sexual Harassment, Gender Orientation, and Job Satisfaction

Marcia A. Brusberg

Tech–Ed Services

Beltsville, Maryland

The topic of sexual harassment in the workplace has captured the interest of researchers in various fields (Gutek, 1982). In the field of communication Booth–Butterfield (1984) and Remland and Jones (1985) have evidenced its recognition as a communication phenomenon. There are numerous definitions of sexual harassment and they include both verbal and nonverbal forms of communication. The institutionally accepted definition that addresses the true nature of sexual harassment is provided by the Equal Employment Opportunity Commission (1980):

> Unwelcome sexual advances, requests for sexual favors, and other verbal or physical conduct of a nature which constitute sexual harassment when (1) submission to the conduct is either explicitly or implicitly a term or condition of employment, (2) submission to or rejection of such conduct by an individual is used as the basis for employment decisions affecting that individual, and/or (3) such conduct has the purpose or effect of unreasonably interfering with an individual's work performance or creating an intimidating, hostile, or offensive work environment.

This definition supplies a foundation from which sexual harassment can be examined. A consideration in defining sexual harassment is that individuals view it differently from one another. In other words, whether or not sexual harassment is communicated depends on the *receiver's* definition of what constitutes sexual harassment. One's tendency to perceive sexual harassment is related both to personal and environmental factors (Booth–Butterfield, 1984; Gutek & Morasch, 1982; Jensen & Gutek, 1982; Powell, 1986; Reilly, Carpenter, Dull, & Bartlett, 1982; Remland & Jones, 1985). While research results allow for the declaration of this statement, few attempts have been made to examine specific elements of the self and their role in the perception of sexual harassment. This study undertakes such an investigation.

Miller (1984) stresses the importance of demonstrating the relationships between concepts when he states that the "proliferation of constructs perpetuates scientific confusion, rather than promoting scientific understanding" (p. 239). He also believes it is vital for students of communication to understand factors influencing people's communication. Sexual harassment may best be understood by exploring factors which may be related to its perception.

Research on sexual harassment has addressed the sexes and their perceptions of this communication phenomenon (e.g. Remland & Jones, 1985; Tangri, Burt, & Johnson, 1982). Benson and Thomson (1982) have suggested that there is a gap between the perceptions of men and women about the frequency and type of harassment that actually occurs in the workplace. Powell (1986) states that "individuals' perceptions of themselves in relation to sex role stereotypes rather than their sex may provide the key to understanding their definitions of harassment" (p. 17). The construct of gender orientation is one way of describing how people perceive and interact with their environment. Psychological gender orientation is the degree to which a person identifies with society's definitions of masculinity and femininity (Bem, 1974). By using gender orientation as a variable for study, in addition to biological sex, we might find further distinctions among perceptions of sexual harassment.

Sexual harassment usually occurs in the workplace, thus providing a specific context in which to focus an examination of this disrupting communication. Our jobs are a dominant part of our lives and most of the working population spends a large portion of time on the job. With so much time spent at work, it is important for employees to experience job satisfaction. While there is little consensus as to what constitutes job satisfaction (Richmond, McCroskey, & Davis, 1982), the presence of disturbing communication would seem to contribute to job dissatisfaction. Therefore, if an individual is very sensitive to sexual harassment, and has a high tendency to perceive it, even when it may not exist in serious forms, that individual may be prone to report more job dissatisfaction.

This study specifically investigates the impact of two personal factors, perception of sexual harassment and gender orientation, on level of job satisfaction. The interrelationship of the two independent variables is also considered.

Review of Sexual Harassment

Recently sexual harassment has become recognized as a social issue (Brewer & Berk, 1982). Scholars in the fields of psychology, sociology, and communication have noted the extent of the problem by looking at its effects, primary targets, and possible solutions as to why it occurs. The effects of sexual harassment are extensive. Targets may suffer any of a number of devastating reactions to it: development of a lower self–image, depression, alcoholism, excessive drug use, family disruptions and even mental illness (Renick, 1980). Psychosomatic illnesses are also reported by victims of sexual harassment (Brodsky, 1976; Renick, 1980). Some common ailments include sleeplessness, chronic fatigue, loss of strength, hypersensitivity, memory loss, and nervousness (Brodsky, 1976). Negative effect also develops as targets experience hurt, sadness, depression, anxiety, anger, disgust, indignation, rage, humiliation, degradation, shame, embarrassment, hostility, feelings of victimization, and feelings of powerlessness (Jensen & Gutek, 1982; Brodsky, 1976; Renick, 1980; Tangri et al., 1982).

These emotional reactions to sexual harassment have work–related consequences as well (Jensen & Gutek, 1982). Renick (1980) and Petersen and Massengill (1982) note a rise in absenteeism among victims, with accompanying lower productivity. Negative affect toward the job in general is reported with receivers feeling distracted, dreading to go to work, becoming accident prone, and experiencing poor motivation (Brodsky, 1976; Renick, 1980; Tangri et al., 1982). Taken together these effects indicate job dissatisfaction. Eventual unemployment is perhaps the most drastic result which could occur (Renick, 1980).

Recipients of sexually harassing communication fear that their complaints will be ignored or disbelieved, that they will be perceived as silly for complaining, or, worse yet, that they will be blamed for the problem (MacKinnon, 1979; Tangri et al., 1982). More men than women see sexual harassment as merely an exaggerated issue (Collins & Blodgett, 1981) which is not difficult to handle; they also believe that incidents labeled as sexual harassment are just "normal sexual attraction between two people" (Tangri, et al., 1982, P. 50). Abbey (1982) suggests that women may be better than men at distinguishing friendly behavior from seductive behavior and this ability may underlie the discrepancy in perceptions concerning the seriousness of sexual harassment. Females' superiority over males in ability to decode nonverbal cues (Hall, 1978; Isenhart, 1980) supports this suggestion. Clearly, reactions to this disturbing communication are problematic.

Women are the primary targets of sexual harassment but some are more prone than others to experience it on the job. Single and divorced women are more likely to be targets than are married women, as are women in entry–level or training positions (Tangri et al., 1982). Women with college degrees are equally likely to be victims as women with lower education (Peterson & Massengill, 1982). Tangri et al. (1982) also found that younger women, who are especially dependent on their jobs for money are vulnerable to harassment. College women fall into several of these groups. Several explanations have been offered as to why sexual harassment occurs in this pattern.

While no single model can account for the occurrence of sexual harassment (Brewer, 1982) they all provide contexts, situations, and person–specific variables to be considered. Models also describe behaviors which may be recognized as sexually harassing communication. Brewer (1982) describes the categories of coercive or physically intrusive behavior, offensive verbalization, and flirtatious behavior (e.g. requests for dates, compliments). The first category is most likely to be recognized as sexually harassing communication, but the second and third classes leave room for vague interpretations. Brewer and Berk (1982) state, "we need to know the circumstances under which sexual harassment is and is not ambiguously interpreted" (p. 3). In response to this need, Booth–Butterfield (1983) developed a self–report instrument which measures the perception of sexual harassment.

Booth–Butterfield notes that the study of sexual harassment has suffered from the lack of "empirical rigor" (p. 2). Most research has used incidence reports, vignettes, and personal perceptions. Booth–Butterfield operationalized perception of sexually harassing communication with scaled responses to written descriptions of harassing communication, and offered evidence for the value of this method. Booth–Butterfield emphasizes the less subjective and emotional nature of responses obtained using the Perception of Sexual Harassment Scale. She also notes the ease in data collection, replicability, and generation of interval data as strengths of the survey (see Appendix A for scale). These assets exemplify the sophistication of this measure. Evidence supports the reliability and validity of the instrument (see Methods).

This review discussed definitions, effects, targets, and explanatory models of sexual harassment. Most importantly, sexual harassment was established as a communication phenomenon, warranting its study from a communication perspective, including an empirical approach and quantitative method of measurement. With this established our concern now turns to the variable of gender orientation, which may be related to perceptions of sexual harassment and level of job satisfaction.

Review of Gender Orientation

For some time communication research has used biological sex as a variable to explain behavior differences (Ellis & McCallister, 1980; Greenblatt, Hasenauer, & Freimuth, 1980). With the emergence of psychological gender orientation, however, many communication researchers have investigated this construct and its relationship to communication variables.

According to Bem (1974), each of us identifies with or endorses differing degrees of society's definitions of masculinity and femininity, and can be categorized into one of four gender orientation groups. The four groups are masculine, feminine, androgynous, and undifferentiated. When a person identifies highly with more masculine characteristics (e.g. independent, dominant, competitive) than feminine characteristics (e.g. sensitive, warm, submissive), that person has a masculine psychological gender orientation. In the case of the person who identifies more with feminine than masculine characteristics, he/she has a feminine psychological gender orientation. The individual who identifies to a high degree with both masculine and feminine traits is labeled androgynous, while the undifferentiated person identifies to a low degree with both masculine and feminine traits.

While this conceptualization (Bem, 1974; Spence, Helmreich, & Stapp, 1975) has inspired much research utilizing psychological gender orientation, the concept of androgyny has received specific attention from communication researchers as well (Wheeless & Dierks-Stewart, 1981). Ellis and McCallister (1980) found that androgynous groups do not use single relational definitions in interactions, do not compete for control, and "seem to develop workable communication patterns" (p. 49). Greenblatt et al. (1980) further concluded that androgynous persons are "better prepared to participate in oral communication situations" (p. 126).

It appears that the androgynous person possesses unique communication skills. Wheeless and Duran (1982) explain this uniqueness in terms of adaptability, saying the androgynous person has a wider repertoire of behaviors from which to draw. Bem (1974) addresses the adaptability idea in stating that androgynous people exhibit behaviors that are "both masculine and feminine, both assertive and yielding, both instrumental and expressive—depending on the situational appropriateness of these behaviors" (p. 155). Therefore, the androgynous individual not only has a variety of behaviors in which to engage, but also exercises discretion in exhibiting certain behaviors in certain situations. Proof of this assertion exists in research results.

Androgynous persons have been found to be interpersonally flexible and more behaviorally flexible than non-androgynous persons (Bem, 1974, 1975; Bem & Lenney, 1976; Wiggins & Holzmuller, 1981). Wheeless and Lashbrook (1982) state the following:

It is our belief that the degree to which a person is seen by self or others as androgynous is a measure of his/her willingness to adapt to the gender orientation of another or, and importantly, to the situations that require something other than a typical gender-based response (p. 30).

This behavioral flexibility and adaptability, then, yields positive outcomes for the androgynous individual, such as being perceived by others as more socially desirable (Lee, 1982) and as more attractive (Rotter & O'Connell, 1982). The androgynous person's ability to adapt to others might require him/her to engage in behaviors that may not be stereotypic of his/her biological sex. Unlike sex–typed persons, the androgynous person is not as securely locked into a sex–role stereotype; thus androgynous people have a greater number of cognitive schemata for processing gender–related information.

With regard to perceptions of sexual harassment, we may find a relationship with an individual's gender orientation. Biological sex differences in the perception of sexual harassment have been studied and reveal a tendency for women to be more sensitive than men to this type of communication. Women are also more likely to label it as harassing (Booth–Butterfield, 1983; Collins & Blodgett, 1982; Gutek, 1985; Powell, 1986; Reilly et al., 1982; Remland & Jones, 1982; Tangri et al., 1982).

While men are generally less likely to perceive this communication phenomenon, we might expect androgynous and cross–sex–typed (feminine) males to be more sensitive to sexual harassment than sex–typed (masculine) males. The same holds true for androgynous and cross–sex–typed (masculine) females over sex–typed (feminine) females. The question of sex role identity and definitions of sexual harassment has recently been addressed by Powell (1986) who found the opposite of this reasoning. In his study, subjects' femininity had an effect on their definitions of sexual harassment. Powell's method comes under scrutiny in comparison to this study. Powell (1986) used a "Which of the following, if any, do you feel is 'sexual harassment' in the workplace? Check all that apply" approach (p. 12). He listed ten behaviors (e.g. sexual remarks meant to be complimentary, sexual touching/grabbing/brushing). It appears that Powell could have significantly influenced subjects' responses with his method (i.e. terminology, format). He labeled the behaviors as sexual a priori, which does not leave room for the subjects' interpretation. Powell's method was directed toward *defining* sexual harassment where this method is aimed at the *communication* of sexual harassment.

Females may not be as likely to label the attention as harassment for several reasons. Feminine females are "predisposed to try to interpret male attention as flattery" (Tangri, et al., 1982, p. 40). Femininity is negatively related to the ability to decode nonverbal cues (Isenhart, 1980). Rosenthal and DePaulo (1979) found that females lose their decoding advantage over males when cues are sent from leaky channels. The researchers suggest that women may lose their advantage because they are more polite when decoding. Feminine females may be especially concerned with manners and courtesy. One could expect that they would refrain from labeling some of the less severe descriptions of behavior as sexually harassing communication. Further, a person's feminist attitudes can determine whether or not certain behaviors are identified as sexually harassing (Schneider, 1982). This is another reason for these expectations.

Another way to look at an individual's gender orientation is to consider the concepts of assertiveness, responsiveness, and versatility (Richmond & McCroskey, 1985). These three elements relate directly to Bem's (1974) masculine (instrumental), feminine (expressive), and androgynous orientations along the dimensions by which they are defined. Bem's conceptualization of masculinity (e.g. willing to take a stand, analytical, takes charge) is very similar to the construct of assertiveness. Femininity and androgyny correspond with the responsiveness and versatility dimensions as defined by Richmond and McCroskey. One can see the similarities by studying Richmond and McCroskey's (1985) working definitions for each of these elements of communication:

Assertiveness is the capacity to make requests, actively disagree, express positive or negative personal rights and feelings, initiate, maintain, or disengage from conversations, and stand up for one's self without attacking another (p. 69).

Responsiveness is the capacity to be sensitive to the communication of others, to be seen as a good listener, to make others comfortable in communicating, and to recognize the needs and desires of others (p. 70).

Versatility is the capacity to be *appropriately* assertive and *appropriately* responsive, depending on the situation (p. 71).

The relationship between Bem's (1974) concepts and these are evident. Based on the work of Wheeless and Dierks–Stewart (1981) Richmond and McCroskey (1985) developed the Assertiveness–Responsiveness Measure (see Appendix B). It measures an individual's endorsement of assertive or responsive behaviors. Throughout the remainder of this study the term "assertiveness" will be used to reference a masculine gender orientation, "responsive" will reference a feminine gender orientation, and "versatile" will reference an androgynous orientation. Based on the literature discussed to this point, the following research questions are proposed:

RQ1: Will gender orientation be associated with significant differences in the perception of sexual harassment?

RQ2: Will gender orientation and the tendency to perceive behaviors as sexually harassing have an effect on job satisfaction?

Method

Subjects and Procedures

Respondents in the study were 659 undergraduates enrolled in basic speech communication courses at an eastern university. Subjects in each class section received a packet comprised of several questionnaires, including the Perception of Sexual Harassment Scale (Booth–Butterfield, 1983), the Assertiveness – Responsiveness Measure (Richmond & McCroskey, 1985), and the Job Descriptive Index (Smith, Kendall, & Hulin, 1969).[1] The subjects were asked to read the instructions preceding each of the scales, to complete the scales in class and to return them to their instructor when they were through. The students who participated in the study received credit for completion of the survey as part of regular class activity.

The respondents (students) were asked to measure their satisfaction with aspects of their current or most recent job (see Appendix C). If a student had never been employed, his/her responses were eliminated from the data analysis. The perception of Sexual Harassment Scale does not measure whether or not a person has been a *victim* of sexual harassment on a particular job, it measures only his/her *perception* of the phenomenon in a work environment. In other words, the approach is "If confronted with, or if you were to observe, the following behavior in the workplace, would you perceive/label it as sexually harassing communication?"

Independent Measures

Two Likert–type format instruments were used to measure the independent variables in this investigation. Both are five–point self–report scales.

Perception of Sexual Harassment.

A 24–item Perception of Sexual Harassment Scale, developed and validated by Booth–Butterfield (1983) was used to assess subjects' tendency to perceive behaviors as sexually harassing communication (see Appendix A). The response format ranges from non–harassing (1) to extremely harassing (5) communication. The two factors extracted from a quartimax rotation are (1) items describing behaviors which "tend to be direct verbal or nonverbal communication where the meaning is focused on target" (p. 19), and (2) items describing behaviors which "tend to be less directly aimed at the subject and more ambiguous in intent than items loading on Factor 1" (p.19). In other words, the items measure behaviors which fall on a continuum from specific, target–centered communication, to less specifically directed communication. This scale is not correlated with the Crowne–Marlowe Social Desirability Scale (r = .087), with Lennox and Wolf's (1984) Self–Monitoring Scale (r = .03), or with McCroskey's (1982) Personal Report of Communication Apprehension – 24 (PRCA–24), r = –.03. Reliability for this scale = .83.

Gender Orientation.

A 20–item Assertiveness–Responsiveness Measure developed by Richmond and McCroskey (1985) was employed to assess subjects' psychological gender orientation (see Appendix B). Half of the items are assertiveness items, while the remaining 10 items measure responsiveness. Both dimensions of this scale appear reliable (e.g. assertiveness = .84, responsiveness = .86). The assertiveness, responsiveness, and versatility concepts parallel Bem's concepts of masculinity, femininity, and androgyny, but focus more directly on communication implications.

Dependent Measure

One seven-point, Likert-type instrument was used to measure job satisfaction, the dependent variable used in this investigation. The Job Descriptive Index (JDI) developed by Smith, Kendall, and Hulin (1969) measured subjects' satisfaction with five dimensions of their current or most recent job. The JDI measures satisfaction with supervision, the work itself, pay, promotion, and co-workers. The adapted version of the JDI employed in this study was the same one used by Richmond and McCroskey (1979). These researchers submitted the scale to factor analysis and subsequently eliminated 14 of the 72 original items because the factor analysis indicated that the items did not load at .50 or higher. Identical factor structures were obtained with the 14 items deleted. All dimensions of this version of the JDI appear reliable, supervision = .92; work = .80; pay = .86; promotion = .80; co-workers = .85 (Richmond & McCroskey, 1979).

Data Analyses

All data analyses were performed using the SAS statistical package. First, t-tests were computed to determine if means of the perception of sexual harassment and means of assertiveness and responsiveness differed significantly for males and females. Second, two multiple regression analyses using a general linear model procedure were conducted. The first regression was to aid in determining the degree to which gender orientation and perception of sexual harassment contribute to the multiple prediction of one's level of job satisfaction. The second regression was to provide the degree to which responsiveness and assertiveness contribute to the prediction of one's tendency to perceive sexual harassment. Probabilities were set at .05 for for all tests of statistical significance.

Results

The results of the t-test for perception of sexual harassment and gender indicated significant differences in males and females tendency to perceive communication behaviors as sexually harassing (male mean = 74.4, female mean = 81.6, $t = -11.29$, $p < .0001$). Significant mean differences were also found in males' and females' responsiveness and assertiveness. The t-test for responsiveness revealed the following: male mean = 38.3, female mean = 41.9, $t = -9.67$, $p < .0001$). The results of the t-test for assertiveness are as follows: male mean = 36.7, female mean = 35.2, $t = 3.31$, $p < .001$).

The results of the first multiple regression analysis revealed a significant prediction only for one's level of satisfaction with co-workers. In this model, the predictor variables were responsiveness, assertiveness, and perception of sexual harassment. The criterion variable was satisfaction with co-workers. This overall model was significant and accounted for 3% of the variance (F = 7.20, d.f. = 3/627, p< .0001). Responsiveness was the only significant predictor of satisfaction with co-workers, accounting for 3% of the sequential variance (F = 19.24, d.f. = 3/627, p < .0001).

The results of the second multiple regression analysis revealed responsiveness as a significant predictor of one's tendency to perceive sexual harassment. In this model the predictor variables were responsiveness and assertiveness. The criterion variable was perception of sexual harassment. The overall model was significant and accounted for 8% of the variance (F = 26.07, d.f. 2/644, p < .0001). Responsiveness was a significant predictor of one's tendency to perceive communication as sexually harassing, accounting for 7% of the sequential variance (F = 50.64, d.f. = 2/644, p < .0001).

Discussion

The results revealed that there is a difference between males' and females' tendency to label communication behaviors as sexual harassment. Specifically, females are more likely than males to perceive sexual harassment. This result is consistent with previous research reports (Booth–Butterfield, 1983; Collins & Blodgett, 1982; Reilly et al., 1982; Powell, 1986; Remland & Jones, 1985; Tangri et al., 1982). Females were also significantly more responsive than males, and males exceeded females on assertiveness. These results reaffirm sex role expectations such that most of the sample was comprised of assertive males and responsive females.

The first research question (Will gender orientation be associated with significant differences in the perception of sexual harassment?) was answered with the results of the second multiple regression analysis. Subjects' responsiveness had a significant effect on their perceptions of sexual harassment such that responsive individuals labeled more communication behaviors as harassing than did assertive individuals. Although no formal hypothesis was stated, this result is not indicative of what was expected. It was previously reasoned that females' responsiveness would not account for a higher tendency to perceive sexual harassment. However, this expectation was focused on responsive females' labeling of less severe descriptions of behavior. In addition, responsiveness in *males* was expected to be related to higher perceptions of sexual harassment. A more detailed data analysis, including interaction effects, may reveal results along these lines.

It is impossible to ignore the similarity of this result to the one obtained by Powell (1986). He found femininity to have a minor effect on subjects' definitions of sexual harassment. Regardless of Powell's emphasis on defining sexual harassment and this study's focus on the communication of it, responsiveness appears to make individuals more sensitive to this phenomenon than does assertiveness.

It may be possible that responsive individuals are more likely than assertive individuals to have sexually harassing communication directed toward them. They may be targets more often because they are open to communication and are not assertive. Highly responsive individuals who lack assertiveness may not express feelings of distaste for the communication directed at them. Failure to confront sources of sexually harassing communication could contribute to the perpetuation of such communication and, subsequently, to responsive individuals' higher tendency to label it as harassing. The amount of variance obtained is small (8%), but this result is highly significant, indicating the effect for responsiveness on perceptions of sexual harassment. However, the significant differences between males' and females' perceptions of sexual harassment as evidenced by the t–test show that the effect for gender is stronger than the effect for psychological gender orientation. It appears that gender is the greatest overall predictor of an individual's tendency to perceive sexual harassment.

The second research question was addressed with the first multiple regression analysis. Gender orientation and the tendency to perceive behaviors as sexually harassing had no effect on overall job satisfaction. Of the five dimensions of satisfaction measured by the JDI (Smith, Kendall, & Hulin, 1969), satisfaction with co–workers was found to be predicted by responsiveness. Although the effect is small, responsiveness accounted for all of the obtained variance (3%), leaving no prediction of co–worker satisfaction in terms of perception of sexual harassment. The failure of the sexual harassment variable to account for variance in this model may be due to the method of data analysis. It is interesting, though, that responsiveness had a significant effect on satisfaction with co–workers. Perhaps one's level of responsiveness allows one to appreciate others and see them as desirable to work with. Responsive people are more affiliative and concerned with developing interpersonal relationships, including on–the–job relationships. They are able to recognize the needs and desires of others. If the responsive person can fill those needs of others, he/she will likely be working with content people and therefore view them as satisfying to work with.

The small amount of variance obtained in this regression analysis (3%) suggests that satisfaction with co–workers may be related to variables other than the ones investigated in this study. This suggestion extends to overall job satisfaction such that it may be better explained by exploring other variables. The results obtained from this study are not generalizable at this point. Interaction analyses may offer more conclusive, generalizable results.

It is clear, though, that gender is significantly related to perceptions of sexual harassment. Organizations should be aware of the discrepancy in males' and females' perceptions of this communication phenomenon. Some incidents of sexual harassment occur with intent on the source's part; some isolated interactions may be labeled as sexual harassment by a woman while the man was unaware that he was offending her. Future endeavors need to address how this discrepancy can be incorporated into definitions of sexual harassment and legal guidelines.

Reference Note

1. This study was part of the author's Master's Thesis which investigated the relationships among gender orientation, argumentativeness, perception of sexual harassment, and level of job satisfaction. The thesis is filed with Marcia A. Verbeeck as author.

References

Abbey, A. (1982). Sex differences in attributions for friendly behavior: Do males misperceive females' friendliness? *Journal of Personality and Social Psychology, 42*, 830–838.

Bem, S.L. (1974). The measurement of psychological androgyny. *Journal of Consulting and Clinical Psychology, 42*, 155–162.

Bem, S.L. (1975). Sex role adaptability: One consequence of psychological androgyny. *Journal of Personality and Social Psychology, 31*, 634–643.

Bem, S.L., & Lenney, E. (1976). Sex typing and the avoidance of cross–sex behavior. *Journal of Personality and Social Psychology, 33*, 48–54.

Benson, D.J., & Thomson, G.E. (1982). Sexual harassment on a university campus: The confluence of authority relations, sexual interest and gender stratification. *Social Problems, 29*, 236–251.

Booth–Butterfield, M. (1983). *Empirical investigation of sexually harassing communication*. Paper presented at the annual meeting of the Speech Communication Association. Washington, D.C.

Booth–Butterfield, M. (1984). *Predicting perception of sexually harassing communication within a communication script framework: A four–part model*. Paper presented at the Conference on Communication, Language and Gender. Oxford, OH.

Brewer, M. (1982). Further beyond nine to five: An integration and future directions. *Journal of Social Issues, 38*, 149–158.

Brewer, M.B., & Berk, R.A. (1982). Beyond nine to five: Introduction. *Journal of Social Issues, 38,* 1–4.

Brodsky, C.M. (1976). *The harassed worker*. Lexington, MA: Lexington Books.

Collins, E., & Blodgett T. (1981). Sexual harassment: Some see it . . . some won't. *Harvard Business Review, 59*, 76–96.

Ellis, D.G., & McCallister, L. (1980). Relational control sequences in sex–typed and androgynous groups. *Western Journal of Speech Communication, 44*, 35–49.

Equal Employment Opportunity Commission. (1980). Interpretative guidelines on sexual harassment. *Federal Register, 45*, [219], 74676–74677.

Greenblatt, L., Hasenauer, J.E., & Freimuth, V.S. (1980). Psychological sex type and androgyny in the study of communication variables: Self–disclosure and communication apprehension. *Human Communication Research, 6*, 117–129.

Gutek, B.A., & Morasch, B. (1982). Sex–ratios, sex–role spillover, and sexual harassment of women at work. *Journal of Social Issues, 38*, 55–74.

Hall, J.A. (1978). Gender effects in decoding nonverbal cues. *Psychological Bulletin, 85,* 845–857.

Isenhart, M.W. (1980). An investigation of the relationship of sex and sex role to the ability to decode nonverbal cues. *Human Communication Research, 6,* 309–318.

Jensen, I.W., & Gutek, B.A. (1982). Attributions and assignment of responsibility in sexual harassment. *Journal of Social Issues, 38,* 121–136.

Lee, A.G. (1982). Psychological androgyny and social desirability. *Journal of Personality Assessment, 46,* 147–152.

MacKinnon, C.A. (1979). *Sexual harassment of working women.* New Haven, CT: Yale Press.

Miller, G.R. (1984). Some (moderately) apprehensive thoughts on avoiding communication. In J.A. Daly & J.C. McCroskey (Eds.), *Avoiding communication: Shyness, reticence, and communication apprehension.* Beverly Hills: Sage Publications.

Petersen, D.J., & Massengill, D. (1982). Sexual harassment – a growing problem in the workplace. *Personnel Administrator, 52,* 79–89.

Powell, G.N. (1986). Effects of sex role identity and sex on definitions of sexual harassment. *Sex Roles, 14,* 9–19.

Reilly, T., Carpenter, S., Dull, V., & Bartlett, K. (1982). The factorial survey: An approach to defining sexual harassment on campus. *Journal of Social Issues, 38,* 99–110.

Remland, M.S., & Jones, T.S. (1985). Sex differences, communication consistency, and judgments of sexual harassment in a performance appraisal interview. *Southern Speech Communication Journal, 50,* 156–176.

Renick, J.C. (1980). Sexual harassment at work: Why it happens, what to do about it. *Personnel Journal, 59,* 658–662.

Richmond, V.P., & McCroskey, J.C. (1979). The impact of communication apprehension on individuals in organizations. *Communication Quarterly,* 55–61.

Richmond, V.P., & McCroskey, J.C. (1985). *Communication: Apprehension, avoidance, and effectiveness.* Scottsdale, AZ: Gorsuch Scarisbrick.

Rosenthal, R., & DePaulo, B.M. (1979). Sex differences in eavesdropping on nonverbal cues. *Journal of Personality and Social Psychology, 37,* 273–285.

Rotter, N.G., & O'Connell, A.N. (1982). The relationships among sex–role orientation, cognitive complexity, and tolerance for ambiguity. *Sex Roles, 8,* 1209–1220.

Schneider, B.E. (1982). Consciousness about sexual harassment among heterosexual and lesbian women workers. *Journal of Social Issues, 38*, 75–98.

Smith, P.C., Kendall, L.M., & Hulin, C.L. (1969). *The measurement of satisfaction in work and retirement.* Chicago: Rand McNally.

Spence, J.T., Helmreich, R., & Stapp, J. (1975). Ratings of self and peers on sex–role attributes and their relation to self–esteem and conceptions of masculinity and femininity. *Journal of Personality and Social Psychology, 32*, 29–39.

Tangri, S.S., Burt, M.R., & Johnson, L.B. (1982). Sexual harassment at work: Three explanatory models. *Journal of Social Issues, 38*, 33–54.

Wheeless, V.E., & Dierks–Stewart, K. (1981). The psychometric properties of the Bem sex–role inventory: Questions concerning reliability and validity. *Communication Quarterly, 29*, 173–186.

Wheeless, V.E., & Lashbrook, W.B. (October 1985). Style and interpersonal communication. Unpublished manuscript, Morgantown, WV: West Virginia University.

Wiggins, J.S., & Holzmuller, A. (1981). Further evidence on androgyny and interpersonal flexibility. *Journal of Research in Personality, 15*, 67–80.

Appendix A

The following statements describe on–the–job situations which may or may not be perceived as harassing. Put the number that best fits *your perception* of the described situation in the blank before the statement.

1	2	3	4	5
non–harassing communication				extremely harassing communication

_____ 1. A prospective employer insists that you spend a weekend with him/her before final hiring.

_____ 2. Your job evaluations begin dropping after you refuse to date your manager. As far as you can discern your behavior has changed in no other way.

_____ 3. Your boss repeatedly touches your shoulder, arm, or hand when giving you instructions.

_____ 4. Your supervisor smiles at you every time you pass by his/her desk.

_____ 5. Your opposite–sex employer makes sexual comments and innuendoes about people when you are present.

_____ 6. Your manager stands very close to you often brushing against you whenever you talk in the office. The person doesn't do this with others in the organization.

_____ 7. Whenever you work late there are invitations to continue at a local drinking establishment or elsewhere.

_____ 8. A promotion is promised if you spend the night with your supervisor.

_____ 9. Your manager sometimes puts sexual cartoons or suggestive pictures on your desk for you to see.

_____ 10. Your supervisor often calls you sexy "pet names."

_____ 11. Your boss often pats you on the bottom in passing or as a greeting.

_____ 12. Two managers enter the meeting room and come over to sit next to you.

_____ 13. Your employer's eyes scan your body as you discuss a business arrangement.

_____ 14. As you go to work each day there are workers who whistle, hoot, or make gestures as you go past.

_____ 15. Your boss consistently cracks sexual jokes while around you after you have expressed your distaste for this practice.

_____ 16. Your manager puts his/her arms around your waist and tries to kiss you as you're working late one afternoon.

_____ 17. You have just been awarded a departmental honor. Your department head (opposite sex) congratulates you with a hug.

_____ 18. While explaining a task, your supervisor places your hand between his or her legs.

_____ 19. A superior in the organization suggests that you would progress faster in the company (or get better grades) if you were physically friendlier with them.

_____ 20. Your employer consistently gazes at your body, looking you up and down as you walk past. This makes you uncomfortable.

_____ 21. Your boss questions you about your weekend plans.

_____ 22. Your female or male manager continually pressures you for a date even though you have explained that you aren't interested.

_____ 23. Though you are uncomfortable with the topic, your supervisor regularly discusses sexual matters with you and questions you about your sexual activities.

_____ 24. In an elevator with your employer he/she starts a conversation.

Appendix B

Please indicate the degree to which you believe each of the characteristics listed below applies to you while interacting with others by marking whether you (5) strongly agree, (4) agree, (3) are undecided, (2) disagree, or (1) strongly disagree that it applies. There are no right or wrong answers. Work quickly and just record your first impression.

____	1.	helpful	____	11. dominant
____	2.	defends own beliefs	____	12. sincere
____	3.	independent	____	13. gentle
____	4.	responsive to others	____	14. willing to take a stand
____	5.	forceful	____	15. warm
____	6.	has strong personality	____	16. tender
____	7.	sympathetic	____	17. friendly
____	8.	compassionate	____	18. acts as a leader
____	9.	assertive	____	19. aggressive
____	10.	sensitive to the needs of others	____	20. competitive

APPENDIX C

The purpose of this questionnaire is to measure *your satisfaction with five aspects of your current or most recent job*. Please respond using the seven point scale that is specified below.

1	2	3	4	5	6	7
strongly disagree	disagree	somewhat disagree	neutral or uncertain	somewhat agree	agree	strongly agree

MY IMMEDIATE SUPERVISOR
___1. Asks my advice
___2. Hard to please
___3. Impolite
___4. Praises good work
___5. Tactful
___6. Influential
___7. Up-to-date
___8. Quick-tempered
___9. Tells me where I stand
___10. Annoying
___11. Stubborn
___12. Knows job well
___13. Bad
___14. Intelligent
___15. Lazy
___16. Around when needed

WORK
___17. Fascinating
___18. Satisfying
___19. Boring
___20. Good
___21. Creative
___22. Respected
___23. Pleasant
___24. Useful
___25. Tiresome
___26. Frustrating
___27. Gives sense of accomplishment

PAY
___28. Income adequate for normal expenses
___29. Satisfactory profit sharing
___30. Barely live on income
___31. Bad
___32. Income provides luxuries
___33. Insecure
___34. Less than I deserve
___35. Highly paid
___36. Underpaid

PROMOTIONS
___37. Good opportunity for advancement
___38. Opportunity somewhat limited
___39. Promotion on ability
___40. Dead-end job
___41. Good chance for promotion
___42. Unfair promotion policy
___43. Infrequent promotions
___44. Regular promotion
___45. Fairly good chance for promotion

CO-WORKERS
___46. Stimulating
___47. Boring
___48. Slow
___49. Ambitious
___50. Stupid
___51. Responsible
___52. Fast
___53. Intelligent
___54. Easy to make enemies
___55. Talk too much
___56. Smart
___57. Lazy
___58. Unpleasant
___59. No privacy
___60. Active
___61. Narrow interests
___62. Loyal
___63. Hard to meet

The data for this study were collected at West Virginia University as part of the author's Master's Thesis(filed with author as Marcia A. Verbeeck).

THOUGHT PROVOKERS

What factors may account for a discrepancy between male and female perceptions of sexual harassment? If females are more likely to perceive sexual harassment on the job, what communication skills are necessary to confront the problems that arise from this discrepancy in perceptions?

CHAPTER FOURTEEN

Male and Female Managers in the 21st Century: Will There Be a Difference?

Linda McCallister
California State University, Long Beach
and
Donald L. Gaymon
Gaymon Resource Management Corporation

In this century, the single most important sociological change affecting the work environment has been the entrance of women into the paying labor force. Women made an initial, but temporary, entrance into the labor force during World War I. After the war, women returned to their jobs as full–time homemakers, and men returned to their jobs and the role of "family bread–winner." During World War II, women returned to the paying labor force, but after the war, many of the women stayed. The number of women in the paying labor force has steadily increased since that time. We now live in a society where men *and* women work. We live in a society where the dual–income family and the female head–of–the–household family is the rule rather than the exception to the rule. This dramatic change brings to light one of the most crucial questions facing organizational America: *What is the relationship between home and work?*

During the 1970's women began moving out of the traditional female professions (nursing, teaching, and secretarial positions) and they began competing for supervisory, management, and male–dominated professional positions. A recent report issued by the U.S. Government Printing Office reveals that women tripled their representation in management positions during the last decade. They also increased their representation in the following professions:

Profession	1970	1980
Dentists	3.5%	6.7%
Doctors	9.7%	13.4%
Economists	15.9%	29.7%
Lawyers	4.9%	13.8%
Judges	8.1%	17.1%

In all probability, a 1987 census might reveal that these figures have doubled. Women are in the paying labor force to stay, and they work for the same reasons men work: (1) to support their families; and (2) to achieve self–actualization.

Michael Keeley (1983) chastises theorists and educators for not responding to—or even recognizing—these societal changes. He raises provocative questions with respect to the basic values in organizational theory and management education; despite claims to the contrary, he contends that values are entailed in general goal models of organization. He suggests that "organizational goals and their attainment are not, in the final analysis, the most important private concerns." He illustrates how, under a goal–model of organizations, Albert Speer, Hitler's Minister for Armaments and War Productions, would be considered as an efficient and productive organizational leader.

Keeley asserts that the needs of the individual and the "preservation of voluntariness" are basic problems in any organization—more basic than goal attainment. He further asserts that individual interests and voluntariness are much too important to be taken for granted. He suggests that a contract model of organizations is an alternative to goal–seeking models because the contract model takes into account individual interests and the idea that individual "rights" might form the basis for organizational solutions. He concludes that the key theoretical question to be answered with respect to organizations is:

What concrete rights would self–interested participants agree to recognize if they were in a position to negotiate freely a set of rules for mutual benefit?

This paper attempts to provide some initial answers to this question and examines the role of sex in determining those answers.

Purpose of the Study

This study attempts to identify prevailing goals and values of young male and female workers/managers. Because it is often suggested that environmental changes, including the widespread presence of working mothers, have produced a generation of individuals who simply expect equal opportunity for men and women in the workplace, this study explores the possibility of unisex work attitudes among 21st century managers.

Specifically, 340 male and female workers/managers who live or lived in a home with a working mother, were asked to complete sentences about home and work. The messages were content analyzed to determine prevailing attitudes and beliefs of a group of individuals who are most likely to be in upper management as we enter the year 2000. This paper reports the results of that content analysis with respect to four revealing questions, and provides some answers to the question: Will there be a difference in the 21st century?

Research Questions

This study attempts to provide answers with respect to the concept of voluntariness as advanced by Keeley (1983). The specific research questions addressed are:

1. What aspects of work do the new generation of workers value?
2. Does sex have an impact on work values?
3. Given a choice, will modern workers adhere to a goal–model of organization or a contract model of organization?
4. Does sex affect the model of choice?
5. Have societal changes brought about unisex attitudes in the workplace?

Sample and Research Design

The sample consisted of 168 females and 172 males with work experience and supervisory or management experience. All subjects had working mothers. The female population consisted of 140 undergraduate, business administration majors and 28 MBA candidates. The male population consisted of 104 undergraduate, business administration majors and 68 MBA candidates. The mean age for both populations was 24.

The subjects were asked to complete a questionnaire that contained 15 statements that dealt with various aspects of home and work. The subjects were asked to complete the statements, and the messages produced by the subjects were content analyzed. The results with respect to four of the statements are presented here. The four statements analyzed for the purpose of this study are:

1. The thing I like MOST about my job is ...
2. The thing I like LEAST about my job is ...
3. If I could be or do anything I wanted, I would ...
4. My experiences and observations lead me to believe that:
   Men make better managers _____
   Women make better managers _____

I believe this because ...

A grounded theory (Glaser and Straus, 1976) approach to content analysis was utilized. Grounded theory suggests that the category system should emerge from the data; thus, the category system becomes part of the results. Open coding procedures (McCallister & O'Brian, 1987) guided the construction of content categories. The coding unit was defined as a thought sequence which may have a subject and predicate but does not necessarily have to be a complete sentence. The context unit was defined as the entire message produced by the subject. Add content categories were mutually exclusive: a thought sequence (coding unit) could only be coded into one category, but it was possible to have more than one thought sequence in a given message (the context unit).

Results

Six categories emerged from the messages produced by subjects in response to the statements: The thing I like MOST about my job and the thing I like LEAST about my job. An additional seventh category emerged from the messages produced in response to the statement: The thing I like LEAST about my job. The categories are defined in Table 1.

Table 1
Liking and Disliking Category System

Category:	Definition:
Independence/Autonomy	These statements make reference to working alone, independently, or with the ability to make autonomous decisions. Personal control of the work environment was frequently cited as a MOST valued work aspect, and bureaucracy and/or organizational control was frequently cited as the LEAST valued work aspect.
Challenge/Creativity	These statements actually use the words challenge and creativity; these statements make reference to the ability to be innovative; and these statements suggest that tasks are stimulating. LEAST liked statements make reference to the lack of challenger and/or creativity.
Task/Job Scope	These statements make actual reference to the variety and diversity of the tasks that are performed and/or the ability to successfully complete a given task. LEAST liked statements make reference to the lack of variety, lack of diversity, the boring nature of the work, and the negative/down aspects of the task activities. In short, these are statements that made reference to the actual work being performed.
People	These statements make direct reference people (workers, managers, customers) as a positive aspect of work. LEAST liked statements make reference to people as a negative aspect of work.
Salary/Benefits	These statements make direct reference to money earned, employee benefits, and hours. LEAST liked statements also include reference to working conditions.
Authority and Status	These statements make direct reference to organizational status and/or authority over others.
Managerial Incompetence	These statements only emerged in the LEAST liked category, and they make direct reference to the manager's inability to manage effectively.

The results reported in Table 1 suggest that men and women have similar attitudes regarding the work they perform. Men and women report that they value people, job scope, and salary in their jobs.

Table 2 reports the frequency with which the most liked work value categories appeared in the messages produced by male and female subjects.

Table 2

MOST LIKED Work Value Categories: Frequency of Occurrence

	Scope	People	Salary	Independence	Challenge	Authority
Females	27%	37%	16%	14%	10%	6%
Males	22%	23%	22%	19%	12%	8%

Graph 1 visually illustrates preference differences between males and females with respect to the things they value most in their jobs.

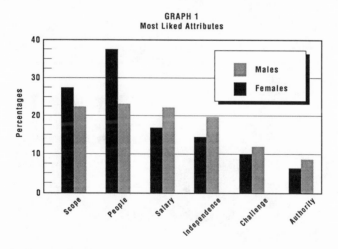

GRAPH 1
Most Liked Attributes

Graph 1 illustrates that women value people and job scope more than they value salary and benefits. Men appear to value people and job scope less than their female counterparts, and they appear to value salary more than their female counterparts.

In stating what they liked most about their jobs, females mentioned the people—their colleagues, managers, and customers. Females also reported that the job scope significantly contributed to the positive aspects of the job. Men reported that people, salary, and job scope equally contributed to the positive aspects of the job; however, they valued people and job scope less than their female counterparts.

Table 3 reports the frequency with which LEAST liked work value categories appeared in the messages produced by male and female subjects.

Table 3

LEAST LIKED Work Value Categories: Frequency of Occurrence

	Scope	People	Salary	Independence	Challenge	Authority Man. Inc.
Females	46%	25%	16%	3%	3%	5%
Males	35%	19%	22%	7%	4%	5%

The results reported in Table 3 suggest that men and women agree on the negative attributes of a job. Job scope, people, and salary are most frequently cited by male and female subjects as negative aspects of the job.

Graph 2 visually illustrates preference differences between males and females with respect to the things they dislike in their jobs.

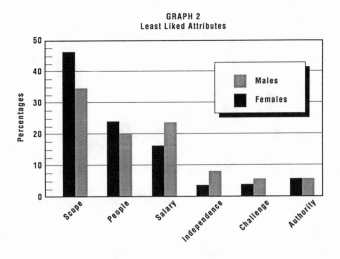

GRAPH 2
Least Liked Attributes

Graph 2 illustrates that men and women report that job scope is the single most important factor contributing to their dissatisfaction with their jobs. Women, however, identify job scope more frequently than do their male counterparts. Women report that people are the second most important factor contributing to their job dissatisfaction, while men report that salary is the second most important factor contributing to their dissatisfaction. People rank third in importance for men, whereas, salary ranks third in importance for women.

Research Question One:

Research question one sought to identify work values of the new generation of workers. In this research, the new generation of workers reported that they are most concerned with the scope of the job, the people they work with, and the compensation they receive for the work they produced. The new generation of workers want a job they enjoy, people they enjoy working with, and a comfortable salary.

Research Question Two:

Research question two sought to identify differences between male and female workers. Males and females alike were most concerned with the scope of the job. Job scope significantly contributes to male and female satisfaction and dissatisfaction with the job. Women, however, cite job scope more frequently as a factor of job satisfaction and job dissatisfaction than do their male counterparts.

The most obvious difference between males and females can be attributed to the value placed on people and salary/benefits. Job scope and salary/benefits contribute to male job dissatisfaction, and job scope and people contribute to female job dissatisfaction. On the other hand, salary/benefits, job scope, and people contribute equally to job satisfaction for men. For women, however, salary/benefits was a distant third with respect to job satisfaction. This could mean that women are not as concerned with hygiene factors (Herzberg, 1968) or it could mean that they aren't receiving enough money to cite it as a reason for liking their jobs.

This research suggests that people—or the human relations factor—is of considerable importance to women. Human relations are also important to men, but not to the same degree. This becomes important as the responses to the third and fourth statements are analyzed.

Preferred Male and Female Work Options

Five categories emerged from the messages produced by subjects in response to the statement: If I could be or do anything I wanted, I would ...The category system is comprised of five themes that reveal personal values and organizational goals. The categories are defined in Table 4.

Table 4
Preferred Work Options Category System

Category:	Definition:
Short Term Goals	These statements express a desire to do something immediate and/or something which appears to be easily attainable. Two types of short term goals are expressed: 1. Home/Personal Goals: (i.e. Take leave from work and complete my studies; and, Get along better with my girlfriends). 2. Work/Career: (i.e., Work for a large corporation; and, Continue my present position until I feel unchallenged then look elsewhere for opportunities).
Entreprenueral Goals	These statements express a desire to own a business or corporation; they express a desire to be a professional with no mention of association with a firm or organization and the profession requires advanced education; they express creative or artistic desires. These statements indicate the career is within the individual and is independent of some large complex organization controlled by others. Examples: Be an entrepreneur; Have my own small business; Own my own CPA firm; and, Be a writer/author, doctor, or lawyer.
Leadership Goals	These statements express a desire to attain a position of leadership within some organization. These positions are not entry level and are not considered easily or immediately attainable given the ages of the subjects in this sample. Examples: Be President; Be C.E.O. for a major development corporation; and, Be an executive in a large corporation that has good benefits and programs for employers.
Fantasy Goals	These statements express a desire to be rich and famous with no mention of a firm or organization; they express a desire to be rich and famous without working; and/or they express a desire to become a professional athlete or movie star. (Given the population tested, these last two goals are considered fantasies and not positions that these people are likely to achieve). Examples: Be a movie star and a musician and later unite the world under a common purpose of love; Be center fielder for the New York Yankees; Be a millionaire; Be pitching for the New York Mets; Travel the world overspending lavishly; Live in every country in Europe so I can learn different languages and cultures; Be healthy, wealthy, wise and most of all happy; and, Be financially secure without having to work.
Family-Career Goals	These statements express a desire to have a family combined with a career or they just express a desire to have a family. Examples: Be "superwoman" top notch CPA, perfect wife, and mother; and, Be a successfully manager in a large corporation and happily married with three children.

The subject's statements were examined to determine the frequency with which each theme appeared. (The frequencies were converted to percentages because of the uneven sample sizes). Table 5 reports the response patterns found in the messages produced by subjects.

Table 5

Personal Values And Organizational Goals: Responses Patterns

	Values and Goals					
	Sht. Trm.	Entprl.	Org. Lead.	Fantasy	Family	No Res.
BY GENDER						
FEMALE*	20%	34%	15%	20%	02%	9%**
MALE	20%	19%	12%	34%	02%	12%

* Female: n=168
  Male: n=172

**Rows total to 100%
  Categories are mutually exclusive. Percentages indicate the percent
  of messages wherein the response preference is present

Graph 3 visually illustrates the differences associated with sex.

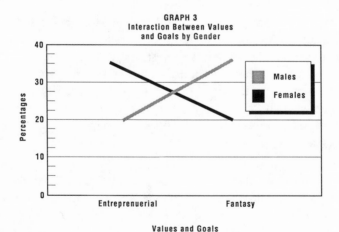

GRAPH 3
Interaction Between Values
and Goals by Gender

Conclusions Regarding Male and Female Goals:

The following statements are offered as a result of the analysis of messages completing the statement: If I could be or do anything I wanted, I would ...

1. No one completed the statement by expressing some greater organizational goal (i.e. I would like to increase profits or productivity for my organization).

2. Everyone expressed goals that would result in some personal benefit or gain.

3. Entrepreneurial goals are the goal of choice for females.

4. Fantasy goals are the goal of choice for males.

5. Fantasy goals for women center on wealth, travel, self–education, and world happiness.

6. Fantasy goals for men center on wealth, fame and heroism.

7. Marriage and children are not expressed goals for males or females.

8. Less than 15% of the male and female populations expressed a desire to achieve a position of leadership within a large organization.

9. Twenty percent of the male and female populations focused on short–term, easily attainable goals as opposed to long–term or higher order goals.

Research Question Three:

Research question three asked if modern workers would, given a choice, adhere to a goal–model of organization or a contract model of organization. These results suggest that the contract model is the model of choice. There is nothing in any of the messages that would suggest a commitment to the greater good of the organization. A commitment may, indeed, be present, but—if and only if—the commitment will produce a personal benefit or gain for the individual.

Research Question Four:

Research question four asked if sex affected the model of choice. The results suggest that the contract model is the model of choice for both males and females regardless of age or education. However, the results also suggest that females choose a professional–success/goals–achievement model, while their male counterparts choose a personal fame/hero–achievement model. This would suggest that when forced to accept an organizational goal–seeking model, females are more likely to adapt and succeed because some degree of professional success can still be achieved and because productivity goals are inherent in the entrepreneurial model.

Given the choice, males would like to be super–heroes who receive fame and attention from the adoring public. This suggests that adherence to the organizational goal–seeking model would be unfulfilling at best.

These results would suggest that women are more likely to find satisfaction in managerial–leadership positions within large organizations because of the emphasis on product oriented achievement. Thus, an analysis of how men and women feel about their roles in management is appropriate.

Men and Women in Management

Research Question Five

Table 6 reports the results of the attitudes regarding men and women in management and provides a preliminary answer to research question five.

Table 6

Attitudes Regarding Men and Women in Management

	Women Better	Men Better	Equal	No Response
TOTAL*	21%	34%	29%	16%
FEMALES**	32%	20%	33%	15%
MALES***	10%	47%	27%	16%

#Rows total to 100%
*n=340
**n=168
***n=172

Graph 4 visually illustrates differing attitudes between males and females with respect to men and women in management.

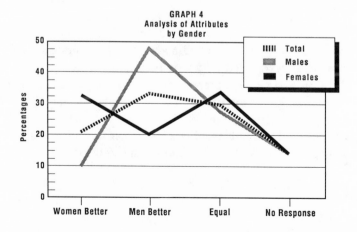

GRAPH 4
Analysis of Attributes
by Gender

Table 6 reports that 21% of all subject stated that WOMEN make better managers; 34% of all subjects stated that MEN make better managers; and 29% of all subjects stated that men and women are EQUAL. This last category is of particular interest because the subjects had to create the category. It was felt that a "men and women are equal" category would have produced a socially desirable response from the subjects so that category was not provided. It was assumed that the degree of socially desirable responses would be decreased and "honest" responses would be increased if the subjects had to create this category.

This initial analysis suggests a shift in attitudes. Prior to 1970, the "men are better" category would have been the socially desirable/acceptable response. A comparison of male and female attitudes provides additional insight into the changing attitudes. Thirty-two percent of the female subjects and 10% of the male subjects reported that women make better managers; 47% of the male subjects and 20% of the female subjects reported that men make better managers; and 33% of the female subjects and 27% of the male subjects reported that men and women are equal with respect to managerial abilities.

The fact that men and women report that men and women are equal with respect to managerial abilities is a definite shift in attitudes. The fact that women and some men report that women are superior to men with respect to managerial abilities is a significant shift in attitudes.

These initial findings would suggest a partial affirmative response to our fifth research question which asked if societal changes have brought about uni-sex attitudes in the workplace. Approximately 30% of the population report that they view men and women as managerial equals. However, 70% of the population still look at sex as a determining factor with respect to managerial competence. An analysis of the messages produced by these subjects provides insight into their reasoning processes and allows for an understanding of the concrete rights recognized by young men and women.

The fourth statement presented to the subjects asked them to indicate if women or men made better managers. They were then asked to complete the statement: I believe this because...

Six critical thinking categories emerged from the messages produced by the subjects. Those categories are defined in Table 7.

Table 7
Critical Thinking Category System

Category:	Definition:
Praise of Male	These statements express some specific behavior displayed by males that makes them better managers.
Praise of Female	These statements express some positive and specific behavior displayed by females that makes them better managers.
Criticism of Males	These statements express some specific behavior displayed by males that indicate they are NOT good managers.
Criticism of Females	These statements express some specific behavior displayed by females that indicate they are NOT good managers.
No Logical Justification	Three types of responses were coded into this category: 1) The lack of a statement of support to justify stated preference (one sex is superior by fiat); 2) Statements that suggest the respondent has not had any experience with one of the sexes, therefore one sex is superior by default; and 3) Statements that indicate quantity causes quality (i.e. there are more male managers therefore they are better).
External Forces	These statements indicate there is something external to the displayed performance of the individual that causes them to be better. There are two types of statements that fall into this category: 1) A statement that suggests evolution or genetic instinct causes one sex to be better than the other. Examples: Women have not stepped up to the same level as men; Men have been managers longer than women; and, Men listen and obey another man before they would listen to a lady. 2) A statement that suggests there are requirements placed on one sex which create or make them better managers. Examples: Women generally have to be more experienced and better at what they do before even being considered for management; and, Women have to work harder to get through all obstacles and that takes determination and other skills beneficial to a good manager.

Table 8 reports the results of the analysis of messages offered in support of the subject's attitudes about men and women in management.

Table 8

Critical Thinking Response Patterns of Subjects Who Stated Men *or* Women Were Better Managers

VERBAL STRATEGIES PRESENT IN MESSAGES

	Praise M	Praise F	Crit. M	Crit. F	No Jus	Ex. Force
Men Better						
FEMALES	42%			28%	14%	28%
MALES	19%			38%	21%	23%
FEMALES BETTER						
FEMALES		53%	18%*		14%	14%
MALES		67%	11%*			20%

COMBINED RESPONSE: Critical of Male + Praise of Females (Criticism of the male never appeared alone without an additional statement in praise of woman).

MEN ARE BETTER:

Table 8 reports that men use an ATTACK STRATEGY to justify their assertion that men are better managers. Thirty–eight percent of the men who felt men were better managers supported their preference by criticizing something women do. Only 19% of the men offered a statement that suggested men actually "do" something that makes them better managers.

Table 5 reports that men use an ATTACK STRATEGY to justify their assertion that men are better managers. Thirty–eight percent of the men who felt men were better managers supported their preferences by criticizing something women do. Only 19% of the men offered a statement that suggested men actually "do" something that makes them better managers.

In addition, 21% of the men who felt men are better managers offered no logical justification—they either stated men are better because there are more men (argument by cause and effect fallacy), or they didn't provide a statement of support (argument by *fiat*).

Finally, 23% of the messages produced by men who report men are better managers made reference to external forces. Primarily, these males suggested a genetic connection—because men have been managers longer than women, they are better managers.

Messages produced by females who state man are better managers tend to praise something males actually "do" with respect to management. These females also support their assertions by criticizing something that women do with respect to management. Their "No

Logical Justification" statements focus on the fact that they have no experience with female managers; therefore, men are better (argument by default). Finally, 28% of the messages produced by females who state men are better managers make reference to external forces (the genetic connection).

Women Are Better:

Verbal strategies produced by males and females who report that women are better managers differ significantly from those reported above. Women who state women are better managers support their assertion by providing a statement that describes a specific, observed behavior (53% Praise of Women). An additional 18% of the messages contained remarks critical of male behaviors, but these remarks were always combined with an additional statement in praise of women. Superiority by fiat was suggested by 14% of the subjects who offered no support for their assertion.

Another 14% of the women who state women are better managers make reference to external forces. These external forces, however, are different from the male external forces. Female external forces refer to the idea that women have to work harder, do more, and have more experience to get the management position, therefore, they are better once they finally make it. Thus, the external forces create a situation where the female manager is actually more qualified for the position than her male counterpart.

Finally, it is important to note that men who state women are better managers use the *same verbal strategies* displayed by their female counterparts. That is, they provided documentation for their assertion (belief) by providing examples and/or illustrations of specific behaviors which help to define their perceptions of "better managers."

Conclusion Regarding Verbal Strategies of Men and Women

The content analysis of the messages produced by all subjects provides additional information about the communication strategies and attitudes of young men and women.

1. Men who state men are better managers tend NOT to provide specific, observed behaviors to support their assertion of male superiority. They make use of generalities and sexual stereotypes to suggest men do something better as managers. They suggest men are stronger, less emotional, and more aggressive. They also say such things as:

   "They handle authority with grace."

   "They have smarts.

   "They are able to put their foot [sic] down."

2. The primary communication strategy utilized by men who state men are better managers is the verbal attack. These men support their assertion of male superiority by attacking

or criticizing some personal female characteristic or activity. Their verbal attacks are also general and stereotypical as opposed to specific and/or described behaviors and/or skills. For example they say such things as:

"They are vulnerable" or "moody."
"They are not strong/aggressive."
"They lose their niceness when they work too much."
"They act impulsively and stupidly."

3. If and when women make critical statements, they combine them with positive statements. They say:

"Women make better managers because the women I've worked under have been very organized, considerate, and productivity oriented. The men seem more distant and uninvolved."

"Women make better managers because they are more sensitive in their interactions and they are less likely to be crooks."

4. Women tend to provide specific, observed, positive behaviors to support female superiority. They say such things as:

"Women make better managers because where I work there is a man manager and a woman manager. The woman does a much better job of organizing."

"Women make better managers because a manager's principle role is dealing with people. On the whole, women are more sensitive in this area and are able to motivate others without threats."

5. Males and females who state women are better managers support their assertions with multiple examples of positive behaviors. They say:

"Women seem to be more organized and have the ability to handle pressure and multiple tasks at one time. They are also better communicators. This comes from working and raising kids."

6. Males who state men are better managers support their assertion with one example of a negative behavior or one generality. They say:

"Men make better managers. Society has led us all to believe this."

"Men make better managers because when our secretary is in charge, things don't run smoothly."

"Men make better managers because the women have not stepped up to the same level as men."

Implications

The most obvious implication from this study is the realization that women and men are NOT vastly different in the kinds of values they have concerning the workplace. When given open–ended opportunities to describe what is important to them, the response profiles are essentially the same for males and females. There is consistency among young people with respect to what is important. Thus, this initial research does suggest the emergence of unisex attitudes regarding work.

Women in response to what they liked most about their jobs consistently make reference to people or the human relations factor. This isn't a surprising result, but the fact that men make reference to people with the same degree of frequency with which they make reference to job scope and salary/benefits is an interesting and to some, a surprising result. For those of us who teach human resource management, it is a welcomed result.

Women also make more reference to Job Scope than their male counterparts. One critical component of the Job Scope category is variety and diversity, and it is interesting that this feature of work appears to be more important to women than men. One explanation for this result might be that women are used to having a great deal of variety in their lives as they attempt to balance home and work responsibilities. As a result, they find that they can handle diversity and, perhaps, enjoy this kind of complex existence.

Another explanation for this result, particularly with respect to Job Scope as a dissatisfier, is that the women in this study may be underemployed. Their responses may reflect the fact that they are capable of performing above their present employment level. Similarly, males make reference to Job Scope as their primary source of dissatisfaction—albeit not as frequently as their female counterparts— which may indicate that these men are also underemployed. In total, these findings suggest that young workers want challenging, interesting, and diversified jobs; they are most dissatisfied when their jobs offer less.

One interesting difference between males and females centers around issues relating to salary, benefits, working conditions, and independence. Men appear to be more concerned with benefits, working conditions, and independence within the organization than women. This may suggest that young men are more concerned with hygiene factors and personal goals than organizational goals. In addition, only 12% of the males in this study express any desire to achieve a leadership position within a large organization. Furthermore, given the opportunity to express a desired goal, the males indicate they want to be wealthy superheroes. These findings are certainly contrary to the popular myth that men are "company men" and/or "team players."

Only 15% of the women in this study express a desire to achieve a position of leadership within a large organization; however, 34% of the women want to be the C.E.O. of their own organization. In addition, the female fantasy goals center on increased education and a peaceful, happier society. These findings suggest a greater concern for society as a whole, and a greater desire to head–up and/or build a successful team within the small organization.

It is important to note that less than 20% of all subjects express a desire to be part of the large, complex, American organization. This certainly isn't good news for organizational America; it is, however, an understandable result. For years, large organizations offered security, benefits, and comfortable salaries to loyal company employees. The age of mergers and takeovers, however, has destroyed the illusion of organizational security. Thus, the primary reason for joining a large organization has been eliminated. For women, the situation is even worse. The tremendous discrimination that still exists in our modern organizations significantly hampers their chances for success. As a result, professional careers and small business ventures are becoming very attractive alternatives for women.

When the results of who makes a better manager are combined with the findings reported above, some puzzling questions appear. Forty–seven percent of the male subjects assert that men make better managers. Yet, when asked to support this position, they fail to provide positive, descriptive, observed behaviors. Instead, they use an attack strategy and criticize something about women, and, in most instances, these attacks are aimed at personal characteristics rather than a behavior associated with effective management. In addition, males report a greater concern for salary, benefits, working hours, and autonomy. This combination of findings suggests the possibility of an anti–organizational bias that shuns the kinds of things (communicating, relating, organizing) that have to be done to make organizations work. In this research, at least half of the males do not appear to be concerned with either task or relationship behaviors that are typically associated with effective management.

To the contrary, women are most concerned with the task and relationship aspects of the work environment. In asserting that women are better managers, females have a much higher propensity to discuss behaviors, rather than to criticize others. Furthermore, the males who assert that woman make better managers also explain their positions by identifying positive, specific, observed behaviors. In short, those respondents, both male and female, who state that women make better managers, display the type of communication skills that are considered critical to effective management.

Finally, it is interesting to note that such a large number of respondents from both sexes created their own responses to suggest that men and women are equal. Perhaps this is a reflection of the basic finding of this study: the profiles of young men and women are more similar than they are different. This may, in part, be due to the presence of the working mother in the home.

Conclusions

This research suggests that young, educated, American men and women reject Scott and Hart's (1979) notion that whatever is good for the individual comes from the modern organization. The majority of the men and women in this research express no desire to be part of large, organizational America. They do, however, express a desire to form their own organizations, and/or they desire professional careers.

It would be easy to explain these results by suggesting that the young generation is the "Me" generation, concerned only with immediate, self-gratification. Indeed, there were subjects in this research who lend credence to this over-generalization. However, 69% of the women and 51% of the men made statements that revealed a strong work ethic and desire to succeed. Furthermore, all of the subjects in this research were working for large organizations and 46% of the women and 35% of the men report that they are dissatisfied with the lack of variety, diversity, and challenge in their jobs. Thus, an alternative explanation for these results is that the organization is at fault. Given a choice, the young men and women of America would prefer not to be part of organizational America. Since most of these people won't be given that choice, large organizations can look forward to a generation of workers who would rather be doing something else.

This generation of workers will eventually become the modern organization and their changing attitudes may bring about positive changes in the workplace. This research reveals that some progress has been made towards unisex attitudes in the workplace, and the research suggests that some people are beginning to examine qualifications rather than stereotypical generalizations. The fact that women are in management positions has obviously helped bring about this change. The 30% of the population that expressed men and women are equal, justified their assertions by citing experiences with both male and female managers.

The comments made in praise of women suggest that women do display skills essential to effective management. Over half of the men in this research did not display those same skills and, in fact, were unable to support their assertions with any degree of verbal sophistication. Thus, if women are truly given equal opportunity, it is possible that they will outrank men in management positions by the year 2000.

By the year 2000, the American society will have moved from the industrial age into the service age. Human relation skills will be crucial to success in service organizations, and the need for brute strength, force, and intimidation will be eliminated. Thus, men will be placed in a position of having to develop the human relation skills that women have already developed and displayed. Since a true concern for people and bigotry are incompatible emotions, discrimination in the workplace should decrease as the male population begins to develop nurturing, supportive, and interaction human relation skills. This study suggests that this change has begun to take place. As importantly, this study suggests that the managers of the 21st century do not adhere to a general goal model of organization. Female and male managers are looking for a construct model that takes into account individual interests.

References

Glaser, B.G. & A. Strauss.(1967) *The discovery of grounded theory: Strategies for qualitative research*, Chicago: Aldine.

Herzberg, F. (1968) "One more time: How do you motivate employees?" *Harvard Business Review*, *47*, 53–62.

Kelley, M. (July 1983) "Values in organizational theory and management education," *The Academy of Management Review*, *8*, 3, 376–387.

McCallister, L. & F. O'Brian. (1987) "Content analysis of text." In *Conducting research in business communication*, P. Campbell (Ed.), Association for Business Communication.

Scott, W.G. & D.K. Hart. (1979) *Organizational America*. Boston: Houghton Mifflin.

THOUGHT PROVOKERS

What social changes may account for a shift to an attitude that views *both* males and females as equally competent to perform as managers? As society becomes increasingly service–oriented, discuss how the role of the manager will adapt to this change.

UNIT V

SEX AND GENDER DIVERSITY IN POPULAR CULTURE

Although the chapters within this unit focus on mediated forms of communication, mass media is but one element of cultural learning. Mass communication scholars focus on the media form, often assuming that the medium alone has primary impact on the forming of individuals' attitudes, values, and beliefs. Scholars of popular culture, on the other hand, assume a complex relationship between mass media and other forms of artistry and communication; therefore, mass media forms are but one way values within a culture are instilled (Cawelti, 1985). It is this complex relationship that the authors within this unit investigate.

Although diverse in the audience (children, adolescents, and adults) and the media form (books, television cartoons, rock and roll music, and print advertisements) they study, all four authors are similar in their view of gender. Each author also assumes, albeit implicitly, that modeling behavior (Bandura) and identification with characters is integral to their research. The authors agree that one media form does not have direct impact on an individual's behavior, but the many messages that pervades one's life do instill gender–specific values. Taken in conjunction with other elements (interpersonal, organizational, intercultural, etc.) of our communication mosaic, mediated messages mesh to reinforce gender specific cultural norms.

Pamela Cooper in "Children's Literature: The Extent of Sexism" investigates the sexism in children's literature, using 31 Caldecott Medal Winners and 30 Newbery Award Winners from 1980 to 1987. Her findings indicate that gender roles in children's books have changed little since the 1970s. Unexpectedly, there is no correlation between the rise of female authors writing children's books and a rise in active female characters within the books analyzed.

Joan Aitken characterizes another form of media targeted at children in "*The Transformers*: An Analysis of Messages in a Product–driven Cartoon for Children." Aitken advances the study of children and media by investigating the impact of the cartoon content in *The Transformers* as well as the relationship between this entertainment form and its prime directive—to sell a product. Although a variety of children's products emerge from various television shows (*Mickey Mouse Club, Sesame Street*, etc.), the Transformers were initially marketed as toys, and then promoted in cartoon form. This promotion provides a different perspective on program content and its intended audience.

In Chapter Seventeen, Lisa Bonelli evaluates fragrance advertisements in magazines targeted to males and females. In "Sex Role Stereotyping in Fragrance Advertisements" Bonelli analyzes the advertisements in three men's magazines (*Esquire*, *Playboy*, and *Gentlemen's Quarterly*) and three women's magazines (*Harper's Bazaar*, *Cosmopolitan*, and *Mademoiselle*), matching each men's magazine to a women's magazine according to age and income of target as well as circulation. Each pair is then analyzed for differences in advertising techniques and appeals. Bonelli classifies these approaches for further analysis.

In Chapter Eighteen, "Declarations of Independence: The Female Rock and Roller Comes of Age," Alan Stewart completes this unit on popular culture with a descriptive analysis of the roles prescribed for female rock performers in the 1970s and 1980s. Stewart's analysis of 1970s female performers and the barriers they broke through to be heard provides a solid understanding of the music they perform and roles they play in 1980. Little documentation of rock and roll history details women's roles with any depth; most ignore it completely. Stewart does more than just fill this void and clearly demonstrates how sex–role stereotypes of the era affects the music of today.

If these four studies are viewed as small components which affect cultural learning, it is obvious that as children we were, and as adults we continue to be, bombarded with sex–role stereotypes and the limits they place on females and males. The frightening aspect of this discovery is that, even in this age of awareness, these stereotypes persist or are replaced by equally restrictive stereotypes.

Bandura, A., D. Ross, & S. Ross. (1963) "Imitation of film–mediated aggression models," *Journal of Abnormal and Social Psychology*, *66*, 3–11.

Cawelti, J.G. (December 1985) "With the benefit of hindsight: Popular culture criticism." *Critical Studies in Mass Communication*, 363–379.

CHAPTER FIFTEEN
Children's Literature:
The Extent Of Sexism

Pamela J. Cooper
Northwestern University

Several researchers have investigated sexism in children's literature (See, for example, Sadker and Sadker, 1977: St. Peter, 1979, and Wigutoff, 1982). The major conclusion of these investigations is that children's literature contains much sexism and the feminist movement has made little impact on changing the sex–role portrayal in children's literature. In addition, what a child reads influences her/his sex–role development (Campbell and Witenberg, 1980). This article examines recent children's literature to determine the degree of sexism and compares the results to previous, similar studies. Implications of the findings are discussed.

Review of Literature

Children's Literature

As indicated previously, children's literature has been extensively analyzed. The conclusion of research studies is that children's literature teaches sexist lessons. In this section several of these studies will be reviewed. Although the emphasis is on the portrayal of females, keep in mind that sexism is a two–edged sword; it is as harmful to males as to females. Thus, some discussion of sexist portrayals of males will be included in this section.

Generally, most research on sexism in children's literature focuses on numerical disparities and sex–role portrayal (stereotyped behaviors and stereotyped professions). In terms of these criteria, a nonsexist children's book is one that recognizes and respects the human qualities of people not demeaned or distorted by sex, race, ethnic or economic background.

One of the first major studies of sexism in children's literature was conducted by Weitzman and her associates (1972). These researchers examined how sex roles were treated in the winners of both the Caldecott Medal and Newbery Award. The Caldecott Medal is given by the Children's Service Committee of the American Library Association for the most distinguished picture book of the year. The Newbery Award is given by the American Library Association for the best book for school–age children.

233

The 18 Caldecott winners and runners–up from 1967–1972 were analyzed. The researchers found that the ratio of males pictured to females pictured was 11:1. When females were illustrated, their traditional, sex–role characterizations were reinforced; girls were passive, boys active; girls followed and served others, boys led and rescued others. Adult men and women in these books were also sex–stereotyped. Women were presented as wives and mothers while men were presented in a variety of occupations. Newbery Award winners fared no better. The ratio of male to female main characters was 3:1.

In an update of the Weitzman, *et al.* study, Kolbe and LaVoie (1981) analyzed Caldecott winners from 1972–1979. Although the ratio of male to female human pictures had changed (1.8:1), the role portrayal of males and females had not. Female roles continued to be stereotypically portrayed.

In his analysis of nursery rhymes and fairy tales (the first literature to which most children are exposed), Donlan (1972) found three recurring types of females: (1) the sweet little old lady; (2) the beautiful young heroine; and (3) the aggressive female. The first two types—sweet little old lady and beautiful young heroine—are both depicted as lovably incompetent. The aggressive female takes many forms—wife, mother, stepmother, and shrew (cruel, vain, greedy, demanding). Donlan concludes that women are portrayed as ineffectual creatures who need to be dominated by men or as aggressive monsters who must be destroyed by men.

Cooper (1987) examined the sex–role portrayal in children's books concerning step–families. Forty–two books (1975–1983) available in libraries in the Chicago metropolitan area were examined. For the most part, stereotyped roles were portrayed. Women in the books worked, but in stereotyped occupations. When women did work, they neglected their children or became aggressive. They were relatively passive and still focused on their appearance. Men were still depicted as the lawyers and doctors and were inept at household duties. Men were portrayed as more caring and sensitive, but only to a point—when problems weren't resolved quickly, they became impatient.

In recent years several nonstereotyped children's book lists have been published. St. Peter (1979) was interested in the sex roles portrayed in one list of nonsexist books. "Little Miss Muffett Fights Back." St. Peter used five scoring categories: (1) sex of central characters, (2) sex of figures portrayed on front cover, (3) sex of character named in titles, (4) numbers of illustrations with males and females, and (5) expressive and instrumental activities. In addition to the nonsexist books, St. Peter also analyzed titles published prior to the women's movement and titles published after the women's movement. Her analyses of 206 picture books indicated that children were presented with sex–typed book models. In general, females were underrepresented in titles and central roles and underrepresented in expressive activities.

Much of what has been reviewed in this article relates to younger children's literature. However, adolescent literature has also been analyzed for sex role stereotyping. Wigutoff (1982) reviewed 300 contemporary realism books for adolescents. All 300 books were published between 1977 and 1980. Traditional role models were depicted—fathers went to work and mothers stayed home. Wigutoff summarized the mother's image in junior fiction in the following excerpt:

> The "good mother" in junior fiction is available when needed, but otherwise invisible. She is on call to prepare food and provide clean clothes, but she never expects gratitude for the services she provides. Her own needs, should they unfortunately exist, are at all times subservient to those of her children. It is an image of motherhood at its most servile. (p 123)

A review of children's literature demonstrates that sexism is a major problem. Both males and females (children and adults) are portrayed stereotypically.

What effect does sex–role stereotyping in children's books have on children? The concern with sexism in children's books results from the belief that books influence children's behavior. The next section of this article discusses the effects of sexism in children's literature on children's sex–role development.

Effect of Sexism

Researchers have shown that book content does influence children's sex–role stereotypes (see research reviewed in Campbell and Witenberg, 1980). Several studies reveal the effect of traditional sex–typed children's books on children. Koblinsky (1979) tested children's recall after listening to stories with males and females in traditional roles and found that boys recalled the masculine characteristics of boys and girls remembered the feminine characteristics of females. In a similar study, Jennings (1975) found that preschool children, when read stories with traditional and non–traditional behaviors of boys and girls, preferred the story in which characters displayed the more traditional behavior for their sex. Kropp and Halverson (1983) found similar results.

Research also demonstrates the effect non–biased stories can have. Lutes–Dunckley (1978) found that children who were asked their career preferences after hearing stories with characters in non–traditional roles, made more non–traditional choices than those children who only heard about traditional characters. Ashby and Wittmarer (1976) found that girls who heard non–nontraditional stories rated male jobs and characteristics appropriate for females more than girls who heard traditional stories. McArthur and Eisen (1976) found more achievement behavior in nursery school girls after they listened to a story about an achieving girl than those who heard a story about an achieving boy. Flerx, *et al.*, (1976) indicated that female role stereotypes can be modified through the use of books that depict egalitarian sex roles. Scott and Feldman–Summers (1979) demonstrated that when females were portrayed in roles traditionally assumed by males, both boys and girls increased their perceptions of the number of girls who could engage in these traditionally male activities.

Some caution is necessary in generalizing these research findings. In her review of the literature, Scott (1980) makes an important distinction between influencing sex–role attitudes and modifying actual sex–role behavior. A change in sex–role attitude does not automatically predict a change in sex–role behavior. Certainly we know that sex–role portrayal in children's books influences children. The magnitude and generalizability of this influence on behavior needs further investigation. No systematic investigation of the effect on adults of their childhood literature exposure has been conducted. However, the point remains that books do have the power to change as well as to instill cultural values, and children's literature can play an important role in eliminating sexism by presenting egalitarian sex roles.

Certainly not all children's literature is sexist. Several authors discuss the available non–sexist literature for children (c.f. Sadker and Sadker, 1977; Rudman, 1984); however, these books are a minority. Much of what children read depicts traditional sex role stereotypes. As a result, children's self–concepts, curriculum choice, and occupational choice are affected (see research reviewed in Stewart, Cooper, and Friedley, 1986).

Method

Selected Books

The books chosen for examination were the 31 Caldecott Medal Winners and Honor Books from 1980–1987 and 30 Newbery Award Winners and Honor Books from 1980–1987. A list of these books is included in the Appendix. Caldecott and Newbery books were selected as a representative sample of children's literature because they are highly regarded for their artistry and content by parents, children's librarians, scholars of children's literature and school systems. As a result, these books have a large mass distribution and are recognized as a major influence in children's literature.

If books are inculcators of sex role models, it seems appropriate to determine whether books written for children continue to show sex role stereotypes given the recent awareness of publishers and the feminist movement (Brooks–Gunn and Matthews, 1979). The Caldecott and Newbery Winners have been determined to be representative of children's literature (Weitzman, et al, 1972; Kolbe and LaVoie, 1981). Thus an examination of these books should provide a general overview of the degree of sexism in children's literature.

Procedure

To enable a comparison with the Weitzman, *et al.* (1972) and the Kolbe and LaVoie (1981) studies, each book was examined to determine the number of male and females present (both human and animal), use of the character in the title, sex of the main character, sex of the author, sex of the illustrator, number of pictures of males and females in each book. In addition, the roles of the main character were analyzed on the following dimensions: expressive/instrumental and stereotyped/nonstereotyped. And expressive role was one which portrayed concern for the well-being of another, affection, warmth and dependency. An instrumental role portrayed the character as task-oriented, somewhat competitive and appropriately aggressive. A role was rated as stereotyped if it portrayed the traditional, culturally-defined sex-role expectations. Nonstereotyped roles were those which could be characterized as androgynous—males and females performed both instrumental and expressive roles.

Results

Caldecott Award Books

The first comparisons are with the Weitzman, *et al.* (1972) and Kolbe and LaVoie (1981) data to determine what changes, if any, have occurred in the Caldecott Award books. The comparisons are presented in Table 1.

As indicated in Table 1, the ratio of male to female human pictures remained the same from 1972–1985, and the ratio of male to female non-human pictures changed slightly. The ratio of male to female names in the book titles has increased from 2:3 in the 1972–1979 sample to 5:3 in the 1980–1985 sample. Finally, the number of books in which the story concerns a female has increased from 3 in 1972–1979 sample to 7 in the 1980–1985 sample.

Two cautions are necessary. Although only one book exists in which no female characters are present, this data is somewhat misleading. In a book such as *Fables* (1981), a series of fables, eleven of the fables are concerned exclusively with female characters.

Although the location of activities seems to suggest a less sex-biased view, such is not the case. For example, in *Outside Over There* (1982), the main character is female and she, Ida, saves her young sibling from the goblins. The major action takes place out of doors. However, Ida is only successful in her venture because her father calls to her to provide direction. In addition, Ida's mother sits in the arbor and "pines" for her husband. She is so lonely she cannot care for her children or wonder where they are while they are gone.

Table 1   Comparison Data on Sex–Role Stereotyping in Caldecott Award Books: 1967–1971, 1972–1979, and 1980–1985.

Comparison Criteria (from Weitzman et al., 1972)	1967–1971 Selections (N = 18)	1972–1979 Selections (N = 19)	1980–1985 Selections (N = 24)
Ratio of male to female human pictures	11:1	1.8:1	1.8:1
Ratio of male to female nonhuman pictures	95:1	2.66:1	3.3:1
Ratio to male to female names in titles	8:1	2:3	5:3
Number of books in which no female characters are present	6	2	1
Number of books in which story concerns a female	2	3	7
Sex–Role Portrayal and Characterization (Passive, dependent female)	most books[a]	17	18
Traditional sex role portrayal	18	17	19
Presence of working women outside of the home	0	0	1
Location of Activities[b]			
Females Indoors	most books	6 of 17	10
Males Outdoors	most books	16 of 17	13

[a]Weitzman, et al. do not indicate the number of books in which females were characterized in this role. Their narrative states "most books."

[b]Only 17 books are involved because male characters were absent in two books, and female characters in two other books.

Similarly, in *Shadow* (1983), a book of African culture, the action takes place out of doors. Both males and females are pictured out of doors. However, the men go to war and the women take care of the children. In *The Glorious Flight* (1984), both males and females are again shown out of doors. The men admire the plane and are pictured near it. The women are pictured standing aloof holding the hands of their children. Thus, simply picturing women out of doors does not in and of itself depict a change in sex role.

In terms of role depiction, little change is apparent. Females are primarily expressive; males instrumental. The mother in *A Chair for My Mother* (1983) is shown having a job outside the home. She's a waitress and her boss is also female. The mother is also a single parent. Thus, the implication is that mothers with husbands don't have occupations outside the home. The only other woman pictured in a job is a receptionist in the bank. This character is only pictured and not mentioned as female in the text. Other occupations for women are mother and babysitter.

Males are portrayed as bankers, sailors, musicians, tailors, mine workers, farmers, magicians, and adventure seekers such as in *The Glorious Flight Across The Channel with Louis Bleroit*, (1984) and *The Treasure*, (1980). Only two males demonstrate expressiveness. The father in *When I was Ten, Nine, Eight* (1984) gives "three loving kisses on cheeks and nose" and holds his daughter in his lap and tucks her in bed. No mother is shown in this book. The implication may be that fathers do such things when a mother is absent.

Males are instrumental. They have the adventures and save the females. They are not pictured engaged in household tasks. Only one male, Peter (*Jumanji*, 1982) is shown as somewhat dependent on a female. His sister Judy decides what they will do when their parents leave. She convinces Peter to play the game Jumanji and also continue when wild animals appear. She "saves" Peter by forcing him to finish the game.

Table 2 presents the results for the 1986 and 1987 Caldecott Award Winners.

Comparison with Table 1 demonstrates that the ratios of male to female pictures (both human and nonhuman), the ratio of male to female names in titles, and the number of books in which no females are present all reflect more sexism than in previous years. The same is true of the remaining categories. No women are portrayed working outside the home. The major role depiction for women in the 1986–87 winners is mother.

Perhaps the most nonsexist book is *The Relatives Came* (1985). In this book, both males and females are shown as instrumental and expressive. Both are shown outdoors and both are shown hugging

Table 2   Comparison Data on Sex–Role Stereotyping in
               Caldecott Award Books: 1986–1987

Comparison Criteria (from Weitzman et al., 1972)	1986–1987 Selections (N = 7)
Ratio of male to female human pictures	2:1
Ratio of male to female nonhuman pictures	18:0
Ratio of male to female names in titles	3:0
Number of books in which no female characters are present	2
Number of books in which story concerns a female	2*
Sex–Role Portrayal and Characterization (Passive, dependent female)	2
Traditional sex role portrayal	7
Presence of working women outside of the home	0
Location of Activities	
Females Indoors	2
Males Outdoors	5

Note: In both books, the story also concerns a male as main character.

children. However, adult women hug adult women, but adult men shake hands with one another. In addition, *Alphabatics* (1986), a book in which letters change to objects, most objects are nondescript. However, when sex is discernible, it is male. For example, L becomes a lion; M a mustache; R a rooster; J a Jack–in–the box.

Newbery Award Books

Weitzman, *et al.*, (1972) indicate that in the Newbery Award Books published from 1967–1971, the ratio of male to female characters was 3:1. Numerically, women were invisible. In addition, women were portrayed as passive and dependent; men were portrayed as active and independent. The only role model for females was mother.

From 1980-1985, the ratio of male main characters to female main characters was 3:4; in 1986-1987, the ratio was 5.6:1. The ratio of total male characters to total female characters was 1:1 in 1980-1985; 2:1 in 1986-87. Thus numerically, females are no longer invisible.

However, in terms of the role models presented for women, little has changed since the Weitzman, *et al* study. Certainly women are portrayed as more than mothers. Occupations include teacher, receptionist, nurse, caterer, musician, crazy woman, professor, doctor, storeowner, salesperson, and warrior. However, numbers fail to tell the entire story. For example, when Ramona (*Ramona Quinby, Age 8*; 1982) becomes ill, her mother stays home from work to care for her. Her father, who is attending college, does not. There is no negotiation on the issue. The mother seems to take it for granted that this is her responsibility. She is also the one who cleans the house and cooks the meals. At one point Ramona's father tells Ramona and her sister Beezus they should cook the evening meal because their mother is tired from her day at work. After the meal he does help Mrs. Quinby with the dishes.

When women have occupations other than mother, they are often unable to be "good" mothers. For example, Jeff's mother in *A Solitary Blue* (1984) leaves Jeff and his father in order to pursue a career of "helping others." She ignores Jeff for six years and then invites Jeff to visit her. However, Jeff is left alone most of the time because his mother is too busy with her feminist work and spending time with her boyfriend Max. Similarly, in *Sweet Whispers, Brother Rush* (1983) Teresa is left to care for her retarded brother Dabl because the mother is a "live-in" nurse. The mother rarely visits. Teresa learns from the ghost Brother Rush that her mother treated Dabl very badly when he was a child. It is only after Teresa's mother marries (and Dabl has died) that the mother returns to live with twelve-year-old Teresa.

Evidently, motherhood and career "don't mix." Harry, the female main character in *The Blue Sword* (1983) is a warrior. In fact, she virtually saves a nation. However, she does so with the magical power of "Kalar" and the blue sword. After the war, she marries the King and bears five children. Her warrior days come to an end as she settles into the mother/wife role. One book, *Sugaring Time* (1984) presents a nonsexist picture of male and female occupations. The story surrounds the gathering of maple sap. The mother is pictured driving the horse drawn wagon which is full of heavy barrels of maple sap. The father is shown in the kitchen cooking and setting the table.

Table 3   Sex Role Stereotypes in
             Newbery Award Winners
             1980–1987 (N = 29)

	1980–1985 N = 23	1986–1987 N = 6*
Ratio of male to female names in titles	7:2	2:1
Ratio of male to female main characters	3:4	5.6:1
Number of books in which no female is a main character	4	4
Number of books in which no male is a main character	1	0
Ratio of male to female characters	1.1:1	2:1
Sex Role Portrayal		
Passive/dependent female	17	5
Traditional sex role portrayal	17	5
Presence of working women outside of the home	13	0

*Volcano: The Eruption and Healing of Mount St. Helen's was eliminated from the analysis since it was the only nonfiction book. It should be noted, however, that no females were pictured in the book. The geologists, scientists, surveyors were all male.

Most books depict stereotyped sex role relationships. For example, Suzy (*A Ring of Endless Light*, 1981) wants to be a doctor or veterinarian. However, her major concern at the present time is boys. She is jealous because her sister Vicky has three boys "in her live." Eleanor (*The Fledgling*, 1981) spends hours sewing herself a new dress. When she wears it, a boy she admires ridicules it. Eleanor runs home crying and refuses to wear the dress again. In this same book Georgie's adventures are the result of the Goose Prince. It is this male character who helps Georgie (female) learn to fly.

The majority of books portray females as expressive, males as instrumental. The heroine in *The Road from Home: The Story of an Armenian Girl* (1980) wants to break away from the contemporary female role and go to college. However, she ultimately forsakes this dream to marry in order to help support her family. Interestingly, the mother in this book dies of grief when her other three children die. Her dependency, caring and warmth are so overwhelming that when her mother role is greatly lessened, she cannot cope. Jeff's father (*A Solitary Blue*, 1984) does not like Jeff to cry and tells Jeff that only boys are reliable. Leigh's father (*Dear Mr. Henshaw*, 1984) cannot express his feelings in his diary. In *Sign of the Beaver* (1984) the father and son are unable to express their feelings. Each is "locked" in the stereotype of male stoicism.

Three books, *Dicey's Song* (1983), *Upon the Head of the Goat* (1982), and *The Whipping Boy* (1986) present female nonsexist roles. In these books the female adult main characters are both instrumental and expressive. However, as previously indicated, males are portrayed primarily as instrumental. In only three books, *Sugaring Time* (1984), *The Moves Make the Man* (1985), and *On My Honor* (1986) do we see any semblance of an expressive, nonstereotyped male.

Sexism occurs in both the Caldecott and Newbery Award Books in terms of sexist language. For example, in *Shadow*, the 1983 Caldecott Winner, the author writes, "That's why a person keeps an eye on his shadow when he wakes up, and takes care not to step on it when he gets up. It could prick him or bite him." Beezus in *Ramona Quinby, Age 8* (1982) worries about a party because "Eighth grade boys act like a bunch of little kids at parties." In the same book, when Mrs. Quinby tells Ramona to clean her room and Ramona refuses, Mr. Quinby "steps in" and tells Ramona, "Young Lady, you do what your mother says and you do it now." In "The Binnacle Boy," one of the tales in *Graven Images* (1983), one daughter is told by her mother, "Girls take after their mothers, Evangeline. Men take after the devil." Later, Evangeline's mother has more to say concerning men: "Men are a stench in God's nostrils."

Conclusion

While the present data show some shift from the sexism presented by previous studies, this changes occurred primarily in the frequency of female characters, not in the role portrayal and characterization. Thus, children and young adolescents who read these books will be exposed to traditional sex roles.

One might suggest that sexist portrayals of males and females continue because most authors are male. Such is not the case. Of the thirty-one Caldecott Award Books, fifteen were authored by males and sixteen were authored by females. In terms of illustrators, fourteen books were illustrated by females, sixteen by males, and one by both. A similar finding occurs in Newbery Award Books—seven were authored by males; twenty-three by females.

One of the major socializing forces, particularly for young children, is books. Through books, children become aware of and understand different social roles people play. If stereotyped roles are the primary roles shown, males and females will fail to realize that people, regardless of their sex, can achieve a wide range of roles. The Association of Women Psychologists (1970) in their position statement on sexism succinctly state the implications of sexism:

> Psychological oppression in the form of sex role socialization clearly conveys to girls from the earliest ages that their nature is to be submissive, servile, and repressed, and their role is to be servant, admirer, sex object and martyr...The psychological consequences of goal depression in young women...are all too common. In addition, both men and women have come to realize the effect on men of this type of sex role stereotyping, the crippling pressure to compete, to achieve, to produce, to stifle emotion, sensitivity and gentleness, all taking their toll in psychic and physical traumas.

Sexism has been shown to affect all areas of life. Stewart, Cooper and Friedley (1986) discuss the effects of sexism in interpersonal relationships, education, self–concept, occupational choice, and moving up the hierarchy in an organization. These authors suggest that sexism has a negative effect for women in all the above mentioned areas.

Certainly changing the sex–role portrayal of women in children's literature will not solve all these problems. However, children decide very early in life what roles are appropriate to males and females. As cited earlier in this paper, when nonsexist literature is used with children, some change towards nonsexist attitudes does occur. Because literature is one of the earliest socializing agents to which children are exposed, it would seem important to make this agent as nonsexist as possible.

The results of the present study indicate that sexism is "alive and well" in children's literature. Numerical increases in female characters are not enough. Nontraditional role portrayal for both male and female must be shown. Only then will children begin to see viable alternatives to their traditional sex role.

References

Ashby, M. & Wittmarer, B. (1976). Attitude changes in children after exposure to stories about women in traditional and non-traditional occupations. *Journal of Educational Psychology*, *68*, 945–949.

Association of Women Psychologists. (Sept. 1970). Statement resolutions and motions. Miami: American Psychological Association Convention.

Brooks–Gunn, J. & Matthews, W.S. (1979). *He and she*. Englewood Cliffs, N.J.: Prentice Hall.

Campbell, P., & Witenberg, J. (1980). How books influence children: What the research shows. *Interracial Books for Children Bulletin*, 11, 3–6.

Connor, J. & Serbin, L. (1978). Children's responses to stories with male and female characters. *Sex Roles*, *4*, 637–640.

Cooper, P. (1987). The communication of sex role stereotypes: The image of stepparents in children's literature. In L.P. Stewart & S. Ting–Toomy (Eds.). *Communication, gender and sex roles in diverse interaction contexts*, 61–82. Norwood, NJ: Ablex.

Cooper, P. (1984). Sexism in children's literature: Extent and impact on adult behavior. Paper presented at the Speech Communication Association Convention.

Donlan, D. (1972). The negative image of women in children's literature. *Elementary Education*, 65–70.

Eakins, B. & Eakins, R.G. (1979). *Sex differences in human communication*. Boston: Houghton Mifflin.

Flerx, V., Fidler, D. & Roger, P. (1976). Sex role stereotypes: Developmental aspects and early intervention. *Child Development*, *47*, 998–1007.

Jennings, S. (1975). Effects of sex typing in children's stories on preference and recall. *Child Development*, *46*, 220–223.

Kolbe, R. & LaVoie, J. (1981). Sex–role stereotyping in preschool children's picture books. *Social Psychology Quarterly*, *44*, 369–374.

Koblinsky, S. (1979). Sex role stereotypes and children's memory for story context. *Child Development*, 452–458.

Kropp, J. & Halverson, C. (1983). Preschool children's preferences and recall for stereotyped vs. nonstereotyped stories. *Sex Roles*, *9*, 261–273.

Lutes–Dunckley, C. (1978). Sex role preference as a function of sex of storyteller and story context. *Journal of Psychology*, *100*, 151–158.

McArthur, L.Z. & Eisen, S.U. (1976). Achievements of male and female story book as determinants of achievement behavior by boys and girls. *Journal of Personality and Social Psychology, 33,* 467–473.

Sadker, M.P. & Sadker, D.M. (1977). *Now upon a time: A contemporary view of children's literature.* New York: Harper and Row.

Scott, K.P. (1980). Sexist and nonsexist materials: What impact do they have? *Elementary School Journal, 81,* 47–52.

Scott, K.P., & Feldman–Summers, S. (1979). Children's reactions to textbook stories in which females are portrayed in traditionally male roles. *Journal of Educational Psychology, 71,* 396–402.

St. Peter, S. (1979). Jack went up the hill...but where was Jill? *Psychology of Women Quarterly, 4,* 256–260.

Stewart, L.P., Cooper, P.J., & Friedley, S.A. (1986). *Communication between the sexes.* Scottsdale, AZ: Gorsuch–Scarisbrick.

Stewig, J. & Higgs, M. (1973). Girls grow up to be mommies: A study of sexism in children's literature. *Library Journal, 98,* 236–244.

Weitzman, L., Eiffler, D., Hokada, E. & Ross, C. (1972). Sex role socialization in picture books for preschool children. *American Journal of Sociology, 77,* 1125–1150.

Wigutoff, S. (1982). Junior fiction: A feminist critique. *Top of the News, 38,* 113–124.

CALDECOTT AWARDS: 1980-1987

1980 *Ox-Cart Man*, Donald Hall, illus. Barbara Cooney
Honor Books: *Ben's Trumpet*, Rachel Isadora
The Treasure, Uri Schulevitz
The Garden of Abdul Gasazi, Chris
Van Allsburg

1981 *Fables*, Arnold Lobel
Honor Books: *The Grey Lady and the Strawberry
Snatcher*, Molly Bang
Truck, Donald Crews
Mice Twice, Joseph Low
The Bremen-town Musicians, retold
and illus. by Ilse Plume

1982 *Jumanji*, Chris Van Allsburg
Honor Books: *A Visit to William Blake's Inn: Poem
for Innocent and Experienced
Travelers*, Nancy Willard
Where the Buffaloes Begin, Olaf Baker
On Market Street, Arnold Lobel
Outside, Over There, by Maurice
Sendak

1983 *Shadow*, Marcia Browon, trans. illus.
Honor Books: *A Chair for My Mother*, Vera B.
Williams
When I Was Young in the Mountains,
Cynthia Ryland, illus. Diane Goode

1984 *The Glorious Flight Across the Channel with Louis Bleroit*,
Alice and Martin Provenson
Honor Books: *Ten, Nine, Eight*, Molly Bang
Little Red Riding Hood, Trina Schart
Hyman

1985 *Saint George and the Dragon*, Tina Hyman, illus., retold
by Margaret Hodges
Honor Books: *Hansel and Gretel*, Paul Zelinsky,
illus., retold by Rika Lesser
Have You Seen My Duckling?, Nancy
Tafuri
The Story of Jumping Mouse, John
Steptoe

1986 *The Polar Express*, Chris Van Allsburg
Honor Books: *King Bidgood's in the Bathtub*, Audrey
Wood, illus. by Don Wood
The Relatives Came, Cynthia Rylant,
illus. by Stephen Gammell

1987 *Hey, Al*, Arthur Yorinks, illus. by Richard Egielski
Honor Books: *Alphabatics*, Suse MacDonald
Rumpelstilskin, Paul O. Zelinsky
*The Village of Round and Square
Houses*, Ann Grifalconi

NEWBERY AWARDS: 1980 – 1987

1980 *A Gathering of Days*, by Joan W. Elos
Honor Book: *The Road From Home: The Story of
an Armenian Girl*, by David
Khercian

1981 *Jacob Have I Loved*, by Katherine Peterson
Honor Books: *The Fledgling*, by Jane Langton
A Ring of Endless Light, by Madeleine
L. Engle

1982 *A Visit to William Blake's Inn: Poems for Innocent and
Experienced Travelers*, by Nancy Willard
Honor Books: *Ramona Quinby, Age 8*, by Beverly
Cleary
Upon the Head of the Goat, by Aranka
Siegal

1983 *Dicey's Song*, by Cynthia Voight
Honor Books: *The Blue Sword*, by Robin McKinley
Dr. Setoto, by William Steig
Graven Images, by Paul Fleischman,
illus. Andrew Glass
Homesick: My Own Story, by Jean
Fritz, illus. by Margot Tomes
Sweet Whispers, Brother Rush, by
Virginia Hamilton

1984   *Dear Mr. Henshaw.* by Beverly Cleary
        Honor Books: *The Wish Giver*, by Bill Brittain
                       Sugaring Time, by Kathryn Lasky
                       A Solitary Blue, by Cynthia Voight
                       Sign of the Beaver, by Elizabeth
                       George Speare

1985   *The Hero and the Crown*, by Robin McKinley
        Honor Books: *Like Jake and Me*, by Lloyd Bloom
                       The Moves Make the Man, by Bruce
                       Brooks
                       One-Eyed Cat, by Paula Fox

1986   *Sarah, Plain and Tall*, by Patricia MacLachlan/Harper
        Honor Books: *Commodore Perry in the Land of the
                       Shogun*, by Rhoda Blumberg
                       Dogsong, by Gary Paulsen

1987   *The Whipping Boy*, by Sid Fleischman
        Honor Books: *A Fine White Dust*, by Cynthia Rylant
                       On My Honor, by Marion Dane Bauer
                       *Volcano: The Eruption and Healing of
                       Mount St. Helens,* by Patricia
                       Lauber (not included in
                       the analysis)

THOUGHT PROVOKERS

Why do sex role stereotypes in children's literature persist when more and more of their authors are women? Are these award winners typical of most children's literature?

CHAPTER SIXTEEN

The Transformers: An Analysis of Messages in a Product–driven Cartoon for Children

Joan E. Aitken

University of Missouri–Kansas City

A relatively new type of cartoon has developed in the 1980s: adventure stories about robots. These animated stories about cyborgs and robots have included: *Robotech*, *The Transformers*, *GoBots*, *Terrahawks*, *Super Saturday*, *Super Powers Team*, *Galactic Guardians*, and *Voltron*, *Defender of the Universe*. Violence, technology, space travel, and galactic adventure have contributed to the new robotic cartoons for children (Fischer, 1983, p. xiii). These cartoons may influence the attitudes and behaviors of their viewing audiences, who are comprised of primarily young, male children. Many of the children's adventure shows are product–driven; that is, they are designed primarily to sell specific toys. *The Transformers* is an example of a product–driven cartoon because the development of the toys took place prior to the development of the television program. Thus, the television program was designed to sell products and ideas.

The Transformers cartoon began with robotic toys able to be transformed into a vehicle, animal, or other form. Enterprising Americans bought the line from the Japanese and developed a television show to promote it (Denison, 1985). In recent years, many successful toys resulted in cartoons (e.g. *The Cabbage Patch Kids* and *Pretty Pony*). Once the Transformers caught the attention of children, several toy manufacturers produced similar toys, and additional animated robotics adventure shows began on television. Now several manufacturers (Hasbro, Tonka, Select, and others) have produced similar toys. The J.C. Penney catalog (1985), for example, contained 66 transforming and 19 related toys. Hasbro (1985) showed their series of Transformer toys as able to convert to over 140 toys, with more "good guys" (43) than "bad guys" (29) available. The characters are supposed to be mechanical beings from another planet who are intent on conquering Earth so as to "enslave its inhabitants and seize its energy resources" (Carlin, 1986, p. 5).

As the field of television analysis has expanded to "become an academically respectable pursuit" (Gronbeck, 1983, p. 138), researchers have considered the analysis of children's programs as an important step in understanding the learning and acculturation of children. Rice and Wartella (1981) warned that researchers need to consider the entire viewing experience. We must consider the situation and child as unique "the child who is interpreting television is an active participant in a dynamic communication of diverse messages that are coded in a number of ways" (p. 372). Thus, one must be careful about drawing conclusions that are supposed to apply to all children. In a study of the arousal of emotions during television viewing, Dorr (1981) expressed concern over the relationship between children's understanding of television and its impact on feelings when she wrote that: "research into the relationship between understanding and impact is sorely needed" (p. 344). Newcomb (1986) contended that television criticism and empirical research can work together to better analyze television effects (p. 226). Thus, this study incorporates a combination of a critical approach with empirical method.

Over the past decades, parents and researchers have speculated on the effects of television on children. The complexity of the media and child development have made it difficult to effectively isolate or analyze effects. Recent research and theories indicate that television affects children, but the full implications are still unclear (Becker, 1983; Bower, 1984; Collins, 1981; Davis & Baran, 1981; Fowles, 1982; Kaye, 1974; Prawat, Anderson, & Hapkiewicz, 1985; Rebel, 1983). The changing nature of the medium and the continual increase in children's television (Tooth, 1985) indicate need for continued concern about what children "take away" from the viewing experience.

The purpose of this study is to analyze the characteristics of *The Transformers* as an example of the animated robotic adventure, by examining language, themes, and characters. The method of research included content analysis of six *The Transformers* episodes by 37 adult raters and questioning of 34 children. The excessive violence, unusual language, and negative portrayal of females raise questions about the effects of *The Transformers* on child viewers.

Method

After viewing several *The Transformers* program episodes, the author developed a series of questions for adult raters that would analyze program content. To analyze the program content, 37 college students from a fundamental communication course and from a communication research course volunteered to rate *The Transformers*. Each person rated one of six episodes of *The Transformers*. Questions pertained to the categories of characters, violence, and language, while using the methods of counting, and answering closed–form and open–form questions. The purpose in using adult raters was to obtain concrete analysis of program content.

To obtain children's perceptions, the study began with interviews of one eight-year-old boy and one eight-year-old girl who demonstrated a high interest in Transformers. The children were asked to explain their interest in and attitudes toward Transformers toys and cartoons. Based on the testimony of these children and issues raised in the literature, a questionnaire was developed with 10 questions relating specifically to *The Transformers*, and four relating to cartoons and interaction with others regarding cartoon-viewing. When the questionnaire was tried on these children, the "yes" or "no" format appeared the most understandable.

Responses were obtained from 34 children who completed questionnaires on the program. The children were given 10 statements, to which they responded "yes" or "no". In addition, there were four open-form questions. These open-form questions were also used as a springboard for discussion after the questionnaires were completed and collected. In some cases, children responded both "yes" and "no" to closed-form questions to indicate that both responses were correct. After completing the questionnaire individually, the children participated in an oral discussion of *The Transformers* and other cartoons. The children were taken from two groups: a third grade public school class and an elementary-aged after-school day care. The children's ages ranged from five to 11. Because of the limited reading and writing ability of young children, the questionnaire was followed by a discussion with the interviewer. Young children were interviewed individually so that the interviewer actually completed the questionnaire.

Findings

Adults. The first set of data came from the 37 college students. One should exercise caution, however, in interpreting this analysis by adult raters who watched only one program. Most viewers come to know characters over time (Piccirillo, 1986), so one-time viewers may have a slanted perception of the program characters. They found that the average number of characters per episode was 15 male characters and 1 female character, which typically included 11 adult nonhuman life forms with no children and no parents.

Regarding violence, raters indicated the following averages per episode: five physically violent acts between characters, 11 shootings, and seven explosions, for an average of 23 violent acts per half hour show. Some raters found more than 40 violent acts in one half hour episode.

Raters were asked to evaluate the use of language in the program. Some raters commented on the Transformer names (e.g. Omega Supreme, Megatron, Bonecrusher, Venom, and Ravage). Of the 37 raters, 33 gave examples of technical language (e.g. "Spectro-galaxy analysis of rock,"), all 37 gave examples of aggressive language (e.g.

"Don't look scared moron, or I will have to destroy you"), 33 gave examples of degrading language (e.g. "You ugly tin can"), and 32 gave examples of complex language (e.g. "Communicate telepathically").

When asked the basic idea of the story line, four raters said they did not know. Many of the answers revolved around revenge, good robots versus bad robots, taking over territory, and saving Earth from invaders. Raters varied in the value they saw in the messages. Some examples of messages of the program included: (a) "Any means of protection available," (b) "If someone doesn't agree with you, shoot them," (c) "Revenge is useless."

Regarding sex, some respondents commented that all characters were male, some noted that females were in subservient positions, and others said that the robots were "sexless." There were no responses to indicate females were portrayed in positive roles.

The rater responses regarding an overall impression ranged from positive to negative. Some example responses included: (a) "While it was very entertaining it did not have any real purpose," (b) "I didn't like it or understand it," (c) "Because these robots change into many different forms, it allows children to use their minds concerning what appears to be one thing could be something else."

Table 1

Item	Male Yes	Female Yes	Male No	Female No	Chi Square
Have watched transformers	20	12	0	2	3.04
Have seen transformers ads	19	11	1	3	2.14
Know good from evil transformer	20	12	0	5	6.80
Cartoons are good for me	18	11	2	3	.85
Parents watched cartoons with me	11	10	11	5	1.01
OK for me to watch transformers	19	12	0	2	2.89
Transformers is more for boys	18	12	1	4	2.75
Transformers have power	19	9	0	4	6.68
I talk while watching cartoons	6	7	15	7	1.65
Transformers are like real life	13	7	12	10	.48

*Denotes differences significant at $p < .01$.

Children. The second set of findings to be reported are from the questions directed to children. Table 1 gives a summary of the children's responses to the true–false (yes–no) statements. A Chi–square independence test was run on the results to determine differences between responses of male and female children. A significance level of .05 was established. Two items showed a significant difference between the responses of boys and girls. Boys were better able to distinguish between "good and evil" Transformers (Chi–square of 6.80, at a significance level of .01, Contingency Coefficient of .39, Cramer's Phi of .43). The second area of significant difference was that boys were more likely to attribute "power" to Transformers than were girls (Chi–square of 6.68, at a significance level of .01, Contingency Coefficient of .42, Cramer's Phi Prime of .46).

The four open–form questions gave insight into the children's perceptions. Representative responses may provide additional explanation. "A Transformer is like:" (a) "a robot," (b) "weird," (c) "a real dummy," (d) "a metal monster," (e) "Superman." "The thing I like about *The Transformers* show is:" (a) "excitement and the way they transform," (b) "they fight a lot of time," (c) "I don't like it," (d) "it has great adventure," (e) "when my brothers are watching it, they can't bother me." "The thing I do *not* like about *The Transformers* show is:" (a) "I like everything about the show," (b) "they transform too fast," (c) "I don't like the evil team," (d) "It is stupid," (e) "killing." "Tell about cartoons:" (a) "*The Transformers* is the best cartoon you can see, (b) "Transformers are good for boys and I like it," (c) "I think everyone should watch them," (d) "I hate Transformers. They are for boys," (e) "They are fun."

Discussion

Based on open–form and closed–form questions, the boys indicated a more positive attitude toward *The Transformers* cartoons than the girls. The girls tended to be more neutral in their interest, and at least some answers indicated a lack of knowledge. For example, one cannot distinguish easily between good and evil Transformers without knowing the use of colors, characters, and plots. Some of the attitudes expressing confusion—indicated by adults and girls—are probably due to unfamiliarity with these complex programs. On the question of power, it is interesting that all boys considered Transformers powerful, although some girls did not. One might wonder if this result is part of an early difference in the perception or definition of power by males and females. If one characterizes Transformers as complex, mechanical, and violent, then one can logically characterize the boys' perceptions of power to include those characteristics.

The similarities of other questions indicate that although both boys and girls are familiar with *The Transformers* and have watched them, both boys and girls consider them cartoons to be viewed by boys. The author was surprised by a strong preference boys demonstrated for certain cartoons and girls demonstrated for other cartoons. Rating services group boys and girls together, but this study indicated that ratings by sex should indicate strong preferences on certain programs. So, one can conclude that although the viewing experience may be similar between boys and girls (e.g. children think cartoons are good for them, their parents approve of their viewing, and some children like to interact with other people while watching cartoons), the program content of boys' programs and girls' programs differs.

Because this study was of a program designed for boys, it appears important to consider the specific attributes of the program and how *The Transformers* may influence male acculturation. In general, the study showed that the animated robotic adventure cartoon *The Transformers* contained: (a) transforming characters, (b) technology and robotics, (c) themes of violence, (d) orientation to school–aged male children, (e) unusual language, and (f) the objective of selling related toys.

Transforming Characters. The characters in the program *The Transformers* are robots which transform into different figures. When one child said the main thing he did not like about the television show was how fast they transformed, he may have hit on a significant idea. The toys appeal to children because of the transformation to robots which takes time and thought. On the cartoons, the transformations happen so quickly that they may fail to stimulate the child's curiosity. If the cartoons emphasized the transformation process rather than the violent themes, they may have more positive appeal to children. When the author watched children playing with the toys, the children appeared to demonstrate creative thinking and problem–solving processes. For those who advocate creativity, the toys and the cartoons may have admirable qualities because they require the child to visualize an object as something it is not.

Technology. Robotic adventures contain characters and language involving robots and computer–generated equipment. Some character voices are distorted to sound mechanical, and dialogue employs technological explanations. Perhaps the time spent watching these cartoons actually helps children grasp technological ideas. In one episode, for example, magnetic power immobilized the computerized Transformers. Children who viewed that program may have learned something about computer technology. One may criticize the program, however, because many technological aspects were scientifically incorrect. The scientific nature of the program appears to be part of its male orientation. Whether or not the information is correct, the children who watch the program may become more comfortable in dealing with technology in other contexts.

Themes of Violence. Although cartoons have long held themes of good versus evil, *The Transformers* cartoons actually use the term of "evil" to clarify the distinction, as demonstrated by the "Heroic Autobots" and "Evil Decepticons." One wonders if a positive message of the episode's moral can permeate the cartoon's violence. The dichotomy between good and evil teaches a black and white perception which may distort children's views of the world.

The significant differences between boys and girls on the concept of being able to distinguish between good and evil merits interpretation. One possible explanation is that boys are more inclined to see a dichotomy, while girls are more inclined to perceive good and bad qualities in various characters. There are several indicators to enable a viewer to identify good from bad Transformer characters. Boys may have watched the program and played with the toys more, so they were better informed of the signs to indicate differences: color, symbols, voices, and behaviors. For example, higher pitched voices, Southern accents, youthful voices, and more pleasant vocal pitch and rate characterize good Transformers. The good Transformers exhibit more positive values and behaviors than the evil Transformers. Hoffner and Cantor (1985) found that perceptual dependence on appearance decreased with age and perceptual dependence on behavior increased with age. Thus, one could expect older children to be able to tell the difference between good and evil Transformers based on the Transformers' behaviors, including their association with other Transformers.

Based on the findings of the adult raters in this study as compared to other studies that analyzed the amount of program violence (Denison, 1985; Harrison, 1981, p. 129; Kaye, 1974, p. 62), *The Transformers* contains up to twice the violence of network cartoons, and eight times the violence of adult programming. Beyond the violence of physical acts—shooting, explosions, whippings, and fights—*The Transformers* also uses violent language. One may wonder if the beginnings of excessive violence in male adult programs and films is nurtured through such extraordinarily frequent violence designed for boys.

School-aged Male Children. This study indicated that *The Transformers* program was preferred by boys, as supported by the content, language, use of male characters, and male actors in advertising. *The Transformers* is one of the most popular syndicated shows for children aged two to 11, but producers gear it to boys aged five to 11, who are in their peak fantasy years (Denison, 1985). Of *The Transformers* episodes analyzed, the only human character was a male youth. The children interviewed indicated strong preferences for cartoons based on their sex. One girl said: "Boys probably play with Transformers more than girls because they probably have more." But the question remains, why do boys have more? According to Lowery and DeFleur (1983), boys prefer adventure programs and girls prefer romantic programs (p. 281). The discussions with children in this study support their conclusion. The excessive violence in cartoons geared for boys makes one wonder about the possible long term effects of such a barrage of violent messages. The author was surprised by how few cartoon programs were regularly watched by both sexes. The findings certainly add support to the concept that Americans define male–female roles early in life.

The lack of competent women in the *The Transformers* not only gives the female viewers negative models, but adds to a general perception that women are excluded from a male world. Because *The Transformers* has a primarily male audience, boys are the primary receivers of these messages. "Research studies have documented that female roles have held at 25 to 30 percent of all TV characterizations. Surprisingly, this percentage has been constant for thirty years!" (Reed, 1980, p. 350). The proportion in most children's cartoons is far more unbalanced. In *The Transformers* cartoons, for example, the ratio is approximately 15 males to one female. In the Smurf cartoons—more popular among female children than males, according to the children interviewed—the male–female ratio is more than 50 males to one female character. One must wonder how male and female children—as they learn about sex differences—perceive the character roles in the cartoons they view. We can assume then that both boys and girls are used to seeing females excluded from their programs. In addition, the nature of the roles of females is subservient in this particular program designed for boys.

Unusual Language. The language of *The Transformers* proved to be unusual. One aspect was that names, titles, and dialogue frequently employed complex and harsh symbols. One can find many specific examples of the technical language use, such as: "...disturb my cerebral–circuitry." (Carlin, 1986, p. 5). Slang sayings were used such as: "tall, dark, and gruesome;" "that should cook that turkey;" "parting is such sweet sorrow;" and "this robot still has a trump card to play." It seems unlikely that children can relate positively to such expressions.

Some adults who watched the program complained that it was complicated and hard to follow. To test the level of language, a segment from the beginning of one episode was analyzed to determine its reading grade–level. Using several indexes, the reading level ranged from third to eleventh grade. Specifically, Spache indicated 3.7 grade, Dale–Chall indicated 9th–10th grade, Gunning–Fog indicated tenth grade, and Flesche indicated eleventh grade. One wonders what effect this language level has for preschool and elementary children. One may argue that the show may be designed to attract high school and college viewers rather than just young children. In fact, according to local Arbitron (1986) ratings, there was a smaller proportion of adult (over age 17) viewers of *The Transformers* than for many other children's cartoons.

One issue in the use of language was that of power. Boys perceived Transformers as powerful more frequently than girls did. The writers of the "Ultimate Doom" (1985) used strong lines, especially as spoken by the evil decepticons. One line used by the decepticon leader was: "Silence you miserable flesh creature, you are to be the first of a new breed—a breed of slaves." A doctor said, "Creating a mindless slave is simplicity itself, thanks to the brilliant complexity of my hypno-chip." The hypno-chip was a special mechanism implanted in the human brain to hypnotize. The father, under hypnosis, told his son, "When next we meet, we are enemies" (Family Home Entertainment, 1985). This use of power appears inappropriate for young viewers. Fiske (1986) discussed the influence of the sense of powerlessness on the part of children (p. 205). Perhaps because children lack power they appreciate cartoon characters who exhibit great power. One may wonder whether the size and power of a Transformer makes children feel a vicarious sense of power or instead magnifies a child's lack of power. Perhaps the boys empathize more with the male characters, or maybe they empathize with the humans who are portrayed as the size of a Transformer hand.

The program encourages boys to accept complex, unusual, and scientific language beyond their reading level. The correct use of language, sophisticated grammatical structure, and multiple syllable words may be the positive aspects of the program. In some ways, the language may be one of the major strong points of the program, but again one may wonder why a program designed to encourage boys to push their language usage fails to have a counter-part for girls. The cartoons appear to be one more vehicle for encouraging male dominance in our society.

Objective of Selling Toys. Researchers have questioned the use of commercial advertisements among children's programs. Commercials send children three messages: (a) all problems are resolvable, (b) all problems are resolvable quickly, (c) all problems are resolvable quickly through technology (Postman, 1981, p. 44). But is selling to children unfair? There are some 40 product-driven children's programs on television (Denison, 1985). Pecora (1986) contends that children's media are a political economy—the product and programs are tied in for marketing and programming success—despite a concern that children should be protected from unscrupulous advertisers. People recognize children as less mature, less educated, and in need of protection (Kaye, 1974, p. 73). Certainly commercialism has been around for years and competition is an important factor (Woolery, 1983, pp. 41–43), as evidenced by Mickey Mouse products. But these new product-driven cartoons start with the marketing before the programs. To the television networks, independent producers, stations, and toy manufacturers, profits come first, and profits are gained through product sales.

Broadcasters have found a built–in, presold audience for their new programs, a boast that has produced may hits. He–Man, for example, sold more than 70 million plastic figures in the last three years. One can easily understand why television broadcasters and toy manufacturers have such a close relationship (Waters & Uehling, 1985, p. 85). In 1985, 51 companies manufactured 121 Transformer logo products from shoes to bedsheets, and Transformer toys grossed over $100 million in 1984, and even more in 1985 (Denison, 1985). The toy manufacturers and producers of animated robotic adventures work together, as evidenced by the advertisement "Challenge of the GoBots. They're Awesome! Check Local TV Listings for Time and Station....Copyright 1985 Hanna–Barbera Productions, Inc. GoBots is a trademark of Tonka Corporation" (Kay, 1986, p. 7). The only difference between a Transformer and a GoBot is the name of the manufacturer, and both manufacturers have television shows about the toys to sell their goods. This blatant use of negative programming to sell toys is unique among certain adventure shows.

Networks only need a few hours of children's programming per week, but independents need five hours per day. Turning out program after program, to be aired twice daily, nearly every day of the week makes extraordinary demands. The sheer economics of producing so many shows explains, in part, why the programs are used to sell toys.

Despite the existence of product–driven programs designed specifically for girls (*Cabbage Patch Kids*, for example), none appears as successful as *The Transformers*. One may wonder if there is additional emphasis on the boy consumer. An analysis of trends in toys designed for boys versus toys designed for girls may give some interesting insights. Perhaps the cartoons for boys are designed to broaden the toy market for boys (encouraging purchase of dolls for boys). Perhaps the future will hold a broadening of the girls' market for toys by using media to promote toys for girls that have traditionally been considered boys' toys. This marketing of toys may have a significant impact on male–female roles and acculturation in future years.

Although one might expect the transforming toys to fall by the way of many previous fads—there is evidence that their popularity is now fading—these new toys have ingenious characteristics that could make them popular for years to come. Just as Superman is 50 years old and the Barbie doll is a quarter of a century, these Transformer dolls and cartoons have lasting potential. With the economic motivation of product–driven shows, it seems likely that manufacturers will continue to try to make children buy adventure toys.

This study indicated potentially serious problems in the product–driven children's program *The Transformers*. In light of the body of research on negative effects of children's television, content charac-teristics of *The Transformers*—including inappropriate technical lan-guage, degrading and violent language; violent actions; superiority of males over females; a complexity of evil lines that use an unnatural dichotomy between good and evil; concepts of control and power; and the commercial motivation of a production–driven children's program—may provide potential for negative effects on the child viewer. The fact that the program is designed for boys makes one question the negative messages boys are receiving about violence and control. Although Transformer toys may give their primarily male consumers a creative and modern puzzle form, the extension of *The Transformers* into a television series has negative associations for children.

References

Arbitron Ratings Television. (1986, July). *Audience estimates in the Arbitron ratings market of Lafayette, LA.*

Becker, S.L. (1983). *Discovering mass communication.* Dallas: Scott, Foresman and Company.

Bower, B. (1984, September). Kids' aggressive behavior linked to watching tv violence. *Science News, 126*(12), 190.

Carlin, M. (Ed.) (1986, February). The menace of megatron. *The Transformers,* Marvel Comics Group, *1*(13).

Collins, W.A. (1981, Fall). Recent advances in research on cognitive processing television viewing. *Journal of Broadcasting, 25*(4), 327–334.

Davis, D.K., & Baran, S.J. (1981). *Mass communication and everyday life.* Belmont, CA: Wadsworth Publishing Company.

Denison, D.C. (1985, December 8). The year of playing dangerously. *Boston Globe Magazine,* p. 14.

Dorr, A. (1981, Fall). Television and affective development and functioning: Maybe this decade. *Journal of Broadcasting, 25*(4), 335–345.

Family Home Entertainment (Producer). The ultimate doom. (1985). *The Transformers.* [Home Video Program].

Fischer, S. (1983). *Kid's t.v.: The first 25 years.* New York: Facts on Film Publications.

Fiske, J. (1986, June). Television and popular culture: Reflections on British and Australian critical practice. *Critical Studies in Mass Communication, 3*(2) 200–216.

Fowles, J. (1982). *Television viewers vs. media snobs: What TV does for people.* New York: Stein and Day.

Gronbeck, B.E. (1983, Fall). The "scholar's anthology:" Televisual studies. *The Central States Speech Journal, 34*(3), 139.

Harrison, R.P. (1981). *The cartoon.* Beverly Hills: Sage Publications.

Hasbro Bradley, Inc. (1985) *The Transformers.* [Advertising Flier]. Pawtucket, RI.

Hoffner, C., & Cantor, J. (1985, November). Developmental differences in responses to a television character's appearance and behavior. *Developmental Psychology, 21*(6), 1065–1074.

Lowery, H., & De Fleur, M. L. (1983). *Milestones in mass communication research.* New York: Longman.

Kay, S. (1986, February). Exploring the unknown. *Fraggle Rock, 1*(6).

Kaye, E. (1974). *The family guide to children's television.* New York: Random House Publications.

Newcomb, H.M. (1986, June). American television criticism. *Critical Studies in Mass Communication, 3*(2) 217–228.

Pecora, N. (1986, October). *The political economy of children's media*. Paper presented at the Culture and Communications Conference, Philadelphia, PA.

Penney, J.C. (1985). *Christmas 1985*. Milwaukee: J.C. Penney Company, Inc., Catalog Division.

Piccirillo, M.S. (1986, September). On the authenticity of televisual experience: A critical exploration of para–social closure. *Critical Studies in Mass Communication, 3*(3), 337–355.

Postman, N. (1981, January) TV's "disastrous" impact on children. *U.S. News and World Report*.

Prawat, R.S., Anderson, A.H., & Hapkiewicz, W. (1985, March). Is the scariest monster also the least real? An examination of children's reality classifications, *The Journal of Genetic Psychology, 146*(1), 7–12.

Rebel, K. (1983, June). *Effects of new electronic technologies on opinion formation and attitudes of young people*. Paper presented at the meeting of the Social Science Education Consortium, Athens, GA. (ERIC Document Reproduction Service No. ED 231 746)

Reed, B. (1980). Sexism in the media world. In M. Emery & T.C. Smythe (Eds.), *Readings in mass communication concepts and issues in the mass media* (4th edition). Dubuque, Iowa: Wm. C. Brown.

Rice, M., & Wartella, E. (1981, Fall). Television as a medium of communication: Implications for how to regard the child viewer. *Journal of Broadcasting, 25*(4), 365–372.

Tooth, G. (1985, January) Why children's tv turns off so many parents. *U.S. News & World Report*.

Waters, H.F., & Uehling, M.D. (1985, May). Toying with kid's tv. *Newsweek*.

Woolery, G.W. (1983). *Children's television: The first thirty-five years, 1946–1981*. Metchen, N.J.: The Scarecrow Press.

Note

The author expresses her appreciation to Lisa M. Latour and Arlene F. Desselles for their contributions to the ideas, research, and presentation of this study.

THOUGHT PROVOKERS

Are there television programs for girls and television programs for boys? What do each type communicate to the intended audience? How is each program style effective in attracting the assigned target?

CHAPTER SEVENTEEN
Sex–Role Stereotyping in Fragrance Advertisements

Lisa Bonelli

Media portrayal of the sexes has been of particular interest to researchers. Specifically, many studies examine the sex–role stereotypes found in magazine advertisements. This research falls into two categories: (1) initial studies which identified the presence of sex–role stereotypes in magazine advertisements (for example, Courtney & Lockeretz, 1971; Lysonski, 1983; Pingree, Hawkins, Butler, & Paisley, 1976; Sexton & Haberman, 1974; Skelly & Lundstrom, 1981; Wagner & Banos, 1973), and (2) later studies which looked beyond identification and examined societal response to stereotypes (for example, Barry, 1985; Lundstrom & Sciglimpaglia, 1977; Wortzel & Frisbee, 1974).

Many studies expanded on an early research design by exploring different sample sources. Some researchers examined sex–role stereotyping in all of the advertisements found within one magazine (Courtney & Lockeretz, 1971; Lysonski, 1983; Skelly & Lundstrom, 1981; Wagner & Banos, 1973). Other researchers looked at sex–role stereotyping in specific magazines (Easton & Toner, 1983) or specific product categories within magazines (Sexton & Haberman, 1974). However, no study has yet examined sex–role stereotyping in advertisements for one product only.

The use of one product for the analysis of sex–role stereotyping in magazine advertisements necessitates special consideration in the choice of that product. Fragrance products, especially, possess a number of characteristics which facilitate the analysis of differences between male and female stereotypes. First, fragrance manufacturers do not make a single product which is marketed to both men and women. Instead, there are men's fragrances and women's fragrances, each of which is marketed exclusively to one sex. As a result of this dichotomy, fragrance advertisers often use different appeals for men and women which correspond to the supposedly different attributes of each product.

Second, fragrance is an image product, and image products need emotional and psychological advertising appeals to compensate for the lack of tangible attributes (Keon, 1984). Since emotional appeals in fragrance advertisements are used to target both the male and female audience, and since men and women are stereotypically seen as differing emotionally, this perceived emotional difference ought to be manifest in most fragrance advertising appeals because they are designed for one sex only.

Finally, the fragrance market is highly competitive. The number of new products introduced each year continues to increase, although most men and women already use some form of fragrance ("Fragrance Foundation Assays Survival," 1984). The advertising strategy that results from this saturated market attempts to distinguish each product from all the others and, in doing so, yields a multitude of different emotional appeals. In their attempt to corner the fragrance market, advertisers use what Larson (1983) calls the "unifying style of persuasion." The goal of this style is to move an audience that already feels positively about a product toward a particular brand by designing an emotional appeal with which the audience can identify. This appeal is filled with emotional elements, such as abstract imagery and poetic language, to entice the audience to participate in the persuasive process. In fragrance advertising this is often accomplished by creating fantasy situations and promising fulfillment of the fantasy through the purchase of the product.

Magazines, because they are a highly specific form of print media, allow advertisers to target specific audiences by advertising in magazines with readers who fit a particular demographic profile. The present study analyzes the advertising appeals used in men's and women's fragrance advertising targeted toward male and female audiences in men's and women's magazines. To explore these appeals more fully, the following research questions guided this study:

1. What are the differences between the number of fragrance advertisements found in men's and women's magazines?
2. What are the emotional appeals contained in fragrance advertisements in men's and women's magazines?
3. What are the differences between the emotional appeals contained in fragrance advertisements in men's and women's magazines?
4. How often do traditional sex–role appeals occur in fragrance advertisements in men's and women's magazines?

Method

To examine the emotional appeals found in fragrance advertisements, a content analysis of the fragrance advertisements found in three men's magazines and three women's magazines was conducted. A primary consideration in the choice of each magazine was the demographic profile of the target audience. This profile was important to assure comparable male and female audiences. The three men's magazines, *Esquire*, *Playboy*, and *Gentlemen's Quarterly*, and three women's magazines, *Harper's Bazaar*, *Cosmopolitan*, and

Mademoiselle were matched based on the age and income of the readers, and circulation size of the magazine.[1]

Advertisers use these men's and women's magazines to target male and female readers. Although these magazines may, in fact be read at times by members of the opposite sex, the number is not large enough for advertisers to change or redirect their advertising appeals. What is important in judging magazine advertising is the target audience, those for whom the advertising appeal is designed, not the readers. The male and female target audience for these magazines can be judged by the 1986 media packages for each magazine. The sample of advertisements was drawn from the April, 1986, issue of each magazine. April is a non–holiday month and did not include any holiday advertisements which sometimes contain emotionally–biased appeals. Also, April is the beginning of a new season in which many advertising campaigns are launched.

First, the fragrance advertisements found in each issue of the six magazines were drawn to form the sample. This yielded a total of 57 advertisements: 47 from the women's magazines, 10 from the men's magazines. After duplicate advertisements were removed, the resulting sample of 45 was divided into four categories: men's fragrance advertisements targeted toward men (n = 7), men's fragrance advertisements targeted toward women (n = 2), women's fragrance advertisements targeted toward men (n = 0) and women's fragrance advertisements targeted toward women (n = 35). One combined men's and women's fragrance advertisement was found in a women's magazine. This advertisement did not fit into any one of the four categories and was excluded from the analysis.

Second, to identify the appeals found in fragrance advertisements, the sample was coded using three emotional appeal categories: (1) *The Emotional Elements in the Style*, (2) *The Persuasive Manner of Delivery*, and (3) *The Emotional Appeal to Different Sexes*. These three content analytic schemes were developed previously by examining a large variety of fragrance advertisements. Certain patterns were apparent in those advertisements which aimed to persuade the audience with emotional appeals. The first, *The Emotional Elements in the Style*, describes the overall emotional image of the advertisement and consists of 11 theme categories: (1) Sexual/Sensual; (2) Beauty/Good Looks; (3) Natural; (4) Humor; (5) Magical/Mystic; (6) Remembered; (7) Love/Emotional Security; (8) Romance; (9) Elegance/Class; (10) Power/Strength; and (11) Unique. The second, *The Persuasive Manner of Delivery*, describes the persuasive way in which the emotional message was presented, and consists of two major categories with three appeals each. The first category is Visually Stimulating Appeals consisting of: (1) Dreamy/Textural; (2) Abstract/Odd; and (3) Concrete/Simple; and the second is Verbally Stimulating Appeals consisting of: (1) No Statement; (2) Short Statement; and (3) Long Statement. The third, *The Emotional Appeal to Gender*, describes sex–role depictions in the advertisements and consists of three categories: (1) Traditional; (2) Non–Traditional; and (3) Neutral.

This study examines how these emotional appeals and techniques differ in terms of the sex of the target audience by comparing the emotional appeals contained in specific fragrance advertisements targeted toward males and females.

Results and Discussion

The analysis of advertising content in men's and women's magazines reveals a number of differences in advertising targeted at women and in advertising targeted at men. When advertisers target women, they use complex, appearance–related emotional appeals. A pattern of stereotyping emerges which characterizes women as externally or "other" oriented, concerned primarily with their appearance and their relationships with men. Conversely, when advertisers target men, they use simple, ego gratification emotional appeals. These appeals stereotype men as internally or "self" oriented, concerned primarily with themselves.

Women's magazines contain almost five times as many fragrance advertisements as the men's magazines. Fragrance, because it is designed to enhance attractiveness, can be categorized as a beauty product. Thus, fragrance is a specific product which, as advertised, reinforces the stereotype that women are more concerned with appearance than men because it is advertised more frequently to women.

In terms of the magazines examined for this study, the most advertising space is devoted to fragrance in *Harper's Bazaar*, followed by *Cosmopolitan* and *Mademoiselle*. In men's magazines, *Playboy* has the largest number of fragrance advertisements, followed by *Gentlemen's Quarterly* and *Esquire*.

The high income magazine for women, *Harper's Bazaar*, contains the largest number of fragrance advertisements, while the high income magazine for men, *Esquire*, contains the least number of fragrance advertisements. Advertisers may feel that wealthy women will spend their money on appearance related products, while wealthy men will not. This again reinforces the stereotype that women in general, and wealthy women in particular, are concerned with their appearance, while men in general, and wealthy men in particular, are not.

Finally, although women's magazines contain men's fragrance advertisements, the men's magazines do not contain any women's fragrance advertisements. This finding stereotypes women and women's relation to men in terms of appearance related products. Fragrance advertisers appeal to women to purchase men's fragrance products, but do not appeal to men to purchase women's fragrance products. This implies that women should be concerned with the selection of men's fragrance and that men should not be concerned with the selection of women's fragrance.

Thus, the fragrance advertising trends noted in men's and women's magazines reveal a traditional depiction of the sexes. The stereotype that women are more concerned with appearance and appearance related products than men is perpetuated by the media—that is, by their perception of what men and women are interested in purchasing.

Table 1 contains the results of the comparative analysis of *The Emotional Elements in the Style* of fragrance advertisements. This scheme is defined as the process of tapping into the emotional state of an individual by offering him or her the opportunity to "be" more attractive or to "possess" some attractive quality. These appeals function on an emotional level because they involve placing oneself into a fantasy situation created by the overall image of the advertisement.

Table 1
Comparative Analysis of the
Emotional Elements in the Style
of Fragrance Advertisements

	Men's Magazines		Women's Magazines	
Category	Ads for Men's Fragrance	Ads for Women's Fragrance	Ads for Men's Fragrance	Ads for Women's Fragrance
Beauty/ Good looks	1(14) *	0	0	17(48)
Elegance/ Class	3(42)	0	0	12(34)
Humor	0	0	0	2(5)
Love/ Emotional Security	0	0	0	3(8)
Magical/ Mystic	0	0	0	7(20)
Natural	2(29)	0	1(50)	7(20)
Power/ Strength	2(29)	0	0	5(14)
Remembered	1(14)	0	0	4(11)
Romance	0	0	0	16(45)
Sexual/ Sensual	2(29)	0	1(50)	19(54)
Unique	2(29)	0	1(50)	6(17)

Numbers of advertisements are listed; percentages are contained in parentheses.

Each emotional element in the style is identified as an obvious appeal in the advertisement and is placed into one or more of the 11 distinct, but not exclusive, theme categories: *beauty/good looks*, *elegance/class*, *humor*, *love/emotional security*, *magical/mystic*, *natural*, *power/strength*, *remembered*, *romance*, *sexual/sensual*, and *unique*.

The most popular emotional appeals directed at men and women reveal a pattern whereby advertisers reinforce traditional sex-role stereotypes. The media appeal to men with ego-gratification appeals, characterized by the exclusion or submission of women. On the other hand, the media appeal to women with relationship oriented appeals which are characterized by the necessary inclusion of men in the advertisement for the emotional appeal to function properly.

Tables 2A and 2B report the results of the comparative analysis of *The Persuasive Manner of Delivery*. Table 2A contains the results of the comparative analysis of *The Visual Persuasive Manner of Delivery*. This scheme is defined by the technique of presenting a message in a manner which emotionally stimulates the audience by creating a visual mood or scene into which the individual can transpose himself or herself. This technique, in many instances, helps reinforce the stereotypes present in the emotional appeals. There are three visual techniques examined in this analysis: *concrete/simple*, *dreamy/textural*, and *abstract/odd*.

Table 2A
Comparative Analysis of
The Visual Persuasive Manner of Delivery
in Fragrance Advertisements

Category	Men's Magazines		Women's Magazine	
	Ads for Men's Fragrance	Ads for Women's Fragrance	Ads for Men's Fragrance	Ads for Women's Fragrance
Abstract/Odd	2(29) *	0	0	7(20)
Concrete/ Simple	3(42)	0	2(100)	14(40)
Dreamy/ Textural	2(29)	0	0	14(40)
TOTAL	7(100)	0	2(100)	35(100)

Numbers of advertisements are listed; percentages are contained in parentheses.

Table 2B contains the results of the comparative analysis of *The Verbal Persuasive Manner of Delivery*. This scheme is defined by the technique of presenting the message in a manner which verbally stimulates the reader. The most frequently used verbal techniques function to enhance the complex emotional appeals targeted at women and to simplify and interpret the emotional appeals targeted at men. There are three verbal techniques examined in this analysis: *short statement*, *long statement*, and *no statement*.

Table 2B
Comparative Analysis of
The Verbal Persuasive Manner of Delivery
In Fragrance Advertisements

| | Men's Magazines | | Women's Magazines | |
| | Ads for Men's Fragrance | Ads for Women's Fragrance | Ads for Men's Fragrance | Ads for Women's Fragrance |
Category				
Non–Verbal	1(14) *	0	0	5(14)
Long Statement	0	0	0	9(25)
Short Statement	6(86)	0	2(100)	21(60)
TOTAL	7(100)	0	2(100)	35(99) **

* *Numbers of advertisements are listed; percentages are contained in parentheses.*
***Percentages may not equal 100 due to rounding error.*

Table 3 contains the results of the comparative analysis of *The Emotional Appeal to Gender*. This scheme is defined as the *traditional*, *non–traditional*, or *neutral* depiction of the sexes. The *traditional* stereotypic portrayal of the sexes is the most widely used in both men's and women's fragrance advertisements.

Table 3
Comparative Analysis of
The Emotional Appeal to Gender in Fragrance Advertisements

| | Men's Magazines | | Women's Magazines | |
| | Ads for Men's Fragrance | Ads for Women's Fragrance | Ads for Men's Fragrance | Ads for Women's Fragrance |
Category				
Neutral	0	0	0	5(14)
Non–traditional	1(14) *	0	0	6(17)
Traditional	6(86)	0	2(100)	24(69)
TOTAL	7(100)	0	2(100)	35(100)

* *Numbers of advertisements are listed; percentages are contained in parentheses.*

Sex-Role Stereotyping in Fragrance Advertisements Targeted Toward Men

The analysis of sex-role stereotyping in fragrance advertisements targeted toward men is based on the three content analytic schemes and reveals a distinct pattern of sex-role stereotyping. The first scheme, *The Emotional Elements in the Style*, reveals the type of emotional appeals found in fragrance advertisements targeted toward men. Seven of the eleven emotional theme categories present in this scheme are contained in the advertisements for men's fragrance targeted toward a male audience.

Elegance/Class is the most popular emotional appeal found in fragrance advertisements targeted toward men. This appeal is defined by any visual or verbal reference to wealth or class such as expensive clothing, jewelry, a luxurious scene or prestigious product name. This appeal directly involves money and status and, when targeted toward men, usually contains a man in a tuxedo or three piece suit, or using a prestigious product. The stereotypical portrayal of men as competitors, striving to achieve wealth and status, is perpetuated by the media with this type of advertising appeal.

There are four other popular emotional appeals found in fragrance advertisements targeted toward men. The *natural* appeal is identified by flowers, nature, water, the sky, trees, clean, crisp clothing or appearance, ruggedness, activity, sports or health. This appeal involves an outdoor scene into which a man can transpose himself to hunt, fish, compete in a yacht race, or just relax. This appeal involves the gratification of the man, alone, and perpetuates the stereotype that men are outdoorsmen and that women are not an important part of the outdoors.

The *unique* appeal in fragrance advertisements targeted toward men also reveals a self-centered orientation. This appeal functions emotionally to set the reader apart from the crowd and is defined by presenting the product or model as unique or extraordinary. For example, the Aramis men's fragrance advertisement reads, "Tradition with a dash of the unexpected," and displays a man holding a briefcase, standing alone in the desert under a red tent. This appeal stereotypes men as individuals or loners who are preoccupied with business matters.

The *power/strength* appeal is defined by references to strength and power, such as largeness in the size of the product or model, or the ability to "make someone else do as you wish."

The *power/strength* appeal does not exclude women from the advertisement. Instead, it uses women for an exploitive purpose: to elevate the man. This ego-gratification appeal works through the belittlement of women. For example, only the hands of the couple are seen in the Drakkar Noir men's fragrance advertisement. The man is clutching a bottle of cologne, while the woman's hands are gently reaching after and touching the man's hands. The caption reads, "Where Gentle Strength Triumphs." This appeal perpetuates dominant and submissive stereotypes and suggests that strength in the man will compel the woman to "follow" him.

Lastly, the *sexual/sensual* appeal to men also involves ego gratification and the submission of women. This appeal is defined by the implication of sensuality or sexiness such as passionate facial expression, exposed body parts, emphasis on suggestive body parts, phallic objects or bedroom scenes. In many instances, when this appeal is targeted to men, there is no indication of a relationship between the man and the woman in the advertisement. Instead, the emphasis is on self gratification. This appeal is evident in the Calvin Klein Obsession advertisement which features only naked women. The male reader is removed from the scene and obviously derives his satisfaction as an observer. This appeal perpetuates the stereotype that men have only a physical interest in sex.

The second content analytic scheme, *The Persuasive Manner of Delivery*, reports the visual and verbal techniques used in the presentation of the emotional elements. These techniques reinforce the stereotypes present in the fragrance advertisements. In *The Visual Persuasive Manner of Delivery*, the most popular visual technique used in men's fragrance advertisements is the *concrete/simple* approach, which is defined by a direct, obvious and easily recognizable picture. This technique reinforces the simple, uncomplicated message of the most popular emotional appeals targeted at men: *elegance/class*, *nature*, *power/strength* and *sexual/sensual*. These appeals remain simple because they do not involve another individual—a woman. Instead they concentrate on the man alone: his emotions, wishes, feelings and desires.

The *dreamy/textural* and *abstract/odd* visual techniques are each used in almost one third of the men's fragrance advertisements targeted toward men. Despite the complex visual imagery associated with these two techniques, the emotional message remains simple and uncomplicated. For example, the *dreamy/textural* technique, defined by the use of devices such as fog, color, clouds, texture or a watery blur superimposed over the picture, is used in an the Old Spice Leather after-shave advertisement. This advertisement is one-half page composed entirely of a textured, worn, brown leather jacket. The most obvious message implicit in this picture is the image of the jacket itself. This realistic presentation entices the reader to imagine himself as the strong, rugged wearer of the jacket.

The Aramis cologne advertisement exemplifies the *abstract/odd* visual approach, defined by the presentation of an altered visual statement with juxtaposed elements, transposed images, odd lighting and abstract designs. This advertisement depicts a man in a three-piece suit, standing alone in the middle of the desert, under a bright red tent. This image visually reinforces the *unique* emotional appeal, yet keeps the message simple. The abstract design and the odd solitary depiction of the man provides the reader with a memorable impression of the man as an individual.

In *The Verbal Persuasive Manner of Delivery*, the most popular verbal technique used to appeal to men is the *short statement*. This technique is defined by a concise yet powerful emotional phrase or caption which interprets or expounds the visual message. This technique appears in well over three–fourths of the men's fragrance advertisements targeted toward men. In these instances, the *short statement* simplifies the advertisements by clarifying the visual message and spelling out the emotional message. In the R de Capucci advertisement, the caption reads, "the new, masculine, long lasting fragrance for men."

The *non–verbal* technique, designed to let the reader interpret the visual message without interference, appears in a small number of men's fragrance advertisements. This technique allows the visual message, which is usually *concrete/simple*, to predominate as the overall theme of the advertisement. An example of this technique is the Calvin Klein Obsession advertisement in which the appeal is explicitly sexual. A verbal interpretation here is unnecessary and might possibly disrupt the emotional processes triggered by the picture.

The *long statement* technique, defined by a lengthy story, poem or dialogue, does not appear at all in the men's fragrance advertisements targeted toward men. This is not surprising because the general tendency regarding advertising to men reveals a simple pattern most accurately illustrated with short, uncomplicated messages.

Similarly, the results of the third content analytic scheme, *The Emotional Appeal to Gender*, reveal that the stereotypical portrayal of the sexes is the most popular in men's fragrance advertisements targeted toward men. The *traditional* appeal to sex differences, which appears in almost all of the advertisements targeted towards men, is defined by the depiction of the male in a masculine, dominant role and the female in a feminine, submissive role. Many of the fragrance advertisements use this stereotypic image of the strong and powerful male as an emotional appeal. In doing so, the advertisers portray stereotypic masculinity as the proper and correct sex orientation for men.

The *non–traditional* appeal appears in few of the men's fragrance advertisements. This appeal portrays men possessing stereotypic feminine attributes such as shyness, tenderness, and passivity, and women possessing stereotypic masculine qualities such as strength and dominance. When targeted to men, however, this appeal is "incomplete." For example, the Drakkar Noir caption reads, "Where Gentle Strength Triumphs." The effect of the word "gentle" is undermined by the presence of the word "strength" and the dominant role of the male in the advertisement.

The *neutral* sex appeal does not appear in any of the men's fragrance advertisements. These *neutral* appeals are devoid of sex–role portrayal entirely and focus on some other element or theme instead. This suggests that men are not really conscious of sex–role portrayal, and that, subsequently, advertisers do not feel it is necessary to avoid sex–role portrayal, sexist or otherwise, in their advertisements which target men.

Sex–Role Stereotyping in Fragrance Advertisements Targeted Toward Women

The analysis of sex–role stereotyping in fragrance advertisements targeted toward women uses the three content analytic schemes to examine both women's fragrance advertisements in women's magazines and men's fragrance advertisements found in women's magazines because they both target women. The analysis of both the women's fragrance advertisements targeted toward women and the men's fragrance advertisements targeted toward women continues to show a pattern of sex–role stereotyping.

The first scheme, *The Emotional Elements in the Style*, examines the emotional appeals in the advertisements. Unlike the the fragrance advertisements targeted toward men, all eleven of the emotional appeals exist in the women's fragrance advertisements targeted toward women. The differing emotional content of advertisements targeted at men and women reveals an obvious sex–role stereotype: that women are emotionally more complex than men.

The most popular appeals found in women's fragrance advertisements targeted toward women require the direct or implied presence of a man. The single most popular appeal to women, *sexual/sensual*, rarely emphasizes physical gratification as it does in the appeal to men. Instead, the advertisements focus on the relationship between the man and the woman. This difference in purpose upholds a traditional, stereotypical portrayal of the sexes in which sex, for women, is depicted primarily as a method to attract a man.

Consequently, although physical gratification appeals appear from time to time in women's fragrance advertisements, they are of secondary importance. For example, the Calvin Klein Obsession advertisement for women, unlike the same product's advertisements for men, has both men and a woman in the advertisement. The theme of physical gratification is important, but the most shocking and obvious message is that this woman has the sexual attention of not one, but three men.

The *beauty/good looks* appeal is the second most popular in women's fragrance advertisements targeted toward women. This appeal features a beautiful model, connecting the fragrance with her attractive and youthful qualities. If women are indeed more appearance conscious than men, which is how advertisers perceive them, it is this type of appeal, repeated time and time again by advertisers themselves, which sets the standards.

The *romance* appeal, defined by moonlit and sunset scenes, wine glasses and candlelit dinners, flowers, especially roses, lace, bows, or a romantic bird such as a swan or a dove, is the third most popular appeal to women. This appeal most certainly involves the presence of a man and strongly reinforces the stereotypical standards associated with romance. By repeatedly pairing specific romantic symbols with relationships between men and women, this type of appeal sets the behavioral norms and expectancies that women hold for romantic relationships.

The fourth most popular emotional appeal found in women's fragrance advertisements targeted toward women is *elegance/class*. Unlike the portrayal of this appeal in advertisements targeted toward men, the emotional message does not emphasize status as an entity unto itself. Instead, the elegant model is beautiful and alluring, and often in the company of an equally attractive and elegant man. When the model is alone, she is posed in some seductive or alluring pose, implying the presence of an man in the advertisement and reinforcing the stereotypic relationship between wealth and attractiveness.

The last popular emotional appeal found in women's fragrance advertisements targeted toward women involves what is stereotypically known as the "feminine mystique." This appeal, *magical/mystic*, is identified by the presence of some "otherworldly" or exotic scene, strange shapes and designs, dark and mysterious colors, the moon or odd lighting. Many of these elements imply secrecy or unnatural powers. The association of these elements with an appearance–related product reinforces the stereotype that women should remain mysterious and secretive if they wish to be considered attractive by men.

Four emotional appeals show large differences in frequency, depending on the targeted audience. The first, *beauty/good looks*, appears in three times as many women's fragrance advertisements targeted toward women than men's fragrance advertisements targeted toward men. This result is not surprising because society in general, and the media in particular, have traditionally emphasized the importance of attractiveness for women and de–emphasized its importance for men.

Second, the *magical/mystic* appeal appears in a substantial number of women's fragrance advertisements targeted toward women and not at all in men's fragrance advertisements targeted toward men. This finding is somewhat surprising because the stereotypic portrayal of the "dark and mysterious" man is a popular image in our society. Perhaps it is because this image deals exclusively with attractiveness, which is not an emotional theme widely used in advertising targeted toward men.

Third, and most indicative of sex–role stereotyping in fragrance advertisements, is the appearance of the *romance* appeal in almost half of women's fragrance advertisements and not at all in men's fragrance advertisements. This finding reveals that advertisers mistakenly assume the emotional appeal to romance is only functional concerning women. Certainly, men too desire romance. Furthermore, the popularity of this emotional appeal in targeting women reinforces the stereotype that women are more relationship oriented than men.

Finally, although the *sexual/sensual* appeal is popular in both the men's and women's fragrance advertisements, it appears almost twice as often in the advertisements for women's fragrance. Again, it is quite possible that the perception of women as relationship oriented is the cause for heavier reliance on this appeal when targeting women.

The results of the analysis of the second content analytic scheme, *The Persuasive Manner of Delivery*, highlight the manner in which the emotional stereotypes are presented and shows that these stereotypes are reinforced with visual and verbal techniques. The *concrete/ simple* visual technique is the most popular in women's fragrance advertisements targeted toward women. However, unlike the men's fragrance advertisements targeted toward men, which are simplified with the use of this appeal, the *concrete/simple* visual technique enhances the emotional message and provides a more complex picture, one which reflects the complexity of the most popular emotional appeals aimed at women: *beauty/good looks, sexual/sensual, elegance/ class* and *romance*. In addition, each of these appeals requires the direct or implied presence of a man, and this is usually accomplished visually.

The *dreamy/textural* visual technique is more popular in women's fragrance advertisements targeted toward women than in men's fragrance advertisements targeted toward men and is used as frequently as the *concrete/simple* approach. This visual technique creates the mood for a complex emotional appeal to function. For example, the two–page Beautiful advertisement contains the face of the Estee Lauder model. She wears a crown of flowers in her hair and is surrounded by waves of beige chiffon. This fabric is a textural device which, combined with the watery blur imposed over the picture, creates a soft, dream–like scene in which the reader can imagine herself.

The *abstract/odd* visual technique appears in the smallest number of women's fragrance advertisements targeted toward women This technique is important in the presentation of certain, other, elaborate messages. For example, Ysatis de Givenchy Parfum uses this approach to depict a complex scene where the emotional message is deeply rooted in the picture. The advertisement is a caricature of a scene between a man and a woman. She is elegantly dressed and reclining in a chair with a costume mask in her hand. An ominous shadow stands in the doorway. The emotional appeals *magical/mystic*, *elegance/class* and *sexual/sensual* are reinforced in this picture by the strange lighting, peculiar visual props and odd depiction of the man as a shadow.

The most popular verbal technique in women's fragrance advertisements targeted toward women is the *short statement*. Unlike the *short statements* in the fragrance advertisements targeted toward men, this technique contains poetic, flowery language and is paired with elaborate visual images and emotional appeals. In the Maxim's advertisement the phrase "hearts beat faster, anticipation soars" accompanies an abstract design of a women leaning over and passionately kissing a man. This combination offers the female reader, who is presumably very emotional, a wealth of appeals with which to identify. When used in targeting women, the *non-verbal* appeal also adds to the complexity of the emotional appeal by not providing interpretation for the complex visual images. Instead, the reader is left to decipher the message according to the emotional stimuli present in the visual image.

The *long statement* verbal technique offers female readers the most elaborate interpretation of complex visual messages. This technique appears in a substantial number of fragrance advertisements targeted toward women and not at all in fragrance advertisements targeted toward men. For example, the Secret of Venus advertisement displays the side view of a naked woman standing in a room of antique furniture. One chair is tipped over, and she is moving out of the field of view of the camera and looking at the ceiling. There is both a *short statement* to the side of the picture, "Know the power of the Secret of Venus," and a *long statement* at the bottom:

> Weil's Secret of Venus Perfume Oil, the tenacious powerful and pulse quickening fragrance lasts for an eternal day and splendorous evening. Secret of of Venus is also a bath oil that perfumes as it envelopes every inch of you.

> Come and know the power of the Secret of Venus and be drawn into its celestial orbit. Great beauties have been made by its mystery for over one–half a century—just as men have been devoured by its power.

Together the visual technique, verbal technique, and a number of emotional appeals function to provide a highly complex emotional message. Also, power in women's fragrance advertisements targeted toward women, is presented as a method to attract men, not as an inherently worthy characteristic.

Finally, the analysis concerning *The Emotional Appeal to Gender* reports that the stereotypic portrayal of the sexes in fragrance advertisements targeted toward women is the most popular, despite the fact that women are supposedly more conscious of, and concerned with sex–role portrayal than men. The *traditional* appeal to different sexes is the most widely–used appeal to target the female audience. Although these stereotypes appear less frequently in women's fragrance advertisements targeted toward women than in men's fragrance advertisements targeted toward men, their significant showing indicates continued sex–role stereotyping by advertisers.

The *non–traditional* appeal to different sexes, defined by the visual, verbal or emotional portrayal of the woman as dominant, strong, or independent and in possession of stereotypically masculine attributes and men as submissive, gentle, and in possession of stereotypically feminine attributes, appears slightly more often in advertisements targeted to women. The women's fragrance advertisement for Emeraude displays this appeal. It depicts a very feminine woman in the dominant position in the picture, with the man standing behind her. The caption reads, "I love only one man, I wear only one fragrance."

The *neutral* appeal to different sexes appears in a significant number of women's fragrance advertisements targeted toward women. This appeal probably exists because advertisers are aware of female consciousness concerning sex–role portrayal. Past studies which looked at societal response to stereotyping (for example, Barry, 1985, and Wortzel & Frisbee, 1974) found that there was segmentation in the female audience concerning preference for traditional or non–traditional sex–role portrayal. Furthermore, women in general are more cognizant of sex–role portrayal than men (Lundstrom & Sciglimpaglia, 1977). This finding explains why advertisers attempt to use the *neutral* appeal to some extent in advertisements targeted toward women and not at all in advertisements targeted toward men.

Advertisers also include men's fragrance advertisements in women's magazines, although there were no women's fragrance advertisements found in men's magazines. This category of advertisements reflects the media portrayal of women's interests regarding men, and contains two levels of sex–role stereotyping: what women supposedly like in men and the actual portrayal of men. These men's fragrance advertisements which target women reveal sex–role stereotyping similar to the other advertisements. The men's fragrance advertisements which target women display only two emotional appeals, *natural* and *sexual/sensual*. These two appeals reinforce the stereotype that men are outdoorsy and sexual, and that women are attracted to these attributes in men.

Concerning *The Persuasive Manner of Delivery* the visual and verbal techniques again reinforce the stereotypical emotional appeals. The presence of the *concrete/simple* technique in the men's fragrance advertisements targeted toward women reveals that in terms of male stereotypes, the media target women with a simple visual technique to reveal the simple nature of the emotional appeals which depict men. The Stetson men's fragrance advertisement illustrates this point. The advertisement simply consists of the bottle and the box. Around the box is a cowboy's lasso. This one visual element is enough to create the stereotypical cowboy image of men and because this advertisement appears in a women's magazine, to create the stereotype that women love cowboys.

The men's fragrance advertisements found in women's magazines all contain the *short statement* verbal technique. This technique uses short simple phrases to spell out the emotional stereotypes present in men's fragrance advertisements which are targeted at women—that is, that men are outdoorsy and sexual.

Finally, the men's fragrance advertisements which are targeted toward women all contain the *traditional* appeal to different sexes. Advertisers appeal to women with the simple stereotypic portrayal of men.

Conclusion

The answers to the research questions illustrate the prevalence of sex–role stereotyping in fragrance advertising. First, the number of fragrance advertisements is higher in women's magazines than in men's magazines, indicating that advertisers appeal to women as if they are more concerned with appearance and attractiveness than men. Second, the most popular emotional appeals used to target women are *sexual/sensual, beauty/good looks, romance, elegance/ class*, and *magical/mystic*. The most popular emotional appeals used to target men are *elegance/class, natural, unique, power/strength*, and *sexual/sensual*.

Third, the differences between the emotional appeals which are used to target men and the emotional appeals which are used to target women are apparent from the nature of the most popular appeals for each mentioned above. The appeals to women concentrate on relationships, romance and looking good to attract men. These appeals, therefore, need the presence of a man in the advertisement to function properly. The appeals to men focus on status, nature, individuality, power, or the physical gratification of sex. These appeals either exploit women for the purpose of emotionally stimulating the male reader or do not include women in the advertisement at all.

Finally, the traditional and stereotypic portrayal of the sexes is still the single most popular image of men and women found in both men's and women's fragrance advertisements. This appeal can be found in almost all of the advertisements which target men, and in most of the advertisements which target women.

In summary, then, fragrance advertising aimed at both men and women reveals a pattern of sex–role stereotyping of both sexes. Women are stereotyped as emotionally complex, externally or "other" oriented, and concerned primarily with their appearance and their relationships with men. Men, on the other hand, are stereotyped as emotionally simple, internally oriented, and concerned primarily with themselves.

Note

1. This information was obtained from the 1986 media package supplied by each magazine. According to the data supplied by the magazines, *Esquire* (a men's magazine) and *Harper's Bazaar* (a women's magazine) are purchased by middle aged readers (median age = 36.2 and 34.7, respectively) with high incomes (median income = $40,000 and $33,987, respectively), and have a small circulation size (700,000 and 737,430, respectively). *Playboy* and *Cosmopolitan* are purchased by younger readers (median age = 32.0 and 28.3, respectively) with lower incomes (median income = $32,168 and $27,543, respectively) and have a large circulation size (4.1 million and 2.8 million, respectively). *Gentlemen's Quarterly* and *Mademoiselle* are purchased by the youngest readers (median age = 25.2 and 27.9, respectively) with moderate incomes (median income = $38,250 and $29,559, respectively). *Gentlemen's Quarterly* has a small circulation size (657,194) while *Mademoiselle* has a slightly larger circulation size (1.1 million).

References

Barry, T.E., Gilly, M.C., & Doran, L.E. (1985). Advertising to women with different career orientations. *Journal of Advertising Research, 25*(2), 26–35.

Courtney, A.E., & Lockeretz, S.W. (1971). A woman's place: An analysis of the roles portrayed by women in magazine advertisements. *Journal of Marketing Research, 8,* 93–95.

Easton, G., & Toner, K. (1983). Women in industrial advertisements. *Industrial Marketing Management, 12,* 145–149.

Fragrance foundation assays "survival." (1984, December). *Drug and Cosmetic Industry,* p. 40.

Keon, W.J. (1974). Copy testing ads for imagery products. *Journal of Advertising Research, 23*(6), 41–50.

Larson, C.U. (1983). *Persuasion.* Belmont, CA: Wadsworth.

Lysonski, S. (1983). Female and male portrayals in magazine advertisements: A re-examination. *Akron Business and Economic Review, 4,* 5–50.

Lundstrom, W.J., & Sciglimpaglia, D. (1977). Sex role portrayals in advertising. *Journal of Marketing, 13,* 72–79.

Madden, T.J. & Weinberger, M.G. (1982). The effects of humor on attention in magazine advertising. *Journal of Advertising, 11*(3), 8–14.

Pingree, S., Hawkins, R.P., Butler, M., & Paisley, W. (1976). A scale for sexism. *Journal of Communication, 26*(4), 193–200.

Sexton, D.E., & Haberman, P. (1974). Women in magazine advertisements. *Journal of Advertising Research, 14,* 41–46.

Skelly, G.U., & Lundstrom, W.J. (1981). Male sex roles in magazine advertising, 1959–1979. *Journal of Communication, 31*(4), 52–57.

Wagner, L.C., & Banos, J.B. (1973). A woman's place: A follow-up analysis of the roles portrayed by women in magazine advertisments. *Journal of Marketing Research, 10,* 213–214.

Wortzel, L.H., & Frisbee, J.M. (1974). Women's role portrayal preferences in advertisements: An empirical study. *Journal of Marketing, 38,* 41–46.

THOUGHT PROVOKERS

Why do advertisers construct different ads for the same product when targeting a predominantly male or female audience? What are the advantages and disadvantages of such a tactic?

CHAPTER EIGHTEEN
Declarations of Independence: The Female Rock and Roller Comes of Age

Alan D. Stewart

Rutgers University

In the past, researchers in the communication field have extensively studied such important mass media as print, television, and radio, but have neglected the major mass medium of recorded music (whether in the form of records, prerecorded cassettes, reel to reel tapes, compact disks, etc.). Popular music, whether directly or indirectly through other mass media, reaches a large audience every day for extensive periods. For example, college students when asked to monitor when they are exposed to recorded music typically discover that they are exposed between one–third and two–thirds of their waking hours, with most being exposed over one–half of their waking hours.

Recorded music, of course, includes many different styles, for example, country, folk, classical, easy listening, and rock and roll—each with its own social milieu and audience. Of these styles, rock and roll has been the culturally–dominant form for the last thirty years. Grossberg (1986) in his study of rock and roll, "Is There Rock After Punk?" complains about "the failure of contemporary communication theory to study this most visible of popular forms" (p. 51). As Christians (1986) suggests, that lack of attention may be changing. There are, however, still numerous important areas to be addressed.

Over the last ten years there have been two important movements in rock music. The first and most obvious of these is the punk rock movement discussed by Grossberg. Less obvious, but equally as important and unstudied except for a few treatments in the popular press (for example, Brandt, 1979; Miller, 1985; Swartley, 1982), is the gradual rise over the last ten years of the female hard–rock artist.[1]

Prior to 1975, most women working in rock music fell into the singer–songwriter genre or the so–called "girl group" genre, either playing soft rock or fronting for a male–led group or a male writer/producer team. This situation has gradually changed. In addition to the many younger female hard rock performers, a significant group of older female artists who are the contemporaries or near contemporaries of major male artists from the sixties have emerged more recently. The music made by these artists represents a declaration of independence from the limited, stereotyped art and lives that women were previously expected to live.

This work is characterized by lyrical and musical rawness, a new emotional depth and complexity, by anger, bitterness, and irony, and by a viewpoint that tends to link power and love and sex. For these women, rock music marks an empowerment freeing them from past stereotypes and limits. These declarations of independence fall into two distinct categories: (1) direct, even anthemic declarations of independence and (2) more indirect declarations of independence in which these women and their audiences are empowered to enter into new and deeper experiential territory.

The direct declarations are made by statements in the lyrics that directly suggest the need for or the existence of the singer's independence. These direct declarations function in one of three forms: (1) by making statements within the context of interpersonal relationships, (2) by making declarations of a more general, often philosophical, nature, and (3) by making statements stressing the importance and primacy of the artist's personal experience.

The indirect declarations are made by the form of the music and the performance and by the types and treatment of content rather than by direct statements. The indirect declarations function in four different ways: (1) in terms of the music itself (just hearing a female voice in this musical context represents a kind of declaration of independence), (2) in terms of the nature of the rough performance with the emphasis on emotional impact rather than prettiness or technique, (3) in terms of transformations of previously–recorded, male–associated material often implicitly challenging traditional sex–role expectations, and (4) in terms of the unexpected and untraditional extreme, violent, obsessive images, subjects, and language.

History and Background

Before female artists gradually started to perform and record hard rock in the time period from 1975 to 1980, most women working in rock music fell into either the singer–songwriter genre or the so–called "girl group" genre. Most of these women, for example, Joni Mitchell or Carole King, played soft rock or fronted for a male–led group or a male writer/producer team like the Holland/Dozier/Holland team which wrote for and produced the Supremes. Even an important seeming exception like Aretha Franklin did her best work singing songs, like Otis Redding's "Respect," which were written by male composers and worked closely with a male producer, Jerry Wexler. Few if any women consistently worked in the harder rock areas of popular music, wrote their own material, led their own bands, played their own instruments, or performed rough, aggressive material with the emotional depth and complexity of important male artists like Bob Dylan, John Lennon, the Rolling Stones, Neil Young, or the Who.

The actual position of women in rock music prior to 1980 can be seen statistically in Denisoff and Bridges' (1982) demographic study of popular music artists between 1970 and 1979 in which they report that only 10 of 268 acts in the rock category of their sample were women or had female group members. Denisoff and Bridges do suggest that "the recent successes of Pat Benatar, Deborah Harry, Christie Hyde (sic) of the Pretenders, Sheena Easton, and others lead one to suspect a comparatively great increase in the number of female performers in rock music, although our figures indicate a rather substantial gap yet to be bridged" (p. 139).

More anecdotally, the traditional position of women in rock music is suggested by the position and naming of female singing groups relative to male groups in fifties and sixties soul music. Many male groups had "sister" groups who formed a kind of women's auxillary whose function was to sing a few songs and serve as cheerleaders for the males. This secondary position was often suggested by group names formed by adding diminutives to the male group name. For example, the Supremes started their careers as the Primettes, the sister group for the Primes who later became the Temptations (Hirshey, 1984). Only later was the name Primettes translated into the Supremes. Many of the "girl groups," though, continued through their careers with names formed with diminutive endings: the Marvelettes, the Ronettes, the Shirelles.

Despite a few glaring exceptions this diminutive, second–class status suggests the place of female performers in rock music, especially hard rock music in the fifties, sixties and well into the seventies. The few exceptions, Aretha Franklin, Grace Slick of the Jefferson Airplane/Starship, and most importantly, Janis Joplin, are basically the exceptions that prove the rule. Most other female artists performed simple, pleasant, polite folk–based music, served as front people for male creators and manipulators, or more frequently sang back–up for male artists. Perhaps only Joni Mitchell consistently made records in a compelling, individual style over a long period of time that challenged the emotional power and complexity of important male artists and dealt with similar themes from a female perspective. Mitchell is in many ways an important precursor and role model for current performers but, despite an occasional hard rock performance such as "Raised on Robbery" and the frequently hard edged quality of her recent jazz rock synthesis, she has mainly stayed away from hard rock both musically and in terms of performance characteristics.

This situation in which female performers had either a secondary status or no status at all started to change in the mid–1970s with the emergence of mainstream performers like Heart led by the Wilson sisters and the new Fleetwood Mac featuring Stevie Nicks and Christine McVie, as well as important less mainstream artists like Patti Smith. Over the last ten years, the number of female rock performers has gradually increased to the point that such performers no longer seem to be an anomalie. Further, there are now a number of important female rock artists who rival their male counterparts in producing significant rock records with a rough sound and emotional depth and complexity.

The current group of important female rock performers falls into two major categories. The first of these is made up of younger women like Joan Jett or the Go–Gos who seemingly do not have any more problem with being female rock artists than they do with mixing supposedly incompatible musical genres like heavy metal and sixties bubblegum (Joan Jett) or sixties girl group sound and eighties punk (the Go–Gos). For these women, performing rock music seems normal and natural.

The second major group consists of older female artists who are the contemporaries or near contemporaries of the major male artists listed above. Unlike the men who emerged in the 1960s, these women only emerged as important artists in the late 1970s and into the 1980s. Some, like Patti Smith, simply did not conceive of themselves as attempting the kind of rock music they had always admired men making. Others, like Chrissie Hynde, had difficulty breaking into the male–dominated area of hard rock. Some, like Tina Turner, had previously merely fronted male–dominated groups. Many, like Ellen Foley and numerous others, had spent their careers singing back–up for male performers. Still others, like Robin Lane, Marianne Faithfull, and Genya Ravan, came to perform the kind of hard rock they are now known for only after years of performing other styles of popular music.

For this second group, the biting, aggressive, emotionally intense and complex, if often unpleasant, music they are now making represents a declaration of independence from the limited, stereotyped art and lives that women were previously expected to live. The work of this second group of female rock performers is characterized by lyrical and musical rawness, a new emotional depth and complexity, by anger, bitterness, and irony, by a viewpoint that tends to link power and love and sex, and by a control over the final product similar to that held by male artists since, like major male artists, these women often write their own material or choose it for themselves when they do not write it, play instruments, lead instead of front bands, and sometimes even do their own producing. For these women, rock music marks a kind of empowerment freeing them from past stereotypes and limits.

There are many significant older female artists whose work might be examined to illustrate this pattern.[2] These include but are not limited to: Tina Turner, Debbie Harry of Blondie, Annie Lennox of the Eurythmics, Yoko Ono, Cyndi Lauper, Ellen Foley, Pat Benatar, Joan Armatrading, Ellen Shipley, Martha Davis of the Motels, and Debra Iyall of Romeo Void. For the purposes of illustrating both direct and indirect declarations of independence by recently–emerged female rock performers, examples will be drawn from the work of five representative and important, older performers: Patti Smith, Chrissie Hynde of the Pretenders, Marianne Faithfull, Genya Ravan, and Robin Lane and the Chartbusters. These examples are drawn from fourteen albums and one EP containing 142 different songs (see attached discography).

These five artists were chosen first of all because they fit the general pattern. They have all emerged as important artists playing the type of hard rock they perform on these records since 1975. All write much of their own material and choose it themselves when they do not write it. Each of the five, except for Faithfull, play instruments at least some of the time, and all control their own bands rather than front for a male group. All make rough, aggressive music and sing with a hard edged quality previously typical mainly of male performers. Perhaps most importantly all make powerful, emotionally complex music which reflects the kind of anger, bitterness and irony that have been the staples of major male performers, and all have songs that clearly exemplify the two kinds of declarations.

Secondly, while none of these five performers are completely mainstream artists neither are any of them minor cult artists. All but Ravan, who produces her own work, record for major record labels, and all are sometimes heard on mainstream radio even if most of them have not had top forty hits. Mainstream performers, such as Tina Turner, Heart, Pat Benatar, or Cyndi Lauper, were avoided because the lowest common denominator factor that often attends mainstream success tends to dilute the clarity and distinctiveness of most new movements in popular culture. Certainly these artists, and other mainstream female rock performers, partake of parts of the larger pattern, but like most mainstream performers, they are apt to provide less clearcut examples of the phenomena. For example, Tina Turner, perhaps the best known of these mainstream hard rock female performers, produces aggressive, emotionally complex work full of anger and irony which makes both direct and indirect declarations of independence. These qualities are especially true of such songs from the *Private Dancer* album as "What's Love Got to Do with It," "Better Be Good to Me," and "Show Some Respect." She does not, however, write her own material or play an instrument, and at least some of the time, for example, on *Typical Male*, the follow–up to *Private Dancer*, she seems to be manipulated by her male producers and writers.

On the other hand, small cult audience artists, such as the Slits or Siouxsie and the Banshees, were also avoided to keep from giving the impression that the emergence of the female hard rock performer was a specialized event limited to a very small audience. Ravan comes closest to cult audience status, but provides an important example since she has been in the music business for over 20 years, first performing and recording as Goldie of Goldie and the Gingerbreads, one of the few all–female bands of the sixties; in addition, she is one of the very few female producers in any type of popular music and probably the only one who works regularly, not only on her own work and that of other female performers such as Ronnie Spector, but also as the producer of many all–male acts.

As a check on the importance and noncult status of these artists, one requirement was that they all had been reviewed positively (at least some of the time) in basically mainstream publications such as *Rolling Stone* and *Stereo Review* and in popular magazines like *Cosmopolitan* and *Mademoiselle* aimed at a mainstream, nonmusic specialized, female audience (see for example, Behan, 1980; Cohen, 1980; Henke, 1984; Hentoff, 1980a, 1980b; Pareles, 1983; Simels, 1978).

In addition, these five performers are all very different artists who were chosen in part because they would not otherwise be discussed as similar. They are stylistically very different musicians and singers with distinctive voices and vocal phrasing; no one familiar with rock music conventions would be likely to mistake the records of any of these women for the work of any of the others or fail to identify a new record by any of these performers.

Secondly, the thematic concerns, world view, and manner of expression of these artists differs drastically. For example, Robin Lane is a born–again Christian. Patti Smith is a published poet whose records are influenced as much by Baudelaire and Rimbaud as by the Rolling Stones and Bob Dylan. Genya Ravan, on the other hand, insists on keeping things close to her rock and roll roots by using typical rock images and teenage metaphors such as fast cars ("put the pedal to the metal"), guns ("Shot in the Dark"), typical teenage sexual language ("Steve . . . go all the way with me"), and teen age references (in "Roto Root Her," she begs her "baby" to "buy me an ankle bracelet").

These artists were chosen, then, because their very differences help to suggest how varied and far–reaching the underlying pattern exemplified by them is—that is, despite differences in the style and content of these five performers, their work all functions in similiar ways to declare independence.

Direct Declarations of Independence

Some of the songs by these artists make direct declarations of independence in which the artists state the fact or condition of their independence or make clear their insistence upon their independence. Sometimes these declarations are only a matter of a line or two within a song; sometimes they form the central statement of the song, even becoming anthemic in nature. Many of these direct declarations concern the relationship between the sexes or the singer's statement of intention within a personal relationship. Some of them, though, deal with more general statements or insist on the primacy and importance of the singer's life and personal experience.

While it was expected that there would be some of these kinds of songs in the work of the five selected artists, an unexpectedly large number of the songs by the five artists studied were either central declarations of independence or contained lines that fit this definition. In fact, all five artists had at least several examples, and the albums by Genya Ravan, whose work is in some other ways the most traditional of the five, were particularly rich in examples with almost half the songs marking direct declarations in some way.

The most obvious, clear-cut examples of direct declarations are those songs in which the declaration forms the central theme of the song. One of the best examples of this type of song is Marianne Faithfull's "Sweetheart," a song in which the singer states her own independence even as she expresses her love:

Sweetheart—I'm changing my role in life,
I'm not re-arranging the main things in my life,
I ain't sacrificing what I hope is true,
I ain't sacrificing, sweetheart even for you.

Later in the song she insists: "My freedom means too much to give up now." She tells her lover that she will be "holding on to find my identity." While the words alone make the point clear, it is Faithfull's insistent, rasping performance that gives them real bite, that makes clear that she really means what she says. Faithfull also exhibits another characteristic of significant rock music in making the point more ambiguous and less didactic by changing "I'm not re-arranging" to "I'm rearranging" when she repeats the first verse—although she is still not "sacrificing." This ambiguity makes clear that such statements are difficult and tenuous, if necessary.

Genya Ravan's "I Won't Sleep on the Wet Spot No More," is even more anthemic, if somewhat earthier in nature, than "Sweetheart." In a pithily inspirational singalong chorus, Ravan echoes the kind of declaration one might find as graffiti in a public restroom:

Oh I had my share, the times I didn't care, my journey made
it clear,
To feel a change and rearrange, and I won't sleep on the wet
spot no more.

Ravan, in fact, sings a number of similarly anthemic songs such as
"The Sweetest One" in which she complains about the tyranny of
trying "to be the sweetest one" claiming that she'd "rather be a
commie out in Tulsa, Oklahoma than to try to be the sweetest one"
or "Pedal to the Metal" in which she reminisces about her teenage
past using a car metaphor typical of male rockers to suggest both sex
and escape: "You put the pedal to the metal and you know it's called
the breaks."

Many of Ravan's and the other performers' direct declarations
involve emphatic statements aimed at former or potential lovers. In
"It's Me" Ravan tells a man who she says would like to have her on
her knees saying please that "if you were the last guy on this earth,
I'd say no because I'd rather be dead." In "Night Owl," she tells a
former lover who wants to return to "sit on it, baby, oh I don't love
you no more." Similar statements mark the work of most of these five
artists. Smith joyously insists in "Revenge" that she is "taking my
revenge, sweet revenge." In "Waiting in Line," Lane tells a potential
lover: "You better watch out cause I strike back." In "Private Life,"
Hynde tells a married lover to "use the door" and to leave her out of
his "private life drama."

In the most violent of these direct declarations, "Tattooed Love
Boys," Chrissie Hynde presents a series of violent images (for example, "I shot my mouth off and he showed me what that hole was for")
in a ferocious hard rock piece that many critics took to be a description of a gang rape, but which Hynde has insisted is about abuse and
women who continue to take it. She declares her own independence
of such violence at the end of the song by mocking another woman
for remaining where she "used to lay." Such songs are unpleasant
and ugly but make their point in the direct powerful way used in the
past only by male performers.

Not all of the direct declarations are this unpleasant or deal with
interpersonal relationships. In one of the most anthemic songs in the
sample, "Imitation Life," Robin Lane in the character of a woman
named Alice who works as a waitress in a diner insists that she is
"glad to be alive" and declares in the anthemic chorus: "I don't want
to lead an imitation life." This assertion connects the song directly
with one of the central ethical themes of rock music: the desirability
of living an intense, meaningful life. The direct, anthemic expression
of this theme places it in a direct line with such earlier important rock
pieces as Pete Townshend's "My Generation" ("Hope I die before I

get old") and Neil Young's "Out of the Blue and Into the Black" ("Better to burn out than it is to rust").

Other songs by these artists make similar general statements or express the importance or primacy of the singer's experience. In "Lovers of Today," Hynde suddenly insists at the end that she will "never be like a man in a man's world," and in "Brass in Pocket (I'm Special)" she continually maintains that she is "special." In one of the most surprising and expansive statements in the sample, Patti Smith declares in "Babelogue": "i am an american artist and i have no guilt. i seek pleasure." She goes on to insist: "i have not sold my soul to god." In the immediately following song, "Rock n Roll Nigger," she declares her intention to live "outside of society." In "Gloria," she similarly insists that "Jesus died for somebody's sins but not mine" and that her "sins are my own/they belong to me/me." In "Aint It Strange," she tells the listener that she will "never end/transcend transcend" and asserts: "i don't get nervous oh i just move in another dimension."

Indirect Declarations of Independence

The songs cited above all make their point directly in the lyrics of the songs as the artists declare independence in any of a number of different senses. Such direct declarations are important in the way that they provide a direct outlet to allow both the artists and their audiences to express and experience a sense of individual selfhood and meaningful independence in a personal, often nonideological manner that places women, as artists anyway, on an equal footing in a genre that had previously been dominated by men. The work of these recently emerged female rock artists, however, also declares independence in other subtler and equally significant ways. The music, the manner of performance, the transformations of older male–produced material, and the extreme, obsessive, often violent images and subjects, which all work together to produce intense, involving subjective experience, all declare independence in more indirect ways.

Such aspects of these songs and performances work, in fact, as all good rock music does, to empower both the artists themselves and their audiences (both male and female) to enter into new, deeper and emotionally more complex experience, in essence to live deeper, fuller, more meaningful, if often less pleasant lives. For these female artists and the female members of their audiences, such empowerment enables them to break through the narrow limits circumscribed by past negative stereotypes.

In one sense, all of these songs mark such indirect declarations just in the sense of existing at all in the form they do. That is, just the fact of hard rock music made by female performers by itself breaks past barriers and in that sense empowers the artists and their audiences to enter new experiential realms. Simply to hear a female voice singing over the pounding beat at the base of most of Marianne Faithfull's material or driven by Chrissie Hynde's savage rhythm guitar or intertwining with the three guitar attack mixing sixties British invasion sound with seventies punk on Robin Lane's recordings is to experience something new which frees the listener from earlier stereotypes and biases.

Much of the earlier discussion of direct declarations focused necessarily on the lyrics, but as Marcus (1986) makes clear any good analysis of rock music as cultural artifacts needs to "focus on the interplay between lyrics and music—the endlessly complex interplay of the musical text . . . the verbal text . . . the performance, the sound engineer's mastering of the recording and so on" (pp. 78–79). Thus, the sound as much as, and maybe more than, the lyrics declares these artists' independence and empowers their audiences.

One especially important part of this sound is the artists' vocal performances. These women, unlike virtually all female rock artists before them, perform their songs vocally as the best of the major male artists in rock music always have. These performers scream, shout, cry, choke, laugh, pout, whisper, rasp, run words together, draw them out, bite them off, and in general twist them so far out of shape that it is sometimes impossible to tell exactly what they are singing even with repeated listenings. The sound and delivery of the lyrics are often more important for their emotional impact than the verbal meaning. In general, the emphasis of the vocal performance is not on pitch and intonation and enunciation and precision in the same way as in other, more traditional, musical forms but on the individuality and emotional impact of the delivery.

The sound and the performance, then, mark important, indirect declarations of independence. The very sound of these records suggests that here is something new and different and powerful. A student who had arrived in a class after the lyric sheet had been passed out once reported that Hynde's "Tattooed Love Boys" (much of which is virtually indecipherable on first listening without a lyric sheet) made her feel as if she had just been assaulted. Such a reaction suggests the power and the nature of such indirect declarations: they provide for deeply, intensely moving, if not always pleasant experience.

Another major form of indirect declarations of independence by the five artists sampled comes in the form of transformations of material previously associated with male performers. Most of these go well beyond the normal idea of cover versions. Some of these transformations are as simple as the change in sex–role stereotypes that occurs when songs invert sexes. A typical example is Genya Ravan's cover of Marvin Gaye's "Stubborn Kind of Fellow" in which the singer forcefully insists that even though the potential lover may be hesitant, the singer is insistent and will not take no for an answer; sung, as it initially was, from a male point of view the song plays on and reinforces typical sex–role stereotypes, but sung from the female point of view, it inverts those stereotypes and works to break them down. The Pretenders' cover of the Kinks' "Stop Your Sobbing" works in a similar manner; the song "means" something quite different when it is a female singer telling a potential male lover that the "one thing" he has to do to make her love him is to "stop sobbing" than it does when the positions are reversed.

Marianne Faithfull's cover of John Lennon's "Working Class Hero" also functions to break down sex–role stereotypes by inverting sex roles, although in a somewhat different social context. Faithfull's assertion that "a working class hero is something to be" works to raise questions about basic sex–role stereotypes. Stereotypically, of course, women are neither thought of as doing the kinds of traditional "men's" work usually associated with the idea of "working class" nor are they stereotypically thought of as heroes. The sex–role inversion provides an ironic twist which suggests that, despite the fact that it breaks the stereotype, women, too, can be "working class" heroes.

Robin Lane's cover of "Shakin' All Over" works in a different way. This song about sexual experience has been widely recorded by males (one of the more recent and best–known versions is a live version by the Who) from whom it usually comes off as a sexual boasting song in which the male performer lets his audience know that he is "getting it." Robin Lane's performance transforms "Shakin' All Over" into a complete submersion into sexual experience that makes the earlier male versions sound impotent by contrast. When she sings that she's got "the shakes in my thigh bone . . . shakin' all over," she sounds not like she is bragging about her sexual experience, but as if she is actually in the throes of that sexual ecstasy. Such a transformation amounts to a declaration of independence to explore and transform material that has previously been the domain mainly of male artists.

Chrissie Hynde transforms "Thin Line Between Love and Hate," a minor seventies soul hit which tells the story of a woman who puts her emotionally abusive lover into the hospital "just that much from being dead," into a virtual anthem expressing her personal credo. The song provides a context within which to understand many of Hynde's own songs of complex love/hate relationships which as she suggests in "Up the Neck" combine "anger and lust" in a combination in which "lust turns to anger."

The most extreme transformations in the sample come from Patti Smith who on her first album *Horses* transforms two standard rock songs by subsuming them into larger structures of her own. In her version of "Gloria," she transforms Van Morrison's simple teenage lust song into a complex investigation of mystical/religious/sexual experience ("Jesus died for somebody's sins but not mine") partially by mixing it with other lyrics and music and partially by continually playing with the pronouns and the point of view so that a listener can never be sure whether she is talking about a lesbian experience or whether she is simply taking on the male role some of the time. In "Land," she goes a step further and combines the simple sixties dance song "Land of a Thousand Dances" with two pieces of her own, "Horses" and "La Mer(de)" to create a large, impressionistic canvas in which disparate, fragmented, sometimes violent images clash against each other and the simple dance song gets subsumed in the larger mystery Smith is attempting to suggest and free her audience to break through to. Smith accomplishes this goal by juxtaposing the names of sixties' dances from the original song (the twist, the pony, the alligator, the mashed potato) against more complex, unsettling images like Johnny either knifed or shot up with drugs in the school hallway, or horses ("white shining silver studs with their noses in flames"), or suggestive but unclear either sexual or violent images and language ("the veins desire get wilder").

These last transformations indirectly declare the artist's independence from the strictures of the past and from the outlook imposed by the male material while simultaneously using that past and that male material to further her own artistic ends.

These last two songs also hint at the last, and perhaps most important, way in which these artists indirectly declare their independence and empower themselves and their audiences. The work of these artists features the kinds of excessive and obsessive, often violent images and subjects often associated with major male rock performers, but rarely previously associated with female performers. Indeed some of these recordings are among the most powerful, effective rock recordings of the last ten years. As should be apparent from the examples already cited, many of these songs deal with extreme and unpleasant subjects like death, suicide, drugs, rape and domestic violence. Even many of the pleasanter songs deal with extreme sexual or romantic emotions.

One last extended example will serve to suggest the power and extremity of much of this material. Marianne Faithfull's "Why d'Ya Do It," a detailed, complex, intense account of sexual jealousy, is undoubtedly one of the most remarkable rock songs of the last ten years. Faithfull put the song together by transforming a poem by Heathcote Williams into six minutes and forty-five seconds of some of the most intense, ugly art ever created. She begins by keeping Williams' male point of view for the outer narrative frame while playing the role of the woman within the song so that one gets the odd, complex point of view of a female artist performing a male's narration of a female's reaction to his sexual infidelity.

The song features extreme language. For example, the woman asks the man: "Why d'ya let her suck your cock?" The male in the

outer narrative frame indicates that he still loves her despite her
"barbed wire pussy." At the emotional peak of the song, the woman
spits out venomously: "Every time I see your dick I see her cunt in
my bed." The song ends with Faithfull repeating over and over again:
"'Why d'ya do it,' she said." Beyond the emotional impact of the
lyrics, though, is Faithfull's performance. She alternately screams,
moans, implores, cries, whispers, shouts, almost literally inhabits the
lyrics, until she brings the situation and the emotions to life in a way
that makes her audience feel the full impact and ugliness. The experience is not pleasant, but it does empower her audience to enter into
new and deeper experiential territory, declaring the indirect independence and right of female performers and their audiences to work
at and experience extremes of human behavior.

Conclusion

Taken as a group, the work of these older female rock artists
indicates that these women who are the contemporaries or near contemporaries of male rock stars who emerged in the sixties have in an
important sense "come of age"—that is, they have finally, if belat-
edly, started to make the same kinds of emotionally powerful, complex popular art as their male contemporaries. In doing this, they
have declared independence for both themselves and their audiences
from limited past stereotypes.

On the most prosaic level, the rise of the female hard rock performer parallels and reflects the movement of women in the general
population into nontraditional jobs and upper level management positions previously held mainly by men. After all, on one level rock
music performing is a job, but it is also something more.

Rock music is a significant, even dominant, part of contemporary
popular culture. Rock music reflects and influences other aspects of
the culture. Rock performers stand as role models and empowerers in
a way no business executive can. The declarations of independence
made by these performers suggest that our popular culture is, on the
one hand, offering female artists significantly changed opportunites
and, on the other hand, offering the female audience important and
more diverse messages. These messages are not, for the most part,
ideological or didactic. Most of these performers undoubtedly recognize the political significance of what they are doing, but they see it as
secondary to their primary jobs as popular artists. That job is to deal
with the non–ideological, the personal, and the specific rather than
the ideological, the general, and the abstract. Obviously, artists like
these are not always "politically correct." If, however, they are to
continue to empower their audiences to enter into new and deeper
experiential territory, then they need to go on to communicating messages which suggest the texture of life and the nature of human experience as they find it.

Notes

[1]These two movements not only occurred over the same time period but are more closely connected than a first glance might suggest. Paradoxically, although punk rock features some of the most mysogynistic songs of a music known for mysogynistic songs, the punk rock movement helped to foster the rise of the female hard rock artist with its populist, democratic, anybody–can–be–a–star attitude. The connection can be observed in the direct relationship of many female rockers to punk. The Patti Smith Group was one of the first and most important American punk groups. Chrissie Hynde was encouraged in her early attempts by members of the Sex Pistols and her band, the Pretenders, was early identified with the punk movement. Genya Ravan produced the first album by the Dead Boys, a seminal American punk rock band. Ellen Foley's second album was produced by and featured songs written for her by Mick Jones and Joe Strummer of the Clash. X, one of the finest and longest lived of the American punk bands, features a female co–lead singer and composer, Exene Cervenka. Many of the younger, or at least newer, female artists credit either Smith or Hynde as role models. In general, despite the sexism exhibited by punk in some contexts, punk seems to have encouraged women to come out of the audience or drop their acoustic guitars and express themselves in the same direct, uninhibited way in hard rock that male performers were.

[2]For the purposes of this paper, "older" is defined as artists who are currently thirty or older—especially those artists who were over thirty when they first began to record or first emerged as hard rock performers. While thirty may not seem "older" in normal terms, it certainly is in terms of rock music which has always been and still remains a youth oriented cultural form. It was in fact difficult, even futile, to try to identify a significant male rock performer who emerged as late as thirty.

References

Behan, K.P. (1980, May). How to make it to the top of the music biz . . . 10 doers tell you everything they know. *Mademoiselle*, p. 150.

Brandt, P. (1979, November). At the top of the charts . . . but are they playing *our* song? *Ms.*, pp. 38-44.

Christians, C. (1986). The recording industry. *Critical Studies in Mass Communication, 3*, 356.

Cohen, D.R. (1980, April 7). Marianne Faithfull: Younger than yesterday. *Rolling Stone*, p. 14.

Denisoff, R.S., & Bridges, J. (1982). Popular music: Who are the recording artists? *Journal of Communication, 32*(1), 132-142.

Grossberg, L. (1986). Is there rock after punk? *Critical Studies in Mass Communication, 3*, 50-74

Henke, J. (1984, April 26). Chrissie Hynde without tears. *Rolling Stone*, p. 17.

Hentoff, N. (1980a, January). And I mean it! (record review). *Stereo Review*, p. 110.

Hentoff, N. (1980b, October). Robin Lane and the Chartbusters. (record review). *Cosmopolitan*, p. 90.

Hirshey, G. (1984). *Nowhere to run: The story of soul music*. New York: Penguin.

Marcus, G. (1986). Critical response. *Critical Studies in Mass Communication, 3*, 77-81.

Miller, J. (1985, March 4). Rock's new women. *Newsweek*, pp. 48-50, 57.

Pareles, J. (1983, June). A child's adventure. (record review). *Mademoiselle*, p. 40.

Simels, S. (1978, August). Patti Smith. *Stereo Review*, p. 78.

Swartley, A. (1982, June). Girls! Live on stage. *Mother Jones*, pp. 25-31.

Discography

Faithfull, Marianne. *Broken English*. Island Records, ILPS 9570, 1979.

Faithfull, Marianne. *Dangerous Acquaintances*. Island Records, ILPS 9648, 1981.

Faithfull, Marianne. *A Child's Adventure*. Island Records, 90066-1, 1983.

Lane, Robin (and the Chartbusters). *Robin Lane and the Chartbusters*. Warner Bros. Records, BSK 3424, 1980.

Lane, Robin (and the Chartbusters). *5 Live*. Warner Bros. Records, MINI 3495, 1980.

Lane, Robin (and the Chartbusters). *Imitation Life*. Warner Bros. Records, BSK 3537, 1981.

Ravan, Genya. *Urban Desire*. 20th Century–Fox Records, T–562, 1978.

Ravan, Genya. *I Mean It!* 20th Century–Fox Records, T–595, 1979.

Pretenders. *Pretenders*. Sire Records Company, SIRE 6083, 1979.

Pretenders. *Pretenders II*. Sire Records Company, SRK 3572, 1981.

Pretenders. *Learning to Crawl*. Sire Records Company, 23980-1, 1982.

Smith, Patti. *Horses*. Arista Records, ARISTA 4066, 1975.

Smith, Patti. *Radio Ethiopia*. Arista Records, ARISTA 4097, 1976.

Smith, Patti. *Easter*. Arista Records, ARISTA AB4171, 1978.

Smith, Patti. *Wave*. Arista Records, ARISTA AB4221, 1979.

THOUGHT PROVOKERS

What rock performers today fit the 1970s sex–role stereotypes of female rock performers? What female rock performers break these stereotypes? What new stereotypes have replaced the old ones?

UNIT VI

NEW DIRECTIONS FOR THE STUDY OF SEX AND GENDER

The final unit advances the study of sex and gender research in communication to include new concepts and directions within that field and, in some ways, challenges basic assumptions of other work presented within the first five units of this book. These new directions include an introduction to culture as an integral component of gender, gender as a hierarchical concept based on power relationships, and a new framework in which to position gender. In previous units, we have seen how each chapter has approached the study of sex and gender in communication differently. Yet even within these innovative studies, there are basic assumptions concerning communication, sex, and gender which remain constant. For example, sex is determined by biology and there are two sexes. Gender is socially constructed and defined through primary classifications: masculine, feminine, and androgynous. Within this final unit, even these basic assumptions are questioned. The "New Directions" unit moves forward into an unexplored frontier to seek new definitions and new frameworks for viewing the study of sex and gender in communication. As one reviewer stated, this unit "stretches me and gets under my conceptual skin."

In the first chapter of New Directions, "Women's Culture and Communication: An Analytical Perspective," Fern Johnson discusses the literature which revolves around the existence of a separate women's culture, discrete from men's. Gender is viewed as a culture, a private realm in public culture, or a silenced separate subculture. Johnson visualizes a model of women's culture with patterns and forms of symbolic meaning of the past which will be changed as women are "freed from male systems to do so." Johnson introduces two cultures, bringing women's separate culture alongside men's culture.

While Johnson sees gender as culture, Cheris Kramarae in "Redefining Gender, Race and Class" posits gender as a hierarchical concept; it is not a separate variable, but a variable which works in conjunction with class, race, and age. With national and international examples, Kramarae makes an intricate argument which views gender as one of many variables within a "power" hierarchy.

David Grimm's chapter, "Toward a Theory of Gender: The Social Construction and Internal Structure of Gender" pushes the definitional perspective of gender to its conceptual limits. From a framework which links biological sex to gender as a socially constructed variable, Grimm argues for the elimination of all discrete variables within sex and gender identification. Instead, Grimm proposes a multi-level model, redefining the categories of sex and gender coding to include 45 variations. Grimm demonstrates that the combination of attributes for males and females is boundless.

Bates, B. Paper review, University of Northern Illinois, 1987.

CHAPTER NINETEEN
Women's Culture and Communication: An Analytical Perspective

Fern L. Johnson
Clark University

"Two different worlds"—men and women live their lives in dramatic separation from one another. Although often not literally separate from one another, women and men diverge in more than superficial ways, and in this sense they are separate. At some experiential level, most men and women know this separation: as they mingle with those of the same sex, as they join in activities with those of the same sex, and as they feel some greater sense of affinity in work as well as in social situations with those of the same sex. The personal knowledge of gender difference may for some be more tacit than for others, but most women and men, girls and boys grasp the difference of the genderized worlds they live in and observe. The grasping of difference is in one way a comprehension of what is in fact distinctive about women's and men's worlds, a reaching out to those of one's own gender to reaffirm the gender bond, to find comfort and support in what is already "given" about women and men. Yet, the grasping is also an attempt to define and create gender in new ways; in this sense, gender is what is socially constructed through affiliation, action, and interaction.

One of the clearest and perhaps best examples of the differing worlds of men and women is found in friendship—the most voluntary and non–institutionalized relationship in society. Lillian Rubin (1985) summarizes her observations about gender and friendship by saying:

> The results of my own research are unequivocal: At every life stage between twenty–five and fifty–five, women have more friendships, as distinct from collegial relationships or workmates, than men, and the differences in the content and quality of their friendships are marked and unmistakable. (pp. 60–61)

Robert Bell (1981) notes in the report of a major study on friendship patterns that "there is no social factor more important than that of sex in leading to friendship variations" (p. 55). Until recently, however, virtually no attention was paid to this important variation. To rectify the historical devaluing and ignoring of women's relations with one another, research conducted by women has been directed to assessing women's friendships in order to correct both the omissions of the past and to provide serious and authentic accounts of the role of friendship in women's lives. Elizabeth Aries and I (Johnson and Aries, 1983) have studied the connectedness of female friends through talk, and Janice Raymond's (1986) provocative book, *A Passion for Friends*, examines the bonds and commitments among women friends—to name just two such accounts.

It is not surprising that the "two different worlds" perspective on men and women led scholars of women to an interest in the general idea that women are culturally distinctive from men. Although research directed to identifying "sex differences" certainly assumes the importance of gender, the differences reported in the literature have been largely attributed to sex–role learning and socialization; much of that work has also assumed that females are in a disadvantaged position because of the specific nature of their learning and socialization. Looking for a more sophisticated framework for understanding the contributors to and consequences of gender, scholars—especially feminist scholars—have either taken cultural differences as a given or asserted the possibility of such an explanation.

My purpose in this essay is to provide an analysis of how gender may be viewed within the framework of cultural systems with an aim toward using this perspective to understand better and to study gender and communication, especially women's communication. The perspective presented here, then, is applicable to domains of inquiry besides communication, but is also specific to communication because it contextualizes work within that domain.

There is growing evidence in various areas of study, including communication, to support the existence of a women's culture separable from men's. Organizing and reviewing the evidence is indeed needed, but it is not my purpose to provide this type of analysis. My focus is on the more general relationship between gender and culture, and in this essay I will argue that there are analytical difficulties with the generally held assumption that culture as a system operates in superordinate, monolithic relationship to women and men. Another way of expressing the problem is to point to problems with assuming that culture is "above" gender and, thus, contains gender within its subsystems.

Specifically, I will propose a definition of culture, review the most prevalent perspective on where women fit into a cultural view, and suggest an alternative perspective to structure research and thinking about women's communication. This perspective posits genders as separate cultural systems, solving the analytical difficulties encountered in the more prevalent, monolithic model. It also gives proper recognition to the roles of women in creating and sustaining a cultural order whose character has been publicly suppressed but which is, nonetheless, pervasive and temporally transmitted.

A Perspective on Culture

Feminists and nonfeminists alike ground their approaches to culture in anthropological notions and assumptions. Looking to anthropology is a logical choice because of the subject matter of that discipline. Culture provides the focus for anthropological inquiry, and culture is in this sense the central rubric of anthropology. Yet, while anthropology claims culture as its center, this concept, similar to the concept of society, serves more as context and background than it does as subject matter and foreground. Anthropology, like most social science disciplines, yields much more research–oriented scholarship than theoretical work. Most anthropologists work to document meaningful differences among groups of people who are distinct from one another in terms of language, values, philosophy, habits, art, religion, and so forth. Theoretical literature on the concept of culture most certainly exists; a useful overview of contemporary theory in anthropology can be found in an essay by Sherry Ortner (1974). Nonetheless, the theoretical literature is overshadowed by the products of anthropological field research which are at the heart of the mission to learn what and how cultures *are* in their everyday, concrete, empirical reality. Much of that work, which the lay person might say exposes the "stuff of culture," is ethnographic—growing from a commitment to studying behavior in its naturalistic setting through methods for recording and then describing that behavior. Although theory always lies implicitly behind, beneath, and around research, the scope in the case of anthropology is one where ethnography has indeed dwarfed theory.

When scholars outside of anthropology take up the concept of culture, then, they must face the high degree to which culture carries tacit meaning for those who have traditionally studied it. Those tacit meanings, divergent as well as redundant within the ethnographic literature, are probably best discovered by studying field reports and methodological accounts written by anthropologists.

In applying the concept of culture to gender, feminist scholars have proceeded in several different ways. Some have assumed the separation of women's and men's cultures, while others have posed two sequential questions: "Do women and men live in different cultures?" and, if the answer is affirmative, "What is the cultural system of women?" In the process of answering the second question, another critical question arises: "How is this cultural system created and maintained?" Theoretically, questions about the cultural system of men could also be asked. The questions might be posed as a way of explicitly comparing women's and men's cultures, or understanding the nature of male culture on its own. But questions about the cultural system of men are rarely raised as a research focus because the assumption is that men's culture has been public and well documented in every society. We read the literature written by men, study their history, see and hear their artistic expression, and study as well as live in the civilization and society they have created. It is the case, however, that the knowledge about men's cultural system that is already available can usefully serve in some instances as contrast with knowledge about women's culture.

In all cultures except the most simple, diversity within the system develops quite naturally as a result of a combination of factors such as contiguity, socioeconomic status, race and ethnicity, occupation, religion, etc. For example, Jewish Americans might be thought of as a subculture, and within that subculture is another subculture of the Hasidic; or teenagers might be thought of as a subculture, but black teenage males as quite another subculture; or professors may seem to us to be a subculture quite distinct from the students they teach. When a patterned form of diversity exists in contrast to the culture but operationally within it, a subculture is said to exist. A subculture functions as a system that is semi–autonomous but that is also subsumed within the larger culture; it is a subsystem within a system. Another way of expressing the relationship between a culture and subculture is to say that a culture is public to a subculture, but unless reported upon, a subculture is private—at least in part—to a culture. Black Americans "know" the white culture that surrounds them, but few whites have any everyday knowledge of the culture(s) of black Americans. Subculture, then, is always conceptually subordinate to culture and exists at a lower level in the analytical hierarchy. The model in Figure 1 demonstrates this relationship. This model assumes that a subculture is both subsumed by and has access to the larger culture in which it resides. Members of a subculture have responsibility for knowing the culture in order to be fully its citizens, but members of the superordinate culture do not have like responsibility for knowing its subcultures.

To present the arguments for viewing genders as cultures, culture must first be given some definition. Two general points are important.

The first important point is that culture has virtually nothing to do with biological inheritance. Eleanor Burke Leacock (1971) made the point in her critique of "the culture of poverty" that, "cultural behavior is recognized as having minimal genetic coordinates, being maximally dependent upon learning, particularly on learning through symbolic means" (p. 9).

The second important point is that culture has everything to do with the symbolic. Clifford Geertz has received considerable recent attention for his contributions to this idea. Geertz (1973) argues that culture exists through the sharing of symbols; it is through public sym-

bols that members of a cultural group communicate their values, mo-
res, and orientations to the world. Using this notion of culture as
consisting of publicly shared symbols, we must then look to what it is
that is symbolically shared. I refer to Figure 1 again to convey what I
believe are the central systems characterizing culture meaning.

What is symbolically constitutive of culture can be understood as
three interrelated and co-equal systems of meaning: (1) language
and communication; (2) artifacts; and (3) abstractions. Together,
these systems represent the common (or at least commonly accessible) grounds and normative standards for members of the culture.

The system of language and communication is made up of the
verbal and nonverbal patterns that characterize the expressions of a
group of people who are its members. All systems of language and
most nonverbal communication systems are symbolic, with arbitrary
links between the system elements and what they represent or interpret. I make no presumption about the criteria for quantitative differences marking contrasting cultural systems of language and
communication. Difference is more a matter of perceptible degrees of
variation marking the character of one system as meaningfully different from another. And the markers are as much matters of interpretive rules as they are production rules. Natural languages, for
example, do not necessarily serve to distinguish cultures from one
another although they often do so. The same natural language such
as Spanish or English may be used in quite distinctive cultures, as
evidenced by the broad distinctions between the language and cultures of South America compared to Spain, and of the United King-
dom compared to North American. Dialects provide a somewhat
better indicator of some cultural differences, but dialect and culture
are certainly not synonymous.

A second major component of a cultural system is its artifacts.
Artifacts are the unique products of a culture which are created as
expressive instruments for re-presenting and re-forming experience
through the manipulation of form and substance. Artifacts carry a
special function because, unlike language, they are commonly understood to be something other than what they represent of interpret.
We think most often of artifacts as types of creative writing (poetry,
drama, prose), visual and plastic arts, design, crafts, music, and
dance. Artifacts serve to communicate the culture across spatial and
temporal boundaries and distances. Some artifacts such as paintings
and written works are physical objects that can be physically repro-
duced, while others such as dance and musical performance must be
passed on through teaching and demonstration (except for the possibility in contemporary culture to photograph, film, and tape such artifacts, in which case the film or tape itself is an artifact).

Finally, a system of abstractions shapes the cognitive possibilities
and structures the choices available within a culture. Cultural abstrac-

tions include the values, morals, ethics, logic, philosophical orientations, laws, and religious beliefs that are held by a people. These
abstractions guide behavior in the broadest manner and govern the
systems of expression that give rise to language as well as art. The
classic treatment of this aspect of culture is found in the work of
Clyde Kluckholm (1951) on value orientations.

The same systems that characterize a culture also characterize a
subculture. Within the subcultures of any culture, there will be systems of language and communication, artifacts, and abstractions that
are distinguishable in some patterned manner from the systems of the
larger culture. Subcultures may be completely discrete and separated
from one another (as are coal miners from Wall Street brokers), or
they may share common elements to varying degrees (as do born-
again Christians and Lutherans). And there is no limit—at least in
theory—to the number of subcultures that may develop and be maintained within a given cultural context. While complete "mutual intelli-
gibility" is not assumed to exist among subcultures, it is presumed that
those within subcultures should know the larger cultural systems and
be able to co-relate to some degree with other members of the culture. The larger culture often overtly oppresses and suppresses a subculture by not legitimizing its systems of communication, artifacts, or
abstractions, or by not recognizing that such systems exist. The best
illustration of such overt action in modern American society is the
negative sanctioning of Black English Vernacular by many educators
and employers.

Women's Culture

In considering women's culture, feminist scholars have taken two
somewhat different approaches, both of which, however, take the
position that a separate women's culture exists and is viable. Both
have roots in the feminist theory of the nineteenth century, although
the second departs some from that base in its assumptions.

One approach assumes that women's culture has existed on a
private level, but it has been denied the opportunity and means for
public expression. In other words, women's culture is ever-present
but always privatized. For this approach, the challenge is to document the systems of language and communication, artifacts, and abstractions that characterize this culture and make those systems
known to women (required) and men (optional). The documentation
functions as the "archaeology" of uncovering what has been kept
from view. The next stage is the "publicity campaign" of exhibiting
the "finds" to members of the culture, some of whom may doubt that
there is more than idiosyncrasy in their own behavior, and to outsid-
ers, many of whom may doubt that any system exists at all. This
particular perspective on women's culture has been designated by

some as *cultural feminism*. Josephine Donovan (1985) in her book *Feminist Theory* says of early (nineteenth–century) cultural feminists:

> While continuing to recognize the importance of critical thinking and self–development, they also stress the role of the nonrational, the intuitive, and often the collective side of life. Instead of emphasizing the similarities between men and women, they often stress the differences, ultimately affirming that feminine qualities may be a source of personal strength and pride and a fount of public regeneration. (p. 31)

The contemporary version of this approach to women's culture places emphasis on preserving certain fundamental values and orientations characteristic of women while rejecting the public–private, work–home division that has marked the separation of men and women. Donovan continues by describing the contemporary version this way:

> Cultural feminists today believe that the traditional realm of women provides the basis for the articulation of a humane world view, one which can operate to change the destructive masculine ideologies that govern the public world. (pp. 61–62)

Within the study of gender and communication, this view has been developed in contrast to earlier interpretations by authors such as Robin Lakoff (1975) that presented women's communication patterns as deprived in some way—a result of discrimination against women which deprived them of fully functional and powerful language and communication forms. I have elsewhere (Johnson, 1983) designated this earlier position as the "deficit position" on women's communication, contrasting it to the "difference position" which takes as given the value and functionality, and in many cases the desirability, of women's communication. The edited volume of work on gender and communication by Barrie Thorne, Cheris Kramarae, and Nancy Henley (1983) also supports the position that women's culture is viable and distinctive from that of men. The editors and authors in this volume assert throughout that women's communication patterns and practices are to be valued.

The other approach taken by feminists posits that women have been categorically denied the opportunity to create culture. They have been silenced and suppressed by male culture through the domination of culture's symbols by men. This view claims that women have no genuine, native systems of language and communication, artifacts, or abstractions. Rather, women must fit "non–native" systems—those developed, controlled, and perpetuated by men—onto their own experiences and realign their experiences so that they are understandable and can be communicated with the alien systems. The lack of some indigenous system is a theme in much of the writing of Adrienne Rich. In one place (Rich, 1979) she says:

Women both have and have not had a common world. The mere sharing of oppression does not constitute a common world. Our thought and action, insofar as they have taken the form of difference, assertion, or rebellion, have repeatedly been obliterated, or subsumed under "human" history, which means the "publicity of the public realm" created and controlled by men. Our history is the history of a majority of the species, yet the struggles of women for a "human" status have been relegated to footnotes, to the sidelines. Above all, women's relationships with women have been denied or neglected as a force in history. (pp. 203–204)

Although this approach stresses the importance of discovering and creating women's culture, it is not typical of what is sometimes understood to be cultural feminism with its valuing of the ways of women. Its assumptions line up more clearly with radical feminism which places patriarchy as the fundamental cause of women's oppression and of the suppression of women's experience not only in the public at large but in women themselves. Feminists who take this approach to women's culture promote the *creation* of culture through systems that are evocative of women's experiences, meanings, and identity; systems that are "authored" by women and in this sense native to women. In the domain of language and communication, Dale Spender (1980) makes the case for this position in her book, *Man Made Language*. Writers such as Mary Daly (1984; 1987) and Adrienne Rich (1978) most boldly put the case to the test of creativity by experimenting radically with language in order to find women's voices.

While the two approaches to women's culture differ, they are not incompatible within the framework on culture that I have presented here. The model—which features interrelated systems of communication, artifacts, and abstractions—serves equally well for both views of culture. In the first, the model organizes and publicizes what we are learning about the patterns in women's symbol systems. In the second, the model serves to guide creative efforts in everyday life as well as in art that are designed to constitute a culture for women which springs from uniquely female experiences, sensibilities, and orders of meaning. The model offers through these two views of women's culture a descriptive and explanatory system as well as a heuristic device for the elaboration of women's culture.

My own view is that women do have a culture distinct from men's, but they will also change and elaborate that culture as they are freed from male systems to do so. In other words, there are patterns from the past that have been brought to the present; and in the present, new patterns and forms of symbolic meaning are being created that will enter the future as the past. The evidence for women's culture as past resource and present creation is found not only in the field of language and communication, but it is growing in the other areas of culture as well. We are seeing more art, reading more literature, listening to more music that is *different* because the creators were or are women and the subject matter is women. Judy Chicago's "The Dinner Party" provides a powerful illustration of publicizing the arts of women that historically were dismissed as trivial and that were relegated to what men have labeled "crafts," which are understood to be subordinate to "pure art." We are also learning more about the abstractions characteristic of women as a cultural group. Carol Gilligan's (1982) work on the system of women's moral reasoning stands as the most widely communicated evidence for this aspect of culture.

Women: Culture or Subculture?

I now turn to the issue of where to place women and their experiences within the model of culture that I have suggested. One traditional view is to see gender as irrelevant to the larger issue of culture. This view simply dismisses gender (either as it marks males and females or as it is socially created to ensure the interpretive distinction between male and female worlds and notions) as not powerful or pervasive enough to originate symbol systems. Another view is to subordinate gender to culture, i.e., to conceive of gender as one of several variables (or variants) serving to organize patterned difference from the larger culture. This is the view depicted in Figure 1, where a gender system would be located, for example, as subculture 2 in a system of n subcultures, where the number 2 is chosen arbitrarily for the purpose of illustration. Within most mainstream disciplines, the study of gender and of females or males specifically would be framed at the subcultural level (or at the social group level if the larger rubric is society).

While seemingly an improvement over the traditional view that disregards the importance of gender, there are analytical problems with placing gender at the level of a subculture in relation to a culture. More specifically, if we see women as a subculture within some larger cultural system, we should, by implication, also see men as a subculture within the same larger cultural system. Yet, men as a group are rarely if ever seen as a subculture, at least not in any general sense; placing men at the subcultural level tends to occur only in relation to some other subcultural marker such as race or social class (e.g., black, urban, teenage males).

But let us assume that we could legitimately take the view that both genders are subcultures. We must then ask about the larger culture to which these subcultures are subordinate. To sustain gender, i.e., both genders, at the lower level of the model requires the higher level of the model to be unmarked by gender. If genders are subcultures, the larger culture must be gender neutral. What we know as culture, however, is not neutral or neuter; it is the product of men

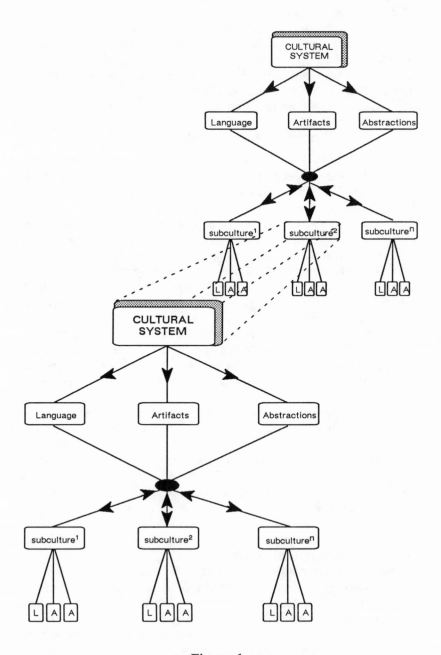

Figure 1

and is maintained through the domination by men over the channels and institutions for the public expression of culture. It is men who have controlled the creation of cultural systems, and it is the province of men that is carried through these systems. It is men who own the "public symbols" about which Geertz writes.

The analytical point is straight forward. To place men's systems of language and communication, artifacts, and abstractions at the levels of both culture and subculture is conceptually inelegant and analytically incorrect. Such placement stipulates as a subclass the class itself to which the subclass belongs. Even though the analytical problems of this model are sufficient to invalidate it, a more important point remains. The model presents an error in socio–political context. Conceiving of the male gender as a subculture parallel to a female subculture masks the patriarchal nature of culture itself as well as the patriarchal manner in which culture is constructed, construed, and communicated; patriarchy shapes and controls culture but is usually transparent to its own creators. A myth is perpetuated which accords an equal status to men and women as creators of what is considered *the* cultural system. This equality does not, however, exist in relation to the larger culture that this model would purport to portray. Women often know this; men usually do not.

The most useful solution to the problems associated with placing both genders within one cultural system is to place them in different systems, acknowledging that women and men reside in separate and hierarchically equivalent cultures. From this vantage point, which is illustrated in Figure 2, we are able to view either one gender or the other on its own terms. With regard to women, the perspective of separate systems removes the tendency to see what women say, do, create, and believe as subordinate to culture itself. It also minimizes the tendency to assume falsely that public manifestations of culture are equally the product and domain of women and men. Of even more importance, the shift in perspective helps to eradicate the assumption that women should know and hold as their own a cultural system that is men's. Only by placing women's culture and men's culture side by side are we able to avoid the presumption that women do and should share "as natives" the broader symbol systems which reflect and reinforce the worldview of men. In a more pragmatic vein, the "two cultures" perspective clearly places interaction between women and men in the domain of intercultural communication, where it belongs.

The "two cultures" perspective should not be taken to suggest that differences among women are unimportant. In fact, one of the major themes of current feminist thinking focuses on differences among women, on correcting a presumption in earlier feminist writing that white women could speak for and represent all women, and on elaborating the differences within women's commonality. Gloria

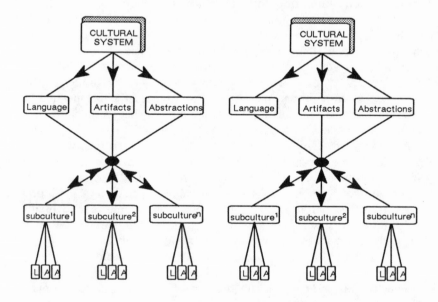

Figure 2

Joseph and Jill Lewis (1981), for example, addressed the need for recognition of differences between black and white women of different classes and sexual preferences. And the full title of a book by Gloria Hull, Patricia Bell Scott, and Barbara Smith (1982) captures the power of oversimplifying gender relations: *All the Women Are White, All the Blacks Are Men, But Some of Us Are Brave.* Positing a women's culture assumes that characteristic patterns tie women together across difference, but it also assumes that subcultures of women exist within women's culture; the two assumptions are inseparable.

The most important point about diversity among women is that it not contribute to the further submersion of issues of both gender and race. The traditional view of culture and its construction of women as a subculture tends to relegate minority women either to a sub–subculture in relation to women or to a sub–subculture in relation to the racial or ethnic group to which they belong. This compounds the socio–political error of that model. At the same time, nonwhite women must not be arbitrarily or artificially placed in either women's culture or their respective minority or ethnic culture. We all carry with us multiple cultural identities, even though certain of those identities have a broader range of implications. Because gender and race have the broadest range of implications within our society, it is nonwhite women who are at greatest jeopardy when it comes to understanding the relationship of culture to communication. Marsha Houston Stanback (1985), who has studied communication differences among black women, cautions that "neither contemporary research on language and gender nor that on black communication coherently describes black women's communicative experiences" (p. 177). It is important that research on women's culture not repeat that problem.

Conclusion

The position I have developed in this paper should facilitate a better understanding of the communication differences between women and men. For a considerable period of time, the paradigms central to our discipline, and to the social science and humanities disciplines as a whole, submerged gender in other presumably larger and more important frameworks for analysis, or they marginalized gender by placing it outside of the mainstream of inquiry. Scholarship is increasingly making us aware that the differences of importance are not simply distributional ones in relation to some specified variables (who uses more tag questions, who self–discloses the most, who becomes an engineer or a nurse) but, rather, are ones reflecting major divergences in both stylistic properties of language and communication and the interpretive systems used to give meaning to language and communication. Once gender is moved to the level of cultural systems, it, rather than some other superordinate construct, focuses and organizes ideas about social and political relations.

More central to feminist theory in general and the study of gender and communication in specific, the "two cultures" view provides the context for turning attention both to uncovering and to creating women's culture. This view can usefully inform and influence new scholarship focused on women. It can also be used to understand anew and refocus work that has already been done. It is only through the elevation of women's experiences from subculture to culture that the burdens and presumptions of patriarchy are cast aside.

References

Bell, R.R. (1981). *Worlds of friendship.* Beverly Hills: Sage Publications.

Daly, M. (1984). *Pure lust: Elemental feminist philosophy.* Boston: Beacon Press.

Daly, M. (1987). *Websters' first new intergalactic wickedary of the English language.* Boston: Beacon Press.

Donovan, J. (1985). *Feminist theory: The intellectual traditions of American feminism.* New York: Frederick Ungar.

Geertz, C. (1973). *The interpretation of cultures.* New York: Basic Books.

Gilligan, C. (1982). *In a different voice: Psychological theory and women's development.* Cambridge: Harvard University Press.

Hull, G.T., Scott, P.B., & Smith, B. (Eds.). (1982). *All the women are white, all the blacks are men, but some of us are brave.* Old Westbury: The Feminist Press.

Johnson, F.L. (1983). Political and pedagogical implications of attitudes toward women's language. *Communication Quarterly, 31,* 133-138.

Johnson, F.L. & Aries, E.J. (1983). The talk of women friends. *Women's Studies International Forum, 6,* 353- 361.

Joseph, G.I. & Lewis, J. (1981). *Common differences: Conflicts in black and white feminist perspectives.* Garden City: Anchor.

Kluckholm, C. (1951). Values and value orientations in the theory of action. In T. Parsons & E.A. Shils (Eds.), *Toward a general theory of action.* Cambridge: Harvard University Press.

Lakoff, R. (1975). *Language and woman's place.* New York: Harper and Row.

Leacock, E.B. (1971). The concept of culture and the culture of poverty. In E.B. Leacock (Ed.), *The culture of poverty.* New York: Simon and Schuster.

Ortner, S. (1974). Theory in anthropology since the sixties. In M.Z. Rosaldo & L. Lamphere (Eds.), *Women, culture, and society.* Stanford: Stanford University Press.

Raymond, J.G. (1986). *A passion for friends: Toward a philosophy of female affection.* Boston: Beacon Press.

Rich, A. (1978). *The dream of a common language.* New York: W.W. Norton.

Rich, A. (1979). *On lies, secrets, and silence.* New York: W.W. Norton.

Rubin, L.B. (1985). *Just friends: The role of friendship in our lives.* New York: Harper and Row.

Spender, D. (1980). *Man made language.* London: Routledge and Kegan Paul.

Stanback, M.H. (1985). Language and black woman's place: Evidence from the black middle class. In P. Treichler, C. Kramarae, & B. Stafford (Eds.), *For Alma Mater: Theory and practice in feminist scholarship*. Urbana: University of Illinois Press.

Thorne, B., Kramarae, C., & Henley, N. (Eds.). (1983). *Language, gender and society*. Rowley, MA.: Newbury House.

THOUGHT PROVOKER

How does viewing gender as culture differ from the ways in which other chapters view culture? How does it change the ways in which other studies were constructed and the results that were found?

CHAPTER TWENTY
Redefining Gender, Class and Race
Cheris Kramarae
University of Illinois at Urbana–Champaign

Here's a discussion between two white, middle class, middle–aged women (but it could just as well be an internal discussion of one white, middle class, middle–aged woman).[1] I've called the voices B and C, for Bewildered and Confused:

Bewildered: I don't know what *white, middle class, middle age*, and *woman* mean any more. These words don't seem stable.

Confused: That's the thing now, isn't it...to be confused about age, race, class, gender.

Bewildered: Well at least it's the thing to be nervous about when you are not "with your own."

Confused: Seems to me that there's not enough talk about class these days. It's dropped out of lots of feminist discussions and literature. For example, where is it in all the spirituality, ecofeminism work? I mentioned this to someone after the seminar we had on feminist critiques of technology—I suggested we were making too many generalizations about women, not paying attention to class differences. She said "If you can't make some generalizations about women, what's feminism?"

Bewildered: Yeah, but what about the fact that so many women in the U.S., particularly women of color, are saying that there is nothing common to all women.

Confused: But there is. Agreed, it's not mothering or nurturing. But I think we can say that in general men think of women as *soft*. That perception, from men, is something all women have in common.

Bewildered: I'm sure not. It may be true of many white men in the U.S. thinking about white women. But all women?

Confused: I'm not talking about *all* women. My part of the U.S. is enough to deal with.

Bewildered: But isn't that one of our troubles? We make statements about *women* and if called on the generalizations we say, "Well we mean U.S. women." Don't we have to say U.S. women all the time if

that's what we mean by women? And then what kind of generaliza-
tion is that—even *if* we could find something we could say about all
U.S. women. And if we can't find anything in common for even all
U.S. women, what does that word mean?

Confused: But all words are generalizations—to help us make sense of
a chaotic world. Sometimes I think feminists who talk about language
get carried away. It's all fine to discuss terminology—language. But it
is *experience* which is meaningful. If I don't *experience* this diversity
among women, it won't do any good just to use words that mean
diversity.

Bewildered: But language is part of your experience. The labels and
descriptions we use help determine what we experience. Experience
is not outside a language system. If we change the labels, it's likely
because we've reconceptualized. We are not thinking in the same
way. The categories are altered. If we say that women's issues are not
monolithic, that subordination takes many different forms, that
women have very diverse interests, concerns, lives, and that considering women's diversity is what is important at the moment...we are
starting to rethink our categories. Marilyn Frye says something about
the importance of the way we use *words*. . . something like "Lesbians
are outside the conceptual scheme and this is something done, not
just the way things are." And it's done partly through our language
categories.

Confused: But I think it's an important political strategy to think of
women as a group. Until we think of ourselves as a group we are not
going to get social change. Using the term *women* in our discussions
of oppression helps move us toward of goals of social change. We can
think of the discussion of what we have in common as a strategy.

Bewildered: But it moves towards *whose* goals? If women do not have
common concerns and goals, this strategy which assumes and names
commonality isn't going to move toward all women's goals. Only
some women's.

Confused: So what do you mean when you use the word *women* like
that? I'm confused.

Race, class, sex, age have become, because of social movements,
standard categories in language research. These categories came into
being and they have undergone revisions in how they are conceptualized because of continued social movements. They continue to be
political issues, although at any one time many researchers, writers
and speakers, ignoring the changes over time in the ways they are
defined, use these categories as unproblematic, as if they had always
been standard, set, apolitical, natural ways of categorizing people and
describing social divisions.

Proposal: Here is what seems to me to be life–giving suggestions for language study and human relations: We stop using *sex* or *gender* as terms to describe a distinct social and personal characteristic of a person or a group of people, and we begin using *gender* as a term to describe an inequality and hierarchy which is also used in the construction of race, age, and class. Further, instead of constructing a pretend research world in which race, age, and class are variables separate from gender, we look at the connections—at, for example, the ways that a gender hierarchy is used in the construction of what we call *class* or *race*.

I am going to elaborate upon viewpoints expressed by others, in several geographical and theoretical locations, who argue that race, age, class and gender are all related divisions which are used to maintain hierarchies within hierarchies. For example, these divisions all incorporate the power relation of gender, although the dominance/submissive dynamic takes different forms in the structuring of gender, race, class and age. There are other perspectives, I'm certain, which will help us rethink these categories; my listening, reading, and thinking are limited and changing. The basic argument I make here is that we are starting in the wrong place if we do our research merely in an effort to describe gender (and race, class and age) through difference, rather than to focus on difference as a result of inequalities. This is not to ignore our important discussions of "common" talk, interests and experiences among women. The intent of this essay is to suggest that our discussions and theories of *relationships* among women, and women and men, include discussions of *hierarchy*.

This argument can aid in the destabilizing of current ways of thinking and of framing research projects. This may seem a strange intention in a culture and in academic institutions which advocate working toward a monolithic, stable, definitive theory with accompanying parsimonious research models. However, since most publicized theories of communication are inadequate, misleading, and dangerous to women (because they ignore and distort women's experiences, ideas, and concerns), we need to suggest new problems, methodologies, and interpretations and to listen to those coming from people outside the academic system. As Sandra Harding (1986) points out, feminist criticism, initially thought to be politically contentious but theoretically innocuous, often becomes a basic challenge to the most fundamental current thought and other social practices (p. 649). We need to point out, again, that statements called "political" and "divisive" are the statements to which those in control of policy would rather we pay no attention.

Feminists are, of course, interested in connections and convergence among our questions, critiques, and proposals. Certainly, revealing relationships and suggesting new connections are central to feminist theory–making. But we realize that our destabilizing questions can help *change* conditions even as they *express* conditions. Many of us want to help establish new social realities. Asking new questions is part of that process, and is more important right now than trying to argue for encompassing theory (or trying to rewrite the old—Marxist, Freudian, Lacanian, or whatever) for ways of perceiving and researching. (Dale Spender notes the number of theories named after men. She is an important feminist theorist, but you don't find men referring to the Spenderian theory.)

What happens to our understanding of *women, gender* and *difference* if we think of the inequities creating the differences as Catharine MacKinnon (1987) suggests? And what happens to our understanding of *gender* and *difference* if we think of gender as embedded in race and class? The importance of these questions is suggested by the work of many feminist analysts in several countries. None of these suggest that we ignore the important distinctions in the lives of girls and women—Black, Hispanic, white, middle–class, young, old, in a variety of relationships and situations. Any researcher or critic who ignores these distinctions will generalize and distort. But what happens if we suggest that gender is *not* just another factor to be added in or not depending upon the research questions, but, rather, is a part of all interactions, as an hierarchical (and therefore evaluating) ordering which is present even if women and girls are not? Gender-ranking locates everyone in a hierarchy, and certainly is a shaping factor in relationships among men who, then, represent mankind. It is, of course, their insistence upon the subordinate category *women*, that allows men to claim their primacy which structures many of their assumptions and behaviors.

"Universals"

Why do we want to make universal statements about women? Or, rather, why do so many white, middle class, heterosexual women want to find commonalities? The reasons offered are not exclusive. Some women want "sisterhood" because it is a way to avoid talking about racism. Others want collective action. Many women have looked for a "feminist standpoint," writes Terry Winant (1987) because it "would supply a shared discourse within which to theorize, strategize, argue, organize, and ultimately mobilize forces intent on bettering women's situation" (p. 126). Some women have spoken and written about "mother's tongue" and about "speaking and writing the female body" — to build a feminist community in this way and thus dethrone men as the self–preclaimed creators of meaning.

This ignores, of course, that not all women think "sisterhood" is possible or desirable (as Lorraine Bethel (1979) writes, "What Chou Mean *We*, White Girl?"). Certainly not all women have the time, energy, and other resources for "writing their body." And who is listening to or reading this body who is writing? White middle class women often have many problems obtaining the needed resources—but in the U.S. most working class women have many more difficulties and other priorities. And the white middle–class women are the gatekeepers of most of the "women's" publications and presses. There is more mention now in these publications of diversity, but usually as asides, as special interests—with universal experience still held as primary concern (Lourdes Arguelles and B. Ruby Rich, 1984).

So we white women need to continue to look at the reasons why we are so eager to find commonalities, to discuss sisterhood.

If white, middle class women *do* talk about *differences,* what do we mean?

Trinh T. Minh–ha (1987) writes: "... '[D]ifference' is 'division' in the understanding of many. It is no more than a tool of self–defence and conquest" (p. 7). Included in the "difference" category are those who need "special care"—the old, the disabled, women of color, Third World women. "Difference" from women so labelled is okay in gentle doses. But please, not too much anger or discussion of white women's racism.

As Kum–Kum Bhavnani and Margaret Coulson (1986) remind us, it is not only *differences* being discussed. These differences often represent conflicts of interest (p. 84). Differences are not the source of separation; the problem comes from refusal to deal with these conflicts. Naming themes *differences* doesn't get at the *hierarchy* and *conflict* that is involved.

Gender. We need also to look at *hierarchy* as we use the word *gender.* In the 1970s we used the terminology *sex* (and *male* and *female*) in our studies of language structure and use. Then, with increasing attention to the social construct of *female* and *male,* many of us moved to the use of *gender.* This term has been used to include many more concepts and experiences than just *female* and *male.* For example, historical and changing concepts of gender—identity, masculinity, femininity, lesbian and gay perspectives, and sometimes even the very popular but problem–ridden discussions of *sex roles* and *androgyny* (see Rae Carlson, 1985; Kay Deaux, 1985; Lapata and Thorne, 1978). Except for the last two, these are still frequently used terms and concepts in language and gender research.

However, just as *sex* and *sex differences* have become problematical as research terms because they carry connotations of biological, bipolar opposites, *gender* and *gender differences* have become problematic because they have, too often, been used as substitutes for the old terms without fresh conceptualization. *Gender differences* have come to mean distinctions resulting from differing socialization of boys and girls. Both *sex differences* and *gender differences,* then, are talked about as if they come about from previous biological and/or

environmental conditions, rather than as an on–going, everyday process. Further, Catharine MacKinnon suggests we hear them not as
labels for static charactersitics but as statements about sexuality,
about the social process "which creates, organizes, expresses, and
directs desire" (1982, p. 516). Monique Wittig also argues that what
appears to be physical features explained by natural order, are actually forced productions. She writes that "Gender is the linguistic index of the political opposition between the sexes" (1983, p. 64).
Gender is only mentioned when so–called girls or women are present
since only they possess gender. " [T]he masculine," Wittig writes, "is
not the masculine but the general." *Woman*, then, is a political concept of opposition, necessary to the maintenance of "the whole con-
gomerate of sciences and disciplines" which she calls "the straight
mind" with its discourses of heterosexuality (Wittig, 1980). Domination, she writes (at least in translation), is denied by the straight
mind, which discusses "difference" to mask the conflicts of interest.
The concept of race did not exist in modern meaning, Wittig (1984)
argues, until the white production of Black slavery. "Woman" is also
an imposed, historical product of a social relationship, not a pre–existing natural given. It is, Wittig writes, "opposition that creates sex
and not the contrary" (1982, 67).

Similarly, Joanne Passaro (1987) writes that in Nicaragua *woman*
and *women* are not parallel to *man* and *men*. Studying the language
used in the literature of the Sandinista National Liberation Front has
made clear to her that the category which translates "women" is limited to "wives of," "mothers, aligned with children," and "victims of
discrimination." The supposed intent of the revolutionary position
papers, the establishment of cultural equality of women and men, is
negated by language categories which make the intent conceptually
and practically impossible.

Race. What does *race* mean to white women and others? During
the past century the study of and theorizing about *race*, and *sex*,
supposedly biological labels, has said much more about the researchers than about any biological differences. Western discussions of *race*
and *sex* by male "experts" have been mostly used (by academicians,
other "experts," and policy makers of mass media) to keep minori-
ties and women in their subordinate place. The pronouncements of
many of these "experts" could better be called applied racism, and
applied sexism. (For an example, see Sheila Jeffreys [1985] on the
work of sexologists in Britain.)

Sociologists and other academicians talk now about some of the
problems with the term *race*. The word in traditional dictionaries (almost always dangerous sources of information because of their biased
sources and perceived authority) is usually described in terms of
physical traits—a definition based, then, on several biological characteristics. In the U.S. much is made—in literature, law, street remark

practices, and social interaction—of the distinctions between whites and Blacks, as belonging to quite different racial groups. Yet, many so-called whites have genes from Black ancestors, and many so-called Blacks have genes from white ancestors (from intermarriages, and from slavery and other rapes). If race were determined by physical traits alone, many people now called "light colored Blacks" would be classified as whites. So *race* categories are not only about physical traits.

Referring to other problems with the concept *race*, some introductory sociology textbooks now even suggest the substitution terms *ethnic group* or *nationality* for people who share language and interaction norms or other features of cultural heritage. Many sociologists now argue there is so much diversity (in interests, income, influence, incarceration rates, etc.) among whites, or Blacks or Native Americans or Hispanics that little can be said about all whites, all Blacks, all Hispanics, all Native Americans, and that it is more accurate to talk about ethnicity and cultural heritage.

In the U.S., it's white (mostly male) sociologists, I believe, who are advocating dismissal of the word *race*, not people of color—who are the ones the white sociologists are usually talking about when *race* is discussed. If white sociologists can talk about "cultural differences" and "ethnicity" then they don't have to talk much about *racism* and it's easier to ignore verbal and physical attacks from whites. (See Kum-Kum Bhavnani and Margaret Coulson, 1986, for a brief discussion of this).

The composition of racism uses a changing variety of verbal and physical assaults to demean a targeted group. A recent film "Ethnic Notions" illustrates the changing, often contradictory ways white entertainers and white-owned media have portrayed Blacks in the U.S.—ways which depend upon the prevailing white fears and designs. For example, to justify white violence toward Black males after the Civil War, they were often portrayed as savage, oversexed, dangerous, animal-like creatures—threatening super-males gone too far.

At other times Blacks were portrayed as rather humorous, docile, simple, sometimes mischievous, child-like individuals, not worth much serious consideration. The "good" Black woman servant was asexual (for example, the heavy, jovial mammy who was happy to be serving, in particular, the white men of "her" family). The Black male "house servant" for the white family was pictured (in film, cartoons, advertisements) as slimmer and smaller—not a threat to white males or to the females of the white males. The image of a happy-go-lucky Black, female and male, obtains its meaning from its opposition to the white male, presented as somber, responsible, hard-working (T.E. Perkins, 1979).

Blacks' own presentations are trivialized by whites. For example, the powerful "Black is Beautiful" phrase expressing a pride in Black

ancestry and history and the beauty of things Black, was genderized
and its political message mocked in a *Cosmopolitan* article "Health
and Make–up Tips to Make the Black Woman Even More Beautiful"
(cited in Gloria Joseph and Jill Lewis, 1981, p. 160).

The ways that white men and women use stereotypes about
Blacks deserves more attention in the U.S.—and elsewhere. But further, we can see that gender hierarchy is used by Black males to
establish hierarchies among themselves. In fact, one has to understand gender hierarchy and sexualized racism to understand many of
the insults among men.

Within the adolescent Black community, gender terms are used
to establish ranking. Why haven't the historians and linguists studying
the "Dozens" or "The Dirty Dozens" as the verbal "games" are
played by young Black males, been interested in investigating the reasons that success in that game is often based on who can say the most
demeaning, outrageous things about the other's mother? (Girls also
know these games [and use retorts such as "Yo mother" as argument
and insult,] but these exchanges are most often among boys.) Most
discussions of "The Dozens" ignore the significance of this phenomenon. For example, Langston Hughes (1966) writes "One of the
quainter Negro contributions to American culture (and common to
jazz musicians) is the ingrained custom among an increasing number
to put one and all into what is vulgarly known as "The Dozens" (p.
119). He mentions that "ancestor belittling" is common in many
parts of the world, discusses the use of "the Dozens" during the times
of whites' slavery of Blacks in the U.S. (when field slaves yelled verbal abuses at the somewhat more comfortable house slaves) and concludes by saying that "The Dozens" are "universal" among Negroes
(p. 119–121).

Gloria Joseph and Jill Lewis (1981) give an example of the content and style of an exchange:

(In a school yard)

Tom: Hey Bill, that gym teacher pushed you around like a dog.

Billy: Pushed who! Man, I pushed him back too.

Tom: Man, you liar, you ain't pushed nobody.

Billy: Who you calling a lie? You can't see straight anyway.

Tom: Yeah, well I can see well enough to know that you're wear-
ing your sister's drawers.

Billy: Your sister ain't got no drawers.

Tom: Your mother wears cement drawers.

In this verbal contest, each player tries to prove he is a man and tries
to establish his leadership role by insulting the sisters and mothers of
other boys and fighting for the honor of your own. Observing these

"games" Joseph and Lewis write "Adults are well aware of the role that the Dozens play in the street life of children, and mothers somehow seem to accept their role in this game without much questioning" (p. 92). But I wonder if we couldn't also usefully note that hierarchical standing within the young Black male community is based on a preceding gender hierarchy; the boys establish their own status in contests in which they try to say the most disgusting things about the sexuality, behavior and appearance of women.[2]

Age and gender: Girls are often considered younger than boys of the same age. I'm not fooled by A *Dictionary of Contemporary and Colloquial Usage* which defines "teeny–bopper" as "a young adolescent who enthusiastically adopts current fads" (p. 29). *Girls* are called teeny–boppers, not boys (except when someone wants to insult them). The words "girl" and "girls" are used long after the words "boy" and "boys" are dropped for male contemporaries.

As Barrie Thorne (1987) points out, modern ideologies of children construct them as linked to women, and as dependents, needing care. So males, of course, take each other out of that conceptual space of children early. "Boy" has become an insult term for adult men, especially as used by whites to put down, belittle Black men. "Boy" is closer in semantic space to "girl" than is "man" to "woman."

Most old people in our culture are considered rather feminine—unfortunate, infantile, small–voiced, irrelevant, physically weak, silly, soft, dependent, frail—traits our culture also associates with females of all ages. If older women have a lot of money they are sometimes moved to the category of *matron*—sterotypically heavy set (or straight–line skinny), idle, pompous women with strings of pearls. Wealthy old men, however, can retain power, potency, strength; many marry young women, illustrating their continued ability to possess youth.

Being old and female *is* more socially and economically devastating, and less physically safe, than being old and male. Old men are sometimes still considered sexual as in "dirty old man." "Dirty old woman" means a slovenly, aged women who has lost her femininity. So within the category "old," we see and hear differences. But in general *old* is a very undesirable social class, and we can see that many of the adjectives associated with "old" comes from the model of the nonessential roles of females.

Class and gender: Given that for the other general categories of race and age the genderizing terms that refer to females are used for the most subordinate people (in this culture Blacks and old people), we seem to have a paradox here. We are likely to associate the working class, the bottom class, with masculinity. This is the rough, tough class—portrayed in popular media—as real men, hardhatted males. The upper class is more likely to be associated with the fastidiousness, and silliness of, particularly, the "idle rich" women. Yet it is the upper class which is more desirable, more powerfully wealthy. How does this work?

In a country which is supposedly built on hard labor and sweat, with physical work the greatest virtue (e.g. "My grandfather built this house with his own hands"), the men who sit at their desks are not the prime examples of physical stamina and honest work. (Working out at the cushy athletic club is not the same.) So it is not surprising that we often hear the middle and upper class men use the language which is associated with lower education status and with masculine toughness. ("We're not going to let the deal get away from us. That ain't the way we work here, damn it.") They appear to be using the forms of grammar and swear words used by upper class males to evoke the qualities of some of the working class perceived masculine roughness and toughness.

Caste and Gender: Caste hierarchy in India is manifested in large part through show of control over women. The higher the caste, the more removed from public life are the women, and the more control men exercise over women's activities. Some of the terms for lower caste males refer to their lack of ability to control women. It seems that the rise of the middle class in India, instead of lessening the gender divisions within the caste system, is built upon them and helps maintain them.[3] Class and caste is structured, in part, through development of a gender hierarchy.

"Deviants" and Gender: We can look at how "deviants" in other social classes are described. In Europe and in the U.S., assailants responsible for gay bashing and hassling often accompany the physical assaults with an explosion of derogatory epithets which state that gay men are, or are like, women— insufficient males, pansies, feminine, and sissy women; the terminology of homophobia relies partly on gender categories.

Starhawk in *Truth or Dare* (1987) writes of how *woman* and *girl* are dirty words, to be thrown at one who is not acting like "a real man." She quotes Sheperd Bliss (1985) who points out that the drill instructor may bark "What's the matter, girl?" to reprimand and embarrass a soldier not following orders given to "the men." Or, he might use a foul description of a part of a woman's body to indicate the soldier's subordinancy. *Woman* is the next thing to The Enemy; the derision of women is an inherent part of basic military training of men. Starhawk quotes Gwynne Dyer (1985): "Marine Corps slang for any woman who isn't the wife, mother, or daughter of anyone present is 'Suzie.' It is short for 'Suzie Rottencrotch."

Varieties, or differences, do not directly *cause* gender—or race or class or age—divisions. The varieties are made and given hierarchical evaluations (with women, old, Blacks at bottom) because dominant groups (men, middle–aged, whites) want to maintain divisions which support their dominance. One of the reasons that the gender inequity is so tenacious is because it forms the basis for so many hierarchical divisions.

"*Variables*". Race, class and age categories are organized through a gender hierarchy. This is not to say, of course, that the gender hierarchy equals race, class or age hierarchy, but only to say that a gender hierarchy is used also to organize other social categories. The relationships are complex, of course. Many researchers have found it useful to see the ways that race, age, and class hierarchies are related to and involved in the construction of gender hierarchies. For example, some analysts have written about how the status of women is like that of minority race groups, or about how women can be usefully considered a class. Some analysts have described how women are described in terms also used for children. But the arguments of this essay have other implications:

1. When we study gender we are studying hierarchies, not differences. Gender is an oppositional, hierarchical division, used by dominant people in varying sexist and opportunistic ways to augment and structure comparisons among people who are also identified as, for example, Black, Hispanic, old, lesbian and gay, and poor.

2. Class, age, race and gender are not autonomous categories. They are political, sexualized hierarchies. There is an interdependency of systems of oppression.

Bibliography

Acker, J. (1984). Class, gender and the relations of distribution. Center for the Study of Women in Society at University of Oregon, working paper #13.

Arguelles, L. & Rich, B.R. (1984). Homosexuality, homophobia, and revolution. Notes toward an understanding of the Cuban lesbian and gay male experience, Part I. *Signs. 9,4*, 683–699.

Bethel, L. (1979). What chou mean *we*, white girl? *Conditions, 5*, 86–91.

Bliss, S. (1985). The enemy: A vet looks back. *Awakening in the Nuclear Age Journal, 11*, 9.

Bhavnani, K. & Coulson, M. (1986). Transforming socialist–feminism: The challenge of racism. *Feminist Review, 23*, (June), 81–91.

Brewer, R.M. (1988). Black women in poverty: Some comments on female–headed families. *Signs, 13,2*, 331–339.

Carlson, R. (1985). Masculine/feminine: A personalogical perspective. *Journal of Personality, 53,2* (June), 384–399.

Deaux, K. (1985). Sex and gender. *Annual Review of Psychology, 36*, 49–81.

Dyer, G. (1985). *War.* New York: Crown.

English–Language Institute of America. (1972). *A dictionary of contemporary and colloquial usage.* Chicago.

Frye, M. (1987). The possibility of feminist theory. Invited paper, Central Division of the American Philosophical Association, May 1.

Harding, S. (1986). The instability of the analytical categories of feminist theory. *Signs, 11,4*, 645–664.

Hughes, L, (Ed.) (1966). *The book of Negro humor.* New York: Dodd, Mead & Co.

Jeffreys, S. (1985). *The spinster and her enemies: Feminism and sexuality 1880–1930.* London and Boston: Pandora Press.

Joseph, G.L. & Lewis J. (1981). *Common differences: Conflicts in Black and white feminist perspectives.* Boston, MA: South End Press.

Lapata, H.Z. & Thorne, B. (1978). On the term 'sex roles.' *Signs, 3*, 4, 718–721.

Macdonald, B., & Rich, C. (1983). *Look me in the eye: Old women, aging and ageism.* San Francisco: Spinsters/Aunt Lute.

MacKinnon, C.A. (1987). *Feminism unmodified: Discourses on life and law.* Cambridge: Harvard University Press.

Martindale, K. (1987). On the ethics of 'voice' in feminist literary criticism. *Documentation sur la Recherche Feministe/Rources for Feminist Research, 16,3* (Sept.), 16–19.

Minh-ha, T.T. (1987). Difference: A special Third World issue. *Feminist Review, 25* (March), 5–22.

Passaro, J. (1987). Conceptualizations of gender: An example from Nicaragua. *Feminist Issues, 7,2* (Fall), 49–60.

Perkins, T.E. (1979). In M. Barrett, et al. (Eds.) *Ideology and cultural production.* New York: St. Martin's Press, 135–159.

Starhawk. (1987). *Truth or dare: Encounters with power, authority, and mystery.* San Francisco: Harper & Row.

Thorne, B. (1987). Re-visioning women and social change: Where are the children? *Gender & Society, 1,1* (March), 85–109.

Walker, A. (1980). One child of one's own: A meaningful digression within the work(s). In J. Sternburg, (Ed.) *The writer on her work.* New York: W.W. Norton & Cie. Quoted in T.T. Minh-ha (1987).

Winant, T. (1987). The feminist standpoint: A matter of language. *Hypatia, 2,1* (Winter), 123–148.

Wittig, M. (1980). The straight mind. *Feminist Issues, 1*:1, 103–111.

Wittig, M. (1982). The category of sex. *Feminist Issues, 2,2* (Fall), 63–68.

Wittig, M. (1983). The point of view: Universal or particular. *Feminist Issues, 3,2,* 63–69.

Wittig, M. (1984). One is not born a woman. In A.M. Jaggar & P.A. Rothenberg, (Eds.) *Feminist frameworks: Alternative theoretical accounts of the relations between women and men.* (2nd ed.) New York: McGraw-Hill.

Zinn, M.B., Cannon, L.W., Higginbotham, E., & Dill, B.T. (1986). The costs of exclusionary practices in women's studies. *Signs, 11,2,* 290–303.

Endnotes

1. The dialogue is based on conversations in the feminist theory seminar at the Center for the Study of Women in Society at University of Oregon (1988), and in seminar at Lewis and Clark (April 1988). I also thank Ann Russo for her comments.

2. We can also recall the many literary games and jokes Jewish men construct by ridiculing their mothers.

3. This analysis was offered in conversations with several women's studies scholars in Bombay, India, 1987.

THOUGHT PROVOKER

What is gender? Is is a discrete variable? Should it be studied as a separate variable?

CHAPTER TWENTY-ONE

Toward A Theory of Gender: The Social Construction and Internal Structure of Gender

David E. Grimm

West Virginia University

Typically, transsexuals have been viewed in terms of the pathology of gender, although they are paradoxically a window to understanding how gender itself is created. Though it is assumed that the transsexual's behavior contradicts anatomy and is, therefore, in some way pathological, the real problem (and one which often does lead to pathology) lies in the bi-polar dichotomization of "feminine" and "masculine" forms of behavior. This paper takes advantage of the perspective granted by transsexualism and reconceptualizes the manner in which the concepts of gender and sexuality are generally viewed. The reconceptualization focuses on the interplay of gender orientation and psychosexuality in nonerotic as well as erotic relationships, and stresses that gender is defined through relationship, not as a static entity. The reconceptualizing has led to concepts such as: "feminine homogenderous," "masculine homogenderous," "woman-with-a-penis," and "man-with-a-vulva"—concepts which accommodate an "appreciation for femaleness" and an "appreciation for maleness" beyond erotic attraction. A visual scheme is presented which illustrates not only stereotypical conceptions of gender and sexuality but, also, ninety alternative possibilities of gender orientation in any given encounter or relationship between two people of either morphologic gender.

Introduction

The existence of transsexuals provides an opportunity to discover what seems to be taken for granted about what it means to be either female or male in our culture. The social construction of gender can be seen most clearly through the window of transsexualism. Using transsexualism as a heuristic has led me to deconstruct and reconceptualize the general concept of gender implicitly related to a model of androgyny.

Ideally, it seems, an androgynous state requires the deconstruction of gender in order to provide the necessary experience with a

331

variety of forms of self–expression in a variety of contexts. To deconstruct gender would mean to take apart the social construction of gender using the same language upon which it was built, including the connections between gender identity and sexuality; and perhaps, show that gender is not what it has been claimed to be, that it's not what we're not, and that we're all composed of what has been considered inherently different in terms of gender.

New concepts arise in the deconstruction of gender, such as, feminine homogenderous for a male who may or may not be sexually attracted to females but who otherwise identifies more with what has been called feminine traits and characteristic expressions of feminine intimacy/sexuality in particular contexts or relationships. Furthermore, for a male who may or may not be sexually attracted to females, but who otherwise identifies with what have been called feminine traits and characteristic expressions across many contexts and relationships, woman–with–a–penis may more accurately describe such a male.

Gender and Transsexualism

It is common for the transsexual to have come upon the idea of reassignment through hearing about other cases and identifying with the expressions used by others, such as, "I am a woman trapped in a man's body." The familiarity with the subject of transsexualism which most transsexuals bring to counselors presents a confounding situation in that transsexuals know the questions and the "correct" answers before the questions are asked (Stoller, 1975). The problem for psychology lies in accounting for the variation within the population of transsexuals of extremely diverse personalities. Transsexuals, then, seem to exhibit as much range in personalities as does the general population.

Money, *et al.* (Money & Ehrhardt 1972, Money & Tucker 1975, Money, 1980), suggest that hormonal changes during critical periods of intra–uterine development may affect the brain of transsexuals to predispose them to cross–gender behavior. The research is very tentative and the conclusions difficult to support. According to Money, it takes a hormonal push to produce a male when otherwise the fetus will always be a female. In general, what the hormonal research seems to be telling us is that nature provides for all combinations of hormonal influence on behavior regardless of the apparent dichotomy between males and females. It seems tenable for a significantly larger percentage to be born biologically predisposed to cross the lines of dichotomous gender beyond what might be considered normal variation among females and males.

Sexton (1969) provides an interesting position which can be used to illustrate social forces which tend to feminize men and, transsexualism as primarily a male problem (perhaps, as a result of variations in the in–utero hormonal push of the male fetus). Sexton feels that home and school both work against boys becoming masculine men. It seems to her that boys are more troubled by social roles and gender norms as well as by genetics. More may be expected of boys, including more limiting emotional outlets, concluding in the male's shorter life span. Sexton suggests that males are particularly vulnerable due to the difference in chromosome structure. If women are protected by the double X chromosome structure which duplicates function, then men are disadvantaged in that their XY structure allows more variation. Considered with the hormonal variations occurring in–utero, the male would seem particularly amenable to feminization by the home and school in spite of the more general pressure of prescribed masculinity for men.

My presentation of Sexton's work is not to propose that the feminization of males causes transsexualism in males or, as she seems to imply, that we need more masculine males, but instead, to point to social situations in which femaleness is appreciated and encouraged in both females and males, and to point to additional biological factors in the preponderance of male–to–female transsexuals.

For Garfinkel (1967), the transsexual presents an opportunity to "dig out" the common sense knowledge about the meaning of being female or male which most of us take for granted. The transsexual presents this opportunity because of a heightened awareness on her/his part of what is required in the recurring act of passing as a member of the other morphologic gender.

Kessler and McKenna (1978) followed Garfinkel's general approach to gender. They take as evidence of a violation of unstated rules in the gender attribution process transsexuals' repeated statements of others' uneasiness toward them until these others decided whether they were female or male. To use Garfinkel's term, a structural strain occurs due to the potential and actual crises involved in passing. Persons do not normally have their status as male or female questioned.

The Gender Attribution Process

In applying the ethnomethodological approach to gender, it was Garfinkel's intention in studying "the case of Agnes" to discover the rules or methods by which members of society attribute gender and to do this by analyzing the methods by which Agnes engaged herself in the recurring act of accomplishing a female status.

Agnes presented herself, not as a transsexual per se, but as a normal female with a physical deformity—male genitals which, by participating in the study, she would have removed and a vagina constructed at little or no cost. Agnes grew up as a boy and claimed that at puberty began spontaneously to develop feminine secondary gender characteristics. What she did not disclose until eight years after her operation (performed in 1959 at age 19) was that she had taken estrogen since age twelve.

Although Garfinkel was unable to obtain information from Agnes regarding a decision to become a female, clearly, in describing situations of passing which she did relate to him, the rationality and calculation in her everyday affairs were revealed. This "management of a texture of relevances," as Garfinkel put it, was provided as a theme from Agnes as, "what do I think everyone else thinks the facts are?" As an example of the kind of method Agnes employed in these situations, Garfinkel describes the secret apprenticeship where she was learning in situations what others assumed she already knew. While thinking she was teaching Agnes how to cook for her son, Agnes' boyfriend's mother was really teaching Agnes how to cook, period (p. 146).

The case of Agnes reveals the intimate connection between the unavoidable effort in accomplishing gender and the practical circumstances in which gender is attributed. Agnes learned how to cook by not revealing how little she knew about cooking. Rather than attempt to defend her lack of experience with cooking and possibly threaten her identity, or offend the realities of her romantic partner and his mother by asking why her partner doesn't know how to cook these meals himself, Agnes complied with the expectations of others (as well as her own).

Agnes was not a feminist. She was a young woman of 19 in 1959 with a serious problem to solve. She was a woman with a penis. As long as she continued to work toward removing "a deformity," her relationship could continue. She and her romantic partner were otherwise happy with the complementarity to their roles and identities which was a rather common expectation in 1959. It should be understandable (rational) that Agnes was more prepared to manage her impression on others, at least until she had more history as a woman in a variety of roles, than she was prepared to expect her partner to accept another penis in the relationship.

Kessler and McKenna agree that seeing only two genders is as much of a socially constructed reality as anything else and that, "Ambiguous cases make the dichotomous nature of the gender attribution process extremely salient" (p. 3). The authors contend that most of the cues people assume play a role in the attribution are really post hoc social constructions of tertiary gender characteristics (those which others label as feminine or masculine). In other words, an individual attributes gender to another individual and justifies the attribution based on the salient behavioral or physical characteristics of that context. The attributer has learned to (algebraically) combine together saliency factors which change in different contexts. Change the context, say by changing the clothes, hair length, perhaps, now carrying a baby, etc. and the "swagger" (that only men are thought to exhibit naturally) will be ignored or disqualified.

In an attempt to learn more about the rules by which people operate in the gender attribution process, Kessler and McKenna devised two studies: the "Ten Question Gender Game" and "The Overlay Study." The former had people ask ten questions to determine the morphologic gender of a person the authors had in mind. The only question participants couldn't ask was the direct question, "is the person male or female?" After asking each question and receiving an answer, the participants were to make a guess and explain their reasons for the choice. Naturally, their choice would also be based on answers to previous questions. The authors had no real person in mind, but instead, a previously made random list of "yes's" and "no's" was given in response to the participant's question. This simple idea produced a wealth of information due to how the participants made sense of the seemingly contradictory information.

The findings in this study indicate that information is socially shared and follows rule guided behavior (e.g., inculcated gender norms), including the participant's belief the answers given them in the study were true. Post hoc construction is revealed in that inconsistencies were made sense of after gender attribution. Furthermore gender attribution is, essentially, genital attribution and penises provided more information than did vulvas (p. 144–145). (Why this is the case becomes a question for their second study). The participants asked more questions about gender role behavior than about physical characteristics such as genitals. The participants tended to believe it was implicit in the rules that they not ask about genitals. Some did ask about genitals and tended to not ask any further questions believing the matter decided, regardless of inconsistencies. These results lead into "The Overlay Study" by Kessler and McKenna.

In this study participants were asked if the drawing they were presented was a picture of a male or a female. They were then asked to rate the confidence of their decision on a scale from one to seven and, finally, tell how they would change the picture to create the other gender. The drawing itself had a non–gender–specific face and to this were added overlays in ninety–six possible combinations of eleven different features: long or short hair, wide or narrow hips, breasts or flat chest, a penis or a vulva, body hair, unisex shirt, and unisex pants.

Even though there were equal numbers of male and female participants, there was a tendency with the genitals covered to attribute maleness to the figure, even in the presence of breasts. The authors assert,

> In phenomenological reality although the presence of a "male" cue, may be a sign of maleness, the presence of a "female" cue, by itself, is not necessarily a sign of female-

ness. . . . [T]he only sign of femaleness is an *absence of male cues* (p. 150, emphasis in the original).

The presence of a penis elicited ninety–six percent agreement that the figure was male, regardless of other features, whereas the presence of a vulva was ignored by one–third of the participants. It was necessary that the vulva be present in addition to long hair and breasts for ninety–five percent agreement to female attribution. These and similar results lead the authors to conclude that gender attribution is essentially penis attribution (p. 153).

Kessler and McKenna see these results as consistent with an androcentric culture where maleness has salience over femaleness. It seems that femaleness is attributed when maleness can't be, that gender attribution is decided by whether or not a penis can be attributed. If it can be, then the person is male. If it can't be, then the person is female. Female attributions, then, are made by default and correspond to the general devaluation of women in our culture. To attribute penis for males and lack thereof for females is again to define women in negative terms. A more positive approach must be taken to counter the phenomenological reality of male salience by defining women in positive terms including the knowledge of the existence of varied and unique genitalia.

"Sex–Difference" Research

The purpose of this section is to suggest the proposition that despite the predilection to highlight differences between females and males, our common humanity may be more fundamental than is any gendered perspective on our behavior. In light of the increasingly tenuous existence of life on earth, I would maintain that the goal of any such research should be to affect our socialization practices and policies for the good of both individual females and males and for a world which needs the talents of all its members. Research on gender must be tendered with the idea that, gender is the expression of socially constructed feminine and masculine forms of behavior, validated by the social recognition of constructed realities and re–created in each generation by individual females and males for portrayal in the reality of a particular culture.

Pearson (1985) discusses the fact that a large number of studies show contradictory results for differences between females and males. Since gender–dimorphic attitudes are socially constructed, contradictions are not surprising because the studies measure the results of specific situations of socialization. Specific socialization practices vary and, thus, differentially affect what might be called natural tendencies in humans e.g., self–disclosure as a fundamental component of intimate relationships.

More specifically, for example, Pearson notes (p. 130) that women may disclose more because they are socialized to do so, and that intimate interpersonal relationships may be more essential to women than to men as a result (with self-disclosing providing opportunities for intimate relationships; an exchange of personal details which underlie an intimate relationship). She seems to imply that women may come to depend upon the dynamics of self-disclosure while men come to employ, perhaps, some other means for cementing intimate relationships other than through self-disclosure. Can we conclude that men do not benefit from self-disclosure in a manner similar to women; or can we conclude that self-disclosure could be just as essential to men, even though they are socialized to think they do not need it and are, therefore, deprived of it; or can we conclude that males are unskilled in one way or another with what to disclose and when?

Post-hoc analyses of socialization tell us nothing about the inherent nature of women and men when these studies are used, as they seem to be, to devise separate strategies of communication for men and women. While it is valid to devise strategies which can be applied to various communication contexts, it is not valid to devise strategies based on "how women and men tend to do things" (except to undermine ill-conceived socialization practices). Such strategies too often seem synonymous with adapting to a bad situation. The trait approach to research is the clearest example of this kind of flawed perspective. Researchers using this approach fail to consider that gender is not a static collection of traits but is the process of learning how to act like women and men. Moreover, they fail to consider that what women and men share as humans is more fundamental to communication processes than is any gendered perspective behind a message conveyed.

To return to the subject of self-disclosure and the nonverbal correlates of self-disclosure in encoding and decoding, Hall (1984), concludes that males are better decoders than they are encoders of the expressive domain. Providing less information or lower quality information (encoding, self-disclosing) has the effect of keeping others from possibly applying control over them by not allowing themselves to be in a submissive or vulnerable position. If males have developed skills as decoders in, what might be called, the psychology of human competition, then, this defensive posture allows little room to trust someone else with their vulnerabilities if self-disclosed. Can it be hypothesized that in this culture, any random male may sooner self-disclose to any random female before he might to a male of some acquaintance?

As Hall points out, "Nonverbal sex-differences are, therefore, most pronounced when one is with one's own sex" and tend to approximate the norms of the other gender in mixed gender encounters (p. 151). The fact that we can manage our communication skills, varying them in the presence of one gender or the other, suggests that there are possibilities for socializing our children towards, as Pearson concludes, psychological androgyny, behavioral flexibility and communication competence, serving our children in a more practical, functional, humanistic and personally satisfying manner.

The inconsistent and overlapping results of "sex–difference" research would seem to indicate that women and men are fully capable of exhibiting and, perhaps, valuing similar personality and social characteristics. The great value in research which studies the effects of socialization on women and men might lie in establishing the useful and the gratifying, and eliminating the destructive and the debilitating in human relationships, rather than in legitimizing post–hoc constructions of gender differences.

Toward A Theory of Gender

Through relationships seems to be precisely how the social constructions of gender and sexuality are born, develop, and are re-created in each generation. Relationships should reveal the underlying constructions and demonstrate how different individuals meet similar desires for self–expression and intimate connection. By examining the notions of complementarity and similarity involved in the social constructions of gender and sexuality, one can see that behavior which is labeled feminine or masculine – believed to be distinct to females or males – is, instead, behavioral variations characteristic to our species for which all of us are capable of exhibiting.

Value and appreciation are assumed to be the minimal cement bonding the relationship. Some relationships are bonded by complementarity; some by sameness. These fundamental notions of complementarity and similarity stem more or less directly from the morphological distinctions between females and males and indirectly through the metaphorical elaborations of sex/gender systems, socialization and the creation of identity.

While genitals are constant (except for visible physical alterations of transsexuals), there is no presumption made in Tables 1, 2, and 3 provided concerning the permanence of gender orientation in the relationships the individual has with others over the life cycle. Gender orientation will be seen as varying in each relationship due to the particular styles of self–expression which each individual exhibits in the relationship.

The distinction in the tables between heterosexuality and homosexuality is based on the potential morphological or physical relationships between individuals in nonerotic and erotic encounters or relationships with other individuals. Predictions for the morphologic gender of nonerotic and erotic partner preferences are based upon expectations of complementarity and similarity which individuals may

TABLE 1. PROFILE OF GENDER ORIENTATION IN NONEROTIC AND EROTIC RELATIONSHIPS (FEMALES)

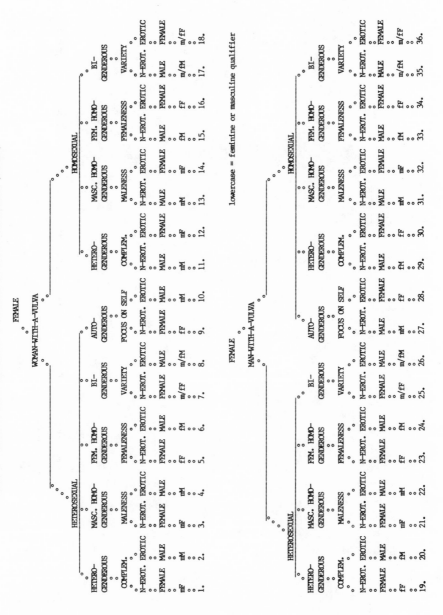

lowercase = feminine or masculine qualifier

TABLE 2. PROFILE OF GENDER ORIENTATIONS IN NONEROTIC AND EROTIC RELATIONSHIPS (MALES)

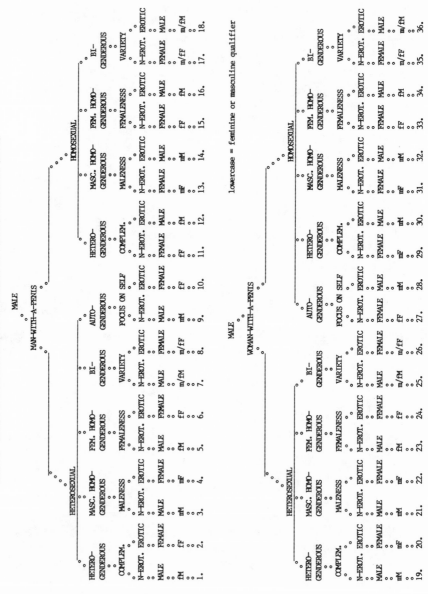

lowercase = feminine or masculine qualifier

TABLE 3 (1 & 2 CONT.). PROFILE OF GENDER ORIENTATION IN NONEROTIC AND EROTIC RELATIONSHIPS

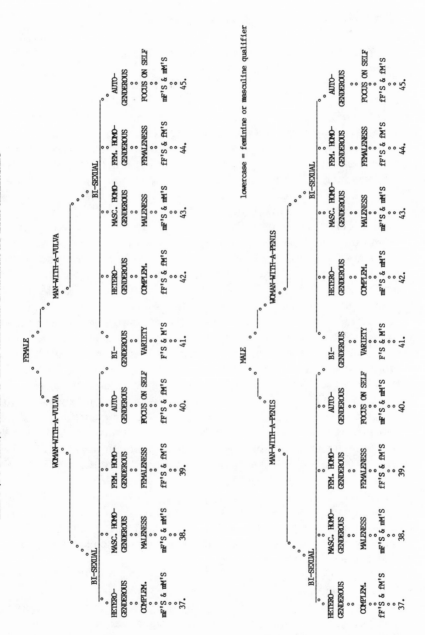

lowercase = feminine or masculine qualifier

bring to an encounter or relationship as well as how these expectations can be satisfied in the encounter occurring in the cultural context of prevailing prescriptions on gender.

Gender Orientation/Identity and Content and Form of Expression

The psychological orientation as more like a man or a woman which is brought to any interaction or relationship is based upon past experiences with, and present expectations about, the meaning of the content and form of a person's own and others' self–expression. It should not be surprising that very often past experiences and present expectations are in agreement with the gender role which has been prescribed by the culture. I am suggesting that this psychosexual component of the relationship may vary with any other individual whom the person is attracted to, finds things in common with, or simply enjoys being around, regardless of their more predominant psychological orientation as more like a woman or a man. Different people elicit different behaviors. These different relationships combine to define our gender and sexual orientations.

The subtle and not–so–subtle manner in which another individual expresses gender is the factor which elicits one's own gendered psychosexual response. The person as well as the content and form of their expression may be attractive or not–so–attractive for one reason or another. Responses to content and form may have nothing to do with sexual arousal, but still, there is the inescapable information concerning the context of the interaction. The context is at least the morphologic gender of the participants (the context is also the various social roles such as economic, political, religious, etc. or more informal and about a specific nonsexually arousing topic). However, the communication of gender includes: a piece of information, in some context, in some style, by some body.

Thus, in addition to a psychological orientation as more like a woman or a man for either morphologic gender, are the possible variations in terms of gendered expression of intimacy/sexuality as more like a man or a woman in the content and form of expression in an encounter or relationship. This conception is to account for individuals who may not go so far as the transsexual in identifying with the other gender, but who do, at times, present a masculine or feminine side to themselves.

The different general ways to communicate with people are: heterogenderously and homogenderously. Within these possible relationship styles exist the following possible combinations: woman to woman, woman to man, man to man, and man to woman. Thus, all the available combinations of orientation and style result from these available options for individuals. Each conversation is handled with a particular gender orientation. Each expression by individuals can be described as more like a woman or a man in form or substance. These styles are not mutually exclusive for different individuals so much as they are descriptive of every individual's different relationships with various other people. Psychosexuality, in other words, is a combination of sexuality and "genderality." Genderality may be seen as a hypothetical construct with which individuals orient the content and form of self-expression in terms of feminine and masculine images.

Just as individuals have learned what it means to be a woman or a man in this culture, so have they learned how it is women and men communicate with each other in various combinations. Thus, every individual has a conception of how women communicate with each other, how men communicate with each other, and how women and men communicate with each other.

Psychosexual Component of Relationships: Complementarity and Similarity

If heterosexuality, in an idealized conception, is the coming together of morphological complements in females and males, then I have taken this conception into the psychosexual domain and defined heterogenderous relationships as the coming together of psychosexual complements in gender orientation and content and form of expression (i.e., the quality of femaleness and maleness involved in the interaction by either morphologic gender).

Heterogenderous relationships exhibit/depend upon complementarity for defining the satisfaction in the relationship. Examples of the nonerotic psychosexual complementary relationships are common in the Mutt & Jeffs, Tom & Jerrys, Ralph & Nortons, Betty & Wilmas, Lucy & Ethels, etc.

If the morphologically heterosexual woman–with–a–vulva is also heterogenderous in a relationship, then she finds a complement on the physical and psychosexual levels of a nonerotic or erotic experience. If the heterosexual woman–with–a–vulva is heterogenderous for both nonerotic and erotic relationships, then her complements logically follow as a masculine male who stimulates sexual arousal or interest and a masculine female who stimulates nonsexually, arousing friendship or otherwise socially–related interest, i.e., the complements to her self–decided feminine identity.

In contrast, in the homogenderous approach to relationships is the appreciation for sameness or qualities which are similar to self. Individuals who take this approach to relationships emphasize sharing qualities between them, whether nonerotic or erotic. The more the erotic qualities are discerned by the individual, the more likely that homosexuality might be explored. However, just as homosexuals are not always sexual in their relationships, this homogenderality has nonerotic components. If one is masculine homogenderous then, there is some sort of appreciation for maleness on the part of the individual in or out of decidedly nonerotic contexts. Logically, this sharing of sameness would take different forms by individuals depending upon their up-to-date assessment of their sexual orientation as well as their gender orientation as more like a woman or a man.

Using the tables, compare the heterosexual woman-with-a-vulva to the homosexual woman-with-a-penis. Both of these individuals take the same approach in their preferences for complementarity and similarity in intimate and sexual, nonerotic and erotic expression in an encounter or a relationship. Both have a gender orientation as more like a woman than a man, and this orientation is complemented in their self-expression by masculine qualities which they perceive in another. However, one is morphologically heterosexual while the other is morphologically homosexual, and one is a morphologic female while the other is a morphologic male.

Both of these individuals correspond to prevailing stereotypes about gender and sexuality, but only in terms of erotic partner preference. Both the heterosexual woman-with-a-vulva and the homosexual woman-with-a-penis are complemented nonerotically by women who express themselves in content or form which is perceived consciously or unconsciously as more like a man than a woman (at least during their encounter or as a predominant aspect of their social relationship).

The homosexual woman-with-a-penis is a male who identifies herself as more like a woman than a man. The heterogenerous component of complementarity is indicated in the attraction to masculine males just as the heterosexual woman-with-a-vulva complements herself on the morphologic level. In essence, these individuals agree with heterosexual standards and carry them out in their relationships with others by complementing what they see as their own feminine qualities with what they think they lack in masculine qualities (thus, psychosexually heterogenerous).

Another implication of this conception regards the stereotypical conception of, for example, heterosexually masculine males in nonerotic relationships (Table 2, #3). While indeed for these individuals, a relationship between two heterosexual masculine males would be identified as decidedly nonerotic, there is an appreciation for maleness shared between them – the same nonerotic component identified with by anyone who appreciates masculine forms of expression and identifies with the expression. So, then, the stereotype of masculine, male friends in this culture is to be viewed as a nonerotic, masculine, homogenerous relationship because of the emphasis on masculine similarities shared between them.

Rosie Greer made as much of a name for himself in retirement from football with his quiet, peaceful demeanor and needlepoint as he did as a "head-hunter" while playing the game. The contrasting forms of self-expression rather than whether or not peaceful demeanors and needlepoint make him more like a woman than a man is a crucial point. The point is that in different contexts he shared with others remarkably different forms of self-expression in a culture which views the two forms as practically incompatible.

Summary and Conclusions

As a phenomenon, transsexualism serves to illustrate the problems which result from gender dichotomous attitudes in a culture which enforces strict adherence to the post-hoc social constructions of gender and sexuality. The complexity of the issue of transsexualism is quite apparent here both on the level of inquiry and as a manifestation of the problems for individuals in a society which has dichotomized (polarized) and stratified (differentially valued) role behaviors of females and males. Many females and males are affected by the restrictions on their behaviors, and both groups can perceive something which is missing in their lives in what is behaviorally permitted to the other gender.

Nurturing dichotomous, individual identities in women and men based on feminine and masculine ideals served to meet the unmet needs of individuals who, by definition, are more one-sidedly developed. A system is created where women and men need each other not as separate individuals, but due to deficiencies in their own repertoires. In general, individuals are discouraged from developing self-contained survival repertoires—arguably necessary for both women and men.

The value of this schema can go beyond (but include) its service to stigmatized individuals. The complexity of sexuality in the workplace troubles many who need a more useful language for their experiences in what is ostensibly a nonerotic domain.

For example, in (but not limited to) traditionally male-dominated professional environments, one could utilize the proposed framework to analyze and articulate heretofore tabooed social structures based on inherent androcentrism and heterosexism. Masculine homogenderous expectations for working together in these environments confound heterosexist norms through the expectation of complementarity in the expressive styles between different morphologic genders. On the one hand, females may be expected to focus the content of their messages homogenderously toward the masculine while presenting their message in a feminine form, thereby satisfying heterogenderous expectations implicitly connected to sexual interest. This presents a seemingly unduly arduous task for females to compartmentalize their expressions, perhaps relatively unconnected to their own gender and sexual orientations in a setting which the female expects to be nonerotically task oriented. On the other hand, heterosexual males in such spheres may resent the eroticization (albeit their own responsibility) of what used to be their nonerotic, masculine, homogenderous approach to working together. It may be difficult for these males to separate how they communicate with potential working partners from potential lovers. The males may sense a previously unexamined erotic quality in their appreciation for masculine homogenderous expression which might threaten their sexual orientation, or perhaps, find themselves fluctuating their gender orientation toward the feminine, an apparent threat to their identity as a man. It would seem to be a simple step (through sexual advances or innuendo) for these males to eroticize, for example, a feminine homogenderous approach in order to maintain their identity as a man and suddenly redefine the relationship heterogenderously.

This very general example may provide some ideas for more comprehensive analyses of settings/relationships in which gender and sexuality may be separated simply by introducing new language not so different from that which we are accustomed. Implicit in this model is a presumption that not only are androcentric and heterosexist norms destructive to human relationships, but as well, that our human tendencies to frame our behavior in terms of gender may be conceptually equalized in order that we may move beyond our historical predilections.

References

Garfinkel, H. (1967). *Studies in ethnomethodology.* Englewood Cliffs, N.J.: Prentice–Hall Inc.

Hall, J.A. (1984). *Nonverbal sex differences: Communication accuracy and expressive style.* Baltimore: Johns Hopkins University Press.

Kessler, S.J. & McKenna, W. (1978). *Gender: An ethnomethodological approach.* New York: John Wiley & Sons, Inc.

Money, J. & Erhardt, A.A. (1972). *Man and woman, boy and girl: The differentiation and dimorphism of gender identity from conception to maturity.* Baltimore: Johns Hopkins University Press.

Money, J. & Tucker, P. (1975). *Sexual signatures: On being a man or a woman.* Boston: Little, Brown, & Company.

Money, J. (1980). *Love and love sickness: The science of sex, gender difference, and pair–bonding.* Baltimore: Johns Hopkins University Press.

Pearson, J.C. (1985). *Gender and communication.* Dubuque, Iowa: Wm. C. Brown Publishers.

Sexton, P.C. (1969). *The feminized male: Classrooms, white collars and the decline of manliness.* N.Y.: Vintage.

Stoller, R.J. (1975). *Sex and gender Vol. II: The transsexual experiment.* N.Y.: Jason Aronson, Inc.

THOUGHT PROVOKERS

Is biological sex a discrete variable? Can we assume that even this basic premise holds in a world of changing sex and socially–constructed gender?

Conclusion

In early studies on communication and language, the norms of communication were tailored after men's communication habits and characteristics. Women's ways of communicating were considered deficient, particularly in the public realm; therefore, women who wished to be "successful" in this realm were trained to think and communicate like men. Universities taught basic public speaking based on men's performance as the "proper" model. Initial studies of communication, language, and gender questioned the assumption that men communicated more effectively. The findings were inconsistent, often dependent on situation, audience, as well as many other variables.

With the onset of the feminist movement, researchers presumed that women's means of communicating were not only equal to men's, but in fact were considered superior. Some studies in communication, language and gender upheld this perspective; others did not. Again, the results were inconsistent. In both instances, sex was presumed to be a controlling variable, a variable which would predict success or failure of a specific communicative act within a specific setting. Even in the face of continually inconsistent results, this perspective has changed little.

In recent years, researchers began studying gender as a socially-constructed variable assigning specific personalities traits as feminine, masculine, or androgynous and its effect in various communication situations. While sex is not an accurate predictor of specific behaviors, gender offers little more. Both serve as a predictive variable only when taken in conjunction with other variables such as setting, task, and audience.

In the final three chapters, new directions for the study of communication and gender were discussed. All three directions demonstrate the limitations of previous studies. Perhaps one of these new directions is the way in which the study of communication and gender research studies will progress: separate yet equal cultures; the integration of gender, age, and race; or the elimination of dichotomous sex roles all together.

This book details the current state of research in communication and gender; in addition, it pushes this state beyond old boundaries. The authors believe it is important for researchers of communication, language, and gender as well as the organizations which support them to resist the complacency of "tunnel vision"—to see only what was seen before.

Index